Critical Essays on
NGŨGĨ WA THIONG'O

CRITICAL ESSAYS
ON
WORLD LITERATURE

Robert Lecker, General Editor
McGill University, Montreal

Critical Essays on
Ngũgĩ wa Thiong'o

edited by

Peter Nazareth

Twayne Publishers
New York

G. K. Hall & Co.
1633 Broadway
New York, NY 10019

Library of Congress Cataloging-in-Publication Data

Critical essays on Ngũgĩ wa Thiong'o / edited by Peter Nazareth.
    p. cm. — (Critical essays on world literature)
    Includes bibliographical references and index.
    ISBN 0-7838-0456-3 (alk. paper)
    1. Ngũgĩ wa Thiong'o, 1938—Criticism and interpretation.
    2. Blacks in literature. 3. Kenya—In literature. 4. Africa—In literature. I. Nazareth, Peter. II. Series.

PR9381.9.N45 Z568 2000
823'.914—dc21
                                                                    00-044318

10 9 8 7 6 5 4 3 2 1

Printed in the United States of America

For Adam David Miller
And to the memory of Phyllis Correa
Two who strengthened my nerve

Drawing by McCeil King.

Contents

◆

Publisher's Note

◆

Producing a volume that contains both newly commissioned and reprinted material presents the publisher with the challenge of balancing the desire to achieve stylistic consistency with the need to preserve the integrity of works first published elsewhere. In the Critical Essays series, essays commissioned especially for a particular volume are edited to be consistent with G. K. Hall's house style; reprinted essays appear in the style in which they were first published, with only typographical errors corrected. Consequently, shifts in style from one essay to another are the result of our efforts to be faithful to each text as it was originally published.

Acknowledgments

◆

I am indebted to McCeil King, who did most of the hard work, such as photocopying material and designing the frontispiece, while continuing her studies as a lawyer; her commitment is similar to that of the lawyer in *Petals of Blood.* I am grateful to Professor Charles Cantalupo, who edited two volumes of criticism in connection with a conference he organized at Penn State Berks campus, Reading, Pennsylvania, April 7–9, 1994, with more than two hundred scholars in attendance to celebrate the work of Ngũgĩ wa Thiong'o; I have included four essays from the volumes. Professor Cantalupo was one of the organizing chairs of the millennial conference "Against All Odds: African Languages and Literatures," held in Asmara, Eritrea, January 11–17, 2000, the other two being Yohanes Zemret and Kassahun Checole of Africa World Press.

Professor Ed Folsom generously shared his expertise on, and commitment to, Walt Whitman. Rina Chaudhary tracked down Harish Narang in India. Carol Sicherman answered my queries with friendly precision.

Michelle Kovacs was infinitely patient and proposed effective strategies for getting past roadblocks. Without her, I would have been wandering in the wilderness.

Most of all, thanks to all the scholars who have interacted with the texts of Ngũgĩ wa Thiong'o.

Introduction: Saint Ngũgĩ

◆

PETER NAZARETH

I first got to know James Ngugi in the early sixties when we were fellow students at Makerere University College, in Kampala, Uganda. We were both in the elite English honors program, although I was two years ahead of him. I was in Mitchell Hall, and Ngũgĩ was in Northcote Hall on the other side of the hill. Everyone knew Ngũgĩ was someone special because of his striking characteristic that turned up in every major character in his novels: eyes that made one realize that he could see deep, that he was going far. Everyone wanted to "touch" him and thus acquire a special kind of grace. This characteristic may provide a hint as to why so many people respond positively to Ngũgĩ the man and the writer even when they are ideologically distant; for example, the Kenyan scholar Simon Gikandi says it was the emotions in Ngũgĩ's fiction that made an impact on him rather than the political analysis.[1]

My play "Brave New Cosmos," produced for the Interhall English Competition in 1961, seemed to contain within it a parody of Ngũgĩ's first play for Northcote Hall, which came later in the program.[2] Not long afterward I arranged to meet Ngũgĩ. I wanted to tell him that I had discovered how to do well on the final exams, which I had just taken; our "elder brother" in writing Jonathan Kariara had not obtained as good a degree as he had merited and I concluded that doing well on the exams required not only knowledge but also strategy.[3] I shared my strategy with Ngũgĩ—I do not know whether he used it since he went mountain climbing the weekend before his finals, feeling nobody had the right to judge him—and he reciprocated by sharing his knowledge of African writers, introducing me to Cyprian Ekwensi, Amos Tutuola, Chinua Achebe, and Wole Soyinka.

While I was waiting for the results of my exams from the University of London I read the manuscript of Ngũgĩ's first novel, *The Black Messiah.* He had written it for a competition organized by the East African Literature Bureau. It won first place but had not been awarded first prize, although the judges did not say what was wrong with it. I told him that I thought the problem was that the ending was not inevitable. If memory serves me correctly, Kamau pulls out a bow and arrow at the end and kills Waiyaki. Ngũgĩ revised the ending two years later when we were postgraduate students at Leeds University in England, after *Weep Not, Child* had been published.[4] The question is thus which of Ngũgĩ's novels comes first. I say *The River Between,* whereas Abdul R. JanMohamed says, "it seems to me that the greater stylistic maturity of *RB* and the more satisfactory reworking of the paradoxes of peripeteia of values justifies an analysis of the two novels in the order of their publication."[5] I disagree. Ngũgĩ's work presents people struggling to wake up from a deep sleep. In *The River Between,* the land is asleep and, being close to the land, so are the people. Waiyaki tries to wake them up, but he also has to wake himself up; after his father Chege's death we are told, "And Waiyaki had gone on like a man drugged, not knowing what to think or do." I interpret JanMohamed's "peripeteia of values" as a crack in the psyche caused by the collapse of values under the sharp blow of colonialism; thus Waiyaki suddenly seems to lose energy and quits the *kiama* even though he should have known it was important to stay in to keep presenting his point of view. But we could instead see his actions as a battle between staying awake and falling asleep. Even if Njoroge is vaguer in his idealism than Waiyaki, he is more awake, certainly by the end of the novel, and this is why I believe *Weep Not, Child* is an advance on *The River Between.*

My comments are not fair to the depth of JanMohamed's *Manichean Aesthetics.* Taking his cue from Frantz Fanon, he says that colonialism introduces a Manichean world (e.g., civilized/savage, advanced/backward, light/darkness). He selects six writers from opposite sides of the line to show the imperative of "manichean aesthetics," and his analysis is "polyphonic," to use the label he gives Ngũgĩ's third novel. His conclusion to the Ngũgĩ chapter is

> Thus with the exception of the analogical center of the novel, which is primarily a condensing device, the interdependence of individuals, and the revelation of meaning through multiplicity of viewpoints and through historical retrospection give *A Grain of Wheat* a formal structure that accurately represents the actual composition of a viable and coherent community. Ngugi's definition of community and the implications it has for present and future African societies makes *A Grain of Wheat* a unique novel in African fiction.[6]

But the full complexity of JanMohamed's analysis emerges when the book is read in its entirety; although there are separate chapters on six writers, each gains by juxtaposition with the others and particularly with its "opposite," Isak Dinesen in the case of Ngũgĩ.

I had been at Leeds for a year when I received a letter from Ngũgĩ in which he wrote that he had been offered a place at Leeds but was not sure whether to accept it. I wrote that he should come. Two years later I was working in the Ministry of Finance in Entebbe; when Ngũgĩ at Leeds heard that I was thinking of returning to continue my postgraduate education, he wrote that I should not come back but should go to America. He suggested that I write a novel, and I began doing so. *In a Brown Mantle,* published in 1972, turned out to be prophetic of the expulsion of Asians from Uganda, announced by Idi Amin nine days after the novel was launched in Kampala, and it brought me to America to accept the Seymour Lustman Fellowship at Yale University.[7] I realized years later that my Goan protagonist and narrator, Deo D'Souza, could be related to Mugo from *A Grain of Wheat;* both are haunted by guilt for having betrayed an idealistic, socialist leader who was killed, both feel lonely, and both feel the need to confess.

At Leeds in early 1965, after Shirley Cordeaux interviewed us for the African Theatre of the BBC, Ime Ikiddeh and I began writing plays for the BBC. "Look at you two!" said Ngũgĩ, who had been interviewed with us. "And I am writing nothing!" After that, he began writing *Wrestling with God,* which he retitled *A Grain of Wheat,* subsequently using the original title as a recurring phrase in his fourth novel, *Petals of Blood.* He wrote the first few lines in class and passed the page across to me, later publishing an extract of the novel-in-progress in a student journal; I read the novel as a whole after buying it at Uganda Bookshop in Kampala in 1967.[8]

So Ngũgĩ and I have known each other for some time, although we are of different ethnic backgrounds (he is Gikuyu, and I am Goan), different countries (he is from Kenya, and I am from Uganda), different relationships to the country (he is indigenous, and I am of immigrant parents), different classes (he is landless, and I am landless, too, but petty bourgeois), and with diametrically opposite notions of British imperialism—which I thought was "good"; this approach to imperialism led to my "breakdown" in England, which was really the "breakthrough" most writers educated under the colonial system must make to decolonize the mind, the imperative Ngũgĩ has made famous.[9] But what we had in common was that we were both workers in the field of writing. We did not draw a distinction between studying literature, writing criticism, and doing our own writing. Thus Angus Calder said in his review of my first book of criticism, *Literature and Society in Modern Africa,* that it and Ngũgĩ's *Homecoming,* published around the same time, strike out in similar directions. "Like Ngugi's, Mr. Nazareth's approach is that of an intellectually flexible, but firmly committed, Socialist," Calder stated, continuing, "and like Ngugi's, his interest doesn't stop at racial or political boundaries."[10] Both of us wrote criticism with a practical edge, without critical jargon, seeking to change consciousness and the world.

I think we had something else in common. Like the Inspector and Munira in *Petals of Blood,* I discovered that Ngũgĩ and I shared a name: *James* was the name given to me at my confirmation. I liked to "twin" with other writings, to create my own "gumbo" by putting in things from elsewhere. My dissertation on Conrad's *Nostromo* bounced off the essay Ngũgĩ had written at Makerere when studying Conrad for his special subject with David Cook. One could argue that Ngũgĩ was rewriting Conrad in *A Grain of Wheat:* I taught the novel in a class I called *Conrad and His Descendants,* in which we studied six texts by Conrad and eight by "descendants."[11] Compare the relationship of Charles Gould and his wife with that of John Thompson and his wife, though Margery Thompson, as the wife of a colonial officer instead of the owner of a mine, is a diminished Emilia Gould. Both men of English origin believe in the civilizing mission of colonialism, although in the case of Gould it is neocolonialism, and both men inspire their women with their idealism; that very idealism leads to oppression of the people they thought they were going to uplift and, as a consequence, emotionally alienates them from their wives. Thompson writes, "Eliminate the vermin," and Robson says "Brutes" as he is dying; Kurtz's famous words scribbled across the manuscript about civilizing the savages in *Heart of Darkness* are "Exterminate all the brutes." The Mugo/Kihika relationship and characterization parallel those of Razumov and Haldin in Conrad's *Under Western Eyes;* the sister of the executed revolutionary plays a similar role in Ngũgĩ's novel to that in Conrad's: Both women save the betrayer morally through their appeal and power. Njeri in her magnificence is comparable to the African woman in *Heart of Darkness,* but the woman in the latter lets out an incomprehensible cry for Kurtz the imperialist agent while Njeri is very articulate about how she is going to join Kihika in the forest and fight for freedom from imperialism. Ngũgĩ's Gitogo is like Stevie in Conrad's *The Secret Agent* in that both are not "normal"; both have powerful imaginations that enable them to see and understand in their mind's eye the suffering of others, and both are killed in their attempts to stop that suffering. Mumbi "jumps ship" metaphorically—from Gikonyo to Karanja in a scene much debated by critics—as Jim does literally. In neither case do we have the omniscient narrator's version of what happened, and both characters deny any responsibility for what they see as something that happened to them beyond their control. Jim and Mumbi want and get a second chance to take responsibility for their actions, Jim for the killing of Dain Waris and other Malays by Gentleman Brown and Mumbi by surrendering to Mugo (Dubem Okafor argued in a paper written for my class that the rhythm of the words reveal the scene is sexual). Neither jumps ship this time; Jim accepts execution, and Mumbi refuses to tell anyone that Mugo is the person who betrayed her brother.

When I was writing about Ngũgĩ's connection to Conrad in *A Grain of Wheat* for my first book of criticism, Tova Raz told me that I was going too far and making it look as though Ngũgĩ was not original.[12] If so, it was probably the result of a linear instead of clustered structuring of my sentences (I was then Senior Finance Officer in the Ministry of Finance); it was also an indication that we were not far removed from the colonial days when a sympathetic critic, Murray Carlin, who had taught Ngũgĩ and me at Makerere, was obliged in his review of Ngũgĩ's novels to deal with the notion that Africans could not write fiction:

> The scene of torture begins by reference to two European officers—with a red beard and grey eyes; I put it that way deliberately, because this feral combination is left just so ambiguous. We are never quite sure whether these two sole attributes are shared between them, or monopolised by one of them; but the result is certainly effective in terms of the rendering of brutality and terror. *I know one cynic on the subject of African writing who is sure to say that this dislocation was accidental—the product of imprecision in language. I don't know about that. What does "accidental" mean, in art? Only good writers have good accidents.*[13] (italics mine)

Imperialism did not take place in a literary vacuum: Scholars such as Mary Louise Pratt and David Spur have shown how writing paved the way for, and justified, imperialism.[14] In the case of Kenya, much was written in England and America about Mau Mau, the guerrilla movement to get back the land, as a savage movement. Ngũgĩ had not only to write, he had also to rewrite. Several African scholars show Ngũgĩ's relationship to Conrad; for example, Abele Obumsele wrote an essay about Ngũgĩ's debt to Conrad.[15] I prefer to see Ngũgĩ in a complex relationship with Conrad—sometimes repeating, at other times reversing or adding and extending, but almost always using Conrad as a literary door to exit the world of colonialism.

Although Wole Soyinka and Nadine Gordimer have both received Nobel Prizes for literature and he has not to date, it is not inaccurate to say that Ngũgĩ wa Thiong'o is the most famous African writer today. In fact, there was a strong rumor in the seventies that he was going to receive the Nobel Prize. Africans, African Americans, and other people worldwide see his fiction as engaged with issues of fundamental concern; he shows the creativity of the folk juxtaposed with the reality of their suffering, identifying and explaining the causes of such suffering—colonialism and neocolonialism—and seeking to end such exploitation. Although he focuses on Gikuyu people and their land alienation, he is dealing with Africa, the Third World, and the whole world. He does so primarily in his novels, but he has also taken up the issues in short stories, plays, essays, public statements, and children's stories. His first major work was a play, *The Black Hermit,* written for Uganda's independence celebrations and produced at the National Theatre in Kampala in October 1962.[16]

Ngũgĩ's work made an immediate impact: *Weep Not, Child* received an award as best novel at the 1966 Festival of Negro Arts held at Dakar. But the amount and range of literary criticism of Ngũgĩ's work are much greater today than they were in the sixties and early seventies. At least nine books and several collections of studies of his work have been published, in addition to conferences held on his work. In the sixties and seventies, the criticism tended to focus on the political ideas of Ngũgĩ's fiction or on its literary techniques, although occasionally a piece on his relationship to Christianity and his use of African folklore appeared. Since the late seventies, the criticism has tended to vary more, with critics discussing the literary techniques, the ideological thrust, the structure, the nature of the language, and so on. In other words, in the eighties and nineties, there was polyphonic criticism of Ngũgĩ.

We are dealing, then, with a writer whose work we cannot classify and file away. For example, debate about the female circumcision presented in *The River Between* continues. Does Ngũgĩ condone female circumcision (clitoridectomy) or is he just saying that it happens, that under colonialism the matrix of the culture hardens in response to a strong colonialism instead of remaining flexible and leading to changes from within? I, too, am continuing a dialogue with Ngũgĩ's works. In the early eighties, I wrote an essay on *Petals of Blood* in Georg M. Gugelberger's *Marxism and African Literature* in which I found fault with the novel.[17] I felt then the speeches could be cut down. Today, I believe that one of the novel's points is that people need to learn from their stories; the characters have to struggle to remember, to tell—in the case of Munira, to write—and to shape their stories. *History* comes from *story,* and as colonialism denied that there was indigenous history, it also denied each "native" the power to tell his or her story, out of which can come awareness of the authentic self. My newer interpretation was reinforced by Ngũgĩ's presentation at the University of Iowa on April 30, 1998. He said that he wrote his novels in longhand and when he revised, rewrote everything. Therefore the slow movement, what one English critic called the "lumbering" style of *Petals of Blood,* is functional, and we need to find out what the function is.

In the seventies, I was very conscious of the political dimension to Ngũgĩ's writing. I disagreed with David Cook's interpretation of *A Grain of Wheat* in his *African Literature: A Critical View,* because, although he had provided the best structural analysis I had read of the novel, he had understated the political vision and ideology, an omission corrected later in the book he cowrote with Michael Okenimkpe.[18] Critics such as Gugelberger have praised Ngũgĩ's radical politics, but James A. Ogude says

> Ngugi's *Petals of Blood* resembles Sembene Ousmane's *God's Bits of Wood,* both in its ideological concerns and, to a large extent, in its subject. But in contrast in Ousmane's novel there is a relationship between a specific socio-historical subject and the individual character experiences, to the extent that the individual expe-

riences and consciousness are shaped by the ongoing social struggle. Even the sense of alienation displayed by certain characters is directly related to the central and political action of the novel. In *Petals* we do not come across workers or even peasants who are directly linked to the political action of the novel.[19]

Ogude's argument is that the "inability to dramatise the working class struggle" could be either because Kenya has not developed a class consciousness and an organized working class so Ngũgĩ has nothing to fall back on from real life or because he is "forced to create an imaginary revolutionary working class modelled after the socialist revolutions." This argument presupposes that Karega is presented by the novel as the ideal working-class hero instead of someone who must go through the process of telling his story and discovering who he is. He must face the fact that his extensive reading, despite his experience as a worker and organizer all over the country, has trapped him in abstract ideological generalizations and blinded him to human beings with real feelings and desires; the situation is similar to the way the protagonist of *The Black Hermit* gets so caught up in his political vision that he insults the woman he loves, who kills herself. It is not that Ngũgĩ tried to write a novel like *God's Bits of Wood* and failed. Ousmane's novel is set during colonial times and Ngũgĩ's during neocolonial, which is why Joseph near the end of Ngũgĩ's novel reads Ousmane's novel. Although of its time, *Petals of Blood* is not bound to its time or to "reality," for there is a spiritual and metaphysical element in Ngũgĩ's work. We can hear in the novel the voices not only of the individual characters but also of the collective, lamenting absence in much the way Taban lo Liyong does in the seminal "Lament to East Africa's Literary Barrenness":

> For there are many questions about our history which remain unanswered. Our present day historians, following on similar theories yarned out by defenders of imperialism, insist we only arrived here yesterday. Where went all the Kenyan people who used to trade with China, India, Arabia long long before Vasco da Gama came to the scene and on the strength of gunpowder ushered in an era of blood and terror and instability—an era that climaxed in the reign of imperialism over Kenya? But then these adventures of Portuguese mercantilism were forced to build Fort Jesus, showing that Kenyan people had always been ready to resist foreign control and exploitation. The story of this heroic resistance: who will sing it? Their struggles to defend their land, their wealth, their lives: who'll tell of it? What of their earlier achievements in production that had annually attracted visitors from ancient China and India?[20]

The collective voice charts the way toward the retrieval of history. Yvonne Vera of Zimbabwe shows in her fiction that the spiritual and metaphysical are tied to nature, bringing the past into the present such that the distant past is still in the collective unconscious.[21] Ngũgĩ tells us in his first and third novels that there was a time when the women were the rulers and warriors among the Gikuyu. Then the men plotted a takeover: When the women warriors returned flushed with victory, they slept with them and got them pregnant. When they were heavy, the men took over. Yet in the collective unconscious remains the knowledge of the time when the women were in charge, which is why the Gikuyu were willing to accept the rule of a queen; it is also why in times of crisis the women are able to act. It is this feeling that makes Mumbi agree to persuade Mugo to come to the celebrations and make a speech, and it is why she believes she has the power to do so. And, indeed, she does: She holds him in her grip through her eyes and exorcises the ghost that has been haunting him. In taking responsibility for her actions, in not exposing the betrayer of her brother to the people because enough blood has been shed, she comes into full knowledge of her strength and now Gikonyo will have to woo a mature woman as an equal.

Ngũgĩ is impatient with the tendency of the people to idealize leaders instead of looking into themselves to find their own power and responsibility. They mythify Matigari in the sixth novel but do not recognize him even as he is standing by their side. It is as though he has materialized out of their unconscious, and at the end takes a running jump back into their unconscious, signified by his disappearing into the river, the reverse of Legatt appearing out of the water in Conrad's "The Secret Sharer." Now the listeners/readers must find the Matigari in themselves. As André-Paul Michaud shows in his essay in this volume, this feature is what makes the sixth novel like the first: the importance of the river, or, as he puts it, nature as agency.

The first book to be published on Ngũgĩ, to my knowledge, was by C. B. Robson in 1979.[22] The next one was by G. D. Killam, who had established credentials as a scholar in the field of Commonwealth literature, doing a fuller analysis of Ngũgĩ's fiction; Killam also edited a valuable and thorough collection of criticism, *Critical Perspectives on Ngugi wa Thiong'o,* published in 1984 and still in print.[23] Putting together some of the best and most representative published criticism of Ngũgĩ from the seventies, Killam included eight general essays, three essays on each of the first two novels, five on the third, and four on the fourth, plus an essay on his first volume of essays, *Homecoming,* opening with an essay by Ngũgĩ, "Literature and Society." It is not my intention to displace Killam's volume but rather to provide newer and fuller interpretations of Ngũgĩ's works, although I have included Killam's essay on *Weep Not, Child* from both his books as representative of pioneering scholarship.

Yulisa Amadu Maddy and Donnarae MacCann have another take on *Weep Not, Child,* about which I shall say more later, and Sigurbjorg Sigurjonsdottir from Iceland reexamines it together with *Petals of Blood* to show that the relationship between Ngũgĩ and Walt Whitman goes beyond

Ngũgĩ's taking of title and epigraphs from *Leaves of Grass*. Written in India, the essay by Harish Narang indicates that, as D. Venkat Rao says, "Ngũgĩ wa Thiong'o is a much admired writer in India," but it also presents a thorough historical and political analysis of *A Grain of Wheat*.[24] Bu-Buakei Jabbi analyzes the same novel in terms of symbolism, comparing the novel with *Under Western Eyes* and arguing that there is a Conradian influence on Ngũgĩ's "water symbolism." Kenneth Harrow does a complex analysis of the elements of fiction in the same novel. The range of critical responses to Ngũgĩ's work is mapped by Joseph McLaren; one of these is Christine Pagnoulle's zeroing in on structure through Part 2 of *Petals of Blood*. Gĩtahi Gĩtĩtĩ begins with the importance of Frantz Fanon to Ngũgĩ's writing but goes on to tell us that when Ngũgĩ wrote his first novel in Gikuyu, he was drawing on the *gĩcaandĩ* tradition; in the process, Gĩtĩtĩ provides information about what the *gĩcaandĩ* tradition encompasses. Alamin Mazrui and Lupenga Mphande do almost the reverse: focusing on Ngũgĩ's use of orature, the word coined by Pio Zirimu, they connect the ideas of Fanon regarding national consciousness with the development and span of Ngũgĩ's fiction. Linking orature with the political situation, David Hulm focuses on music in Ngũgĩ's work, showing that what Gatuĩria was struggling to create in the fifth novel was in fact created by Bob Marley in accordance with the Rastafarī way of life.

The volume does not include any items that deal exclusively with Ngũgĩ's books of essays (he has published five volumes) or his plays (he has published four full-length plays, two of them cowritten, one with Micere Githae Mugo and the other with Ngũgĩ wa Mirii, and one volume of one-act plays). But reference is made to these works when presenting something of a "total" picture of Ngũgĩ's work, as in the essay by Christine Loflin. A "complete" picture is also found in Carol Sicherman's thorough scholarship, which is sympathetic to and yet objective about Ngũgĩ's ideological commitment. She provides details about Ngũgĩ's education, formulating four hypotheses about his development as a writer and thinker and indicating the way he seeks to subvert the mind control of colonial education. In her second essay, she shows how he writes and rewrites African history. Loflin, for her part, explores the full implications of landscape in Ngũgĩ's work, in its spiritual, economic, and political dimensions, indicating the ways it includes even the social and political dimensions of the publishing of the work. Yulisa Amadu Maddy and Donnarae MacCann argue that Ngũgĩ has kept growing in exile: In his children's fiction, he is fighting not only to decolonize the mind but also to help prevent it from being neocolonized in the first place, as Andrew Salkey of Jamaica did before him when he published nine children's novels in addition to his five novels. (Ngũgĩ told me that when he was studying in England, it was Salkey who first treated him as a writer.) Before providing the context of children's stories in modern Africa, Maddy and MacCann analyze *Weep Not,*

Child almost as a children's novel, proving that Ngũgĩ has long been in an ideological battle to resist the miseducation of young minds. It should be no surprise that this novel received the UNESCO prize.

I recall a presentation in the International Writing Program in the mid-seventies by a writer from Central America. He spoke in a language resembling English for 50 minutes, of which the audience understood only one sentence: "It is dangerous being a writer." It is also dangerous being a publisher, as revealed in Henry Chakava's courageous concluding piece.

Ngũgĩ has published six novels and, after a hiatus of more than a decade, is completing his longest novel to date, 1,200 pages, *Murogi wa Kagoogo* {*The Wizard of the Crow*}. Almost all the critics in this volume see a connection between the earlier works and the later, although Ngũgĩ himself has insisted that there is a break when he stops writing "Afro-Saxon literature" and writes instead in his mother tongue. The story of how he wrote *Devil on the Cross* in Gikuyu on toilet paper while he was in detention in 1978 is well-known: To surprised audiences, he points out that in detention, toilet paper is not provided for one's comfort.[25] He has stated that just as English had been imposed on the African people by the colonizers, its continued use in writing is detrimental to the development of African languages and furthers the creation of an elite alienated from the people. This view has led to an intense debate among African scholars. Dubem Okafor, in *The Dance of Death: Nigerian History and Christopher Okigbo's Poetry,* has made a case against Ngũgĩ's position. Okafor says that followers of Obi Wali, named by Ngũgĩ as the person who made him realize the importance of writing in African languages, are actually preaching marginalization of "African cultural productions" because international scholars ignore African writing in indigenous languages. He concludes:

> such cultural productions in indigenous languages do not get called "Literature"; they belong in that undignified category of "verbal art." One is not surprised by that relegation of *Third World* "verbal arts" to the dust-bin of inconsequence, which has nothing to do with the quantity or literary/aesthetic quality of such vernacular labors. The truth is that "no one will learn the language of a people without any economic or political power." And economic and political disenfranchisement remains the fate of the laboring peoples of the Third World.[26]

Ngũgĩ answered in his presentation at the University of Iowa in 1998. He read the school scene from *Weep Not, Child* in which Njoroge and the class are learning English. When we read it on the page, it seems simple; when Ngũgĩ read it aloud, it demonstrated dramatically the early stages of alienation through the imposition of a foreign language. Ngũgĩ has convinced increasing numbers of people of the importance of language, which is why the debate rages with both passion and pragmatism. One can argue, as proven by

Gĩtahi Gĩtĩtĩ in his analysis of *Devil on the Cross,* that through using Gikuyu, Ngũgĩ has been able to access indigenous art forms that were blocked out when he used English. I recall Ngũgĩ telling me after the publication of *Weep Not, Child* that readers asked him why he did not use proverbs like Achebe. "Can I help it if my people don't speak in proverbs?" asked Ngũgĩ. There is no question about that now; the use of Gikuyu became a channel for proverbs, aphorisms, folktales, and oral structures in his fifth and sixth novels (although we also see them to some extent in *Petals of Blood*). Ngũgĩ wants to develop Gikuyu and other African languages by using them and by thus speaking not only about and for the people but also to them. His success can be seen in the fact that after he cowrote the play with Ngũgĩ wa Mirii in Gikuyu he was detained for almost the whole of 1978.[27] His success can be further seen in "Against All Odds: African Languages and Literatures into the 21st Century," a conference held in Asmara, Eritrea, January 11–17, 2000, at which he was a presiding chair.[28]

Ngũgĩ is not new to proposing and carrying out literary revolutions. In the late sixties, with the support of Taban lo Liyong and others, he succeeded in abolishing the Department of English at the University of Nairobi and replacing it with the Department of Literature, which emphasized East African, African, and other relevant literatures. This change was no small achievement in an ex-British colony. Alamgir Hashmi, in a presentation entitled "Bill Shakespeare's Laundry Bills and Beyond: English Studies in Pakistan," says, "When the present writer began his university teaching career in Pakistan in 1971, the departments of English were very much the same as they had been in the 1950s and 1960s."[29]

There is the question of why Ngũgĩ appeals to so many people in the West. One reason, I believe, is the way he opposes formal education with a deeper kind of learning, one that comes from within, from knowledge and self-knowledge because his novels provide true education. Although he states that today one must take sides with either the robber or the robbed, his fiction always provides the possibility of and responsibility for choice. Ole Masai in *Petals of Blood* chooses to fight for Kenyan freedom instead of siding with his Indian shopkeeper father; he dies for his country. Although we doubt John Thompson in *A Grain of Wheat* will be born again, he could do so if he chose to, as is the case with Mugo and as is a possibility presented to Karanja. This ability to choose is empowering to the reader, whether Western, African, or Eastern. And Waiyaki's struggle to wake up his people and himself in *The River Between* reflects humanity's struggle to move to a higher level of consciousness, as argued by Ken Wilber in *Up from Eden: A Transpersonal View of Human Evolution.*[30]

Although much of Ngũgĩ's writing has focused on Mau Mau, the role of Mau Mau keeps changing and growing in the texts. Abdulla, who had lost a leg fighting for Mau Mau, comes to a Sufi-like conclusion:

Maybe . . . maybe, he thought, history was a dance in a huge arena of God. You played your part, whatever your chosen part, and then you left the arena, swept aside by the waves of a new step, a new movement in the dance. Other dancers, younger, brighter, more inventive came and played with even greater skill, with more complicated footwork, before they too were swept aside by yet a greater tide in the movement they had helped to create, and other dancers were thrown up to carry the dance to even newer heights and possibilities undreamt of by an earlier generation.[31]

We know that Abdulla will be leaving behind Joseph, whom he had brought up as a brother. We also know that Abdulla has just impregnated Wanja, who was waiting for a second chance to be a mother, to mother a child who may be the new messiah. But we could interpret Abdulla's thoughts, because they are in a text, as implying that the new dance will be done by the artist, the writer, who will take it to newer heights of consciousness.

The writer could take the dance to newer heights, but mediators are required. In *A Grain of Wheat,* Mugo follows through on Kihika's notion that Christ failed because he died on the cross without his message passing into the hearts of the people and letting them realize they could be messiahs for one another. Mugo had tried to rationalize his betrayal of Kihika by asking what would have happened to Christ if Judas had refused to play his part. Ngũgĩ gives Judas a second chance; Ngũgĩ's Judas is not damned but can become a messiah. Mugo completes Kihika's message through his public confession in dry words that do not let people fly to heights of ecstasy but force them to look inside. Gikonyo is one who ponders Mugo's courage, thus recognizing his own betrayal and beginning the healing process; he decides to work on the stool he had once planned for Mumbi as a wedding gift, and now it will be carved for her big with child.

As I write, Ngũgĩ has been out of Kenya physically for nearly two decades. He was born near Limuru, Kenya, in 1938, which means he is now in his sixties. He went to England in 1982 for the launching of the English translation of his first Gikuyu novel, entitled *Devil on the Cross,* but was warned by friends not to return because he was to be arrested and blamed for the coup that allegedly briefly deposed President Moi. He has lived in exile ever since, in Europe and now in the United States. How ironic that he has achieved status in the United States—he is currently Erich Maria Remarque Professor of Languages and Professor of Comparative Literature and Performance Studies at New York University. Is his position hypocritical, as one scholar said a few years ago, attacking neocolonialism and yet benefiting economically by being in the center? One answer is that human beings are full of contradictions, and these contradictions are presented in Ngũgĩ's characters. For example, Karanja uses his position as chief of the Home Guards to sexually exploit women, yet he does not force Mumbi to submit. But is this really a contradiction or the dialectics of being human? A better answer is that

Ngũgĩ must do whatever he can to create the work that brings the message out to the people. A Guinean scholar said cynically at a conference about the African Writer and Commitment, "The primary duty of the writer is to stay alive." Perhaps there is a contradiction between the revolutionary and the revolutionary writer: The former may want to sacrifice everything and everybody for the revolution, whereas the latter is concerned about both the revolution and the literature, about the form and structure and aesthetic shape of the latter. And also with the moral shape: The revolutionary writer allows for the possibility that people can change. The critic can change, too. A comparison of my essays on *A Grain of Wheat* and *Petals of Blood* with this introduction will reveal that I continue to be involved with Ngũgĩ's work in ways beyond those of a detached scholar.

One more reason why Ngũgĩ may be so popular with readers in the West is that he does not really reject Christianity, despite having dropped his "James," but is reevaluating its radical potential, like Kihika who argues that we can all be messiahs for one another. When Ngũgĩ visited the University of Iowa in the late eighties, a student, Mike Zmolek, said to him, "Peter Nazareth says that you are the most Christian writer Africa has produced. What do you say to that?" Ngũgĩ gave a reply worthy of Christ's answer to the question of whether it was right to pay tribute to Caesar. He played with my name and said that with that kind of name, I had no choice but to say what I had said.[32] I would retort that in his account in *Detained,* Ngũgĩ beats down the chaplain sent in to break his spirit with a superior knowledge of the Bible and an alternate interpretation of Christ and the prophets as revolutionaries. Christianity without doubt, but not the kind colonialism uses to keep the people in subjection.

The purpose of this volume is to show Ngũgĩ as artist and Ngũgĩ as fighter against colonialism and neocolonialism, continuing to expand his thinking, aesthetic strategies, and concern for humanity. The emphasis is on recent criticism because it became much more dynamic as the twentieth century closed. African literature has been educating its critics; the essays reveal that Ngũgĩ is a polyrhythmic writer, such that later works make one see greater depth in his earlier ones. The volume opens up Ngũgĩ as an artist and thinker about whom we can, do, and should have numerous analyses and discussions.

The book proves Ngũgĩ lives.

Notes

1. Simon Gikandi, "Moments of Melancholy: Ngũgĩ and the Discourse of Emotions," in *The World of Ngũgĩ wa Thiong'o,* ed. Charles Cantalupo (Trenton, N.J.: Africa World Press, 1995), 70. It could be argued, contrariwise, that it is precisely because they are drawn to him despite his ideology that some people are hostile to Ngũgĩ.

There is the question of how to write Ngũgĩ's name. He initially wrote under the names "James Ngugi" or "N. T. Ngugi." He did not use the tilde then or when he reverted to his original name. I believe he started using it when he began publishing work he wrote in Gikuyu. Critics have tended to use the tilde above the *u* and *i* only where they have been used in the publication they were addressing—but not always, for critics also did not use it when they or their publishers apparently found it too difficult to do so. Therefore, there is some variation in how the name appears throughout this volume; similarly, the spellings "Kikuyu," "Gikuyu," and "Gĩkũyũ" appear as originally published.

2. Peter Nazareth, "Brave New Cosmos," in *Origin East Africa,* ed. David Cook (London: Heinemann, 1965), 167–78.

3. See Jonathan Kariara, *The Coming of Power and Other Stories* (Nairobi: Oxford University Press, 1986), the only volume he published before his untimely death.

4. James Ngugi, *Weep Not, Child* (London: Heinemann, 1964); James Ngugi, *The River Between* (London: Heinemann, 1965).

5. Abdul R. JanMohamed, *Manichean Aesthetics* (Amherst: Massachusetts University Press, 1983), 298.

6. JanMohamed, *Manichean Aesthetics,* 223.

7. Peter Nazareth, *In a Brown Mantle* (Nairobi, Kampala, and Dar es Salaam: East African Literature Bureau, 1972).

8. James Ngugi, *A Grain of Wheat* (London: Heinemann, 1967); Ngũgĩ wa Thiong'o, *Petals of Blood* (London: Heinemann, 1977). Ngũgĩ later made changes in *A Grain of Wheat;* the revised edition was published in 1986. For example, Koinandu became Koina, the Party became the Movement, and the rape of Dr. Lynd became the killing of her dog. Apparently the reason for the last change was that Ngũgĩ discovered that no white woman had been raped during the Mau Mau movement, but I believe that something is lost through the change. Koinandu had taken out his frustration by participating in the rape, but he was haunted thereafter, and it was Kihika's leadership that channeled his frustration into a *political* objective. It could be argued, however, that the revised scene is ambiguous and it is left to the reader to decide whether Dr. Lynd was raped; in reply to my request for clarification, Ngũgĩ answered by e-mail: "I cannot remember exactly why I changed but obviously the dog incident works better."

Another important change, which I think was unnecessary, is the addition of a line at the end of chapter 6 when Gikonyo says to Mugo, "God, I sold my soul, for what?" This line makes explicit what Gikonyo is only willing to come to terms with after the public confession of Mugo.

But there is one change that undoubtedly improves the novel. In the original version, Kihika said, "I despise the weak. Let them be trampled to death. I spit on the weakness of our fathers. Their memory gives me no pride. And even today, tomorrow, the weak and those with feeble hearts shall be wiped from the earth. The strong shall rule. Our fathers had no reason to be weak. The weak need not remain weak. Why? Because a people united in faith are stronger than the bomb" (217). In the new version, he says, "I despise the weak. Why? Because the weak need not remain weak. Listen! Our fathers fought bravely. But do you know the biggest weapon unleashed by the enemy against them? It was not the Maxim gun. It was division among them. Why? Because a people united in faith are stronger than the bomb" (1986 edition, 191). Kihika now presents a sharper and more humane understanding of the long fight against colonialism.

9. Ngũgĩ wa Thiong'o, *Decolonising the Mind: The Politics of Language in African Literature* (London: James Currey; Nairobi: Heinemann; Portsmouth, N.H.: Heinemann; Harare: Zimbabwe Publishing House, 1986).

10. Angus Calder, "Peter Nazareth's *Literature and Society in Modern Africa,*" *Afras* (University of Sussex) 1, no. 4 (1973): 16.

11. See Peter Nazareth, "Conrad's Descendants," *Conradiana* 22, no. 2 (1990), 173–87.

12. Peter Nazareth, "Is *A Grain of Wheat* a Socialist Novel?" in *Literature and Society in Modern Africa* (Kampala, Nairobi, and Dar es Salaam: East African Literature Bureau, 1972), 128–54.

13. Murray Carlin, "Politics and the Artist," *Transition* (Kampala) no. 18 (1965): 53.

14. Mary Louise Pratt, *Imperial Eyes: Studies in Travel Writing and Transculturalization* (New York: Routledge, 1992); David Spur, *The Rhetoric of Empire* (Durham, N.C.: Duke University Press, 1993).

15. Abele Obumsele, "Ngugi's Debt to Conrad," in *Critical Perspectives on Ngugi wa Thiong'o* (Washington, D.C.: Three Continents Press, 1984), 110–21.

16. James Ngũgĩ, *The Black Hermit* (London: Heinemann, 1968). The published version is a little different from the one produced in 1962.

17. Peter Nazareth, "The Second Homecoming: Multiple Ngugis in *Petals of Blood,*" in *Marxism and African Literature,* ed. Georg M. Gugelberger (Trenton, N.J.: Africa World Press, 1985).

18. David Cook, *African Literature: A Critical View* (London: Longman, 1977), 95–112; David Cook and Michael Okenimkpe, *Ngugi wa Thiong'o: An Exploration of His Writings* (London, Ibadan, and Nairobi: Heinemann, 1983).

19. James A. Ogude, "Imagining the Oppressed in Conditions of Marginality and Displacement: Ngugi's Portrayal of Heroes, Workers, and Peasants," *Wasafiri* (Queen Mary and Westfield College) no. 28 (1998): 8.

20. Ngũgĩ, *Petals of Blood,* 67. Taban lo Liyong's "Lament to East Africa's Literary Barrenness" was published in *Transition* no. 19 (1965), the issue that contained Murray Carlin's review of Ngũgĩ's *The River Between.*

21. See, for example, Yvonne Vera, *Nehanda* (Toronto: TSAR Books, 1995).

22. C. B. Robson, *Ngugi wa Thiong'o* (London: Macmillan, 1979). The most recent book on Ngũgĩ is Oliver Lovesey, *Ngũgĩ wa Thiong'o* (New York: Twayne, 2000); this volume is published in Twayne's World Authors Series, African Literature, edited by Bernth Lindfors.

23. G. D. Killam, *An Introduction to the Writings of Ngugi* (London: Heinemann, 1980). G. D. Killam, ed., *Critical Perspectives on Ngugi wa Thiong'o* (Washington, D.C.: Three Continents Press, 1984).

24. D. Venkat Rao, "A Conversation with Ngugi wa Thiong'o," *Research in African Literatures* 30, no. 1 (Spring, 1999): 162–68.

25. See Ngũgĩ wa Thiong'o, *Detained: A Writer's Prison Diary* (London, Nairobi, and Ibadan: Heinemann, 1981). For an account and analysis of the detention, see Bernth Lindfors, "Ngugi wa Thiong'o's Detention," in *The Blind Men and the Elephant and Other Essays in Biographical Criticism* (Trenton, N.J., and Asmara: Africa World Press, 1999), 93–108.

26. Dubem Okafor, *The Dance of Death: Nigerian History and Christopher Okigbo's Poetry* (Trenton, N.J., and Asmara: Africa World Press, 1998), 82–83.

27. Ngũgĩ wa Thiong'o and Ngũgĩ wa Mirii, *I Will Marry When I Want* (London, Ibadan, and Nairobi: Heinemann, 1982).

28. On January 17, writers and scholars from all regions of Africa issued the Asmara Declaration on African Languages and Literatures. Stating that "African languages must take on the duty, the responsibility, and the challenge of speaking to the continent," they stressed the importance of promoting African languages, of recognizing the rich diversity of African languages, and of recognizing the vitality and equality of African languages "as the basis for the future empowerment of African peoples." The declaration states further that "democracy is essential for the equal development of African languages and African languages are vital for the development of democracy based on equality and social justice." It was noted that African languages like all languages contain gender bias, which needs to be overcome to achieve gender

equality. The last of ten sections states, "African languages are essential for the decolonization of African minds and for the African Renaissance."

The full text of the Asmara Declaration can be obtained from Africa World Press/The Red Sea Press, P.O. Box 48, Asmara, Eritrea, or P.O. Box 1892, Trenton, NJ 08607.

29. Alamgir Hashmi, "Bill Shakespeare's Laundry Bills and English Studies in Pakistan," *The Toronto Review of Contemporary Writing Abroad* 17, no. 1 (1998): 10–17.

30. Ken Wilber, *Up from Eden: A Transpersonal View of Human Evolution* (Wheaton, Ill., Adyar, and Madras: Quest Books, 1996).

31. Ngũgĩ, *Petals of Blood,* 340.

32. My third name is Joseph and my wife's name is Mary.

Ngugi's Colonial Education:
"The Subversion . . . of the African *Mind*"

CAROL SICHERMAN

Of course [after graduation from high school] some things go, whistles, lights-out, uniform, parades, prefects, . . . and yet all the central ideas go on. There will still be chores to be done, and done well, without grumbles; there will still be the need to discipline, for men who can obey and can therefore—when called upon—rule . . . (Francis 1957, 2).

What we are practicing at Makerere, day in and out, . . . is the subversion . . . of the African *mind;* the breaking down of mental tissues; their reconstruction in the Western mode; the reordering of thoughts, feelings, habits, responses, of every aspect of the mind and personality. This is what we *are doing,* and cannot avoid doing—this is the core of our activity (Murray Carlin in Stanley 1960, 11).

In 1957 a solemn third-former at Alliance High School wrote in the school magazine: "Superstition used to play an important role in Kikuyu society. . . . It was the chief reason why the older order changed more slowly than many people desired" (Ngugi 1957, 21). Unequivocally rejecting "rigid" traditional society, the writer declares approvingly that with the advance of Christianity—"without doubt the greatest civilising influence"—many Gikuyu have come to regard "superstition and witchcraft . . . with derision." After a well told anecdote tinged with humorous self-mockery, the essayist ends with sermonizing gratitude for "a most valuable lesson" (22).[1]

This parrot-like bagatelle in *The AHS Magazine*—signed "J. T. Ngugi, Form 3A," and his first published work—echoes the high moral tone of the missionary headmaster of Alliance High School, E. Carey Francis (Greaves 1969; Kipkorir 1980; Sicherman 1990, 389–92). The motto of the school, "Strong to Serve," implied the kinds of "chores" that boys thus educated would have to do in Kenya when they became—in Ngugi's later caustic paraphrase of his headmaster's goal—"efficient machines for running a colonial

Reprinted, by permission, from Carol Sicherman, "Ngugi's Colonial Education: 'The Subversion . . . of the African *Mind,*'" *African Studies Review* 38, no. 3 (1995): 11–41.

system" (Sicherman 1990, 20). A few of them, Francis said, might even be admitted to his own Cambridge University—as a friendly gesture, not on merit. "Of course we protested," Ngugi later recalled, "but inwardly we believed it" (Marcuson 1966, 6).

The present paper examines the mental subversion effected upon Ngugi and his fellow students by the higher-educational system in late-colonial East Africa. While this subversion was itself later subverted by Ngugi and some other victims, it remained indelibly imprinted on those who became (in Ngugi's term) "neocolonialists." One measure of the power of colonial mental subversion is the venom with which the neocolonial Kenyan government pursued its vendetta against Ngugi even after he had gone into exile (Sicherman 1992); another is the failure to effect a true revolution in higher education even in Tanzania, the East African country where such an effort had the greatest chance of success (Samoff 1990, 209–14, 257).

The complex processes of decolonizing (and recolonizing) African minds during the past 35 years demand an analysis that would probably be best performed by African intellectuals. The present paper has a more limited purpose: to describe the impact of two institutions on Ngugi's intellectual development—Alliance High School, the premier secondary school in Kenya and a model for Siriana in *Weep Not, Child* and *Petals of Blood;* and Makerere College in Uganda, the only university college in all of East and Central Africa, and a legendary mecca throughout the region.[2] Yet this story is not only Ngugi's: his gifts notwithstanding, he was by no means unique in either his vulnerability to subversion or his later resistance to it. When, in the early and mid-60s, he and several others proceeded from Makerere to postgraduate work at Leeds University, the colonial blinkers fell off. Indeed, with individual variants, what happened to Ngugi at Alliance, Makerere and Leeds happened to many other African intellectuals who grew up in late-colonial Africa. The present narrative features Ngugi as a cultivated product of the kind of colonial academic hothouse that, with local variations, the British built wherever they deemed there were among their imperial subjects a few whose intellects might be forced into something rather like a Western shape.

Four hypotheses govern this paper, which develops mainly the second and third: first, that Ngugi's primary education in a Gikuyu independent school (1948–55) gave him an awareness "of colonialism as an oppressive force" and a pride in peasant culture, which itself had provided an informal education in "songs, stories, proverbs, riddles" (Sicherman 1990, 19–20); second, that at Alliance High School, the combination of flexible ethnic pluralism, rigid and proselytizing Christianity, and colonial doctrinalism—along with high intellectual demands—made a lasting impact on its most famous graduate and gave him intellectual tools with which he later attacked the colonial mind-controls; third, that the same combination of pluralism, doctrinalism, and intellectual rigor appeared as well at Makerere but differently proportioned: with the doctrine muted, with the intellectual demands increased, and—perhaps most important—with a much greater encouragement to write creatively; fourth, that at Leeds, Ngugi found in Fanon and Marxist theory a doctrine to replace the Christian-imperial model that was inculcated at Alliance and assumed at Makerere—and that this way of thinking took root in the nationalist soil prepared in the Gikuyu Independent School.

ALLIANCE HIGH SCHOOL

Alliance High School— Ngugi's ticket to Makerere, Leeds, and the world— had been founded by a coalition of missionary groups in 1926. A programmed world modeled on the British public school, it served the cream of the cream.[3] Carey Francis, a workaholic "martinet," maintained Alliance as "an adobe of peace in a turbulent country" convulsed by the anti-colonial struggle (Kipkorir 1980, 114, 136; Ngugi 1964h, 108). Prefects, appointed on grounds of character rather than academic ability, operated as the headmaster's agents in a Lugardian system of indirect rule—a "knightly order of masters and menials" in which prefects were responsible not to any student constituents but to the all-powerful headmaster (Njoroge 1978, 97–101; Ngugi 1977, 170; Kipkorir 1980, 125–27). Ngugi himself served as a bottom-rank prefect in 1957 and 1958.

Alliance, like all such schools, "systematically conditioned [the boys] to disassociate themselves from the very people who had brought them up and who were now breaking their necks to earn their school fees for them back on the farm" (Hower 1980, 73). The school's ardently Christian ideology and distance from home sharply diminished the "traditional influence of their kinfolk and age-mates" (Goldthorpe 1965, 52). The implied associations between English-medium education and urban advancement, and between indigenous languages and rural backwardness, created class lines, separating the tiny nascent elite from their peasant origins. Because colonial education policies insisted that primary education be conducted in African languages, only the minuscule elite who passed through the eye of the needle into secondary school could know English well.[4]

Yet there were potential benefits for the pupils. As a national boarding school, Alliance brought boys from the country's many ethnic groups to a "paradise" of "harmony" (Ngugi 1964h, 115), which thus supplied a model for the multicultural independent Kenya that Ngugi has always advocated (Ngugi 1962b). In a nice irony, it supplied significant personnel for the anti-colonial leadership through its graduates and also through students and staff expelled by Francis (Kipkorir 1980, 114, 133–47; Njoroge 1978, 102–04). Even (or particularly) the Mau Mau movement recognized that an Alliance education could help overthrow the colonial hegemony that Francis intended to uphold. Illustrating this irony, Ngugi made his first trip to Alliance (in 1955) hidden—by the nationalist forces—"in the guardroom of a goods train": the colonial authorities, knowing that his brother was fighting in the forest, had refused him the requisite pass (Ngugi 1981a, 73; Greaves 1969, 118–19).

Perusal of the annual *AHS Magazine* for 1956–59 reveals an institution controlled through the colonial examination system, through extracurricular activities, and through the muscular Christianity characteristic of such missionary ventures. Religion was central. In his Foreword to the November 1956 magazine, Francis rejoices that, with the "dark days" of Mau Mau over, AHS students no longer needed to fear when they went out to teach Sunday Schools "packed tight with eager boys and girls" (1).[5] Sports loomed large, and there were clubs for academic subjects and for chess, scouting, music, and the like. More than half the school belonged to the Dramatic Society, which put on annual productions of Shakespeare. A few extracurricular activities attempted discreet innovations: an Intertribal Society to bring "the various tribes here more closely together" (1958, 16); productions of plays in Kiswahili, some of which toured (1957, 15; 1958, 18; Ngugi 1986, 39); a History Society concerned with "subjects outside the school's history curriculum" (1959, 33).[6]

While the *AHS Magazine* consists mainly of reports of student organizations, it also includes a number of brief and expectable student essays such as accounts of vacation trips (among them Ngugi's report of a European/African "Voluntary Service Camp" in 1958, 29–30) and moralistic exhortations to "exercise your mind" (1957, 20) or to "put away the shame of 'African Time' " (1956, 18). A few essays on cultural practices show glimmers of independent thought even while also suggesting cultural alienation, as when a writer laughs at the "curious" and "superstitious" customs of pre-European Gikuyu (Ngini 1956).

In this generally stifling atmosphere, the Debating Society—one of the most popular clubs—and the library afforded Ngugi ways to catch his breath. Fresh from his Gikuyu Independent school, he took part in a debate on a motion "that western education had done more harm than good" in Kenya; "trembling with anger," he declared "that western education could not be equated with the land taken from the peasants by the British" (Sicherman 1990, 20).[7] Small wonder that Francis once warned him against becoming a "political agitator" (Sicherman 1990, 21). In the library, which held nearly 2000 books (*AHS Magazine* 1959, 27), he found "cherished companions" in the characters of Dickens and Stevenson (Ngugi 1993, 136) and "stumbl[ed] across" Tolstoy's "Childhood, Boyhood, and Youth," which influenced his first published writing (Sicherman 1990, 21). He remembered "litera[ll]y trembling" when he saw Peter Abrahams's *Tell Freedom* in the hands of an Alliance teacher (Sicherman 1990, 22). But for all his reaching toward an African identity, he was so affected by Francis's "strongly messianic influence"

(Tejani 1973, 106) that he came to Makerere "very much a product of Carey Francis" (Dinwiddy 1987)—a devout Christian with a first-division pass in the School Certificate exam.

MAKERERE AND THE UNIVERSITY OF LONDON

Although Alliance proudly sent more students to Makerere than did any other school (Greaves 1969, 112), Carey Francis—a member of the Makerere College Council—reviled the staff as "a bunch of Bolshies" who were "letting down all the good work being done in the schools" (de Bunsen 1987). In other words, the all-European staff was "liberal." There were even a few European students; when Ngugi arrived in 1959, he felt initially "on my guard against the sprinkling of white faces" in his classes (Ngugi 1963b).[8] During the 1950s, a period of great change, Makerere became even more European, for it began to operate as the University College of East Africa under a "special arrangement" that gave the University of London oversight over both the curriculum and the examinations.[9] While Makerere was in effect a "residential English university" (Kozoll 1962), it differed in one respect from its model: because African secondary schools lacked A-level courses, Makerere students spent their first two years studying three subjects at A-level in order to pass the London Preliminary Examination; after that, General Degree students studied three subjects for two years, and Honours students devoted three years to a single subject. Hence Ngugi, who took the Honours course, spent five years at Makerere.

Margaret Macpherson, a veteran member of the English Department, recalled the "traumatic . . . hammering out of the syllabus" in the early 1950s, when London prevailed over local pleading for accommodation to East African circumstances (Macpherson 1987). The affiliation with London established Makerere "as an international centre of learning" (Ngugi, 1963c); the African pass rate was similar to that of internal University of London candidates (Ashby 1961, 18). A decade of control from abroad, however, undoubtedly contributed to Makerere's "aloof" postcolonial relationship with East Africa (Ngugi 1963c).

The tight tether anchoring Makerere to London is evident in the Honours literature curriculum, which spanned Chaucer—defiantly taught in the original despite a London University "ban on Middle English" (Warner 1956, 56)—to T. S. Eliot. Jonathan Kariara's arch essay on preparing for the English examination indicates an Honours curriculum that was dense and demanding for anyone, far more so for non-native speakers: *Emma* ("humorous and lovely to read"), *Cry, the Beloved Country* ("my Bible, noble book," the only "African" work studied), *Hamlet* ("good for my soul"), "Synge's lovely Plays," *Great Expectations, Joseph Andrews, Antigone,* the "odious" *Odyssey,* and two other disliked works, *Typhoon* and *Much Ado About Nothing* (1958, 8). At the end of three years came an oral examination and eight three-hour written examinations—one on language, one on Theory and Practice of Criticism, and six on literature divided into periods or major authors.[10] Enrollment in the English Department was high; in Ngugi 's final year there were 122 students taking various options, 22 of them in the Honours course (*Makerere University Annual Report for the Year 1963–64,* 8).

The staff took an Arnoldian, Leavisite approach to the texts (Whittock and Cook 1965, 26; Warner 1954, 26).[11] In his inaugural address as first Professor of English, *Shakespeare in the Tropics,* Alan Warner explained the underlying premise: African students would study English literature in order to "become citizens of the world" (1954, 16–17). In keeping with Warner's belief that "the stimulus of English ideas and forms" would be essential to the development of Africans' "own written literatures" (1954, 20), the staff singled out European authors who might provide models for budding African writers—Dickens[12] (from the Great Tradition), Homer (oral tradition) and Synge (peasant culture). A drama survey starting with the Greeks particularly influenced Ngugi and others; among the student plays that showed the "obvious influence of Synge" (Ngugi 1989) was Erisa Kironde's "The Trick"—" 'The Shadow of the Glen' by J. M. Synge transposed into an African setting" (Kironde 1968, 103).

In the curriculum Ngugi found possibilities for a countersubversion that had to be confined to his journalism. In one column he recommended the use of Shakespeare "to hit back at the white man" (Ngugi 1964e); in another, he found Dickens's *Hard Times* a useful brick with which to beat a Makerere lecturer who demanded that Ugandan education be put on a "scientific basis" (Ngugi 1963a, 12).[13] Endorsing Shelley's call for a society of the "equal, unclassed, tribeless, and nationless" (1962e), he turned imperialist language on its head: "new beacons" would shine from Africa to enlighten "the Dark Continent of Europe as well," as Africa became the "saviour" of European "civilisation on the verge of decay" (1963a, 35). And "there was Conrad, sneaking through as a member of Leavis's Great Tradition, actually undermining that tradition" (Nazareth 1983, 178).

NGUGI'S HONORS PROJECT ON CONRAD

Two deities in Leavis's pantheon, Lawrence and Conrad, were the prescribed authors who most affected Ngugi as a creative writer. While Lawrence's spirituality and "way of entering into the spirit of things . . . influenced [him] quite a lot" (Duerden 1964, 122), Lawrence's lush style tempted him toward a "dangerous" imitation (Nazareth 1990). Between Conrad and Ngugi lay a more fruitful "affinity of sensibilities" (Nazareth 1972, 132), and he chose

Conrad for the "special project" required of Honours English students. Conrad's appeal lay both in his examination of alienation, self-betrayal, and heroism—topics Ngugi explored with sensitivity—and in his use of a "borrowed language" that he "beat . . . into various shapes to give . . . meaning to the physical and moral world" (Ngugi 1993, 5; Abdullahi 1964, 126). Perhaps more important were Conrad's questioning of "the morality of action" (Duerden 1964, 124) and his political and economic themes—topics omitted from Ngugi's project.

Supervised by David Cook during Ngugi's final term, these three essays (one each on *Lord Jim,* "The Secret Sharer," and *Nostromo*)[14] are written in the "clean English" expounded in Warner's *Short Guide to English Style,* written in 1961 with Makerere students in mind. "Cut the cackle," Warner advised (Hindmarsh 1962, 32). Did he reflect that "clean English," as a reviewer of his book remarked, "is a style which lends itself particularly to the rebel, the debunker, the enemy of hypocrisy, loftiness, atmosphere and enthusiasm" (Hindmarsh 1962, 32)? While Ngugi aspired to these roles in his journalism, his Conrad essays demonstrate the morality-sniffing, close-reading approach favored at Makerere, where "many seminars [were] spent on detecting . . . moral significance in every paragraph, in every word, even in Shakespeare's commas and fullstops" (Ngugi 1986, 90). Despite such retrospective disdain, close reading of great literature is good for budding writers and critics, and Cook's careful and respectful annotations imply high expectations of his student. As discussed below, Ngugi later condemned Cook for his patronizing readings of neophyte African writers; but surely Cook had something to teach him with respect to discriminating literary criticism.

Ngugi's Conrad essays have some bearing on his later development, as when he hints agreement with Conrad's belief that "condemnation or even praise should be born of understanding" (1964b, 6). The paper on *Lord Jim* responds to Cook's request for an analysis of the structure in light of an allegation that "the book is broken backed" (Ngugi 1964a, 1). Ngugi's argument for a unified structure enables him to discuss questions of passivity and moral responsibility that he had been forced to consider while growing up during the Independence struggle and that he was later to deal with in his own fiction. Some of his comments apply as much to Mugo in *A Grain of Wheat* as they do to Conrad's Jim. Jim (and Mugo like him) "must keep on tormenting himself, slowly destroying himself[,] for it is in his nature to annihilate himself"; in the end, Jim (like Mugo) accepts both that side of us that is "perpetually turned to the light of day, and that side of us which exists stealthily in perpetual darkness" (7–8). Other thematic parallels include the "opposition between the conscious self that takes decisions and wills to achieve great heroic deeds[,] and the subconscious which betrays him," and the impossibility of forgetting the past (4). Commending its "energy," Cook awarded this essay the "exceptional mark" of A; not one word of his comment betrayed his awareness that the author was himself a novelist.

Only the paper on *Nostromo* suggests, briefly, Ngugi's own interest in politics, then expressible only outside the classroom. While most of the paper examines the title character's significance "in the definition of . . . moral issues"—a properly Makererean topic—Ngugi starts by describing *Nostromo* as "a political novel" that examines relationships among social, political, and economic institutions (1964c, 1–2), a description that could apply equally to Ngugi's own work to come. The most evident proof of the Conradian pudding was to lie in *A Grain of Wheat,* in which he transmuted *Under Western Eyes* into a tale of Kenya at the moment of independence, on the model already exemplified in Kironde's transposition of Synge. As Cook wrote on Ngugi's essay on "The Secret Sharer," he had "a very considerable grasp of Conrad as a whole," briefly discussing *Heart of Darkness, The Secret Agent,* and *Under Western Eyes,* and mentioning *The Nigger of the Narcissus* and *Victory.* If, as Ngugi claims today, "Conrad always made me uneasy" because he saw no "redemption arising from the energy of the oppressed" (1993, 6), or on account of his "ambivalence towards imperialism" (1986, 76), he concealed this doubt in his senior project. Then—and now—Conrad's "techniques had impressed me" (1986, 76).

DEFICIENCIES IN THE SYLLABUS AND THE CRITICAL APPROACH

If you were in prison for life or if you were shipwrecked on an island, what books would you like to have with you and why? That used to be a favorite question of literature teachers at Alliance High School, and later at Makerere College. The normal response was to mention, not really the books one would have liked to have . . . but the novels or the volume of plays or poetry that one had studied in depth, on which one could do an adequate critical appreciation to earn a good mark (Ngugi 1981a, 131).

It would have been useless to answer the examiners' question with a discussion of the books by African and African-diasporic writers that Ngugi read at Makerere, for there were no such books on the syllabus. While the staff were earnestly encouraging student writing through Synge and Conrad, there was, right there in the Makerere library, "literature that told [Ngugi] of another world, a world which was in many instances my own": the writing of Peter Abrahams, Chinua Achebe, George Lamming, Cyprian Ekwensi, Aimé Césaire, Léopold Sédar Senghor, and others (Sicherman 1990, 22).[15] Ngugi could also find such books in the library of Northcote Hall (his dormitory) and in the private library of a political-science lecturer, Cherry Gertzel, who invited students to her apartment to discuss politics—another topic thought unsuitable to the classroom (Ngugi 1989; Bown 1990; Ingham 1990). For a student from a book-banning country like Kenya, it was heady stuff to read such "forbidden fruit" as Montagu Slater's *The Trial of Jomo Kenyatta* (Ngugi 1962c). One book he read extracurricularly, Lamming's *In the Castle of My Skin,* gave him a "special . . . mission to study non-English literature" (Ngugi 1976). Not until *Petals of Blood,* completed in 1975, did he transfer what he learned from African literature to his own writing; lonely and alienated Conradian heroes populate his first three anglophone novels, in which only the secondary characters exhibit active resistance.

Isolated from emergent African literatures, a Makerere education was, in David Rubadiri's apt phrase, a "pot plant"—"able to grow in its own confined boundary, but failing to take root and nourishment from mother earth itself" (1966, 9). With a syllabus and critical approach remote from local cultures, the English Department promoted "universal" moral values, interiority, and individualism—emphases ill-suited to the development of distinctively East African writing and criticism for at least four reasons. First, a curriculum composed of acknowledged Western classics might well be "totally alienat[ing]" to neophyte writers and critics because it implied all Western writing was "great"; of course, inferior works form the bulk of European as of all writing (Whittock 1968, 91). Second, the focus on isolation and alienation discouraged any challenge to British cultural hegemony by distracting attention from East African communitarian traditions. Third, woolly espousal of "universal" values tended to distance the specific and local—that is, what the students knew most intimately; furthermore, "universal values" (if they exist) "are always contained in the framework of social realities" (Marcuson 1966, 8). Fourth, the curriculum excluded the verbal art most familiar to East Africans—orature, "vivid and alive," in constant evidence at funerals, on political platforms, by the fireside, during moonlight dances and at weddings (p'Bitek 1966, 70–71).

Even though anglophone writers like Ngugi were acquainted with orature, it does not figure prominently in their work. It was Okot p'Bitek—significantly, neither a Makerere product nor formally trained in literature beyond the secondary-school level—who first blazed a path toward distinctively East African writing and who became an influential researcher on, and teacher of, orature. It was no accident that the Acholi original of *Song of Lawino,* Okot's most important work, was indebted to a non-literate poet, his own mother (Lindfors 1983, 282–83). The English version affected early listeners "like a bombshell" exploding European verities; its publication by a local firm was another strike against European hegemony (Rubadiri 1968, 150–51). Okot, who "directed *{Song of Lawino}* to the students at Makerere" (Serumaga 1967, 152), skewers Lawino's husband as a Makerere man contemptuous of traditional culture (p'Bitek 1966–67, 87, 138). "Cultural slavery," Okot told a Makerere audience, pervaded the entire educational system (1967).

Absence of indigenous critical standards remained a problem for writers and critics. The gadfly Taban lo Liyong looked in vain for critics "to guide our tastes and choices" (1968, 5); as yet, he said, East Africa had only "non-us" critics (1968, 5)—outsiders like David Cook at Makerere, who called for a vaguely defined "positive" criticism (Cook 1971). Before long, some of Cook's former protégés, including Ngugi and Nazareth, condemned his encouragement of creative writing for lacking judgment and rigor (Nazareth 1990).[16] In response to such criticism, a visiting BBC official, Edward Blishen, explained that "Mr. Cook is . . . just being hopeful" (*Makererean* 6.49 [22 Mar. 1967], 8). Yet even those who felt that Cook had merely appropriated Africa admitted his contributions: his yeoman work in co-editing the first anthologies of East African writing (Cook 1965; Cook and Lee 1968; Cook and Rubadiri 1971); the extraordinary energy he put into the Makerere Travelling Theatre; his interviews with writers for Radio Uganda and the BBC (Cook 1976); his urging young writers to send their works for broadcast and publication; and numerous other activities, such as founding a student play-reading group and conducting Writers' Workshops.[17]

Developments in the Early 1960s: The Teachers for East African Scheme, *The Makererean* and Other Publications, the Conference of African Writers of English Expression and *The Black Hermit*

At Makerere the early 1960s were a time of heightened political consciousness that sometimes affected intellectual activities outside if not inside the classroom. Despite a reputation for political inactivity (Langlands 1977, 3, 5), students "linked arms and sang" in euphoria when Kenyatta was released (Dinwiddy 1985, 8), critiqued a Kenyan government report purporting to account for Mau Mau (Sicherman 1990, 381–83), celebrated Tanzanian independence as "a new dawn in the region" (Ngugi 1993, 165), and cheered the East African political leaders in 1963 when they assembled to discuss Federation (Ngugi 1993, 168). Besides such political events, four developments at Makerere affected literary affairs: the arrival of a large number of young Americans in the Teachers for East Africa scheme (TEA), the founding of a student newspaper under TEA auspices, the Conference of African Writers of English Expression and the production of Ngugi's play *The Black Hermit*.

In 1961 Makerere became the host institution for the TEA scheme, a joint British–United States effort to staff the rapidly expanding secondary schools until sufficient numbers of African teachers were trained. The TEA selection process emphasized professional competence and creativity; the TEA participants, unlike their successors from the Peace Corps, did not represent their nations (Bing 1989). The TEA students—initially nearly all American, most of them white—received varying amounts of training at Makerere; eventually all took the one-year Dip.Ed. course. "It is easy to admire the

Americans, difficult to like them," a student wrote anonymously, ticking off the complicated responses elicited by the first cohort of 152 Americans: "admiration, antagonism, horror, disgust, curiosity" (*Makererean* 1.2 [11 Dec. 1961]: 2). While the TEAs were well received at first, in the late 60s the resentment of some East African students over alleged pro-white favoritism by the Education faculty became public. Meanwhile, the Americans were "impressed with the industry and friendliness" of Makerere students, with whose "hopes, interests and concerns" they "closely identified" (Shields 1962).[18]

The Americans made a considerable impact on Makerere, above all on extracurricular activities. In the first year of the "American invasion" (Macpherson 1964, 84), one of the TEAs, Nat Frothingham, directed a *Macbeth* notable as the first full-length Shakespeare play produced at Makerere with an all-African cast, costumes, and setting (Nazareth 1990). This *Macbeth* was, furthermore, the first full-length Makerere production to take place at the so-called National Theatre.

The most lasting American contribution was a student newspaper called *The Makererean,* founded by several TEA students in 1961—the first Makerere publication initiated by students that lasted more than a few issues (on *Penpoint,* founded by staff, see below). Until its demise early in the regime of Idi Amin, *The Makererean* afforded an important outlet for student ideas and maintained a record of events. Serious, energetic, challenging, and at times humorous, the paper infused a salutary American brashness in the previously timid public persona of the Makerere student. The irreverent tone persisted when the American progenitors dropped away (as they soon did), and the staff became entirely local, including Ngugi in 1963–64.

At the same time, Ngugi wrote for the Kenyan press (Lindfors 1981) and was associated with two ephemeral Makerere magazines. As an Information Officer of the Student Guild, he revived *The Undergraduate* as the Guild organ;[19] and he co-edited *Makerere Horizon,* sponsored by the Students Discussion Group at Northcote Hall, where he lived. An unsigned inaugural editorial in the latter, noting sternly that "not a single novel has so far appeared" in East Africa, demanded that writers "examine our Historical evolution, [and the] political and social problems surrounding us and throw light on them. . . . East Africa—wake up!" ("Editorial," 1961, 3–4).[20] Makerere staff and students, among them Ngugi, also contributed commentary and fiction to *Transition,* a magazine founded in Kampala in 1961 by Rajat Neogy, a Ugandan political-science graduate of London University.

The landmark African writers conference, which was organized by Gerald Moore of the Department of Extra-Mural Studies, took place in Northcote Hall in June 1962. It was at this conference that Hugh Dinwiddy, the Warden of Northcote, introduced Ngugi to Achebe, who advised him on the half-finished manuscript of *Weep Not, Child* and referred him to the Heinemann representative (Dinwiddy 1987).[21] Several speakers anticipated Taban's famous lament for East African "literary barrenness" (lo Liyong 1965;

Mphahlele 1962, 8). The more established writers from West and South Africa were "avuncular" toward the inexperienced East Africans (Ngugi 1972, 67), who had most to gain from the conference: from the impassioned public debates on the definition of "African writing," on "negritude," and on the role of publishers; from the no-holds-barred public discussions of participants' work and the closed workshops arranged by genre; and from the public readings by participants. "What I remember most about the conference," Ngugi wrote two decades later, "was the energy and the hope and the dreams and the confidence" (1981a, 142). Still later, "from the self-questioning heights of 1986," he saw "absurd anomalies": because he had published two stories in English, he qualified to attend, while long-established writers in African languages like Shabaan Robert and Chief Fagunwa were excluded (Ngugi 1986, 6).

A few months after the conference came Ugandan Independence. During the festivities, Ngugi's *The Black Hermit* was put on at the National Theatre—the first performance of the first full-length anglophone East African play. Whatever the merits of the script,[22] the play was "written from *inside*" and as such was "what Makerere, and, indeed, East Africa had been waiting for" ("Northcote Hall Newsletter," no. 6, 6 Dec. 1962: 1). The opening performance moved many in the audience to tears:

> . . . a modern African writer had analysed our alienation, had understood the process of history that made us, had exposed the acculturation imposed upon us by our foreign education and reminded us in the tears of joy and independence of the bitterness of the struggle which lay ahead (Tejani 1979, 52).

Pan-African pride swelled: a Kenyan writer's play for Ugandan Independence was performed by actors from Kenya, Uganda, Tanzania, Malawi, India, and Britain (Ngugi 1968, cast list; cf. Ngugi 1993, 164). The *Hermit* group anxiously awaited the *Makererean* review by Trevor Whittock, a member of the English Department; it was substantially favorable: "The faults fall away beside what is achieved" (1962). Other significant theatre productions soon followed, and Kampala seemed to be "the one place in East Africa where foundations for a living theatre are being laid" (Ngugi 1964d).

"LIBERAL" STAFF, STUDENTS AS "DISEMBODIED SPIRITS"

As European staff paved the road to intellectual growth at Makerere, their liberal decency dampened without fully squelching the students' stirrings of rebellion. In the late 1950s,

> Makerere offered as good a chance to mould a young mind into an educated one as any place anywhere of equal standing. It was even better because it was

a local institution. You were encouraged to understand and learn to evaluate your own environment, so that you had an explanation of your own on what went on around you . . . (Ruheni 1973, 22).

These features of liberal ideology at Makerere are precisely those enumerated by the historian Kenneth Ingham (1990), who taught at Makerere 1950–62.[23] Both Ingham and Mwangi Ruheni (a Kenyan civil servant, novelist and Makerere graduate) valued "hav[ing] an open mind even if all the others are closing theirs around you" and the "ability to change one's mind in the face of new evidence" (Ruheni 1973, 22). With regurgitation of facts and ideas prevalent in East African secondary schools, Makerere encouraged (or seemed to encourage) a bracing independence—behind which lurked an incurable Eurocentricity.

That Eurocentricity, strengthened by the respect for authority inculcated by African and Western cultures, powerfully countered the value supposedly placed on independent thought. Even when Ngugi asked questions in his Kenyan journalism—"Can the Educated African Meet this Challenge [of staffing a modern civil service]?" (Ngugi 1962a)—his addressee was another "educated African," in other words, a Makerere graduate; he rarely challenged the educated African's liberal teachers, whose assumptions still controlled the discourse of Makerereans and Old Makerereans. Very few staff or students at Makerere recognized any connection between liberal ideology and colonial intellectual repression. Hardly any could acknowledge what a much-admired member of the English Department, Murray Carlin, wrote in the late 1950s, his blunt honesty fueled by sympathy for the students' plight: the central activity at Makerere, Carlin declared, was a kind of mental subversion, "breaking down" the students' "mental tissues" and reconstructing them along Western lines (Stanley 1960, 11). Small wonder that Ruheni's fictional hero thinks of founding "an SUSS, the Stomach Ulcer Sufferers Society" (1973, 23).

The SUSS implies not only stress but also students' attempts to deal with it through humor and talk among themselves. The staff meant well but, hardly aware of their students' private selves, were friendly only according to their own limited understanding (hence the warmth with which Ngugi, decades later, recalls the exceptional Hugh Dinwiddy, discussed below). And there *was* friendliness. As the only university-level institution in all of East and Central Africa, Makerere welcomed students of many ethnic backgrounds, who co-existed with relative comfort. But the developing countries of East Africa needed an institution that would enable intellectuals to form closer ties to their peoples more than they needed comforting Makerere, "a community [literally and figuratively] fenced in" (Mazrui 1978, 254).

Whether from Britain or elsewhere,[24] the rather cloistered, idealistic, but unconsciously conservative young scholars who enlarged the staff in the 1950s were nearly all dedicated to African political independence. Most of them graduates of the great British universities, they reproduced at Makerere "a pale shadow of Oxford or London" (Apthorpe 1965, 12). With only a vague sense of their students' social and cultural context, most of the staff regarded them as "disembodied spirits" (Ingham 1990). Untroubled that everyone in positions of power was white, the staff believed themselves free of racial prejudice (Bown 1990). Whatever the racist tinge of their kindly remoteness, and whatever its deleterious later effects, they succeeded in creating a sanctuary gratefully recalled by many of the students of the period: "an island isolated from the tides and waves around" (Ngugi 1963b). Buffeted by these "tides and waves," most graduates in the early Independence period expressed modest hopes for secure civil-service or teaching jobs rather than the careers at the top in politics, business, and the professions for which it seemed they were being prepared (Barkan 1968, 26).[25] Possibly Makerere made its graduates "feel too heavenborn, too much a mandarinate, . . . to bother to communicate with other classes" through the rough and tumble of politics (Apthorpe 1965, 7). If true, this suggestion may help to explain the extraordinary energy that Ngugi later invested in the Kamiriithu experiment,[26] as he recoiled from isolation amid the academic elite.

THE IMPOSITION OF ALIEN CUSTOMS IN A TIME OF TENSION

Secret Lives, Ngugi's title for his short story collection, describes as well the coexistence of Makerere staff and students, each pretending to understand the other, few succeeding in doing so. With so much at stake, students found it wise to separate the public self from the "personal core" (Prewitt 1966, 39), collaborating to create Europeanized public selves. "Makerere under De Bunsen,"[27] one of Ngugi's characters reminisces, featured "worsted woollen suits, starched white shirts and ties to match . . . proper dressing" (Ngugi 1975, 115). Students dressed better than staff (Macpherson 1987)—"very elegantly . . . [appearing] confident of their social position" as professionals-in-the-making (Tejani 1971, 59; Apthorpe 1965, 8; Goldthorpe 1965, 77). The tolerant and patronizing attitude of the staff shines cheerfully through blinkered British eyes:

> The first dances held at Makerere in 1947 caused tremendous excitement. There were even tutorials in ballroom dancing and tutors found themselves required to remember greater elegance of slow foxtrot or tango steps than they had done for many years and this in itself produced much laughter (Macpherson 1964, 168).

How could anyone be angry amid such gaiety? Some students reciprocated by teaching African dances to the staff. Only after Independence was there a

Department of Music, Dance and Drama for serious study of these inter-twined aspects of African cultures.

The Europeanizing of the students had long been a goal of educators in East Africa. Acting on the premise "that European civilisation . . . is the high-est known scheme of relationships," teachers who knew "little of the African, his language, and his mind" were given "full authority over African boys and girls" (Smith 1926, 258). This education produced "young Africans . . . ashamed of their own tribes, and very sensitive to European contempt" (Smith 1926, 258)—the very students who populated Makerere 40 years later. "In a country that was almost entirely agricultural," Makerere students regarded agricultural work—in fact, "anything indigenous, native, [or] voca-tional"—as "a shameful activity" or "an attempt to keep them subservient" (Hower 1980, 74; Nanka-Bruce 1988, 17). They "behaved like aristocrats—snapping their fingers at waiters, ordering taxi drivers to pick up girls for them along the roadside" (Hower 1980, 74).

Such apemanship, however, failed to persuade the staff that their stu-dents had true culture because, lacking such commonplace European resources as major newspapers, the BBC, and public libraries, Makerere stu-dents had no general knowledge to share with their teachers at the tea- or supper-parties that the bored staff felt bound to conduct. Ruheni's depic-tion of students struggling through "highly academic" conversations about the Warden's "latest Renoir" (1973, 20) captures the students' uncertain grasp of Western values both literal and figurative; if the Warden had a Renoir, it was a cheap reproduction. Few of the equally confused staff—amused and dismayed that students mistook "Father Christmas" for an early Church Father—realized that it was *they,* in the African context, who were ignorant; they could not admit that there was " 'missing background' on *both* sides of the dialogue," and that they needed to "build up a field of African reference" for themselves while teaching English cultural back-ground to their students (Warner 1958, 3, 6; Dinwiddy 1985, 3). In the meantime, students puzzled over conversational etiquette, picked doubt-fully at strange food, and wondered "which knife to pick up for what" (Ruheni 1973, 20).

Even as they complained of the students' passivity, the staff often made no effort to contact them outside the classroom (Stanley 1960, 4). And despite retrospective claims to have been aware of the pressures felt by the students (especially the Gikuyu), the staff thought they could do little "except make life as normal as possible" (Ingham 1990) in the only proper setting for a "normal" academic life—the ivory tower. During and shortly after Mau Mau, this studiously apolitical atmosphere actually exacerbated tensions for Gikuyu students, one of whom wrote that when talking with a staff member, "you don't know whether he regards you as a smartened up murderer, a sympathiser of the movement or what" (Kariara 1959, 7).

STUDENTS' PERCEPTION OF STAFF'S MISSIONARY ATTITUDES

The Kenyan students' political awareness built to a new height just before Independence (*Makererean* (3.2 [27 July 1963], 3). One anecdote told by a former student illustrates both their political consciousness and the chasm in perception between them and staff. About 1960, Grant Kamenju (1987) recounted, a member of staff took him and other Kenyan students on an outing to Lake Victoria. The students talked Kenyan politics nonstop, the staff member remaining silent. At the end of the day, he dropped them at their halls of residence and spoke for the first time: "Everything you have said today is straight from the devil."[28] While so frank an expression of the missionary attitude was unusual, attenuated versions were common. Unwitting "captives of the colonial experience" (Bing 1989), most staff took Western cultural values for granted, their beliefs all the "more harmful because they [were] unmeditated and largely unconscious" (Ngugi 1964g). Because even overtly missionary types intermingled "selflessness and spiritual arrogance" (Mukherjee 1993, 127), students found it difficult to condemn their teachers outright. Ngugi, later rechristening Carey Francis as Cambridge Fraudsham, admitted that he "was great in his own way" (1977, 168).[29]

The students knew that their teachers were governed by a seductive mindset radically different from the one with which they had grown up. Some worried that "we were all being glazed/With a white clay of foreign education" (Cook 1965, 100).[30] Kariara observed that students and staff—greeting one another with "a suspicious, timid smile, pretend[ing] to understand one another's points of view"—were "all very cautious not to hurt other people's feelings" (1959, 7). Repression of personal opinion thus formed the foundation of the "open-mindedness" supposedly endemic at Makerere, and a poor foundation it was for the cultivation of creativity.

CREATIVE WRITING AT MAKERERE—PRE-*PENPOINT* LOCAL PUBLICATIONS AND COMPETITIONS

Ali Mazrui told a 1971 conference at the University of Nairobi: "The Department of English at Makerere can still claim to have produced more creative writers in English in East Africa than any other Department, at home or abroad" (1973, 41–42). The staff saw their central task as "stimulat[ing], maintain[ing] and extend[ing] the conditions for creativity" (Whittock 1968, 94).[31] In Ngugi's day, three members of the English Department were especially significant for their encouragement of creative writing—Margaret Macpherson (at Makerere 1946–81), who contributed greatly to the development of theatre; David Cook (at Makerere 1962–76), who, in addition to the work noted above, published criticism of African literature; and Hugh Dinwiddy (at Makerere 1956–70), who was Warden of Northcote Hall, Dean of Students, and part-time lecturer in English.[32]

Earlier staff attempts to foster writing included the publication of thoroughly colonial student essays in the *Makerere College Magazine* (founded in the mid-1930s). Beginning in 1947, the year the Makerere College Literary Society was founded, these efforts often took the form of College competitions. The first two such were the Interhall English Competition (at first only for plays) and the Literary Competition for short stories, which attracted nine entries in the first year and inspired the judge, Elspeth Huxley, to recommend that African short-story writers "study deeply the methods and art of the masters . . . Rudyard Kipling and Somerset Maugham" (Huxley 1947, 40). Notwithstanding her own recommendation that "the young African writer," like Homer and Malory, "draw on the folk-lore and tradition of his people for inspiration and fresh plots," Huxley denied the prize to "the best told of the tales"[33] because it was derived from folk material and was therefore "reportage" (Huxley 1947, 38). Other genres besides fiction later got their contests, some sponsored by outside bodies. Since the favored forms were short, writers were discouraged from attempting major works. One important exception was the Literature Bureau's competition for novels, for which Ngugi wrote *The River Between.*

The influence of publications and competitions—nearly all sponsored by expatriates and all aimed at a tiny minority of the population—may ultimately have been pernicious, for they "almost stifled any indigenous attempt at [original] expression through the newly-acquired language" (Rubadiri 1968, 149). Language itself was a problem. Most prizes were for writing in English, although in the early 60s competitions occasionally sought writing in African languages as well.[34] For the most part, East African writers used English with careful skill "but without any of the relish and abandon" of West Africans (Mahood 1966, 20). A Makerere student summed up the "haunting tragedy of multilingual Africa": "We can all communicate in English but very few of us can express ourselves in English" (Sentongo 1967, 6).

PENPOINT AND MAKERERE LITERARY TASTE

Penpoint, founded in 1958 as *The English Department Magazine,* developed rapidly from its first issues heavy with staff contributions—poems, quizzes and moralistic essays that modeled "good" writing. Michael Kaggwa's "The Journey of the Shepherds" (no. 6, Dec. 1959, 6), a serious parody of David Rubadiri's already celebrated "Stanley Meets Mutesa," was an heartening sign, for the inspiration came from an African rather than a Western poet (Rubadiri's poem, published in *Penpoint* no. 1 [1958], itself parodied T. S. Eliot's "Journey of the Magi"). Kaggwa's and Rubadiri's poems both exhibit

Makerere literary values, which put a premium on "lucidity . . . linguistic discipline . . . delicate sureness in making fine points and subtle descriptions" (Cook 1961b, 1). The head of the English Department praised a student writer (whom he didn't trouble to name—Elvania Zirimu, in fact) in patronizing terms that he surely would not have bestowed upon British undergraduates: she presented "African material . . . in English with simplicity and freshness . . . with charm and skill, and without naiveté or self-consciousness" (Warner 1963, 52). Fortunately, *Penpoint* did not remain completely in thrall to expatriate standards. African writers outside the Makerere orbit occasionally provided more varied stimulus; Ngugi co-edited an issue (no. 15, July 1963) that included work by three South Africans who were becoming famous: Richard Rive, Dennis Brutus, and Ezekiel Mphahlele. Thus African writers sidled into Makerere, albeit not into the syllabus. In the following year, *Penpoint* went from cyclostyled to printed form; in 1971 it was renamed *Dhana*.[35]

The kind of writing valued at Makerere during the earlier 1960s appears in the anthology selected by Cook and Ngugi from the pages of *Penpoint* (including four stories by Ngugi).[36] Some of the writing, Cook claimed, was "of a very high quality on an absolute standard" (1965, x); by the more appropriate relative standard of Western university student writing, the poems, stories and short plays collected in *Origin East Africa* are, like most such writing, apprentice work with a few pieces showing exceptional talent. Most of the authors apply foreign narrative techniques to indigenous subjects, a few implying disdain for "backward" rural people; two folk tales employ more traditional narration. Recurrent themes include the conflict between Christian and traditional religion, and the struggle against an often hostile nature. Ngugi's "The Return" is among the few works that address political issues. The perennial faults of undergraduate writing appear: stiff, unidiomatic dialogue in the stories and plays (with the notable exception of Tunde Aiyegbusi's and Peter Nazareth's plays), archaic diction and unnatural syntax in the poetry. With the blessed exception of the plays, humor is in short supply.

Besides Kariara's poem lamenting the "disease" of "foreign education" (Cook 1965, 100), the one work in *Origin East Africa* that directly concerns Makerere is Nazareth's satirical play "Brave New Cosmos," which beat Ngugi's "The Rebels" in the 1961 Interhall Competition (Sicherman 1990, 5). The urbanized, quotation-spouting Kaggwa, an undergraduate studying English, expects the world to be his oyster once he takes his degree; scorning "cheap literature" and *Time Magazine,* he prefers "great books of criticism like Bradley's" (Cook 1965, 170–71). Writing a play called "The Yellow Maize-Patch" for the Interhall Competition, Kaggwa has decided to "take a theme from a play by Ibsen or some other dramatist and Africanize it" (Cook 1965, 174), responding to English Department efforts to foster African literature on Western models and blithely ignoring African orature. As he mocks the adjudicators' response the year before to Kariara's "The Green Bean Patch"

(Nazareth 1990), Kaggwa's friend sneers: "Don't forget to throw in the usual set, with bamboos, and to dress your actors in barkcloth"; the adjudicators favor plays set in villages, with the chief's "son dramatically returning home from civilization in time to save his people" (Cook 1965, 174)—rather like Ngugi's black hermit, who appeared the following year. So separate are literature and life for Kaggwa that he laughs dismissively when a village friend envies him the joys of "sit[ting] on the green grass under a tree and read[ing] . . . Wordsworth" (Cook 1965, 177). Only a "caveman" would study in the open; "a modern civilized human being" reads in a library.

PERSONAL INFLUENCE: DINWIDDY AND MACPHERSON

The success of Nazareth's play in the competition reproves his mockery of the adjudicators, less hidebound than he imagined. Several staff members personally encouraged the most talented students. It was to Dinwiddy, Warden of his own hall of residence, that Ngugi showed his first novel; indeed, Dinwiddy—a man beloved for his encouraging kindness, intellectual stimulus, and sheer fun—worked with him "page by page" on what became *The River Between* (Dinwiddy 1987). Dinwiddy recalls giving unwitting stimulus to the writing of Ngugi's first novel when he remarked during a lecture on *Othello* in 1960:

> "It's time we had some African novelists. We can't go on with Elspeth Huxley." And so about three weeks later, at ten o'clock at night, there came a knock on our front door, and there was James [Ngugi]. He said, "I've done something awful." I said, "What can I do? How can I help?" He said, "I've started writing a novel, and I've got stuck! There it is." He'd brought the manuscript with him, stacks of paper. I said, "For goodness sake, come in" (Dinwiddy 1987).[37]

No wonder that Ngugi was then, as the artist Elimo Njau remembered, "an innocent child of Dinwiddy" (E. Njau 1991). But he was more: genuinely encouraged by Dinwiddy to think for himself, he was beginning to form, in his extracurricular journalism, the critique of colonialism that took firmer shape in Leeds a year or two after his graduation from Makerere. "About the last thing he did at Makerere in public," Dinwiddy (1987) recalled, was to speak at the traditional end-of-year dinner, "in a state of trembling emotion," against "bourgeois teaching" in the Department of Fine Arts—a department that, in the view of Europeans, "had done its absolute utmost to introduce . . . the spirit of African feeling about the pictorial world" (Dinwiddy 1987).[38]

Although Ngugi was already surpassing what even Dinwiddy had to teach him, he insists on the latter's valuable influence (Ngugi 1987). Along with his own effort to know each student personally, the engagingly nonconformist Warden created what became known as the Northcote "spirit," emblematized today by an abstract sculpture outside the main entrance. Urging students "to contribute to the general well being," he fostered informal debates, sports, and dances (Dinwiddy 1987). Among his efforts to "bring people together" were his periodic "Northcote Hall Newsletter," full of information and humor, and his invitations to visiting dignitaries to meet with students (Dinwiddy 1987). On one such occasion in 1961, Ngugi was among the Kenyan students who, "muttering angrily," departed in protest when the visiting Colonial Secretary, Alan Lennox-Boyd, thoughtlessly described them as "Kenya boys" (Dinwiddy and Twaddle 1988, 198).

The other major influence on creative work at Makerere came from the redoubtable Margaret Macpherson, to whom Rubadiri traces the flowering of theatre in Kampala in the 1960s (Lindfors 1989, 69). Early in her 35-year tenure she built upon the use by the colonial Department of Social Welfare of what is now called "theater for development"; and well before orature became a subject of formal study, she encouraged the collection of oral literature and the use of folklore in African drama.[39] She tirelessly produced classic English plays and, by the late 1950s, plays written by Makerere students.

A DISAPPOINTED ELITE SUFFERING "SOUL MUTILATION"

No matter how sympathetic, the staff could sense only dimly the huge psychic burden shouldered by Makerere students, who were not "disembodied spirits" at all but complicated people "torn two ways" between "the West and . . . the tribe" (Ngugi 1962a). The students themselves were painfully aware of the "filtering process" that had selected them from the thousands of students discarded during the rough and almost arbitrary sequence of examinations (Ruheni 1973, 18). But instead of glorying in their achievement, they felt inferior to the only beings who seemed to matter—Europeans. "We were supposedly the elite," Nazareth recalled, "yet somehow there was this feeling that we were not good enough. We were not Europeans" (Lindfors 1980, 84). The 1958 Makerere commencement orator in Ruheni's novel *The Future Leaders* praises the graduates in a premonitory fashion, calling them "the future leaders of this country," on whom depend "the hopes of the peoples of the great territories of Uganda, Kenya and Tanganyika" (1973, 1). Not long after, the narrator dismisses the speech: "How can they all be the future leaders? And who will do the work?" (1973, 66). That question—the relationship between intellectuals and workers—was increasingly to preoccupy a few Makerere graduates, particularly those who, like Ngugi, went abroad for further education and were caught up in the international swirl of ideas of the 1960s.

At home or abroad, most Makerere graduates struggled with the effects of their teachers' unwitting "mental subversion." No one could expect, "after sowing so many purely European seeds in one's mind, a harvest that was

African or even tolerably half-caste" (Bukenya 1972, 29).[40] The alienated hero of a Makerere undergraduate's short story describes himself and his fellows as "doomed to sterility and civilization" (Nagenda 1965, 26). The young African elite suffered from something like "soul murder," a traumatic experience that the psychiatrist Leonard Shengold defines as "instances of repetitive and chronic overstimulation, alternating with emotional deprivation, that are deliberately brought about by another individual" (1989, 16–17). The Makerere hothouse did indeed "deliberately" provide "repetitive and chronic overstimulation." The phrase "emotional deprivation" aptly describes the African student, estranged from his home environment and placed among paternalistic Europeans who appeared to have the students' best concerns at heart while often cruelly disappointing them. "Mutilation" may be a more appropriate term than "murder," however, for it has less finality. A mutilation may be amended by some sort of prosthesis, or a new part may grow to replace the lost one; the soul may even emerge stronger.

Some late-colonial Makerere graduates came eventually to a revision of their Makerere experience that enabled them to enjoy an integrated culture rather than remaining "ugly half caste[s] of Westernism and Africanism" (*Makererean* 3.1 [13 July 1963], 5). They had first to recover from colonial brainwashing, "an inevitable part of psychic murder, resulting all too often in what Nietzsche called the worst form of slavery: that of the slave who has lost the knowledge of being a slave" (Shengold 1989, 16). It is impossible to say how many Makerere graduates were slaves of this sort. Thinking retrospectively, one Old Makererean caricatured a member of the English Department, a man he had earlier admired, as "a sort of giant brain with no heart."[41] Those Makerere graduates who themselves became giant brains with no heart were far more likely to become slaves than were those like Ngugi, whose "enormous warmth" (Dinwiddy 1987) mediated the later ideological fixities of his brain.

At Makerere, Ngugi adapted well, learning to speak out of both sides of his mouth: Leavisite when writing for his teachers, incipiently socialist in his journalism. On the one hand he asserted that Makerere was "wholly colonial with all its prejudices and intellectual slant in favour of the West"; on the other, he complained like any African intellectual in the twilight of colonial rule about the customary problems: the frustrations "of writing for a foreign audience," the indifference or ignorance of African readers, and the lack of an East African literary tradition or "an intellectual community in which ideas will throb" (1963d; 1964f). Then, as he later recalled, "Leeds came to my rescue" (1993, 7).

CURATIVE EXPERIENCES AT LEEDS UNIVERSITY

Ngugi came to Leeds University in 1964[42] with much more than his Master's degree on his mind. Of course, he had ideas for a thesis on West Indian litera-

ture. At last able to read widely, he found particularly compelling the persistence of "African consciousness . . . in West Indian awareness"; this was itself
part of a "larger theme" typical of 60s intellectuals from the supposedly
"postcolonial" world: "the search for an identity in an essentially colonial situation" (1972, 83, 89). The identity he chose was that of the African teacher-
novelist moving "with a whip among the pupils"—readers in Africa—while
"flagellating himself as well as them" (Ngugi 1966, 54). That dynamic
stance, along with the implied violence, was to mark Ngugi's writing hence-
forward.

As part of his re-formation of identity, Ngugi began speaking aloud his
doubts about the very foundation of both his colonial education and his existence as a writer: the English language (in Marcuson 1966, 8). Thus the articulation of his most essential creative principles evolved far from home; distance makes the eye see clearer, and the 60s produced many kinds of distance.
A good vantage point from which to understand the homeland better, the
ugly industrial/proletarian city of Leeds gave the lie to "England's green and
pleasant Land"—Makerere graduates in English literature would be familiar
with Blake's preface to his prophetic poem *Milton*—in ways that enchant-
ingly beautiful Oxford or Cambridge could not. The Blakean spirit of revolution rooted in Leeds's "dark satanic mills" turned out to be a valuable part of
the African colonial heritage.

In grimy Leeds, its own contradictions undermining reverence for things
British, Makerere graduates could better perceive the "colonial character" of
their alma mater and resolve to build a Blakean "Jerusalem" in their own
countries (Ngugi 1989).[43] Their socialist faith, growing organically out of
their East African experiences, was fertilized at Leeds University by a rich mix
of extracurricular intellectual activity and nurtured in Arnold Kettle's courses
in the English novel—their first experience of "relevant" intellectual life
within the academy. Steeped in Kettle's humane socialism and imbued with
Marx and Fanon, they restored their "mental tissues," undoing the "reconstruction in the Western mode" that Makerere had attempted (Stanley 1960,
11). And so they returned from Leeds ready to cry out to the British: "I shall
no longer simply ride on your shock absorbers—I wish to walk on the ground
and feel this soul of my mother under my feet" (Rubadiri 1966, 12). For some
at least, the subversion of the mind had been undone.

Notes

Research for this paper was partly funded by the Research Foundation of the City
University of New York. An earlier and much abbreviated version was presented at a 1994
conference on Ngugi and appears in the conference proceedings, *Ngugi wa Thiong'o: Texts and
Contexts* (Trenton, NJ: Africa World Press, 1995).

1. Years later, a selective memory gave Ngugi only the confirmatory example of
magic, not the failed effort that taught him a Christian lesson (Ngugi 1981a, 128).

2. Makerere College, founded as a technical high school in 1922, became an institution of higher learning in 1938. Enormous growth took place in the 1950s—from 213 students and some 40 staff in 1951 to 696 students and some 100 staff in 1957–58 (Goldthorpe and Macpherson 1958, 351).

3. In 1958, 0.61 percent of the boys and 0.04 percent of the girls in the eligible age group were enrolled in the final year of high school (Goldthorpe 1965, 7).

4. There were many variants of this policy. When Ngugi's Independent school was taken over by the government during the Emergency, English became the language of instruction and pupils were punished for speaking Gikuyu at school (Ngugi 1986, 11).

5. According to the *AHS Magazine* for 1956 (p. 11), 70 percent of the student body belonged to the Christian Union, and 130 AHS students were teaching over 2000 children. Most of the participants were Gikuyu who taught in their mother tongue.

6. Here, too, the colonial mindset prevailed, as in Peter Kinyanjui's essay on his namesake, "A Great Kikuyu Chief," applauded for welcoming the first British traders (*AHS Magazine* 1959, 44–45).

7. The 1957 issue notes a debate on the motion that "Education is the chief source of discontent" (*AHS Magazine,* p. 15); "Political Science should be taught in African Secondary Schools" was among the topics in 1958 (*AHS Magazine,* p. 17).

8. Although the College had been open to all races since 1951, in the 50s there had been only five European undergraduates, along with a few British and American graduate students (Goldthorpe 1965, 13). In 1961, the Teachers for East Africa scheme (discussed below) began bringing substantial numbers of white students.

9. Makerere joined in 1961 with the fledgling university colleges in Nairobi and Dar es Salaam in preparation for full academic independence as the short-lived University of East Africa (see Maxwell 1980, 196ff.).

10. During the early 60s, there were minor variations in the syllabus and examination system. Ngugi was apparently governed by an even more prescriptive curriculum, since he had to produce a ninth exercise on a "special subject," the Conrad project discussed below.

11. Ngugi names T. S. Eliot in addition to Arnold and Leavis as a main influence at Makerere, noting that "Eliot's high culture of an Anglo-Catholic feudal tradition" was "suspiciously close to the culture of the 'high table' and to the racial doctrines of those born to rule" (1986, 90).

12. The staff in the departments of History and English thought that 19th-century England provided apt models for Uganda in the 1950s. In a political protest in 1958, three students paraded through Kampala bearing a banner reading: "DOWN WITH EARLY NINETEENTH CENTURY TORY DESPOTISM," enraging the British and making no impact on "the necessarily uncomprehending populace of Uganda" (Dinwiddy 1985, 4–5).

13. In a paper delivered at a seminar in Zimbabwe in 1981, Ngugi expanded the analysis of *Hard Times* (1981b, 90–91).

14. I am grateful to Peter Nazareth for providing photocopies of these essays and to Ngugi for permission to use them. "Why Nostromo?" quotes Leavis, 1948 (the chapter on Conrad's "Minor Works and *Nostromo*")—the only secondary source cited in the essay. The paper on "The Secret Sharer" is a pendant to the one on *Lord Jim.* On Cook, see below.

15. Given the size of the Makerere library (64,000 volumes in 1961, exclusive of the Medical Library—Macpherson 1964, 139), the acquisitions policy was respectable. My unscientific sampling of holdings in African and West Indian literature and criticism published by 1964 yielded the following data (parenthetical figures indicate the number of titles under each author's name): Abrahams (7), Achebe (3), Ekwensi (7), Hearne (3), Lamming (3), Mphahlele (4), Naipaul (7), Soyinka (4), and Tutuola (5).

16. Nazareth's hostile opinion of Cook appears in an anonymous letter from a civil servant—as Nazareth then was—in support of a scurrilous anonymous attack on Cook (unnamed but easily recognizable) by a London-based Makerere graduate (in *Transition* 6.30 [1967]: 8);

the supportive letter accuses Cook of having "discouraged and killed local creative talent" by forcing writers to "run while they are learning to walk" (*Transition* 7.32 [1967]: 7).

17.   Cook wanted to credit Ngugi as co-editor of *Origin East Africa,* but the department chair (Geoffrey Walton) thought it inappropriate to put a student's name on the cover (Nazareth 1990); Cook says that he "discussed the whole matter with James Ngugi, then a second year student, and we began sifting" (1965, ix–x). The Travelling Theatre began in 1965 during the long vacation, when nine undergraduates toured Uganda and Kenya with a repertoire of eleven short plays in Kiswahili, Luganda, Runyoro/Rutoro, and English, seven of the plays being by Makerere students (Cook 1966; see Cook and Lee 1968, "Introduction"); see also Horn 1978, 24.

18.   In describing local assessments of the TEA, I rely mainly on Shields, supplemented by *Makererean* 6.46 (24 Jan. 1967): 4. For an extensive analysis, see Nanka-Bruce 1981, 116–46. The Americans were all sponsored by Columbia University's Teachers College and the U.S. Agency for International Development. The United States government funded recruitment and training while the East African governments provided salaries and allowances; the U.S. withdrew its support in 1966, when it began sending Peace Corps volunteers instead. The program continued for another two years, with mainly British participants. By 1963, the British government was sharing costs of recruitment and training equally with the U.S., and intake numbers were evenly balanced between the U.S. and the U.K. (134 from each); the total to date was 404 (U.S.) and 191 (U.K.) (*Reporter* [Nairobi] 8 June 1963, 26); the final U.S. total was 461 (Nanka-Bruce, 1981). The TEAs were taught separately from the local students in some Dip. Ed. courses (Psychology and Principles of Education); this and other allegedly discriminatory practices aroused controversy; see the series of accusatory and defensive letters in *Transition* in 1968 (7.34:34; 7.35: 8–10; 7.36: 12–13). One thing is certain: the percentage of Makerere graduates who entered the Dip. Ed. program between 1961–62 and 1968–69 actually declined from 24 to 16 percent (Nanka-Bruce 50), as employment opportunities broadened and teachers salaries continued to be low.

19.   *The Undergraduate* had published sporadically in 1955–59. The issue edited by Ngugi (4.1, March 1962) was apparently its last. There were four Information Officers, described as members of the Guild Publications Bureau.

20.   The editors of *Makerere Horizon* were Ngugi and A. C. Juma. The editorial bears evidence of Ngugi's extracurricular reading, referring to Abrahams, Achebe, Tutuola, and Ekwensi. A similar call to "wake up and get on with the job" appears in Ngugi's account of the 1962 writers' conference published in *The Makererean* (1962d).

21.   *Weep Not, Child,* dated "Northcote Hall July 1962" (Ngugi 1964h, 136), was "written and re-written in Room 75" (Dinwiddy, "Northcote Hall Newsletter" no. 11 [14 Nov. 1963]); it was accepted for publication in 1962 (*Makererean* 2.4 [8 Oct. 1962], 1). The other Makerere students at the conference were Jonathan Kariara, John Nagenda, and Rebeka Njau; the only other East Africans present were Okot p'Bitek and Grace Ogot. Nagenda and Okot were Ugandan; the others, Kenyan. All of the East Africans present became significant players on the East African literary scene—Kariara (d. 1993) as a writer, anthologist, actor, editor, and "master of the art of conversation" whose poems "are known to literally hundreds of thousands of Kenyan students" (Williams 1993); Nagenda as a writer of fiction and poetry, as well as a broadcaster (see the biographical note in Nagenda 1986); Njau as a writer of fiction and plays, as well as a teacher (see the out-of-date biographical note in R. Njau 1975); Okot (d. 1982) and Ogot as writers of international as well as regional repute (see Zell, Bundy, and Coulon 1983, 441–42 and 463–64). For Nagenda's later comment on the conference, see Nkosi 1962; for a detailed analysis of the conference, see Fonlon 1963.

22.   Ngugi later laughed at himself for having made "a peasant mother . . . speak in a poetic language reminiscent in tone of T. S. Eliot" (Ngugi 1986, 43). Gerald Moore's review (1963) singled out the "bizarre syntax" of Ngugi's "curiously jerky and short-winded" verse, a fault that Nazareth (1963) claimed had been eliminated during rehearsals. The text was pub-

lished later with some revisions. According to Ngugi (1989), he changed the names to seem generally African, rather than "recognizably from Central Kenya"; but Nazareth (1990), who once owned a copy of the original script, says there were also substantive changes that injected slightly anachronistic post-Independence political ideas. Ngugi refused to give Mahood a copy of the script because he was "dissatisfied with its present form" (Mahood 1966, 30). The play was performed the following year in a Ugandan high school, according to Dinwiddy's "Northcote Hall Newsletter" no. 14 (4 July 1964), 2.

23. After leaving Makerere, Ingham became Director of Studies at the Royal Military College (Sandhurst) and, later, Professor of History at Bristol University. In order to fill the curricular void, while at Makerere he wrote the first two of his books on African history, with titles indicating the Eurocentric bias of the time: *Europe and Africa: A School Certificate History* (1953) and *The Making of Modern Uganda* (1958).

24. Several members of the English Department were South African—Whittock, Carlin, and D. D. Stuart.

25. Barkan's research "confirm[ed] what observers of Makerere have felt for some time," that most students were "pragmatic and non-ideological, and not prepared to fight for principles" (*Makererean* 6.50 [18 July 1967], 7). His findings fit both the colonial period (when Makerere graduates were being trained for the colonial administration) and the 1960s (when Obote's informers infiltrated Makerere classrooms more effectively than had their colonial predecessors—see Mazrui 1978, x–xi; Langlands 1977, 6). For the actual occupations of the 1481 people who had graduated from Makerere by 1959, see Goldthorpe 1965, 61; he describes them as a "white-collar elite" shaped by the needs of the colonial administration (p. 63). On the changing connotations of a career in politics during the 1950s, see Goldthorpe 1965, 84.

26. Ngugi and Ngugi wa Mirii's creation of *Ngaahika Ndeenda* in his home village of Kamiriithu in 1977 led to his detention. See Ngugi 1981a (75–80) and 1981c (39–51).

27. On Bernard de Bunsen, the Makerere Principal, see Sicherman 1990, 109–10; he died in 1990.

28. The responses of former staff members to Kamenju's story may be calibrated according to their degree of politicization. At one end of the spectrum, a long-serving staff member pronounced the story "totally unlikely." In the middle, a historian "could think of one" person who might have spoken the offensive statement but added emphatically that "that was *not* the [general] mentality." At the other extreme, a member of the Extramural Department—who had taken "Marx for granted" (in general, Marx appeared at Makerere, if at all, "only as an incidental rather eccentric figure" [Ngugi in Marcuson 1966, 6])—responded immediately and energetically: "Actually, I *can*," adding that the likely suspects were "not the most intelligent people of the strongly Christian group." Arthur French, a member of the Education faculty, belonged to "the strongly Christian group": " 'Child-centred education' without Christ-centred religion," he declared, was "a very horrid thing" (1958, 8).

29. Francis was also the model for Rev. Livingstone, the headmaster in *Weep Not, Child*. Njoroge (1978, 239) sees the change from allusion ("Livingstone") to outright allegorical mockery ("Fraudsham") as evidence of Ngugi's "anger with Kenya's post-independence and his determination to condemn . . . missionaries and the Christian religion."

30. Borrowing Kariara's metaphor, an old man in Ngugi's story "A Meeting in the Dark" says that "those coated with the white clay of the whiteman's ways are the worst. They have nothing inside" (1975, 62).

31. Whittock is quoting and endorsing his former Makerere colleague R. G. Harris's inaugural lecture at the University of Malawi.

32. Macpherson served from 1946–48 as Headmistress of Makerere College School—the Education faculty's demonstration school—and then joined the English Department, which she chaired before her retirement in 1981; she has continued to publish alumni newsletters and also to sponsor reunions in England. Among her publications were a "chronicle" of

Makerere (Macpherson 1964), *If It Works, It's Right: A Handbook of Play Production for East African Schools and Colleges* (East African Publishing House, 1979), and a collection of short plays for school production, *The Cooking Pan and Other Plays* (Heinemann 1979). Cook embarked on his "love-affair with East Africa" when he visited and taught briefly at Makerere in 1961 (Cook 1961a, 31). He returned in 1962 as a staff member, became chair (1967), oversaw a renovation of the curriculum (1968–72), was named Professor of Literature in 1971, and left in 1977 to teach in Nigeria. Having taught at the University of Southampton from 1957, he was one of the few expatriate staff members to give up a promising career in the U.K. in order to come to Makerere. Dinwiddy, after his return to England, wrote searching articles, reviews, and conference papers on East African education, literature, and religion; he has also returned to East Africa on several occasions.

    33.   This was A. M. Nhonoli's "The Chief's Beautiful Daughter," *Makerere* 2.5 (1948), 86–93. The winning story was Nicholas C. Otieno's "The Adventures of Oingo" (*Makerere* 2.4 [1947], 33–37).

    34.   The East African Creative Writing Committee received a £3,000 Rockefeller Grant to finance prizes for short stories in English, Gikuyu, Kiswahili, or Luganda; in a previous competition for a novel in English, Kiswahili, or Luganda, there were 48 entries (*Reporter* [Nairobi] 25 May 1963, 30–31).

    35.   Virtually suspended during the Amin and Obote II regimes—vol. 7.1 appeared in 1977; vol. 8.1, in 1981—*Dhana* (Kiswahili for "thought" or "imagination") was revived in 1993; my thanks to William Shullenberger for a copy.

    36.   The four stories are "The Return," "The Village Priest," "Gone with the Wind," and "The Fig Tree" (Cook 1965, 53–76); all but "Gone with the Wind" appear in *Secret Lives,* where "The Fig Tree" is retitled "Mugumo." For the publication history of the *Penpoint* stories, see Sicherman 1989, (nos.) 50–63, 65–68, 75–79. For an analysis of Ngugi's significant revisions of "The Village Priest" between *Origin East Africa* and *Secret Lives,* see Cook and Okenimkpe 1983, 145–47. An inveterate reviser, Ngugi had already tinkered with the ending of "The Village Priest" between its first publication in the *Kenya Weekly News* (28 Apr. 1961, 44–45) and the second version in *Penpoint* no. 13 (Oct. 1962), 2–6. At the same time as he published stories in *Penpoint* (in which he also published two plays—Sicherman 1989, (nos.) 73–74 and 109–10), he published other stories in the *Kenya Weekly News*—basically a settlers' paper—and *Transition,* the voice of his own emergent African generation—Sicherman 1989, (nos.) 60, 65, 80, 83, 85.

    37.   Dinwiddy (1987) gives the date as 1959. Ngugi reports writing "a shy little note" to Dinwiddy confessing his wish to be a writer—before he had written anything (1972, 47). A variant has Ngugi telling Kariara that he had written a story for *Penpoint,* and then proceeding to write it (Nazareth 1990).

    38.   Ngugi's undiminished animus against the Makerere School of Art is evident in his complaint in "Education for a National Culture" that "the European lecturers used to import clay from Europe. Ugandan soil was not good enough for art, even though the students were all Africans" (Ngugi 1981b, 95), and local people produced clay pots.

    39.   Information from comments at the Uganda Literature Festival (London, 24–25 May 1991) by Macpherson and by Rose Mbowa of the Makerere Department of Music, Dance and Drama. Macpherson's collaborations included *Let's Make a Play* with her student E. C. N. Kironde (East African Literature Bureau, 1960), and she directed many student plays, including Kariara's "The Green Bean Patch."

    40.   The setting of the novel is actually the University of Dar es Salaam, although it is often mistaken for Makerere; Bukenya, a graduate of Dar es Salaam, proceeded to Makerere for graduate work.

    41.   Nazareth (1990), crediting someone else (unnamed) with the phrase.

    42.   A more detailed analysis of this topic appears in Sicherman 1995.

    43.   In another irony, "Jerusalem" is a depressed residential area of Nairobi.

References

Abdullahi, Aminu. 1964. "Ngugi wa Thiong' o," in Dennis Duerden and Cosmo Pieterse (eds.) *African Writers Talking: A Collection of Radio Interviews*. London, Ibadan, Nairobi: Heinemann; New York: Africana Publishing Corp., pp. 124–31.

Apthorpe, Raymond, Margaret Macpherson, David Rubadiri, and James Allen. 1965. "A Symposium Discussing J. E. Goldthorpe, *An African Elite: Makerere College Students 1922–1960. . . .*" *Makerere Journal* no. 11 (Dec.): 1–16.

Ashby, Eric. 1961. *Patterns of Universities in Non-European Societies*. London: School of Oriental and African Studies, University of London.

Barkan, Joel D. 1968. "What Makes the East African Student Run?" *Transition* 37: 26–31.

Bing, John. 1989. Telephone interview, 28 July.

Bown, Lalage. 1990. Interview, Glasgow, 16 July.

Bukenya, Austin. 1972. *The People's Bachelor*. Nairobi: East African Publishing House.

Cook, David. 1961a. "Ten Weeks," *Transition* 1.2: 31–34.

———. 1961b. "Judge Not that Ye Be Not Judged: Confessions of an Adjudicator," *Penpoint* no. 11: 1–2.

——— (ed.) 1965. *Origin East Africa: A Makerere Anthology*. London, Ibadan, Nairobi: Heinemann.

———. 1966. "Theatre Goes to the People!" *Transition* 25.2: 23–33.

———. 1971. "Literature: The Great Teaching Power of the World: Inaugural Lecture . . . Nairobi: East African Literature Bureau. [Unpaginated.]

———. 1976. *In Black and White: Writings from East Africa with Broadcast Discussions and Commentary*. Kampala, Nairobi, Dar es Salaam: East African Literature Bureau.

Cook, David, and Miles Lee (eds.). 1968. *Short East African Plays in English*. London, Nairobi, Ibadan: Heinemann.

Cook, David, and Michael Okenimkpe. 1983. *Ngugi wa Thiong' o: An Exploration of his Writings*. London, Ibadan, and Nairobi: Heinemann.

Cook, David, and David Rubadiri (eds.). 1971. *Poems from East Africa*. London, Ibadan, Nairobi: Heinemann.

de Bunsen, Bernard. 1987. Interview, London, 12 August.

Dinwiddy, Hugh. 1985. "Makerere and Development in East Africa in the Colonial Period." Unpublished paper presented at the Conference on Uganda, University of Copenhagen, 25–29 Sept.

———. 1987. Interview, Bognor Regis, 20 July.

Dinwiddy, Hugh, and Michael Twaddle. 1988. "The Crisis at Makerere," in Holger Bernt Hansen and Michael Twaddle (eds.) *Uganda Now: Between Decay and Development,* pp. 195–204. London: James Currey; Athens: Ohio University Press; Nairobi: Heinemann Kenya.

Duerden, Dennis. 1964. "Ngugi wa Thiong' o," in Dennis Duerden and Cosmo Pieterse (eds.) *African Writers Talking: A Collection of Radio Interviews*. London, Ibadan, Nairobi: Heinemann; New York: Africana Publishing Corp., pp. 121–24.

——— and Cosmo Pieterse (eds.). 1972. *African Writers Talking: A Collection of Radio Interviews*. London, Ibadan, Nairobi: Heinemann; New York: Africana Publishing Corp.

"Editorial." 1961. *Makerere Horizon* 1.1: 2–4.

Fonlon, Bernard. 1963. "African Writers Meet in Uganda," *Abbia* 1 (Feb.): 39–53.

Francis, E. Carey. 1957. "Foreword," *The AHS Magazine,* Sept.: 1–2.

French, A[rthur]. 1958. "A Christian Approach to Education," *The Undergraduate* 2.4 (Apr.): 7–8.

Goldthorpe, J. E. 1965. "An African Elite: Makerere College Students 1922–1960," *East African Studies 17*. Nairobi: Oxford University Press for the East African Institute of Social Research.

Goldthorpe, J. E., and Margaret Mcpherson. 1958. "Makerere College and Its Old Students," *Zaire* 12.4: 349–63.

Greaves, L. B. 1969. *Carey Francis of Kenya*. Foreword by Oginga Odinga. London: Rex Collings.

Hindmarsh, Ronald. 1962. "Cut the Cackle" [review of Alan Warner, *A Short Guide to English Style* (London, Oxford University Press, 1961)]. *Transition* 2.3: 32–33.

Horn, Andrew. 1978. "The Golden Decade of Theatre in Uganda," *Literary Half-Yearly* 19.1: 22–49.

Hower, Edward. 1980. *The New Life Hotel*. Reprint. London: Robin Clark, 1983.

Huxley, Elspeth. 1947. "Best Original Short Story: Judge's Comments," *Makerere* 2.4: 37–40.

Ingham, Kenneth. 1990. Interview, Bristol, 11 July.

Kamenju, Grant. 1987. Interview, Nairobi, 5 May.

Kariara, Jonathan. 1958. "On Revising for an English Examination: A Soliloquy," *Penpoint* no. 1: 8–9.

———. 1959. "What Is Wrong with Makerere Society," *The Undergraduate* 2.4 (Feb.): 7–8.

Kipkorir, B. E. 1980. "Carey Francis at the A.H.S., Kikuyu[,] 1940–62," in B. E. Kipkorir (ed.) *Biographical Essays on Imperialism and Collaboration in Colonial Kenya*. Nairobi: Kenya Literature Bureau, pp. 112–59.

Kironde, Erisa. 1968. "The Trick," in David Cook and Miles Lee (eds.) *Short East African Plays in English*. London, Nairobi, Ibadan: Heinemann, pp. 103–14.

Kozoll, C. 1962. "To Be—or What To Be," *The Makererean* 2.2 (20 Aug.): 2.

Langlands, Bryan. 1977. "Students and Politics in Uganda," *African Affairs* 76.302: 3–20.

Leavis, F. R. 1948. *The Great Tradition: George Eliot, Henry James, Joseph Conrad*. Reprint. Harmondsworth: Penguin Books in Association with Chatto and Windus, 1962.

Lindfors, Bernth (ed.). 1980. *Mazungumzo: Interviews with East African Writers, Publishers, Editors, and Scholars*. Athens, OH: Ohio University Center for International Studies.

———. 1981. "Ngugi wa Thiong o's Early Journalism," *World Literature Written in English* 20.1: 23–41.

———. 1983. "An Interview with Okot p'Bitek," *World Literature Written in English* 12: 281–99.

———. (ed.). 1989. *Kulankula: Interviews with Writers from Malawi and Lesotho*. Bayreuth African Studies Series 14. Bayreuth: Bayreuth University.

lo Liyong, Taban. 1965. "Can We Correct Literary Barrenness in East Africa?" *East Africa Journal* 2.8 (Dec.): 5–13.

———. 1968. "Post Script," *Nexus* 4: 5–6.

Macpherson, Margaret. 1964. *They Built for the Future: A Chronicle of Makerere University College 1922–1962*. Cambridge: Cambridge University Press.

———. 1987. Interview, Bowness-on-Windermere, 9 July.

Mahood, M. M. 1966. "Drama in New-Born States," *Présence africaine* 32: 23–39.

Marcuson, Alan, assisted by Mike Gonzalez, Sue Drake, and Dave Williams. 1966. "James Ngugi," *Union News* 18 Nov.: 6–8.

Maxwell, I. C. M. 1980. *Universities in Partnership: The Inter-University Council and the Growth of Higher Education in Developing Countries 1945–70*. Edinburgh: Scottish Academic Press.

Mazrui, Ali A. 1973. "Aesthetic Dualism and Creative Literature in East Africa," in Andrew Gurr and Pio Zirimu (eds.) *Black Aesthetics: Papers from a Colloquium Held at the University of Nairobi, June 1971*. Nairobi, Kampala, Dar es Salaam: East African Literature Bureau, pp. 32–51.

———. 1978. *Political Values and the Educated Class in Africa*. Berkeley and Los Angeles: University of California Press.

Moore, Gerald. 1963. "*The Black Hermit*" [review]. *Transition* 3.8: 34.

Mphahlele, Ezekiel. 1962. "The Makerere Writers' Conference," *Africa Report* (July): 7–8.

Mukherjee, Bharati. 1993. *The Holder of the World*. New York: Alfred A. Knopf.

Nagenda, John. 1965. "And This, at Last," in Cook (ed.) *Origin East Africa: A Makerere Anthology.* London, Ibadan, Nairobi: Heinemann, pp. 23–28.

———. 1986. *The Seasons of Thomas Tebo.* London: Heinemann.

Nanka-Bruce, Suzanne. 1988. "Teachers College Projects in East Africa: A History of Educational Cooperation, 1961–1971." Ph.D. Diss. Teachers College, Columbia University.

Nazareth, Peter. 1963. "Verse in *The Black Hermit,*" *Transition* 3.9: 5.

———. 1972. *Literature and Society in Modern Africa: Essays on Literature.* Nairobi, Kampala, Dar es Salaam: East African Literature Bureau.

———. 1983. "Out of Darkness: Conrad and Other Third World Writers," *Conradiana* 14.3: 173–97.

———. 1990. Interview, Iowa City, 2 June.

Ngini, D. K. 1956. "The Kikuyu Before the Coming of Europeans," *The AHS Magazine* Nov.: 21–22.

Ngugi wa Thiong' o (James Ngugi). 1957. "I Try Witchcraft," *The AHS Magazine* Sept.: 21–22.

———. 1962a. "Can the Educated African Meet This Challenge?" *Sunday Nation* 27 May: 31.

———. 1962b. "Let's See More School Integration," *Sunday Nation* 8 July: 25.

———. 1962c. "Why Not Let Us Be the Judges?" *Sunday Nation* 29 July: 4.

———. 1962d. "Writers Conference," *Makererean* 2.1 (6 Aug.): 2.

———. 1962e. "Here's the Kenya *I* Want," *Sunday Nation* 12 Aug.: 28.

———. 1963a. "Don't Forget Our Destination," *Sunday Nation* 10 Feb.: 12, 35.

———. 1963b. "The Oasis That Is Makerere," *Sunday Nation* 24 March: 30.

———. 1963a. "Don't Forget Our Destination," *Sunday Nation* 10 Feb.: 12, 35.

———. 1963b. "The Oasis That Is Makerere," *Sunday Nation* 24 March: 30.

———. 1963c. "Now Let's See More Flexibility from University Colleges," *Sunday Nation* 7 July: 31.

———. 1963d. "The Writer and the Public," *Makererean* 3.4 (24 Aug.): 5.

———. 1963e. "A New Mood Prevails," *Sunday Nation* 24 Nov.: 14.

———. 1964a. (Jan.?). ["Are there two parts of *Lord Jim?*"] Untitled, undated, unpublished essay.

———. 1964b. (Jan.?). "The Significance of 'The Secret Sharer.' " Unpublished, undated essay.

———. 1964c. "Why Nostromo?" Unpublished essay dated 26 Jan. 1964.

———. 1964d. "Theatre," *Transition* 3.12 (Jan.–Feb.): 55.

———. 1964e. "Why Shakespeare in Africa?" *Daily Nation* 22 Apr.: 6.

———. 1964f. "More Is Needed from Educated Africans," *Sunday Nation* 7 June: 9.

———. 1964g. "Teachers, Too, Want Cash!" *Sunday Nation* 21 June: 6.

———. 1964h. *Weep Not, Child.* Reprint. London, Ibadan, Nairobi: Heinemann, 1976.

———. 1966. "Chinua Achebe: A Man of the People," *Omen,* Oct. (Leeds University). Reprinted in Ngugi 1972, 51–54.

———. 1968. *The Black Hermit.* Nairobi, London, Ibadan: Heinemann.

———. 1972. *Homecoming: Essays on African and Caribbean Literature, Culture and Politics.* Foreword by Ime Ikiddeh. London, Ibadan, Nairobi: Heinemann.

———. 1975. *Secret Lives and Other Stories.* London, Nairobi, Ibadan: Heinemann.

———. 1976. "The Black Experience," *Umma* 3 Nov.: 20.

———. 1977. *Petals of Blood.* Reprint. New York: E. P. Dutton, 1978.

———. 1981a. *Detained: A Writer's Prison Diary.* London, Nairobi, Ibadan: Heinemann.

———. 1981b. "Education for a National Culture." Reprinted in Ngugi, *Barrel of a Pen: Resistance to Repression in Neo-Colonial Kenya.* London and Port of Spain: New Beacon Press, 1983: 87–100.

———. 1981c. "Women in Cultural Work: The Fate of Kamiriithu People's Theatre in Kenya." Reprinted in Ngugi, *Barrel of a Pen: Resistance to Repression in Neo-Colonial Kenya.* London and Port of Spain: New Beacon Press, 1983: 39–51.

————. 1986. *Decolonising the Mind: The Politics of Language in African Literature.* London: James Currey; Nairobi: Heinemann; Kenya, Portsmouth, NH: Heinemann; Harare: Zimbabwe Publishing House.

————. 1987. Interview, London, 4 Aug.

————. 1989. Interview, New Haven, 6 May.

————. 1993. *Moving the Centre: The Struggle for Cultural Freedoms.* London: James Currey; Nairobi: EAEP; Portsmouth, NH: Heinemann.

Nkosi, Lewis. 1962. "John Nagenda," in D. Duerden and C. Pieterse (eds.). 1972. *African Writers Talking: A Collection of Radio Interviews.* London, Ibadan, Nairobi: Heinemann; New York: Africana Publishing Corp., pp. 115–17.

Njau, Elimo. 1991. Interview, Nairobi, 25 June.

Njau, Rebeka. 1975. *Ripples in the Pool.* Reprint. London: Heinemann, 1978.

Njoroge, Samuel Ngugi. 1978. "The Influence of Traditional and Western Religions on the Cultural and Political Thinking of Ngugi wa Thiong' o and Okot p'Bitek." M. Phil. thesis, Leeds University.

p'Bitek, Okot. 1966. "Future of the Vernacular Literature," in East African Institute of Social and Cultural Affairs (ed.) *East Africa's Cultural Heritage.* Nairobi: East African Publishing House, pp. 70–77.

————. 1966–67. *Song of Lawino & Song of Ocol.* George Heron (ed. and intro.) Reprint. London, Ibadan: Heinemann, 1984.

————. 1967. "We Must Preserve Our Culture," *Makererean* 6.51 (5 Aug.): 3.

Prewitt, Kenneth. 1966. "Makerere: Intelligence vs. Intellectuals," *Transition* 6.27: 35–39.

Rubadiri, David. 1966. "The University Role in the Development of East African Culture," in East African Institute of Social and Cultural Affairs (ed.) *East Africa's Cultural Heritage.* Nairobi: East African Publishing House, pp. 9–12.

————. 1968. "The Development of Writing in East Africa," in Christopher Heywood (ed.) *Perspectives on African Literature: Selections from the Proceedings of the Conference on African Literature Held at the University of Ife 1968.* Ibadan: University of Ife Press; London: Heinemann; New York: Africana Publishing Corp., pp. 148–56.

Ruheni, Mwangi. 1973. *The Future Leaders.* Nairobi, Ibadan, London: Heinemann.

Samoff, Joel. 1990. " 'Modernizing' a Socialist Vision: Education in Tanzania," in Martin Carnoy and Joel Samoff (eds., with Mary Ann Burniss, Anton Johnston, and Carlos Alberto Torres) *Education and Social Transition in the Third World.* Princeton: Princeton University Press, pp. 209–73.

Sentongo, Noah. 1967. "Emotional Identity," *Makererean* 7.55 (2 Nov.): 6, 8.

Serumaga, Robert. 1967. "Okot p'Bitek," in D. Duerden and C. Pieterse (eds.) 1972. *African Writers Talking: A Collection of Radio Interviews.* London, Ibadan, Nairobi: Heinemann; New York: Africana Publishing Corp., pp. 149–55.

Shengold, Leonard. 1989. *Soul Murder: The Effects of Childhood Abuse and Deprivation.* New York: Fawcett Columbine.

Shields, James J. 1962. "Researcher Examines American Teachers at Makerere," *Makererean* 1.4 (19 Feb.): 4.

Sicherman, Carol. 1989. *Ngugi wa Thiong' o: A Bibliography of Primary and Secondary Sources 1957–87.* Bibliographical Research in African Written Literatures, 1. Oxford: Hans Zell.

————. 1990. *Ngugi wa Thiong' o: The Making of a Rebel: A Source Book in Kenyan Literature and Resistance.* Documentary Research in African Written Literatures, 1. Oxford: Hans Zell.

————. 1992. "Ngugi wa Thiong' o as Mythologizer and Mythologized," in Anna Rutherford (ed.) *From Commonwealth to Post-Colonial.* Sydney: Dangaroo Press, pp. 259–75.

————. 1995. "The Leeds-Makerere Connection and Ngugi's Intellectual Development," *Ufahamu* 23.1.

Smith, H. Maynard. 1926. *Frank Bishop of Zanzibar: Life of Frank Weston, D.D. 1871–1924.* London: Society for Promoting Christian Knowledge.

Stanley, Manfred. 1960. "Student-Staff Relations in an African University [Makerere]: Some Comments on the Social Context of Higher Education." Unpublished paper read at conference of the East African Institute of Social Research, Dec.

Tejani, Bahadur. 1971. *Day After Tomorrow.* Nairobi, Kampala, Dar es Salaam: East African Literature Bureau.

———. 1973. "Local Significance and the Importance of the Local Audience in Modern African Writing (Studied in Ngugi, La Guma, Mphahlele, Okara and Peters)." Diss. University of Nairobi.

———. 1979. "Modern African Literature and the Legacy of Cultural Colonialism," *World Literature Written in English* 18.1: 37–54.

Warner, Alan. 1954. *Shakespeare in the Tropics: An Inaugural Address as First Professor of English, Makerere College, University College of East Africa, Kampala, Uganda. Delivered on 10 May 1954.* London, Nairobi, Ibadan: Oxford University Press.

———. 1956. "Teaching English to East African Students: An Interim Report," *English Language Teaching* 10.6: 51–61.

———. 1958. "African Students and the English Background," *English Language Teaching* 13.1: 3–7.

———. 1963. "A New English in Africa?" *Review of English Literature* 4.2: 45–54.

Whittock, Trevor. 1962. "Black Hermit: Ngugi Speaks to Africa," *Makererean* 2.7(22 Nov.): 1.

———. 1968. "The Function of an English Faculty in an African University," *English Studies in Africa* 11: 81–94.

Whittock, Trevor, and David Cook. 1965. " 'English' in Africa Now," *Penpoint* 19 Oct.: 26–28.

Williams, Aidan. 1993. "Jonathan Kariara (1935–93): A Tribute," *Weekly Review* 24 Dec.: 16.

Zell, Hans M., Carol Bundy, and Virginia Coulon. 1983. *A New Reader's Guide to African Literature.* 2nd ed. London, Ibadan, and Nairobi: Heinemann.

Nature as Agency in Ngũgĩ's
The River Between

ANDRÉ-PAUL MICHAUD

Never trust the teller, trust the tale.

—D. H. Lawrence

Ngũgĩ's first novel flows likes a river: cool, smooth, meandering, and some-times in rapids yet deceptively calm amidst powerful eddies. In his first novel (published after *Weep Not, Child*), Ngũgĩ crafts a vehicle for his political, edu-cational, and philosophical messages and, equally, his own passionate forum for self-discovery. This novel has been generally ignored, both by scholars and by Ngũgĩ himself.[1] Those who treat this work frequently analyze its mes-sages and qualities in relation to the author's successive novels, often ignoring or missing the unique literary strategies of *The River Between*. Although it is informative and rewarding to follow the literary, intellectual, and philosophi-cal progress of a talented author such as Ngũgĩ, it is necessary to investigate each work on its own terms.

In this critique I endeavor to illustrate the importance of *The River Between* as a foundation for Ngũgĩ's successive evolution as artist and thinker. In this interpretation, I first illuminate *The River Between*'s literary value and then demonstrate how this same value can be found in Ngũgĩ's latest work, *Matigari*.

Ngũgĩ introduces the reader to his homeland and his fictional land-scapes as if the reader is surveying the geography and later witnessing—per-haps even participating in—the story.

> A river flowed through the valley of life. If there had been no bush and no for-est trees covering the slopes, you could have seen the river when you stood on top of either Kameno or Makuyu. Now you had to come down. Even then you could not see the whole extent of the river as it gracefully, and without any apparent haste, wound its way down the valley, like a snake. The river was called Honia, which meant cure, or bring-back-to-life.[2]

This essay is published here for the first time by permission of the author, with whom the copyright remains.

In this opening passage the reader enters into this "wordscape," entranced by the dreamlike, mythic-time-tinted description: It is as though the reader is viewing what will become through a geographical prism. Ngũgĩ quietly paints Nature as allegory, symbol, manifestation, reflection, and active participant in the story that will unfold. Most critics of this work have noted the importance of Honia river. Some critics imagine Nature as an observer or geographic foil, whereas Lloyd Williams sees the river as a symbol of "tribal and Christian unity."[3] However, although it appears that Ngũgĩ wishes to portray Nature as both observer and literary mirror, more importantly it is as an active, guiding force in the Gikuyu people's struggle for life and unity for which he creates this elemental presence, illustrating its power and participation.

In this critique, I focus on Ngũgĩ's literary strategies to encompass Nature and how Nature as a literary force continuously advances, retreats, and inundates the story line. The geography of the ridges illustrates and foreshadows the sociopolitical and religious conflict in the two villages while simultaneously creating banks to guide, contain, and define the lifeblood's presence.

> The two ridges lay side by side. One was Kameno, the other Makuyu. Between them was a valley. . . . When you stood in the valley, the two ridges ceased to be sleeping lions united by their common source of life. They became antagonists. You could tell this, not by anything tangible but by the way they faced each other, like two rivals ready to come to blows in a life and death struggle for the leadership of this isolated region. (*RB*, 1)

These first pages of text must be studied carefully. Humans do not join Ngũgĩ's delicately crafted geography until chapter 2. Although this technique was a common, even classic, convention during the eighteenth and nineteenth centuries, its use in this novel and this time is both refreshing and powerful. The author's painstaking description and treatment of the natural surroundings are too profound to only cradle the story. Nature as a dynamic, eternal force will guide and shape humanity's actions and development through its symbolic geography and its lifeblood, Honia river. This eternal, "drought-scorning" current and its evaporative transformations—rains, mist, and fog—provide a varied, flexible water symbology that easily enters into the narrative, altering the tone and flow or course of events. Also, this element seems to voice Nature's wisdom and concern and, perhaps, Ngũgĩ's personal perspective.

The first quote describes Honia in its frame, its banks formed by the valley. Trees obscure the observer's and the characters' view of the river, and, through this symbolic foliage, Nature identifies the future conflict. The antagonistic villagers have, both literally and figuratively, lost touch with and sight of their soul, their "lifestream." The labyrinthlike forest that encompasses the whole isolated region, surrounding the two villages and shrouding the river, suggests a literary rendition of a mist or fog: this "labyrinth of bush thorns and creeping plants" (*RB*, 14). It appears safe to presume that these variations symbolize and reflect the confusing slumber in which the two villages are imprisoned. These vaporous, scarcely tangible blankets provide a natural symbol that identifies and illustrates the state of sociopolitical and spiritual hibernation, the indeterminacy that while characterizing the Gikuyu villagers' consciousness also threatens to suffocate them. This symbolism of confusion and unconsciousness permeates the novel, often enhancing or modifying vital events, descriptions, or monologues. The first paragraph identifies this "deep-sleep," while foreshadowing what is to come. These villagers, all "sleeping lions," will awake to fight, to reestablish their past glory.

The most powerful element of this wordscape must be brought to light. Firstly, Ngũgĩ magnified and reinforced the dominance of Nature in the novel by changing the title from *The Black Messiah*. Secondly, in the text itself, Honia river is the physical manifestation of and symbol for the eternal and dynamic, healing and rejuvenating qualities of Nature. "Honia river never dried: it seemed to possess a strong will to live, scorning drought and weather changes" (*RB*, 1). This passage asserts Nature's efficacy and power. An undercurrent seems to suggest that colonialism is but a single droplet amidst infinite tides, a momentary depression in an endless and ever-changing weather cycle. Having identified and elaborated on the fundamental literary strategies with which Ngũgĩ flavors and navigates his work, I will begin to describe the story line and its sociopolitical and philosophical components through this prism.

Ngũgĩ's wordscape methodically illustrates the setting that cradles the narrative while also echoing, directing, and influencing its denouement. The second chapter disturbs Nature's deceptive calm. Two young boys fight. Kamau and Kinuthia reflect parental behaviors and dislikes while hurling insults, replicating this symbolic dichotomy. Waiyaki charges onto the scene. Immediately, he dominates the situation, forcing Kamau to disengage. His power over his fellows is clear. "The tremor in the boy's [Waiyaki's] voice sent a quiver of fear up Kamau. He quickly looked up and met the burning eyes. . . . Meekly he obeyed the unspoken command" (*RB*, 6). This first human interaction introduces the dialectic that exists throughout the novel, encompassing the ideological and philosophical conflicts between the two villages. Waiyaki is already drawn as a powerful leader. However, although Kinuthia will be loyal to the end, Kamau's hatred and humiliation in regard to this younger boy foreshadow the intensity of conflict that will unfold. These sons reflect and personify the same divisions that Ngũgĩ's landscape defines. Kamau and his father, Kabonyi, will soon characterize the Kiama, intensely violent as "converts" to traditional customs. Kinuthia will conceptualize a more rational, removed force; his less immediate proximity fosters perspective. His views reflect those of the more moderate villagers. And Waiyaki, in his person, seems to encompass two major dialectical forces. On the one hand, he shall personify the "modern" African's identity crisis, wishing to maintain his tradition while incorporating those Western values that appear beneficial. On the other hand, this dialectic is both reinforced and confused further in his views on education and progress. He believes his goal is to raise his villagers' consciousness and sociopolitical power through the white man's education. Yet immediately it is apparent that his vision is unclear, even blinded by this very dream of education. His nearsighted vision typifies theoretical and actual aspects of colonialism, especially the "false consciousness" with which the colonists governed, pacified, and encouraged the Africans.[4]

This early scene, which foreshadows the novel's antagonistic forces, precedes the pivotal discussion between Chege, the father, and Waiyaki, the son. This forest scene, strongly reminiscent of a rite of passage (notably p. 14), identifies the messianic path with which Chege burdens his son: "Arise. Heed the prophesy. . . . Learn all the wisdom and all the secrets of the white man. But do not follow his vices. Be true to the people and the ancient rites" (RB, 20). Chege's speech clearly enunciates the Promethean task with which he and the Gikuyu tradition have burdened Waiyaki. This initiatory passage, which describes the dilemma that will course through the novel, hints at the dangers with which this path is fraught, telling of Mugo, Waiyaki's ancestor, "People did not believe him. Some even poured scorn on him, laughing at him. . . . The seer was rejected by the people of the ridges" (RB, 19).

Throughout the early chapters, which frame the pivotal events and ideas of the novel, Nature remains relatively passive. Rarely does it dramatically voice its position. However, in several notable scenes Nature seems to flavor or alter the plot's course. As Waiyaki and then Kamau and Kinuthia leave the villages and remain at Livingstone's school, Nature quietly pleads with the elders to awaken and question their actions, loyalties, and surroundings. Famine gnaws at Chege and the other elders' conscience and tradition-conditioned reasonings (RB, 37). Here, Ngũgĩ cleverly voices his concerns, employing Nature as a kind of warning, judgment, and punishment. Waiyaki's initiation into manhood closely follows this passage. Nature and Muthoni seem to join forces with the rite itself to enhance its inherent meaning and to clarify and define the struggle with which Waiyaki has been laden. These two forces enhance this essential empowerment, better jarring Waiyaki from his blind or unconscious state; in short, they join to define the fluency of his rebirth. Reactions that seem appropriate in light of the ritual's fundamental tribal meaning and to the physical pain are emphasized and also redirected to illustrate how Waiyaki's intellect is already active in his attempts to understand and deal with this mission in its contemporary cultural context.

> What was Muthoni feeling, he wondered. He thought that if he had been in her position he would never have brought himself into such pain. . . . And that day when Chege took him to the sacred grove . . . strange how that old man defied time. . . . Livingstone in his way was like Chege . . . standing for the other side . . . no . . . confusing the two. (RB, 45–46)

This stream of consciousness emphasizes the already confusing state of affairs and the difficulty in resolving the tribe's problems. Waiyaki sees the parallels that exist between the elders and vaguely connects with Muthoni but does not recognize a more direct linkage or interconnectedness between the younger generations. An essential aspect of Waiyaki's character, noted by Sekyi-Otu, must be highlighted. In the earlier citation, the first two sentences suggest a fundamental lack of commitment or desire on his part. Although the words are directed at the act of circumcision, it seems safe to assume, in light of its true nature as a response to Muthoni, that his query is in regards to his mission. Why undertake this task? This short passage echoes later monologues that support this interpretation. Nature contributes to this scene, emphasizing its indeterminacy while also drawing on one traditional symbol for the ritual death aspect in rites of passage.

> There was mist everywhere. It covered Kameno, Makuyu and the other ridges in its thin white greyness. It was chilling, chilling the skin. But Honia river flowed on as if defying the mist. The water, however, was cold. (*RB, 45*)

This paragraph, which introduces and tints the chapter on Waiyaki's initiation, also redirects the reader's attention to Honia river. Again, Ngũgĩ reminds us that the narrative's concern is temporary and transcendable. Ngũgĩ's ideas involving transformation may be seen in this passage also; both mist and its liquid form are present in the same description. Natural and social transformations will always occur, bringing fresh insight and perspective. Honia will always flow, bearing its curative properties.

These early scenes and the chapters that relate their particulars, which make up the first half of the narrative, suggest or directly voice the questions to be asked or resolved in Waiyaki's ultimate initiation into leadership. The second half of the novel begins when Waiyaki is forced to leave school and then decides to found his own schools to educate the children of the two ridges. An important aspect of the dialectic that exists between tradition, colonialism, and the "white man's education" and the concept of transformation in Ngũgĩ's novel is the timeliness of Chege's death and news of Waiyaki's need to leave Siriana. At the exact moment Chege dies, Waiyaki learns of Siriana's order to expel all students who have been circumcised. This scene appears to illustrate the natural growth cycles present in Nature: the transformation of decaying or dead matter to fertile *prima materia,* from Chege to Waiyaki. Chege's life and death will provide Waiyaki with nourishment in his mission to uphold tradition while realizing his Promethean task of stealing the white man's knowledge. Here he realizes that his work has begun. Tradition is dying with his father and must be replaced with a supportive and equally powerful institution.

As Muthoni—who was to be the bridge that spanned and connected Honia river and its ridges—dies, the three camps begin to wage war. Waiyaki fights for his schools, Joshua for his Christian flock, and Kamau for tribal purity. The young girl's courageous and idealistic death both clarifies and deepens the chasm between these villages and their leaders. It is important to note that an early passage admonishes all three for one fundamental failing. Each leader advocates and embodies a single issue, blindly ignoring the complete sociopolitical and traditional context.

Ngũgĩ's idea of transformation and a constant negotiation and renegotiation of realities and possibilities become more and more apparent. Muthoni, in death, transcends her earlier psychosocial and human limitations and becomes a powerful spirit who affects everyone, hastening the people's awakening and the ultimate denouement. Muthoni's physical death frees her soul to pursue its personal religion, while creating the most divisive and unbridgeable gulf between the two parties of opposition. This result is utterly contradictory to what Muthoni would have wished. Her reasonings behind her forbidden initiation translate into an appeal for unity, of both spirit and religion but also of polity. In a better world, Muthoni's death could have been symbolized as the riverbed that bridged and united the two opposing ridges. Instead, this death broke the remaining connections that linked the two factions. Before Muthoni's death, Chege's death, and the chain of events that follow, Nature is relatively calm and quiet. However, this agency soon breaks on the wordscape, eroding and reshaping the main characters' outlooks, ideas, and actions. These twin forces of erosion and reconfiguration, or, more precisely, transformation, shape the story line that cradles the sociopolitical and ideological struggle. Increasingly, Nature makes itself felt. It questions, admonishes, threatens, or merely shapes the moods of the villagers and most certainly the main characters.

One notable discussion between the sisters precedes Muthoni's death. It is important to portray it to demonstrate the symbolic division between the ridges and between the sisters and the one river that unites them. This conversation, which characterizes the dichotomy that threatens both ridges, asserts Muthoni's desire for unity: " 'Father and mother are circumcised. Are they not Christians? Circumcision did not prevent them from being Christians. I too have embraced the whiteman's faith. However, I know it is beautiful . . . to be initiated into womanhood. You learn the ways of the tribe. Yes, the whiteman's God does not quite satisfy me. I want, I need something more.' . . . She spoke now, looking beyond Nyambura as if to some other people" (*RB,* 26). These words suggest that the two sisters' dialogue echoes that of other villagers and clearly emphasizes the complex and somewhat unnatural division between Joshua's daughters. Immediately after this discussion, Ngũgĩ returns to Nature: "Honia river flowed on. The insects went on with their incessant sound mingling with the fall of the river" (*RB,* 27). This return recenters the text, reminding the reader of the central and fundamental influence and importance of the river and the interconnectedness and the limited magnitude of human experience. An interesting occurrence (which has been interpreted in both a varied and a generally contradictory manner) closes this chapter. On leaving the riverbank burdened with tin water barrels, Muthoni drops hers, and it rolls down the hill toward the river. Many scholars perceive this as a bad omen (*RB*, 27), much like it appears in the text. However, it seems reasonable to assert, in keeping with the present interpretation, that the river is "blessing" Muthoni's belief in oneness. By repossessing an extension of its being that has been taken by Muthoni, and is thus hers, it is incorporating the raw and natural curative force present in her action and integrating it into its eternal source. In the context of Muthoni's life and death, and the harsh dichotomy that it represents and elucidates, I will proceed to illustrate Nature's agency and how it interacts with its human constituency.

> Drip! Drip! All along the edge of the corrugated-iron roof. Drip! Drip! All in a line, large determined drops of rain fell on the ground. . . . And the rain came down in a fury, the straying thin showers forming a misty cloudiness so you could hardly see a few yards away. (*RB*, 61)

Rain tattoos the intensity of the novel's second half on paper. This crushing storm asserts Nature's fury at the two ridges' disunity and colonialism's brutality. Chapter 13 is the structural center of the text; it is separated from the end by 13 additional chapters. Here, the reader witnesses Waiyaki in contemplation. Rain invades his mood, his spirit, and even his school. "The barrack-like mud-walled building, made of poles and thatch, could vaguely be seen through the misty rain. . . . Waiyaki knew only too well what was happening inside. The rotting grass thatch was no deterrent to rain. Numerous pools of water must have already formed on the floor" (*RB*, 61). In this passage, Ngũgĩ communicates the decrepit nature of Waiyaki's institution. Only three years since its formation and Muthoni's death, the building has fallen into disrepair. And Nature demonstrates its irate concern with this education. Both literally and symbolically, holes have already appeared in Waiyaki's belief and theories supporting the white man's education as a necessary and fundamental tool for the ridges' liberation from the increasingly heavy colonial yoke. The tension and a mounting feeling of the immediate need for action become more and more clear. Rain pours, reminding Waiyaki of the sleeping lions. Ngũgĩ skillfully and concisely depicts the white man's expansion and the troubles that haunt the ridges. The division between Kabonyi and Joshua and the formation of the Kiama are hinted at, and the central dialogue between the ridges is voiced by Waiyaki's "fellow teachers," Kamau and Kinuthia. As the discussion between his two companions intensifies, Nature reflects and magnifies the brewing storm: first, emphasizing the present indeterminacy, with the "misty rain," then the torrent of rhetoric and rain combining to produce a powerful stream of tension. And in the first quotation, Nature seems even to respond to Kinuthia's discourse—"The rest was drowned out by the falling rain" (*RB*, 62)—marking colonialism as the enemy. And the lashing storm grows stronger with the dialogue: "The rain came down with greater vigour . . . the downpour almost slashing the sunscorched grass" (*RB*, 63, 65).

Waiyaki, strongly influenced by the powerful rainstorm and his friends' discourse, cannot but think of flooding, Nature's ultimate response to human incompetence or injustice. "[N]arrow streams . . . mingled and flowed on to join the main stream, like a small river, like Honia. Or like a flood. Only this one would end and Honia river would for ever flow" (*RB*, 64–65). This passage, alone, beautifully defines Nature's, and especially Honia river's, incredible and eternal life force. It also provides strong support for the argument behind the river's evaporative transformations and Nature's agency on human action and thought.

Chapter 13 offers a rich framework within which to present the events and developments that have occurred in the three years separating it from the previous chapter. Most importantly, however, the chapter reemphasizes the childhood fight that continues into the present. And it reasserts Waiyaki's lack of awareness and understanding in regard to the true needs of the tribe. "Perhaps Kinuthia was speaking for the sleeping hills, for the whole of Gikuyu country. Then he suppressed the feeling and thought of the new drive in education" (*RB*, 64). These few words express Waiyaki's fundamental flaw in regard to tribal leadership and his goals of education, until it blocks out all external sounds.

This blind obsession with education as salvation, of which Africans were constantly taught and reminded, encompasses all of Waiyaki's hopes and dreams. Ngũgĩ, here, suggests how arduous is the battle to overcome colonialism and, more specifically, its psychological mechanisms. False consciousness, which both pacifies and guides the dominated, clearly illustrated by the oppressed's dream for advancement through education, grips Waiyaki. Hope, however, is present. His internal monologue voices a concern that suggests a consciousness of the artificiality or falsity of his obsession:

> He wanted to concentrate on education. Perhaps the teaching of Livingstone, that education was of value and his boys should not concern themselves with what the government was doing or politics, had found a place in Waiyaki's heart. (*RB*, 65)

The narration voices the cries of the villagers, angry and hungry to win back their land. Ngũgĩ ends the chapter, once more asserting the fluency of Nature's voice and the magnitude of its power and concern with the present sociopolitical environment:

> [Waiyaki] was angry with the rain. The rain carried away the soil. . . . For a time, he felt like fighting with the rain. . . . Even here in this natural happen-

ing, he could see a contradiction. The rain had to touch the soil. That touch could be a blessing or a curse. (*RB*, 65–66)

Before I proceed to illuminate Nature's increasingly influential and powerful agency and the dependent interpretation of the denouement, I will digress from the novel's temporal development to critique Waiyaki's literary value—his position and value both as archetype and as a unique character—to better understand Ngũgĩ's message and the evolution of his thought. And, at the conclusion of this work, I will identify this process in a brief analysis of some key characteristics of *Matigari*.

The text slowly reveals Waiyaki's development. From the moment at which Chege has burdened him with his mission, Nature and his psyche have been continually striving to awaken Waiyaki's leadership qualities and his consciousness. Throughout the text, he builds his schools and speaks for education, yet his is not leadership in its ideal philosophical definition. Even when he is an important member of the Kiama, Waiyaki does not actually lead or guide his people on the righteous path. Oftentimes, external forces and events, and most certainly Nature, erode his tunnel vision momentarily. At such times, Waiyaki realizes that he has been acting without reflection. Yet he never realizes his incredible talent for leadership. It is important to reemphasize Ngũgĩ's original title, *The Black Messiah*. In light of later works and the author's philosophical obsessions and dilemmas with messianic figures, it is noteworthy that he retitled this text, abandoning, altering, or lessening the impact of this theme. Waiyaki never attains the position of messiah or leader in the tribe. However, it is not for lack of attributes; rather, his commitment, consciousness, and courage are lacking. This example illustrates the power of revision. Knowing the original title, we can reinterpret Waiyaki's position in the novel's sociopolitical context. It seems safe to deem Waiyaki a failed prophet. Or, perhaps more accurately, he represents the laborious birth, the beginnings of African leadership and revolution. In light of Waiyaki's messianic potential and realities, we will continue to elucidate Nature's influential presence.

The next two chapters highlight Waiyaki's tribal position. The omniscient narrator voices the tribe's sentiments, in addition to asserting and clarifying the protagonist's feelings. Both elements are apprehensive and concerned with his apparent leadership. Elders fear age-related problems, whereas Waiyaki himself, proud of his role "in awakening the hills, the sleeping lions" (*RB*, 69), is conscious of and wishes to "reconcile all these antagonisms" (*RB*, 69). This awareness clearly shows the reality of the hills' struggle. Waiyaki's role in awakening the hills is dangerous and premature. It is disastrous to awaken people without afterward providing clear and wise sociopolitical insight. The antagonisms will increase as the white man's education stimulates thought and the politicoreligious division is caught up with this focused yet blurry goal to educate the villagers. This intensification soon focuses all the villagers' fear, concern, and anger on the struggle that incorporates education, tribal purity and unity, and Christianity and colonialism.

This apparently unbridgeable chasm is reflected in the anthropomorphism of Nature in Ngũgĩ's description of the antagonistic ridges. We may see Kabonyi and his goal of tribal unity as Kameno ridge, Joshua as Makuyu, and Waiyaki attempting to bridge these opposing hills. As Muthoni tried unsuccessfully to heal this artificial division by crossing Honia river, so Waiyaki tries to reconcile these parties by seemingly embracing both the tribe and the white man's education. This precarious middle position acts as the pivotal crisis in the text. Chege's words, which enjoined Waiyaki to steal knowledge from Siriana and the whites without becoming tainted with their faith, a Promethean task, leads him to a juncture at which he must choose between them or act to fuse the two into a new and unified whole. In this struggle, Nyambura also joins her force to Waiyaki to help bridge the ridges and their opposing parties. The pressure mounts as Kabonyi, Joshua, the elders, and Nature increasingly enjoin or attempt to force Waiyaki to choose.

> He could not sleep. Thin rays of the moon passed through the cracks in the wall. . . . It was no good staring blankly at the hazy darkness in which every object lost its clear edges. (*RB,* 71)

Nature enters Waiyaki's home, assailing his conscience, forcing him to remain awake. A feeling of guilt embeds itself in his soul, growing increasingly hard and heavy. He vocalizes concern, questioning whether "the education he was trying to spread in the ridges [was a] contaminant" (*RB,* 72). Now Kabonyi and his Kiama begin to needle him, declaring him a convert to the white man's faith, addressing the villagers' concerns that he is now a stranger and "the oilskin of the house" was not for them (*RB,* 3). Joshua attacks him as a heathen, a barbarian who believes in circumcision. Here, Waiyaki, feeling claustrophobic among such antagonistic and contradictory forces, has a vision that presumably holds the answer to his and the tribe's survival. "It was the shape of a woman and he could not make out who she was" (*RB,* 72). Later, he walks, drawn by the moon's "glare." He collides with Nyambura at Honia river and "recognize[s] the shape in his mind that had refused to melt" (*RB,* 74). This passage and its surrounding pages identify four important elements present throughout the text: (1) Nature's agency, here incorporated by the moon; (2) the interconnectedness of Waiyaki's and his two peers' lives (*RB,* 73); (3) the need to cross Honia river to gain its curative powers by bridging its physical manifestation; and (4) the draining nature of Waiyaki's position between these opposition parties, caused and exacerbated by colonialism, this "peripetia of values" of which JanMohammed writes.[5] "He had now for many seasons been trying to drain himself dry, for the people. Yet this thing still pursued him" (*RB,* 73).

This complex and threatening dance continues to hold Waiyaki and the other participants. It becomes more and more frantic and demanding as the sociopolitical struggle and its rhetoric build, concentrating everyone's attention and energy into this debate. The powerful concentration that imprisons the energy and minds of the villagers reinforces the brutal dichotomy that may destroy any and all who attempt to cross or heal its fault. Here, one character holds council with himself, remaining clearheaded, graced with perspective. Kinuthia often, and increasingly so as the climax builds, warns Waiyaki, voicing concerns and rumors that circulate freely among the villagers but to which Waiyaki appears deaf.

> "Be careful, Waiyaki. You know the people look up to you. You are the symbol of the tribe, born again with all its purity. They adore you. They worship you. You do not know about the new oath. . . . But they are taking the new oath in your name. In the name of the Teacher and the purity of the tribe. And remember Kabonyi . . . hates you. . . . And he is the one who is doing all this. Why? The Kiama has power. Power. And your name is in it, giving it even greater power. Your name will be your ruin." (RB, 112)

This warning follows Kinuthia's question about whether Waiyaki will marry Nyambura. Waiyaki answers in the negative, but the damage is done. Although he has been rejected, it is all the same. His desired alliance is seen as treason to the tribe, showing accord with Joshua's party. Even Kinuthia, Waiyaki's truest friend, interprets it as such. Perhaps guilty, perhaps embarrassed, Waiyaki speaks to no one, refusing to clarify the situation. This is the pivotal event. From this moment, Kabonyi and his son, Kamau, see no possibility for reconciliation. He is guilty of treason; while pretending to hold the tribe's best interests, he is negotiating an alliance with Joshua's faction. Their verdict will determine their subsequent actions.

Waiyaki becomes more and more aware of his dilemma. He realizes that his dream of education has not addressed his tribe's true needs and concerns and has entirely ignored the present sociopolitical climate. However, each time he has the opportunity to alter his course or address the need for reconciliation and unity, he refuses to speak. Sometimes this muteness is the result of pride, sometimes a lack of courage. No matter, Waiyaki's actions are interpreted as treason. The end approaches. Waiyaki, fearing for Joshua's and Nyambura's lives, runs to their aid. Kamau witnesses this interaction, and the verdict must be acted on. Waiyaki is imprisoned, along with Nyambura, to await their formal trial and its verdict.

Here, Waiyaki's fundamental error is his belief that as a leader he was irreplaceable. For this reason, perhaps, he continues to procrastinate, calling for unity, and withdraws from the Kiama. His attempt to warn Joshua and, in so doing, to demonstrate his desire for unity, leads to his capture. Without Waiyaki's explanation of his strange actions, Kamau and Kabonyi have no alternative but to view this event as a treasonous meeting.

Finally, Waiyaki and Nyambura stand trial. Beside Honia river, the tribes unite to witness and assist in this process, still separated by the river's expanse. Too late, Waiyaki realizes the power of the Kiama. He understands that as a social phenomenon, it is a real and valid entity that identifies a need of the community's. At this late moment, Waiyaki realizes he must preach unity. However, all he can manage is mute acceptance of Nyambura, thus defining his treason.

> Yet the oath did not say that he should not love. . . . And how could he tell them now that he had not betrayed them, but this was not what he meant by unity. . . . How could he tell them that he meant to serve the hills[?] (*RB,* 151)

This internal monologue defines what is necessary to the tribe and what is necessary to lead the tribe.

Communication will foster and nurture respect and confidence. But communication is not yet possible; further transformations and experiences must come first. The novel ends, and Ngũgĩ stresses two fundamental ideas. First, he emphasizes the people's guilt. It is not only Waiyaki's burden and fault; the people themselves were not active or thoughtful enough. "They went away quickly. . . . For they did not want to look at the Teacher and they did not want to read their guilt in one another's faces" (*RB,* 152). Second, he emphasizes the eternal nature of Nature, the curative powers of the river and of time:

> The two ridges lay side by side, hidden in the darkness. And Honia river went on flowing between them, down through the valley of life, its beat rising above the dark stillness, reaching into the hearts of the people of Makuyu and Kameno. (*RB,* 152)

Having demonstrated Ngũgĩ's ideas, including Nature's agency, individual and collective responsibility, and other interrelated concepts, I will proceed to illustrate how important *The River Between* is, both alone and in demonstrating how Ngũgĩ returns to its themes in *Matigari.*

One important element of Ngũgĩ's philosophical search for understanding resides in his use of messianic figures. Although he attempts to dismiss messiahs in the works that fall between *The River Between* and *Matigari,* he returns to this theme, presumably satisfied with this concept. Its presence in his latest work strongly suggests that he believes a messianic figure is vital and important, although he does not preclude it being a temporary measure. However, another possible explanation could enhance or contradict Ngũgĩ's approval of the messianic figure. In the text, the fluid, ephemeral quality attributable to Matigari could suggest that he is not a messiah figure in the real sense but rather a "hallucination" or, better still, a holograph,[6] which is both individual and collective at the same time. This approach suggests that a messiah as focal point for the people's dreams and energies is good and worthy, rather than and in contrast to a lone and strong leader with inactive or passive followers, like the villagers from Makuyu and Kameno.

> Some say that he is as tall as a giant. . . . Others say that he is as little as a dwarf. Some say that Matigari is a woman, and others maintain that he is a man.[7]

History strongly supports this possible interpretation. Kenyan authorities went door to door, attempting to arrest Matigari, fearful of such a revolutionary. Then, he was found to be a text.

Nature as agency and literary device recenters Ngũgĩ's latest text. The mugumo tree, the mythic and sacred tree of the Gikuyu, appears. This home of Murungu, which Chege reveals to Waiyaki in the Sacred Grove, in *Matigari* guards the weapons of Matigari and the Gikuyu among its roots. This tree reminds us of the Gikuyu myth, while reasserting *The River Between* as a foreshadowing agent. The presence and textual importance of the tree connect the two works and symbolize how more weapons and strategies can be drawn from Nature and tradition than from any other source. "Once I wear my belt, none of them will be able to cross the river, even if they come in thousands" (*Matigari*, 172). This passage also has an element of Ngũgĩ's idea of transformation. His few weapons can hold so many off, being powerful symbols more than physical objects. A later passage suggests that Matigari has evolved beyond the physical realm. Although he can bleed, he seems immortal, "for the bullets did not hit him. . . . It was as if on reaching him they turned into water" (*Matigari*, 173). This passage reinforces the earlier interpretation that Matigari is united with Nature and his people, an irrepressible idea in the minds of the masses. Also, the transformation of bullets into a harmless, if not vital and nourishing, element suggests that Ngũgĩ links the earlier Maji Maji revolt of Tanganyika against Germany—that is, the major anticolonial movement in East Africa prior to Mau Mau—to his fictional present. This incorporation illuminates Ngũgĩ's desire not only to unite East Africa in its struggles but also to establish and emphasize history's continuity, suggesting that one revolution gives birth to another and strengthens both.

The denouement of *Matigari* witnesses Matigari's race to reach the mugumo tree and his weapons cache. As Muriuki crosses the river and attains the tree's roots, Matigari carries Guthera to the river. At the last moment before hundreds of enemies reach the couple, they fall into the river. Simultaneously, Nature erupts, protecting its human representative from his neocolonial hunters.

"Matigari and Guthera fell into the river. Drops of water splashed . . . wetting the dry earth by the banks of the river" (*Matigari*, 174). Nature embraces the revolutionaries, and their sacrifice causes the water to erupt, sowing the arid banks with nourishing fluid. "And suddenly lightning flashed, and a peal of thunder rent the sky. At first a few drops of rain fell, one here, another there. Then a deluge came from the skies. . . . The rain poured as if all the taps of heaven had been turned on full blast" (*Matigari,* 174).

Nature as agent is no longer a suggestion. Here Nature unleashes its rains and its power in a twofold manner. First, this sudden storm is to protect Matigari and his companions from death, so that they may fight again. And then it pours to illustrate its transformation. Matigari's and Guthera's probable physical deaths have been a sacrifice. This material is transformed by Nature and unleashed on the Earth as healing nourishment to thirsty soil and the souls it supports. Nature, incorporating Matigari, gives back to humankind its leader in what is perhaps a more useful and nourishing form. And one from the next generation, Muriuki, escapes to continue to fight the neocolonialists and to heal his people. Thus, Matigari lives, greatly empowered by his unification with Nature.

In this interpretation I clearly define the literary importance of *The River Between,* both as a unique and clever illustration of Nature's agency and as a guiding text for Ngũgĩ's evolution as author and thinker. The value of Ngũgĩ's first novel can be seen in its completeness. It stands, on its own merits, as a well-written, thoughtful work. Its importance and wholeness are further established and reemphasized by Ngũgĩ himself in his latest novel. Ngũgĩ returns to his original ideas of *The River Between* to rework or reassert them in *Matigari,* thereby illuminating their worth. This essay, hopefully, will encourage both writers and critics to determine the value of a text on its own merits rather than only in relation to subsequent texts. "Trust the tale."

Notes

1.   It is noteworthy that Ngũgĩ did not offer a dedication in *The River Between.* The absence of such a passage when all his other works have dedications further reinforces the argument that Ngũgĩ was embarrassed or uncomfortable with the quality or message of his first novel. Ime Ikiddeh, in his essay "James Ngugi as Novelist," provides additional support in this debate. In reference to the author's concern over the timeliness of the publication of *The River Between,* Ikiddeh writes, "Ngugi in fact felt slight embarrassment on this account, needlessly I thought, when *The River Between* was published in 1965" (Ime Ikiddeh, "James Ngugi as Novelist," *African Literature Today* 2 [1969]: 4).

In general, artists and critics have not offered positive feedback on Ngũgĩ's first novel, published after *Weep Not, Child. The River Between,* with few exceptions, has been treated with indifference. Worse still, it appears that critics have almost completely ignored it, publishing few essays on it. Critics seem to be pained by its existence, hoping to will it away by ignoring or belittling its message or its literary techniques. Its current status in the published criticism as the perceived outsider to Ngũgĩ's respected and carefully read work is denigrated most by the fact that, to this date, the Modern Language Association (MLA) has only three references for criticisms of *The River Between* whereas other Ngũgĩ novels have warranted over a dozen analyses.

It is unfortunate when a talented author has misgivings or is embarrassed about his or her first novel. Perhaps more importantly, it is unfortunate that critics have neglected to carefully read *The River Between* as a unique and individual work, a separate entity from the author's subsequent novels. Should the richness, intensity, and literary genius of Ngũgĩ's successive novels act as a kind of punishment for his first endeavor, which shares the aforementioned qualities veiled artfully in simple language, this language that can easily lull the critic into a complacent reading of the text?

2.   James Ngugi, *The River Between* (London: Heinemann, 1965), 1; hereafter cited in this essay as *RB*.

3.   Lloyd Williams, "Religion and Life in James Ngugi's 'The River Between,' " *African Literature Today* 5 (1971): 54–66.

4.   Ayi Sekyi-Otu, "The Refusal of Agency: The Founding Narrative and Waiyaki's Tragedy in 'The River Between,' " *Research in African Literatures* 16, no. 2 (1985): 167.

5.   Abdul R. JanMohammed, *Manichean Aesthetics: The Politics of Literature in Colonial Africa* (Amherst: University of Massachusetts Press, 1983), 194.

6.   "A hologram is produced when a single laser light is split into two separate beams. The first beam is bounced off the object to be photographed. . . . Then the second beam is allowed to collide with the reflected image of the first, and the resulting interference pattern is recorded on film" (Michael Talbot, *The Holographic Universe* [New York: Harper Perennial, 1993], 15).

This image, when focused on by a laser, or in some instances a bright light source, projects a three-dimensional image of the original object or subject. The three dimensionality of such a hologram can be eerie. One can study it from all directions. The image appears solid until one attempts to touch it or place one's hand through it, only to discover nothing is there. The astounding quality that makes the hologram both a rich physic and a rich literary metaphor is found in its unusual wholeness.

The film can be cut into segments, no matter how large or small, and when these parts are viewed again with the laser, one finds that the complete image is present on even the smallest portion of the film. The complete image is projected. The only proof that it has been cut is that there is a loss of resolution the smaller it becomes.

This trait of the hologram has lent itself to its use as a scientific metaphor or model for the entire universe. Many leading physicists are convinced that each atom, each molecule, each particle, has the entire blueprint for the universe in its boundaries—the entire consciousness, if you will, of what we know as the universe.

Michael Talbot posits, in his work *The Holographic Universe*, that if we all are both a part of and the complete whole of the universe, then we should be able to determine, to some extent, our reality and the rules that govern it. He believes that what we "see" in fact is not what our eyes actually perceive. We perceive waves and patterns that our visual cortex then interprets. His idea is that if in a way we are creating visions continually, due to our belief in what we are "seeing," it is reasonable to suggest that if a number of people believe strongly in something, it will manifest. The author illustrates this possibility in describing a number of famous miracles and mass visions or "hallucinations" that were corroborated by highly skeptical contemporary scholars, thinkers, and religious leaders. In one instance, the Catholic Church declared that the miracles had indeed happened. Due to this potentially damaging rivalry, the Church declared that it was the work of the Devil (Talbot, *Holographic Universe*, 130).

Talbot believes that the sightings of the Virgin Mary and the many collaborated accounts of the stigmata prove that we can "see" or create what we believe and what we want to manifest.

This idea becomes a rich metaphor that seems tailored to Ngũgĩ's *Matigari*. As the author describes this messiah through the eyes of the people, he leaves the impression that Matigari is a manifestation of the people's desires for a messiah figure, that he is real in the sense that he has come from them, that they all believe in him and in his existence, but in essence he is but a holograph. This perspective is not a negative. It seems that this view is what Ngũgĩ, ultimately, is comfortable with. The lone messiah is not a healthy nor viable idea, whereas a messiah that comes from inside each individual to create a collective focal point for energies and desires is a much more powerful and incredible manifestation of the people's will for change. In this I believe the holographic universe is manifest, and here lies the beauty and power of Ngũgĩ's latest novel.

7. Ngũgĩ wa Thiong'o, *Matigari* (Oxford, England: Heinemann, 1989), 159; hereafter cited in the text in this essay.

Bibliography

Chevalier, Jean. *Dictionnaire des Symboles: Mythes, Rêves, Coutumes, Gestes, Formes, Figures, Couleurs, Nombres.* Paris: Laffont Jupiter, 1982.

Ikiddeh, Ime. "James Ngugi as Novelist." *African Literature Today* 2 (1969): 3–11.

JanMohammed, Abdul R. *Manichean Aesthetics: The Politics of Literature in Colonial Africa.* Amherst: University of Massachusetts Press, 1983.

Ngugi, James. *The River Between.* London: Heinemann, 1966.

Ngũgĩ wa Thiong'o *Matigari.* Oxford, England: Heinemann, 1989.

Nnolim, Charles E. "Background Setting: Key to the Structure of Ngugi's 'River Between.' " *Obsidian* 2, no. 2 (1976): 20–29.

Sekyi-Otu, Ayi. "The Refusal of Agency: The Founding Narrative and Waiyaki's Tragedy in 'The River Between.' " *Research in African Literatures* 16, no. 2 (1985): 157–78.

Stratton, F. "Narrative Method in Ngugi." *African Literature Today* 13 (1982): 122–35.

Talbot, Michael. *The Holographic Universe.* New York: Harper Perennial, 1993.

Williams, Lloyd. "Religion and Life in James Ngugi's 'The River Between.' " *African Literature Today* 5 (1971): 54–66

Weep Not, Child

G. D. KILLAM

... [D]ecolonization is always a violent phenomenon. ... Its unusual importance is that it constitutes, from the very first day, the minimum demands of
the colonized. To tell the truth, the proof of success lies in a whole social structure being changed from the bottom up. The extraordinary importance of this
change is that it is willed, called for; demanded. The need for this change exists
in its crude state, impetuous and compelling, in the consciousness and in the
lives of the men and women who are colonized. But the possibility of this
change is equally experienced in the form of a terrifying future in the consciousness of another "species" of men and women: the colonizers.

—Frantz Fanon

Weep not, child, Ngugi's first published novel, belongs in subject-matter to
the period shortly after the close of the Second World War when nationalist
sentiments came to a head in Kenya. The events those sentiments provoked,
culminating in the Mau Mau emergency, are seen as they influence the lives
of the family of Ngotho and, though less fully elaborated, the families of
Howlands, a white settler-farmer, and Jacobo, a Kenyan landowner. The
events the novel describes are seen principally from the point of view of
Njoroge, the youngest son of Ngotho, from the time he enters school to a
point in the midst of the emergency, some twelve years later, when, disillusioned by the destruction of his family, denied the education by which he
sought to fulfil himself and enrich the life of his family and his country, he
tries to take his life.

The novel reveals how all the members of Ngotho's family—his sons
Boro, Kori and Kamau by his wife Njeri and Njoroge by Nyokabi—become
involved in the crisis and suffer the violence it provokes. Through these experiences Ngugi examines three separate but related themes: first, the appropri-
ateness of a young Kenyan getting a western education, secondly, the influence of Christianity in the Kenyan context (since the education is provided by
a mission school) and thirdly, the causes and prosecution of the independence

Reprinted, with permission, from G. D. Killam, *"Weep Not, Child,"* in *An Introduction to the Writings of Ngugi* (London: Heinemann, 1980), 36–52.

struggle. Ngugi treats this material in a straightforward manner and his examination of the three themes runs more or less parallel, mingling in the life of Njoroge, whose progress in the various schools he attends takes place as the political situation in Kenya deteriorates to the point where Jomo Kenyatta, the political leader of the nationalists, is arrested, tried, found guilty and imprisoned. At the same time a state of emergency is declared, sides in the struggle are drawn up, a number of Kenyans, among them Njoroge's older brothers, Boro and Kori, go into the forest to become freedom fighters. Poised against them are British forces, joined by white farmers who are sworn in as political officers in the emergency, and by Kenyan constabulary. Violence and atrocities are committed on both sides as Mau Mau soldiers seek to drive Europeans from the land from which they have alienated Africans, a land by legend, law and custom rightfully theirs.

The land was given to the Gikuyu people at the time of the creation of the earth, of Gikuyu and Mumbi the archetypal forebears of the Gikuyu. Ngugi discusses the creation thus:

> . . . There was wind and rain. And there was also thunder and terrible lightning. The earth and the forest around Kerinyaga shook. The animals of the forest whom the Creator had recently put there were afraid. There was no sunlight. This went on for many days so that the whole land was in darkness. Because the animals could not move, they just sat and moaned with the wind. The plants and trees remained dumb. It was, our elders tell us, all dead except for the thunder, a violence that seemed to strangle life. It was this dark night whose depth you could not measure, not you or I can conceive of its solid blackness, which would not let the sun pierce through it.
>
> But in this darkness, at the foot of Kerinyaga, a tree rose. At first it was a small tree and grew up, finding a way even through the darkness. It wanted to reach the light, and the sun. This tree had *Life*. It went up, up, sending forth the rich warmth of a blossoming tree—you know a holy tree in the dark night of thunder and moaning. This was Mukuyu, God's tree. Now, you know that at the beginning of things there was only one man (Gikuyu) and one woman (Mumbi). It was under this Mukuyu that he first put them. And immediately the sun rose, and the dark night melted away. The sun shone with a warmth that gave life and activity to all things. The wind and lightning and thunder stopped. The animals stopped wondering and moved. They no longer moaned but gave homage to the Creator and Gikuyu and Mumbi. And the Creator who is also called Murungu took Gikuyu and Mumbi from his holy mountain. He took them to the country of ridges near Siriana and there stood them on a big ridge before he finally took them to Mukuruwe wa Gathanga about which you have heard so much. But he had shown them all the land—yes, children, God showed Gikuyu and Mumbi all the land and told them,

> 'This land I hand over to you. O man and woman
> It's yours to rule and till in serenity sacrificing
> Only to me, your God, under my sacred tree . . .' (pp. 23–4)

Ngugi conveys two fundamental things in this passage. The land is the source of life to the Gikuyu because it provides food. As important as the material needs it supplies, is the spiritual needs it satisfies. Jomo Kenyatta describes the Gikuyu belief in this way:

> Communion with the ancestral spirits is perpetuated through contact with the soil in which the ancestors of the tribe lie buried. The Gikuyu consider the earth as the "mother" of the tribe, for the reason that the mother bears her burden for about eight or nine moons while the child is in her womb, and then for a short period of suckling. But it is the soil that feeds the child through a lifetime; and again after death it is the soil that nurses the spirit of the dead for eternity. Thus the earth is the most sacred thing above all that dwell in or on it. Among the Gikuyu the soil is especially honoured, and an everlasting oath is to swear by the earth.[1]

Kenyatta writes further in *Facing Mount Kenya* that "a culture has no meaning apart from the social organization of life on which it is built."[2] He refers to the systematic alienation of the land by the British, which was conducted by the British dating from 1902. Ime Ikiddeh discusses the history of British intervention in Kenya in these terms:

> From the attempt by Joseph Chamberlain in 1902 to found "a national home for the Jewish race" on thousands of square miles of land in Kenya and the official appropriation for British ex-soldiers after the World War, to the open seizure and illegal speculation by white settler-farmers that went on all the time, the record of British usurpation of land in Kenya must be one of the most sordid scandals in colonial history.
>
> The Crown Lands Ordinance of 1902 and subsequent laws in 1915 and after, far from controlling land dealings, led, in fact, to more profitable speculation by Europeans and greater loss to the African population.
>
> What individual settlers could own—and before 1902 they could have it for nothing—is illustrated by the case of Lord Delamere, the one-time indomitable leader of the Europeans in Kenya. In 1903 he applied for 156 square miles of leasehold at ½d (pence) per acre, to be held for ninety-nine years with the right of purchasing it permanently at 8d (pence) per acre. Delamere, who already held large tracts of land, was granted 100,000 acres on lease. Such was the rush to acquire land that the Land Commission reported in 1905 that 200% of Masai grazing grounds had been applied for. Forced labour, which included the indiscriminate use of women and children went hand in hand with land, and so did increase in the taxes extracted from the 'natives.' . . . Further Land Commissions were set up between 1928 and 1934, but the situation was not much better when Kenyatta returned to his country (in 1946). . . .[3]

The effect of this alienation process is described by Kenyatta in these terms:

When the European comes to the Gikuyu country and robs the people of their land, he is taking away not only their livelihood, but the material symbol that holds family and tribe together.[4]

Weep Not, Child is the artistic expression of the truth of this assertion. Ngotho works on land, once the ancestral land of his forebears, now owned by Howlands, and he lives on land, again once his but now owned by Jacobo. Ngotho acquiesces to his circumstances because he is confident that the prophecy of the Gikuyu sage, Mugo wa Kibiro, that the land will be returned to its rightful owners, will be fulfilled. He believes this despite the experience of dealings he has had with whites and the example his father who, too, had trusted in the prophecy:

"Then came the war. It was the first big war. I was then young, a mere boy, although circumcised. All of us were taken by the force. We made roads and cleared the forest to make it possible for the warring white men to move more quickly. The war ended. We were all tired. We came home worn out but very ready for whatever the British might give us as a reward. But more than this, we wanted to go back to the soil and court it to yield, to create, not to destroy. But Ng'o! The land was gone. My father and many others had been moved from our ancestral lands. He died lonely, a poor man waiting for the white man to go. Mugo had said this would come to be. The white man did not go and he died a *Muhoi* on this very land." (p. 25)

Boro and Kori have been to war for the British, too. They have seen a brother, Mwangi, Njoroge's older brother die in an alien cause on alien soil. But they draw different conclusions from their experiences of fighting in Egypt, Jerusalem and Burma. They have met members of other "subject races" who have had similar experiences to their own, and have learned of movements in other parts of the world to repossess land taken from its hereditary owners by imperial conquest. Boro and Kamau can be taken to stand for that generation of Kenyans who were moved to fight for the land when all other forms of appeal were suppressed, often violently. They prefigure Kihika in *A Grain of Wheat,* symbolic of figures who, frustrated by having no land to work, by having fought for little gain in an alien war, take to the forests and effect the return of the land to the rightful owners. They realize that passive waiting will not win them back the land. Moreover, Boro's anger with the status accorded his people by the British spills over on his father. Ngugi presents the situation in plain terms:

Boro thought of his father who had fought in the war only to be dispossessed. He too had gone to war, against Hitler. He had gone to Egypt, Jerusalem and Burma. He had seen things. He had often escaped death narrowly. But the thing he could not forget was the death of his stepbrother, Mwangi. For whom or for what had *he* died?

When the war had come to an end, Boro had come home, no longer a boy but a man with experience and ideas, only to find that for him there was to be no employment. There was no land on which he could settle, even if he had been able to do so. As he listened to this story, all these things came into his mind with a growing anger. How could these people have let the white man occupy the land without acting? And what was all this superstitious belief in a prophecy?

In a whisper that sounded like a shout, he said, "To hell with prophecy."

Yes, this was nothing more than a whisper. To his father, he said, "How can you continue working for a man who has taken your land? How can you go on serving him?"

He walked out, without waiting for an answer. (p. 26)

The anger Boro expresses for his father is the first rent in the "feeling of oneness [which] most distinguished Ngotho's household from many other polygamous families." This, Ngugi tells us, "was attributed to Ngotho, the centre of the home." The breakup of the home, which the novel dramatizes from this point forward—and the breakup of the homes of Howlands and Jacobo, a comparison which Ngugi sustains to good artistic effect—becomes a metaphor for the breakup of Kenyan society, preparing the way for it to be replaced by a new order, a process not completed by the novel's close and with no suggestion of what the new order might be.

Ngotho continues to work the land for Howlands. Boro and Kori go to work in Nairobi and become involved in the independence movement. How-lands' whole life is in the land. Although his family is about the same size as Ngotho's we learn little of them except that his wife after an initial romantic response to Africa comes to find life almost intolerable and spends her time hiring and firing servants in a futile attempt to work out her frustrations. We know that he has a daughter overseas, that he, like Ngotho, has lost a son overseas in the war and that he has another son, Stephen, about Njoroge's age and with whom Njoroge has a fleeting moment of intimate understanding. Howlands has come to Kenya after the First World War. Described as a "typ-ical Kenya settler":

He was a product of the First World War. After years of security at home, he had been suddenly called to arms and he had gone to the war with the fire of youth that imagines war and glory. But after four years of blood and terrible destruction, like many other young men he was utterly disillusioned by the "peace." He had to escape. East Africa was a good place. Here was a big trace of wild country to conquer. (p. 30)

The irony is that Howlands, disillusioned with his own land, dispossesses the Kenyan of his. When Howlands' son, to whom he planned to pass on the land, is killed in the Second World War his reaction is to turn wholly to the land:

Mr Howlands lost all faith—even the few shreds that had begun to return. He would again have destroyed himself, but again his god, land, came to the rescue. He turned all his efforts and energy into it. He seemed to worship the soil. (p. 31)

It is in this scene with Howlands, when Ngugi reveals most clearly the irony arising out of the parallel lines their lives have followed. For just as Howlands would have no idea that Ngotho might experience guilt comparable to his own at the loss of a son, so Howlands would have no idea of the force of the idea which binds Ngotho to the land and, ironically draws from Howlands feelings amounting to affection:

Not that Mr Howlands stopped to analyse his feelings towards him. He just loved to see Ngotho working in the farm; the way the old man touched the soil, almost fondling, and the way he tended the young tea plants as if they were his own. . . . Ngotho was too much of a part of the farm to be separated from it. (pp. 29–30)

This scene carries a weight of foreshadowing. It is here that Ngotho is disarmed of his view that Howlands will leave the land to return to its hereditary owners, that the prophecy of Mugo wa Kibero will be fulfilled:

Ngotho's heart jumped. He too was thinking of his children. Would the prophecy be fulfilled soon?
"*Kwa nini Bwana.* Are you going back to—?"
"No," Mr Howlands said, unnecessarily loudly.
". . . Your home, home . . ."
"My home is here!"
Ngotho was puzzled. Would these people never go? But had not the old Gikuyu seer said that they would eventually return the way they had come? And Mr Howlands was thinking, would Stephen really *do*? He was not like the other one. He felt the hurt and the pain of loss. (p. 32)

Shortly after this Ngotho attends a meeting, organized by Boro, Kori and others, to organize a strike. Kiarie, one of the organizers, reminds the crowd of people of their history under colonialism, of their alienation from the land. His speech ends in the familiar pleas of Moses to Pharaoh: "Let my People go," noting the association between Moses and Jomo, the Black Moses, sent by God to liberate the Kenyan people.

But when Jacobo, "crystallized into a concrete betrayal of the people," is brought in to pacify the people, Ngotho leads a charge against Jacobo, riot police break up the meeting and the strike fails.

Jacobo is the fourth representative figure in the novel. Howlands, when the emergency is in effect, enunciates a policy of divide and rule—get the blacks to fight each other and the white man will be safe. But in fact a policy such as this has been in effect for a long while before the emergency. Jacobo represents that small number of Africans who were allowed to own and farm land, who were thus able to accumulate wealth. But their position depended on the goodwill of the whites and thus people like Jacobo, both pitiable and contemptible, become their toadies. More than this, such people become agents of division within the African community. Boro and his peers are in accord about the reasons for reclaiming the land but lack agreement over how to do this. Jacobo and those like him (figures whose mentalities we find explored at greater depth in Ngugi's later writing) help perpetuate this disarray.

Ngotho's action in the strike further alienates him from Boro who holds his father accountable for the failure. Moreover, it marks the beginning of the decline of Ngotho and his family.

It is an irony that Ngotho, in a public act of protest against the victimization of Africans by Africans, prompted by his clear recognition of the truth of Boro's claims, destroys his sons' cause. But it is equally an irony that the revolution which Boro mounts to retrieve the land for the peasantry has the effect of alienating completely the last generation of genuine African peasantry, symbolized by Ngotho, from the land.

Ngotho's nadir occurs after the ill-fated strike which fails because Ngotho, recognizing the treacherous behaviour of Jacobo, on impulse attacks the latter and provokes a riot. He is fired from his job, his reputation destroyed as he resides, a supplicant, on the farm of Nganga, a compassionate farmer.

It is against this background of deepening stress that Njoroge grows from boyhood to adolescence. When the novel opens his mother asks him "would you like to go to school?" and he holds his breath, fearing she may withdraw her words. But she does not and we see in a series of vignettes how Njoroge's schoolboy career progresses, how he persistently does better than others. At school he makes a close relationship with Mwihaki, the daughter of Jacobo. And it is at this time, in listening to discussions in his father's hut about the problems in the country that he begins to conceive an important mission for himself:

> Njoroge listened to his father. He instinctively knew that an indefinable demand was being made on him, even though he was so young. He knew that for him education would be the fulfilment of a wider and more significant vision—a vision that embraced the demand made on him, not only by his father, but also by his mother, his brothers and even the village. He saw himself destined for something big, and this made his heart glow. (p. 39)

Njoroge accepts the teaching of the missionaries and his callow mind elaborates a dream compounded of education and Christian teaching, exploiting the analogy between the two religious forces he is submitted to:

His belief in a future for his family and the village rested then not only on a hope for sound education but also on a belief in a God of love and mercy, who long ago walked on this earth with Gikuyu and Mumbi, or Adam and Eve. It did not make much difference that he had come to identify Gikuyu with Adam and Mumbi with Eve. To this God, all men and women were united by one strong bond of brotherhood. And with all this, there was growing up in his heart a feeling that the Gikuyu people, whose land had been taken by white men, were no other than the children of Israel about whom he read in the Bible. (p. 49)

But the dream is stalemated, even as Njoroge, "now a big boy, almost a young man" . . . and the "full force of the chaos that had come over the land was just beginning to be clear in his mind" (p. 84). And it is reduced by the false consolations offered out of the Bible to account for the chaos:

"Turn to the Gospel according to St Matthew, Chapter 24, and begin to read from line 4."

There was a shuffle of leaves.

"Let's begin to read . . ."

"And Jesus answered and said unto them: Take heed that no man deceive you.

"For many shall come in My name, saying, I am Christ; and shall deceive many.

"And ye shall hear of wars and rumours of wars: see that ye be not troubled: for all these things must come to pass, but the end is not yet.

"For nation shall rise against nation, and kingdom against kingdom: and there shall be famines, and pestilences, and earthquakes, in divers places.

"All these are the beginning of sorrows.

"Then they shall deliver you up to be afflicted, and shall kill you: and ye shall be hated of all nations for My name's sake.

"And then shall many be offended, and shall betray one another, and shall hate one another.

"And many false prophets shall rise, and shall deceive many.

"And because iniquity shall abound, the love of many shall wax cold.

"But he that shall endure unto the end, the same shall be saved . . ."

He read on. But when he came to verse 33, he stopped and stared at all the people in the church. Then he raised his voice and went on:

"Verily I say unto you. This generation shall not pass till all these things be fulfilled . . ."

It was as if darkness too had fallen into the building and there was no one to light the way. (p. 90)

It survives the brutal murder by the Christian police of the revivalist, Isaka, who professes his Christian faith singing with the protection of God he needs no pass. He is beaten and shot, almost before the eyes of his young catechists.

But the dream is not really enough to sustain Njoroge. Its weaknesses are probed by Mwihaki on one of their meetings. All he has is faith and she knows faith is not enough:

> He became serious and a little distant. He was again in his vision.
> "Our country has great need of us."
> "Do you think the country really needs you?"
> "Yes," he said rather irritably. Was she doubting him? "The country needs me. It needs you. And the remnant. We must get together and rebuild the country. That was what your father told me the day I was at your home."
> "The country is so dark now," she whispered to herself.
> "The sun will rise tomorrow," he said triumphantly, looking at her as if he would tell her that he would never lose faith, knowing as he did that God had a secret plan.

Mwihaki's disillusionment is juxtaposed to Njoroge's faith. Mwihaki is a foil to Njoroge throughout the novel. She experiences despair as the horror of the emergency spreads over the land. When he expounds his "vision" to her she retorts angrily, and out of fear:

> "You are always talking about tomorrow, tomorrow. You are always talking about *the* country and *the* people. What is tomorrow? And what is *the People* and *the Country* to you?" She had suddenly stopped what she had been doing and was looking at him with blazing eyes. Njoroge saw this and was afraid. He did not want to make her angry. He was pained. He looked at her and then at the plain, the country beyond stretching on, on to the distant hills shrouded in the mist. (p. 106)

Njoroge's faith is in his belief that:

> "If you knew that all your days life will always be like this with blood flowing daily and men dying in the forest, while others daily cry for mercy; if you knew even for one moment that this would go on for ever, then life would be meaningless unless bloodshed and death were a meaning. Surely this darkness and terror will not go on for ever. Surely there will be a sunny day, a warm sweet day after all this tribulation, when we can breathe the warmth and purity of God. . . ." (p. 106)

His words offer optimism of a kind and are a reflection of his duty to prepare himself for his role once the troubles have been passed. But Mwihaki has struck a chord of doubt in him and for a moment his faith, couched in vague abstractions, looks threadbare. Moreover, the speech offers an ironic foreshadowing of Njoroge's ultimate disillusionment. So that when the scene between him and Mwihaki is replayed, in mirror fashion, after his torture by Howlands, it is Njoroge who repudiates his vision and pleads with Mwihaki to fly to Uganda with him. And it is she, always realistic in her appraisals, who speaks of duty:

"We better wait. You told me that the sun will rise tomorrow. I think you were right."

He looked at her tears and wanted to wipe them. She sat there, a lone tree defying the darkness, trying to instil new life into him. But he did not want to live. Not this kind of life. He felt betrayed.

"All that was a dream. We can only live today."

"Yes. But we have a duty. Our duty to other people is our biggest responsibility as grown men and women."

"Duty! Duty!" he cried bitterly.

"Yes, I have a duty, for instance, to my mother. Please, dear Njoroge, we cannot leave her at this time when—No! Njoroge. Let's wait for a new day."

She had conquered. She knew now that she would not submit. But it was hard for her and as she left him she went on weeping, tearing and wringing her heart. The sun was sinking down. Njoroge's last hope had vanished. For the first time he knew that he was in the world all alone without a soul on whom he could lean. The earth went round and round. He saw everything in a mist. Then all of a sudden, he fell on to the ground and cried "Mwihaki, oh Mwihaki." (pp. 133–4)

Njoroge, for all his hope, achieves none of the things he sought and much of what he did not—expulsion from school and employment in the shop of an Asian merchant, both humiliating experiences.

Yet the lyrical possibilities of the dream are most profoundly experienced by Njoroge at the secondary school:

Njoroge was often surprised by these missionaries' apparent devotion to their work. One might have thought that teaching was to them life and death. Yet they were white men. They never talked of colour; they never talked down to Africans; and they could work closely, joke, and laugh with their black colleagues who came from different tribes. Njoroge at times wished the whole country was like this. This seemed a little paradise, a paradise where children from all walks of life and of different religious faiths could work together without any consciousness. (p. 115)

Ironically it is at this moment the dream is dealt its death blow. Police officers come to take Njoroge away to his village. Jacobo has been murdered, Ngotho has confessed the crime and Njoroge has been denounced as an oath taker. Ngotho has been castrated and Njoroge is threatened with the same mutilation. Howlands, now a maniacal District Officer, turns the full fury of his hatred against Ngotho for whom he once held a special fondness. Ngotho is the most treacherous of the Gikuyus in his eyes.

Ngugi brings the novel swiftly to a close. Boro comes out of the forest to kill Howlands but not before he and his father, in one of the genuinely moving scenes in the novel, have been reconciled:

"Forgive me, father—I didn't know—oh, I thought—" Boro turned his head. The words came out flatly, falteringly. "It's nothing. Ha, ha, ha! You too have come back—to laugh at me? Would you laugh at your father? No. Ha! I meant only good for you all. I didn't want you to go away—"

"I had to fight."

"Oh there—Now—Don't you ever go away again."

"I can't stay. I can't," Boro cried in a hollow voice. A change came over Ngotho. For a time he looked like the man he had been, firm, commanding—the centre of his household.

"You must."

"No, father. Just forgive me."

Ngotho exerted himself and sat up in bed. He lifted his hand with an effort and put it on Boro's head. Boro looked like a child.

"All right. Fight well. Turn your eyes to Murungu and Ruriri. Peace to you all—Ha! What? Njoroge look . . . look—to—your—moth—"

His eyes were still aglow as he sank back into his bed. For a moment there was silence in the hut. Then Boro stood up and whispered, "I should have come earlier. . . ." (p. 124)

In a sense the spirit of the family is revived and Ngotho, even in death, is once again the centre of the home.

Ngugi takes the opportunity, just before Boro kills Howlands, to examine the circumstances which have converted Howlands from an introspective farmer who takes more consolation from his work on the land than in his family, into a brutal killer who only half understands the forces which sweep round him and who, in the midst of his brutal behaviour, finds repugnant the system which has cast him in this role:

He now knew maybe there was no escape. The present that had made him a D.O. reflected a past from which he had tried to run away. That past had followed him even though he had tried to avoid politics, government, and anything else that might remind him of that betrayal. But his son had been taken away. . . . It was no good calling on the name of God for he, Howlands, did not believe in God. There was only one God for him—and that was the farm he had created, the land he had tamed. And who were these Mau Mau who were now claiming that land, his god? Ha ha! He could have laughed at the whole ludicrous idea, but for the fact that they had forced him into the other life, the life he had tried to avoid. He had been called upon to take up a temporary appointment as a District Officer. He had agreed. But only because this meant defending his god. If Mau Mau claimed the only thing he believed in, they would see! (pp. 76–7)

When Boro confronts him with the reasons for fighting the war, Howlands reveals he does not comprehend that Africans have any rights whatsoever:

"I killed Jacobo."

"I know."

"He betrayed black people. Together, you killed many sons of the land. You raped our women. And finally you killed my father. Have you anything to say in your defence?"

Boro's voice was flat. No colour of hatred, anger or triumph. No sympathy. "Nothing."

"Nothing. Now you say nothing. But when you took our ancestral lands—"

"This is my land." Mr Howlands said this as a man would say, This is my woman.

"*Your* land! Then, you white dog, you'll die on your land."

Mr Howlands thought him mad. Fear overwhelmed him and he tried to cling to life with all his might. But before he could reach Boro, the gun went off. Boro had learnt to be a good marksman during the Second World War. The white man's trunk stood defiant for a few seconds. Then it fell down. (pp. 128–9)

This is as much insight as Howland achieves.

Njoroge works in a shop owned by an Asian for a time. But such is his desolation that he does the job badly and is fired from it. At his last encounter with Mwihaki he asks her to escape from Kenya with him for Uganda—just as she had sought him to do in the past. This time it is she who refuses, and echoing Njoroge's words, speaks to him of "duty" and "responsibility." There is no talk of misty dreams, but merely the need to accept the stark reality of the terror and wait it out. Mwihaki, it seems can do this, but not Njoroge.

He attempts to hang himself but is saved from doing so by his mother. The novel ends on a deeply gloomy note:

But as they came near home and what had happened to him came to mind, the voice again came and spoke accusing him: *You are a coward. You have always been a coward. Why didn't you do it?*

And loudly he said, "Why didn't I do it?"

The voice said: *Because you are a coward.*

"Yes," he whispered to himself. "I am a coward."

And he ran home and opened the door for his two mothers. (p. 136)

Weep Not, Child is a small novel with few complexities either of plot or in the creation of characters. There is a symbolic quality in the novel. Ngugi admits having had a certain symbolism in mind when he wrote this book. He says, for example, that he saw Jomo Kenyatta as a kind of saviour or Black Messiah but admits that they are not saviours as such but:

symbols of certain social forces which are started, and the individuals are mere agents of those forces which are already in society.[5]

Similarly, Njoroge conceives an analogous symbolic role for himself, seeing the equation between Jomo and Moses and his own potential relation to it. In a way all of the characters and situations, though unmistakably real, present something more. Howlands is a typical Kenyan farmer with notions as callow and imperfectly thought through as Ngotho's unquestioning faith in Mugo's prophecy or Njoroge's callow dream of being a Messiah.

The small village of Ngotho is a microcosm of Kenya at the time of the emergency and the principal characters—Ngotho, Njoroge, Howlands, Boro, and Jacobo—represent the various points of view, possibly too obviously, which obtain in it. Certain scenes, as well, have a symbolic reference. The most notable of these is when Howlands, now partly crazed and demented with fatigue and killing, threatens to castrate Njoroge as he has done Ngotho. It is suggestive of the desire of Europeans to deprive Africans of their rights and manhood.

The creation of Njoroge is the weakest part of the book. Njoroge, we are told, "had always been a dreamer, a visionary who consoled himself faced by the difficulties of the moment by a look at a better day to come." This represents a weakness in the character and, by implication, in his creator. Often throughout the book he retreats into vague phrases, a measure of his inability to control, at the age he is, his destiny. Often throughout the novel he is powerless to act and does not want to contemplate the possible consequences of certain hard facts that have to be faced. Ngugi gives Njoroge more to do than a youth of his age can do and more to understand than a youth with his limited intellect can cope with.

If the viewpoint of the novel is not wholly adequate to a full examination of the theme—how much more would be gained, for example, to see the events of the novel through Boro's eyes—the disinterestedness Ngugi achieves in his rendering of the events of the book accounts for its convincingness. Njoroge's point of view is severely limited. He, like Waiyaki, never grows to intellectual maturity. His Messianic dream, not unlike Waiyaki's, of saving his people in time of trouble by means of education, vaguely defined, and the large charity found in the sacrifice of Christ, equally vaguely apprehended, is founded on adolescent romanticism. As such it is vulnerable and crumbles when pressure is applied, pressure of a kind even an adult, mature in body and will, would find difficult to withstand.

Njoroge is delicately moulded and we watch him grow from boyhood into adolescence with an interest and compassion similar in kind to the emotion which prompted Ngugi to create him. We know his boyish dream is callow and we do not mind that. It is a dream that a boy can have. Equally we feel no great pity when the dream dies. We share his fear in the forest when the teacher is murdered by the colonial troops and sense the horror and the pain of the castration with which the maddened Howlands threatens him.

But this is not an idyll, not a tale for children. And so it is the events taking place in the society in which Njoroge lives which matter most to readers.

The dream of education, too, is another weakness in the book. The suggestion is made that Njoroge's acquisition of western education is the means to a better future—of acquiring the understanding of the white man and thus of achieving what he has achieved of re-acquiring the land. But little is made of this. Nyokabi, it seems, wants Njoroge to be educated so that she will be able to feel the same as the Howlands women or Juliana, the wife of Jacobo:

That was something. That was real life. It did not matter if anyone died poor provided he or she could one day say, "Look, I have a son as good and as well educated as any can find in the land." (p. 16)

And while Ngotho is prepared to say that "Education is everything" it is the land that is everything and education is useful only if it leads to the recovery of the land. Kamau and Kori contribute to Njoroge's education but say little about why they do so. Perhaps it is simply assumed that readers know and nothing more needs be said.

The question of the value and the kind of education which is best for African people is something Ngugi is much concerned with of course. It is a central theme in *The River Between,* where the discussion is more clearly focused than here. In this novel we see, perhaps, the beginning of the analysis which will consume many pages in *Petals of Blood,* the suspicion that the sort of idyllic formal education doled out in the remote safety of such schools as Siriana merely shields people from life and that the real lessons are learned in the informal, sometimes terrifying experiences which one is left to synthesize for himself. But the matter is left up in the air here.

The book makes passing implicit comment on the morality of various related actions and enterprises which form familiar themes in Ngugi's writing. Howlands expounds the morality of paternal colonialism in conjunction with a belief in his right to the land. So great is his obsession with the land and his sense of betrayal on the part of Africans, that the violence he vents on them ultimately rebounds to derange him:

He had remembered himself as a boy, that day so long ago when he had sat outside his parents' home and dreamt of a world that needed him, only to be brought face to face with the harsh reality of life in the First World War. . . . Mr Howlands could now remember only drinking to make himself forget. He cursed horribly.

And this Ngotho. He had let him go home more dead than alive. But still he had let him go. Howlands had not got the satisfaction he had hoped for. The only thing left to him was hatred. What had made him release Ngotho was a notebook that had been found behind the lavatory from where apparently Jacobo had been shot. The notebook had Boro's name. At first Mr Howlands had been unable to understand. But gradually he realized that Ngotho had been telling a lie, in order to shield Boro. But Boro was in the forest? Slowly he arrived at the truth. Ngotho too had thought that it was Kamau who had done the murder. He had taken on the guilt to save a son. At this Mr Howlands' hatred of Ngotho had been so great that he had trembled the whole night. (pp. 127–8)

Howlands and Boro, who eventually kills him, are not unalike in the views they hold and practise. Ultimately simple expedience determines and justifies how they act. Boro's thinking is somewhat confused as this passage shows; but he honours necessity:

"And Freedom?" the lieutenant continued.

"An illusion. What Freedom is there for you and me?"

"Why then do we fight?"

"To kill. Unless you kill, you'll be killed. So you go on killing and destroying. It's a law of nature. The white man too fights and kills with gas, bombs, and everything."

"But don't you think there's something wrong in fighting and killing unless you're doing so for a great cause like ours?"

"What great cause is ours?"

"Why, Freedom and the return of our lost heritage."

"Maybe there's something in that. But for me Freedom is meaningless unless it can bring back a brother I lost. Because it can't do that, the only thing left to me is to fight, to kill and rejoice at any who falls under my sword. But enough. Chief Jacobo must die." (pp. 102–3)

Boro's actions are consistent with his beliefs: when he kills Howlands he experiences no emotion at first. He has killed out of a sense of duty.

Ngugi comments as we have seen on the morality of the preaching of the Christian missionaries as it seeks to deflect the African from a just consideration of his circumstances. The passage from St Matthew which Ngugi cites offers an ironic reflection on how the missionaries, in collusion with other European forces—a policy of Howlands in the emergency is "to set these people fighting amongst themselves instead of fighting with the white men . . ." (p. 77)—have been instrumental in perpetrating the divide-and-rule policy against which the passage preaches.

Finally, this is a novel which examines various attitudes toward "duty." Each of the characters acts out of a sense of commitment to an idea, each believes his idea defensible and each, as the events of the novel proceed, is given cause to re-examine the strength of his position. Ngotho and Njoroge's positions change as a result of their experiences but not those of other principal characters; rather, their positions harden and they pay with their lives. Ngotho gives his life in order to save his son's, reversing the attitude which caused him to reject the oath when Boro sought to administer it to him at the emergencies' beginning—in Ngotho's mind Boro had "no right to reverse the custom and tradition for which he and his generation stood." In the actions and reactions of his characters, in the way he probes into motivations, in the compassion he shows for Njoroge, Ngotho, and Mwihaki especially but also for Nyokabi, Nyeri and the brothers of Njoroge, Ngugi's humanism is revealed and tempers his anger.

As with *The River Between* Ngugi achieves a notable effect in a small book which in plain language and with plain and neatly balanced plotting conveys an impression of an important period in contemporary history by displaying the experiences of a variety of sensitive human beings.

Ngugi was aware of the shortcomings of the novel and its limited perspective which accounts for the uncomplicated nature of the story it tells and the motifs it examines. He accounts for this by saying that he was a child growing up during the emergency period and because of this was not aware of all the implications of the struggle. But, he says:

> One did get the impressions. You are so young. You see your uncles being killed. British soldiers come to collect your uncles. You see some of your friends being taken from their homes. These things stay with you. You see an old man you respected being emasculated as a condition of war. These things leave you with the impression though you take these things for granted and just go on.[6]

The novelist then synthesizes the personal experience into the imaginative work and is fully successful in realizing his aim which he describes in the following fashion:

> In *Weep Not, Child* I just wanted to capture as much as possible the atmosphere of the situation, what it felt like to actually live in the small village at this time. So I wasn't trying to capture anything that was very deep, but I was trying to capture what it felt like to live in a civil war. So that even if I didn't use my experience in many of the episodes, there are things which I may have seen or heard or felt at the time.[7]

There is a sparseness of concrete details of the lives of the characters, even Njoroge the most fully perceived figure in the book, and of the society in which the action takes place. So, too, there is a sparseness about the inner lives of the characters. This sparseness, accentuated by virtue of the village setting in which Ngugi places the action of the novel, makes the book more a history of the changes wrought by the emergency than an experience of the change in the way a novel can convey a sense of how such changes come about.

Weep Not, Child is a small book and in some respects a naive one. But in it, as in *The River Between,* Ngugi puts down a blueprint for the mature writing in *A Grain of Wheat* and *Petals of Blood.*

References and Notes

1. Jomo Kenyatta, *Facing Mount Kenya* (London: Martin Secker and Warburg 1938; New York: Vintage, 1965), p. 22.

2. *Ibid.,* p. 305.

3. Ime Ikiddeh, "Ngugi wa Thiong'o; the novelist as historian" in Bruce King and Kolawole Ogungbesan (eds.), *A Celebration of Black African Writing* (Zaria: Ahmadu Bello University Press; London: OUP 1975), p. 210.

4. Jomo Kenyatta, *op. cit.,* p. 317.

5. Reinhard Sander and Ian Munro, "Tolstoy in Africa," *Ba Shiru,* vol. 5 (1973), p. 26.

6. *Ibid.*

7. *Ibid.*

Escape or Rebel? The Case for Anticolonialist Education in *Weep Not, Child*

Yulisa Amadu Maddy and Donnarae MacCann

Education is "a mirror unto" a people's social being. It has been a major ideological battlefield between the economic, political, and cultural forces of oppression and the forces for national liberation and unity.

—"Literature in Schools"

The aim of imperialism whether in its colonial or neocolonial stage is to steal the wealth generated by the people. . . . The aim of colonial education is to bring up a partly developed native only fit for brute labor, a native who has internalized a consciousness that blinds him[1] into not seeing the loot and the plunder going on around him. . . . Education and culture are in fact class education and culture.

—"Education for a National Culture"

Ngũgĩ's work as novelist, playwright, and educator has been significant over a 40-year time span. With the publication of *Weep Not, Child* in 1964, educators received an object lesson as well as a compelling story. In this novel, the colonist-controlled school provides a curriculum that is purely Anglo-Saxon with respect to language, art history, and geography. This curriculum is fully supportive of colonialist expansionism and warfare. But the war of independence in Kenya entails a war against this alien and debilitating indoctrination.[2] The Mau Mau war of liberation constitutes a united force that creates a kind of "school" for the people. In Ngũgĩ's words in *Barrel of a Pen:*

> [I]t's both an act of education and an educational process to struggle to seize back the right and the initiative to make one's own history and hence culture which is a product and a reflection of history.[3] (87)

By downgrading things African and inculcating "values of self-doubt, self-denigration, in a word, a slave consciousness," the British-run colonial school

This essay is published here for the first time by permission of the authors, with whom the copyright remains.

achieves a large degree of dominance over the child's mind, spirit, and behavior (*BP,* 92).

In the 1990s, American educators were replicating the intellectual imperialism that Ngũgĩ portrayed in his novel, as we will show by critiquing the *English Journal* (one of the official publications of the National Council of Teachers of English). In an African focus issue, most of the articles describe classroom assignments that distort and falsify images of Africa. By devising negative conceptions of blackness, the teachers are giving African American children biased conceptions of themselves. And the purpose is the same as in African colonialist schools—namely, to produce mental enslavement, to create notions of inferiority in children of African descent, and to create notions of superiority in the European-descended students. Throughout the years Ngũgĩ has spoken directly to the teaching profession about such racism in education, but apparently the message has not reached America. Our aim here is to reintroduce that message by revisiting *Weep Not, Child* and Ngũgĩ's essays about education. It is important to take a close look at some American classrooms to underline the value of Ngũgĩ's insights to the present educational establishment. His perception that education and politics are overlapping phenomena is demonstrated in American classroom practices.

WEEP NOT, CHILD: AN OBJECT LESSON IN EDUCATION

Two school types are consistently present in *Weep Not, Child,* but each is revealed indirectly. The young hero, Njoroge, is all but hypnotized by the false hopes and imperialistic brainwashing supplied by the colonizer or the colonizer's native surrogate. If the national liberation struggle had not intervened, the boy would have undoubtedly ended up like Jacobo—a neighbor who has gained wealth and other material advantages over other Africans but has suffered great spiritual and moral losses. In the second "school" (the Mau Mau Liberation Movement), Njoroge's elder brothers have preserved their self-respect, cultural integrity, and social responsibility but have faced the ultimate self-sacrifices: exile, torture, or death. These contrasting intellectual journeys were the choices available to Ngũgĩ and his generation of Kenyans. He writes:

> In my second book, "Weep Not, Child," I was primarily interested in evoking what a simple village community felt, caught between forces which they could not quite understand. I lived through the period myself.[4]

The colonialist forces that confronted Ngũgĩ were not really complicated, despite their insidiousness. In *Barrel of a Pen* he defines the terms of the colonized society without resorting to jargon or abstruseness: "It's the slave, the peasant, the worker who does all the production, who creates the wealth of that society, and yet is not able to control the disposal of that which his sweat has generated" (*BP*, 91). The opening chapters of *Weep Not, Child* lay bare the relationship between this unethical seizure of another's life and the treatment of children. We see four perspectives by four family members: the boy (Njoroge), his father (Ngotho), his mother (Nyokabi), and one of his brothers (Kamau). To the newly enrolled schoolboy, a formal education means riches, which in turn mean "a bright future."[5] To the boy's father, this new opportunity is seen in relation to Jacobo, a lackey of the British and owner of the land on which Ngotho and his family are allowed to reside. The narrator reports:

> When anybody now asked him whether he had taken any of his sons to school, he would proudly say, "Yes!" It made him feel almost equal to Jacobo. (*WNC*, 12)

This is not a case of sophomoric envy. Ngũgĩ sketches a scene at the nearby barber shop that uncovers the deep anguish of Ngotho. The barber is full of tales of the Second World War—a mindless ritual in which European men had slaughtered each other while European women had slept with black soldiers. These wartime memories helped to demystify the arrogance of white, male Europeans. The barber's reminiscences counter the superiority myth that the colonizers are continually reinforcing. For Ngotho, schooling for a son is another means of gaining some leverage over a colonized existence.

For Njoroge's mother, Nyokabi, "a lot of motives had indeed combined into one desire, the desire to have a son who had acquired all the learning that there was" (*WNC*, 16). We have access to Nyokabi's thoughts: if this educational goal were fulfilled, "would Ngotho even work for Howlands [the British plantation owner]" (*WNC*, 16)? And would this British settler's family even "continue living as *Ahoi* in another man's land, a man who clearly resented their stay" (*WNC*, 16)? Moreover, "Why should [one of her sons] have died in a white man's war [Second World War]? She did not want to sacrifice what was hers to other people" (*WNC*, 16). Finally we learn that her "mother's instinct . . . yearned for something broader than that which could be had from her social circumstances" (*WNC*, 16). Nyokabi's anticolonialism, like that of her husband, is finding an outlet in the youngest son's schooling. But she has been swept up by the same empty fantasies as her child.

The next-to-youngest son, Kamau, represents Ngũgĩ's clear admiration for the artisan. Kamau is apprenticed to a carpenter and is philosophical about the way his prospects are deemed a lesser opportunity: "Don't you worry about me. . . . Get education, I'll get carpentry. Then we shall, in the future, be able to have a new and better home for the whole family" (*WNC*, 4). Kamau thinks collectively, a mental process that does not come easily to young Njoroge and one that his beloved school will not encourage.

By placing these family fantasies in juxtaposition with the daily school-room realities, Ngũgĩ builds the background for his anticolonial commentary. Also, the economic structure of the region unfolds as we learn about each character and, in particular, about who owns what. Given the power of ownership in Ngũgĩ's story, plus the accompanying power to dominate, any hopes centered on schooling seem truly a case of wishful thinking. Even if Njoroge had enjoyed a more viable and meaningful educational environment, the boy and his family would have been in an unequal fight. In "Education for a National Culture," Ngũgĩ makes this point clear:

> [I]n a situation where one nation or race or class is dominated by another, there can never be any neutral education transmitting a neutral culture. . . . In such a society, there are in fact two types of education in mortal struggle, transmitting two opposed types of culture and hence two opposed consciousnesses or world outlooks or ideologies. (BP, 89–90)

Under colonial domination, Njoroge's world outlook does not reach beyond his own childlike dreams for "a bright future." But this self-involvement soon changes as the country moves toward a revolutionary war. Njoroge's idealism expands: "[He] saw himself building the whole country. For a moment he glowed with that possibility" (WNC, 92). This hope that he will become a heroic, saving influence is stated intermittently as the narrative progresses. But it is clearly unrealistic. For one thing, the violent British reaction to impending Kenyan independence translates into increasing danger for Njoroge's own family. As the boy fantasizes, his father and brothers are hunted down, tortured, imprisoned for life, executed, and/or held in a detention camp indefinitely. Moreover, the physical persecution has a counterpart in the schoolboy's intellectual persecution as the white supremacy myth permeates his learning environment. At his mission high school, the headmaster seems outwardly evenhanded, but "he believed that the best, the really excellent could only come from the white man" (WNC, 115). The schoolboy has become so submerged in this myth of white infallibility that he does not recognize its repercussions for himself and all blacks. He comforts himself with a dogged faith in the future, but the story's narrator adds a commentary on that delusion: "He [Njoroge] did not know that this faith in the future could be a form of escape from the reality of the present" (WNC, 111).

From this point forward we see the protagonist's literal efforts at escape. His British education has not suggested any means by which a Kenyan can serve his nation; on the contrary, the British have appropriated Njoroge's nation and are planning to keep it. All that remains for Njoroge is an escape to Uganda (an idea that his girlfriend, Mwihaki, rejects) or an escape via suicide (an act that his mother successfully interrupts). These two women have less education than Njoroge, but they are the saviors of human life. Mwihaki's scholarly achievements allowed for nothing better than admittance to a teacher-training institution. But she knows her duty toward her own mother, now the widow of Jacobo, and remains with her. Njoroge has promised his dying father that he will care for his mother and stepmother, but in the end it is the mothers who look after him.

Ngũgĩ succeeds in evoking "two types of education in mortal struggle"—a condition that traumatizes any dominated people. But he is explicitly proeducation, even while he is uncovering its usefulness to tyrants. When Njoroge wins admittance to the secondary school, the whole neighborhood rejoices:

> Whatever their differences, interest in knowledge and book-learning was the one meeting point between people such as Boro [a Mau Mau leader], Jacobo [a counterrevolutionary and spy for the British] and Ngotho [Njoroge's father who believes a spiritist's prophecy about freedom but must, in the end, resort to direct action]. (WNC, 184)

If a young activist, a traitor, and a traditionalist can unite behind education, the people have truly found a common ground.

But the anguish accompanying colonialist education is emphasized in Ngũgĩ's essays, and this anguish "is not of course peculiar to Africa. It is true of the whole black world, the colonized world" (BP, 37). Furthermore, formal emancipation has not proved sufficient. Ngũgĩ writes:

> During the neocolonial stage of imperialism education and culture play an even more important role as instruments of domination and oppression. . . . Since the petit-bourgeoisie grew up accepting the world-view of the imperialist bourgeoisie, it will drive the youth even more vigorously into educational factories producing the same world-view. (BP, 97)

This program is accompanied by "the continuation of the colonial state, the colonial economic structure, with, of course, a few cosmetic reforms" (BP, 97).

The neocolonialism under discussion here has its counterpart in America. We can see the importance of Weep Not, Child to Western educators if we note the way American children encounter Africa in their classrooms. Many American educators give lip service to multiculturalism, but their pluralistic curriculum seems more cosmetic than real. Essays in the English Journal show how far the contemporary curriculum has developed in its distortions of African realities.

ANTI-AFRICAN ASSIGNMENTS FOR AMERICAN CHILDREN

In December 1990, the English Journal featured three articles about teaching the African experience. Two of the three authors represent the worst kind of imperialistic, anti-African propaganda. The third suggests ways to amend the ubiquitous use of Alan Paton's *Cry, the Beloved Country,* but he does not suggest that this novel be replaced. The essayist comments that Paton's novel is "the most frequently taught work of South African literature in American classrooms," and he is apparently not willing to take on "the system" by rejecting it. Other problems are also evident in his approach to South Africa, as we will see. But we begin with Nick Spencer's *English Journal* article: "The African Tale."

Spencer tells his eighth-grade Iowan students about his Peace Corps assignment in Cameroon. His essay describes how his "houseboy," Ipanda, broke ranks with traditionalists in his community by killing a poisonous snake rather than respecting it as a possible omen. The snake had taken up residence in Spencer's house while Spencer was out of town, and the neighbors would not help evict it.

> "They wanted to," [explains the teacher]. "But the villagers wouldn't remove the snake because they considered the task impossible; they thought it was a guardian, an immortal spirit, of my house, a product of *my* magic."[6]

These words elicit peals of laughter from the American teenagers, which is apparently what their teacher intended. He goes on to explain the perceived superiority of white over black and the way the "houseboy" joined the whites. Spencer explains that by becoming "white," Ipanda is "no longer a boy." And his students get the message. A girl explains to him after class: " 'It's not a snake story.' 'It's the story of an African boy who crosses a cultural line into a white man's world.' " Spencer tells the reader, as he has told his eighth graders year after year, that an African boy's "life was changed forever by the death of a snake."

> "Ipanda became a white man," I say.
> "A white man?"
> "Yes." I assure them. "In every way that mattered to the villagers, he became a white man."[7]

That is, Ipanda "left his village, attended secondary school in Yaounde, graduated from the University of Cameroon, took a degree in law, and became a lawyer for his nation's Supreme Court."[8] Spencer seems to be using every symbol at his command to tap into the American children's ideas of what is excellent and progressive. They know what "Supreme Court" means to them. They had perhaps not associated "law" with "whiteness" in such explicit terms, but their teacher has made the point unequivocally. The idea of "spirits" and "omens" is placed in contrast to "law," and there is no one to explain to the children the actual significance of metaphysical concepts and holistic African worldviews.

Nowhere do we see even the merest hint of what excellence means to the people of Cameroon. We are given no opportunity to experience African self-definition or glimpse what an African self-authenticating perspective might be. We see no effort on the teacher's part to explain a perspective that unifies animals, humans, and spirits in an interconnected cosmic pattern. Religious and cultural traditions are, instead, held up for derision and mockery. In short, a valid oppositional knowledge is totally lacking. One wonders whether Spencer, as a Peace Corps volunteer, knows anything about African traditions and values. What has his preparation for life in Africa included? Was the point of his cross-cultural journey only a newfound capacity to tell "funny" stories? Is he a much-prized teacher because he can appear before his American students as a stand-up comic?

Such an intellectual model hardly coincides with what *English Journal* subscribers are led to expect. And, in fact, they are misguided even by the essay that introduces the focus articles about Africa, an essay in which Jerry L. Martin of the National Endowment of the Humanities explains the importance of "sameness" and "difference." Martin's words are actually a contradiction of what follows, but because they are intended as an introduction, they seem to be validating the colonialist perspective of Spencer. In his opening comments Martin seems to be suggesting an unbiased viewpoint:

> Why does the emphasis on Difference matter? Not just because other ideas and times and places are interesting. Certainly not because they are intrinsically superior. It matters because the ability to conceive things as different than they are is a condition of human freedom. Those who lack that ability are prisoners of the present moment, of the present place.[9]

He continues by noting that "we must have the capacity to enter into other worlds—imaginatively—if we are to conceive and to create our own world." And he suggests a two-way entering process by stating that "the study of Difference is meaningful only if there is also Sameness. . . . The Same does not have to remain the Same: it can become Different."[10]

As Nick Spencer's "African Tale" fails to move students to other "ideas and times and places," so an essay by Robert Mossman misleads readers about the independence struggle in South Africa. Mossman recommends the use of works by blacks as a supplement to a curriculum centered on Alan Paton's *Cry, the Beloved Country,* but he misreads history when he lends credibility to Paton's so-called prophetic vision. Paton, he says, predicted black-on-black violence, and to Mossman the warring factions in Natal in the eighties and nineties are confirming evidence. He writes:

> The sagacity of Paton's famous prediction [voiced by a black] "that one day when they [the whites] turn to loving they will find we [the black Africans] are turned to hating" has been proven on the streets of Sharpeville, Soweto, Alexandra, Johannesburg, and Capetown. The very rolling hills of Natal on which Paton eulogized so rhapsodically are now the killing fields between ANC proponents and Inkatha advocates.[11]

To reduce the democratization struggle in South Africa to a case of Africans "hating" each other is a common colonialist ploy. There is ample documentation that apartheid forces were implicated in black-black factional fighting, and black South Africans have been well aware of this complicity. Also, additional evidence has become known to a wider audience through the work of the Mandela government's Truth and Reconciliation Commission.

Mossman critiques the Paton narrative as "at worst, simplistic and patronizing," but this response is hardly sufficient. He does not see the white political agenda of 1948 (the year of publication), as Paton also refused to recognize it. For Paton and Mossman it is easy to reduce a nationalist struggle to a human relations controversy between individual white people and black people and to overlook the larger political program. There were political reasons for portraying the preeminent black characters as "always trembling with humility" to use Es'kia Mphahlele's terms.[12] And Ngũgĩ does not mince words about Paton's self-serving creation of native African functionaries. He comments:

> [T]he African character held for admiration and presented as worthy of emulation is the non-violent, spineless type, the type who turns the other cheek, the right cheek once the left cheek has been hit by a racist colonialist whitey. Such for instance is Rev. Stephen Kumalo in Alan Paton's poisonous novel *Cry, the Beloved Country.* . . . [T]he most racist of white characters . . . would be quite happy to have a Bishop Stephen Kumalo for a prime minister! (*BP,* 95)

Mossman, who teaches at St. Gregory School in Tucson, Arizona, combines *Cry, the Beloved Country* with Peter Abrahams's *Mine Boy* as a way to teach his students how to compare white and black literary artists—to show "what biases they have, and how these are conditioned by their color."[13] It would seem that the horrific conditions of apartheid are reducible to biases embraced equally by the entire population—hardly a credible conclusion.

The good intentions of teachers such as Mossman have clearly not been enough to meet the multicultural requirement. And another case in point is Patricia Spencer, who states her good intentions in the *English Journal:*

> It is with open eyes that I wish my students to view their world, aware of inconsistencies, injustices, aware of penetrating evil, probable change, potential rebirth. . . . The "heart of darkness" deep within us all surfaces, searches to find familiarity, brotherhood.[14]

Here we are all charged with a dark heart, but throughout Patricia Spencer's article it is Africa that is linked with benighted and degrading features. Any other "darkness" is kept well offstage. She uses the eyes of the colonizer in describing her experiences in Africa in her personal journal. She passes this journal around for her ninth-grade students to read, and the students exchange their own journal entries. For example, Spencer gives an account of a boat ride in West Africa and presents her first glimpse of members of the San group (which she mislabels as Pygmies):

> The boat slows. A glistening black arm and tiny buttocks appear barely visible in dense vegetation yards from the river's edge. . . . A huge Bantu with a Samson-like torso operates this concession. Local residents and tourists alike take advantage of this opportunity to view the tribe of monkey men hiding naked in the inner jungle. Swinging from vines, chanting in high-pitched voices.[15]

Is this picture one that will achieve the goal of helping students view their world "with open eyes"? These eyes are hard to distinguish from the eyes of Edgar Rice Burroughs's "Tarzan" (1911).[16] Spencer sees Africa in extremist terms ("tiny buttocks" and "Samson-like torsos"). She sees "monkey men . . . swinging from vines." She criticizes the other tourists for photographing the inhabitants on the mainland, but she is herself debasing these people in explicit terms. There is no satiric tone or hint of irony but rather a throwback to turn-of-the-century pulp writing. She contradicts her insistence that she is providing students with a noble method—a way of "ventur[ing] into archetypes, the Greek word for 'original pattern.' "[17] Her journal seems less a repository of archetypes than a collection of psychological assaults.[18]

With reference to this type of violence, Ngũgĩ makes the following observation:

> [Subsequent to the scramble for Africa in 1884], the night of the sword and the bullet was followed by the morning of the chalk and the blackboard. The physical violence of the battlefield was followed by the psychological violence of the classroom. But where the former was visibly brutal, the latter was visibly gentle.[19]

Ngũgĩ continues with novelist Cheikh Hamidou Kane's metaphors about the cannon as well as the magnet (the school's seductive force). Kane sees new schools in the wake of imperialist incursions, schools that have the "efficiency of a fighting weapon." "But better," he says, "than the cannon, [the new school] made a conquest permanent. The cannon forces the body and the school fascinates the soul."[20]

Ngũgĩ's concern for schools and their pupils is coupled with his understanding of much larger forces—for example, the shifting international alignments and their impact on schools and other social institutions. His wide-ranging insights and analyses can potentially make the overlap of educational and political policy a positive rather than a negative phenomenon.

CONCLUSION: UNDERSTANDING THE CHALLENGE

Imperialist depictions of Africa are designed to serve the interests of dominating nations. Ngũgĩ offers a succinct explanation of cause and effect connections:

The sum total of this [colonialist] type of education . . . is to socialize the African youth into a culture embodying values and hence a consciousness and world outlook which on the one hand is in total harmony with the needs of imperialism and on the other, is in total antagonism to the struggle for liberation. (*BP,* 95)

The needs of imperialism correspond to the needs of the haves in contrast to the have-nots in the countries of the African diaspora as well as the African continent. When Ngũgĩ describes the Western producers of African underdevelopment, he could just as easily be making a reference to the conservative agenda makers in America. He notes:

For the Western imperialist bourgeoisie, civilization, stability, progress, mean the continuation of the colonial state . . . with, of course, a few cosmetic reforms (like allowing a few natives to own farms, businesses, and go to live and drink in places that were formerly for whites only) to deceive the populace. (*BP,* 97)

As noted earlier, when specific groups of people are locked into a recurring cycle of disadvantage, "education and culture play an *even more important* role as instruments of domination and oppression" (*BP,* 96–97; italics ours). To give such people any viable tools of education would alter their status as a subjugated class. Thus such tools are consciously or unconsciously withheld, and the kind of debilitating education described here in American schoolrooms is proclaimed valid. There is, however, a constructive vision of schooling, and Ngũgĩ describes it:

Ideally, education should give people the knowledge about the world in which they live: how the world shapes them and how they shape the world. Education should transmit a culture that inculcates in the people a consciousness that man through his labor power is the creator of his social environment and that in the same way that man acts on nature and changes it, he can also act on his social environment and change it. (*BP,* 90)

This is not a description of Njoroge's formal education in *Weep Not, Child,* nor is this ideal education discernible in the lessons about Africa in American classrooms. In an interview in May 1998, Ngũgĩ noted the importance of creating stories that "truly reflect a more positive self-image of the African child. . . . Narratives tend to be strong enough to carry the child along without the child recognizing what is actually happening. . . . Children may not question how the 'bad guys' are defined—how the successful colonizer is allied with the 'good' and those opposing colonization are associated with the 'bad.' " He suggests that "we need to re-locate what is 'good' and 'bad'—be clear about whose side we are on class-wise, oppression-wise. . . . The child's capacity for wonder is clear, and we need to also make the world more understandable to children." He reminds us that there are always new, power-exerting conditions; "we need to be aware of the whole network of connections between colonizing capital and the industries that produce books for children."[21] Ngũgĩ is echoing here a warning presented at the 10th conference of the African Literature Association. His warning stresses the risk of an "inadequate grasp of . . . the international and national realignment of class forces and class alliances."[22] As is usually the case, he is keeping within the same line of vision the massive forces operating in institutions and the specific needs of individual scholars and learners.

Ngũgĩ's contribution to education has continued throughout his career. His vision as educator, playwright, and novelist is remarkably consistent. Although there is beauty in life despite the problems, and although children need to be clear about this reality, their education and culture "must not only explain the world but must prepare the recipients to change the world." With this agenda for change, the child will become "a producer, a thinker, and a fighter all integrated in the same individual" (*BP,* 99).

The school is potentially an integrating force or a destabilizing force because it shapes a mental universe. Ngũgĩ explains:

> [Colonialism's] most important area of domination was the mental universe of the colonized, the control, through culture, of how people perceived themselves and their relationship to the world. Economic and political control can never be complete or effective without mental control. To control a people's culture is to control their tools of self-definition in relationship to others.[23]

Weep Not, Child is a brilliant object lesson about selfhood and superimposed power. The American classroom has sometimes been an object lesson in reverse—a means of debasing the self and abusing the image-making powers of literature. But a mitigating, progressive, uncompromised voice is present. As a "new assertive Africa" finds expression in the creative works of Ngũgĩ, so it finds expression in his educational philosophy—in his consistent, liberating efforts on behalf of the young.

Notes

1. Ngũgĩ has included the following explanatory note in his 1986 work *Writing against Neocolonialism:* "The terms 'he' and 'his' . . . are not used to denote the 'maleness' of a person. It should be read to indicate an individual person, whether male or female" (p. 20).

2. Elsewhere in this collection we have analyzed this theme as it appears in Ngũgĩ's first children's book: *Njamba and the Flying Bus* (Nairobi: Heinemann Kenya, 1982, 1986). We have called that essay "Freedom's Children: Antiracist Juvenile Literature by Ngũgĩ wa Thiong'o and Other African Writers."

3. Ngũgĩ wa Thiong'o, *Barrel of a Pen: Resistance to Repression in Neo-Colonial Kenya* (Trenton, N.J.: Africa World Press, 1983), 87; hereafter cited in this essay as *BP.*

4.   James Ngugi, interview, *Union News,* Leeds University, November 18, 1966.
5.   James Ngugi, *Weep Not, Child* (1964; Oxford, England, and Portsmouth, N.H.: Heinemann, 1987), 3; hereafter cited in this essay as *WNC.*
6.   Nick Spencer, "The African Tale," *English Journal* 79, no. 8 (1990): 37.
7.   Spencer, "African Tale," 37.
8.   Spencer, "African Tale," 37.
9.   Jerry L. Martin, "Sameness and Difference," *English Journal* 79, no. 8 (1990): 19.
10.   Martin, "Sameness and Difference," 19.
11.   Robert Mossman, "South African Literature: A Global Lesson in One Country," *English Journal* 79, no. 8 (1990): 42.
12.   Ezekiel Mphahlele, *The African Image* (New York: Praeger, 1962), 157.
13.   Mossman, "South African Literature," 42.
14.   Patricia Spencer, "African Passages: Journaling through Archetypes," *English Journal* 79, no. 8 (1990): 40.
15.   Spencer, "African Passages," 39.
16.   Edgar Rice Burroughs, "Tarzan of the Apes," *All-Story Magazine,* 1912 (Chicago: A. C. McClurg, 1914; New York: Ballantine, 1983).
17.   Spencer, "African Passages," 38.
18.   It should be noted also that Patricia Spencer assigns her students one of the worst conceivable novels about Africa: Clayton Bess's *Story for a Black Night* (Boston: Houghton Mifflin, 1982). Bess was a Peace Corps volunteer in Liberia, and his story portrays unspeakable degrees of black-on-black fratricide. The weapon used for afflicting one another is the smallpox disease, as community members protect their households by secretly spreading the disease to relatives and neighbors. The work is a classic example of the imperialism that assigns both incompetence and incredible barbarity to the African population.
19.   Ngũgĩ wa Thiong'o, *Decolonising the Mind: The Politics of Language in African Literature* (London: James Currey; Nairobi: East African Educational Publishers; Portsmouth, N.H.: Heinemann, 1986), 9.
20.   Quoted in Ngũgĩ, *Decolonising the Mind,* 9.
21.   Ngũgĩ wa Thiong'o, interview with Donnarae MacCann, University of Iowa, May 1, 1998.
22.   Ngũgĩ wa Thiong'o, *Writing against Neocolonialism* (Middlesex, England: Vita, 1986), 11.
23.   Ngũgĩ, *Decolonising the Mind,* 16.

Bibliography

Abrahams, Peter. *Mine Boy.* London: Faber and Faber, 1946; New York: Knopf, 1955.
Burroughs, Edgar Rice. "Tarzan of the Apes." All-Story Magazine, 1912; Chicago: A. C. McClurg, 1914; New York: Ballantine, 1983.
Martin, Jerry L. "Sameness and Difference." *English Journal* 79, no. 8 (December 1990): 18–19.
Mossman, Robert. "South African Literature: A Global Lesson in One Country." *English Journal* 79, no. 8 (December 1990): 41–43.
Mphahlele, Ezekiel. *The African Image.* New York: Praeger, 1962.
Ngũgĩ wa Thiong'o. *Weep Not, Child.* 1964; Oxford, England, and Portsmouth, N.H.: Heinemann Educational Books, 1987.
———. Interview. *Union News.* Leeds University, November 18, 1966.
———. *Writers in Politics: Essays.* London and Exeter, N.H.: Heinemann Educational Books, 1981.

————. *Barrel of a Pen: Resistance to Repression in Neo-Colonial Kenya*. Trenton, N.J.: Africa World Press, 1983.

————. *Decolonising the Mind: The Politics of Language in African Literature*. London: James Currey; Nairobi: East African Educational Publishers; Portsmouth, N.H.: Heinemann, 1986.

————. *Writing against Neocolonialism*. Middlesex, England: Vita, 1986.

————. Interview by Donnarae MacCann, University of Iowa, May 1, 1998.

Paton, Alan. *Cry, the Beloved Country*. New York: Scribner's, 1948.

Spencer, Nick. "The African Tale." *English Journal* 79, no. 8 (December 1990): 36–37.

Spencer, Patricia. "African Passages: Journaling through Archetypes." *English Journal* 79, no. 8 (December 1990): 38–40.

Voices of Many Together in Two:
Whitman's America and Ngũgĩ's Kenya

SIGURBJORG SIGURJONSDOTTIR

Can Walt Whitman, born in America in 1819, and Ngũgĩ wa Thiong'o, born in Kenya in 1938, have a "dialogue" on these pages? I believe there is a valid reason to talk about their voices together in one sentence: two voices, including the many, holding a meaningful dialogue. It will be my task here to focus on two of Ngũgĩ wa Thiong'o's six novels, *Weep Not, Child* and *Petals of Blood,* in the light of two poems by Walt Whitman, from which the novels take their epigraphs. I will argue for Whitman's relevance to the struggle against the oppressive political situation that Ngũgĩ effectively portrays. *Weep Not, Child* takes its title and epigraph from Whitman's poem "On the Beach at Night," and *Petals of Blood* uses epigraphs from Whitman's poem "Europe." The poems provide a frame of reference for the novels, and there are important similarities between the two writers and relationships between their political concerns.

Ngũgĩ's novels all deal with a precarious period in the political history of Kenya. The first three novels—*The River Between, Weep Not, Child,* and *A Grain of Wheat*—are set in colonial Kenya, the third one taking place when the country is on the verge of independence. They depict the oppressive life under colonial rule and people's feeling of alienation from the soil, their country, which is perhaps most memorably portrayed in how the protagonist's father in *Weep Not, Child* experiences the land crisis. The three novels portray the oppression and the tensions in society at large and how the situation affects the individuals. They also depict the increasing resentment toward colonialism and people's hopeful vision of new and better times to come. Ngũgĩ's last three novels—*Petals of Blood, Devil on the Cross,* and *Matigari*—all deal with neocolonialism in postindependence Kenya.

Whereas *Weep Not, Child* is a youthful novel, characterized by the struggle against colonialism but also enveloped in hopeful uncertainties of a "new" future, a vision of independence hanging in the air, *Petals of Blood* explicitly describes and deals with the grim political reality of postindependence Kenya.

This essay is published here for the first time by permission of the author, with whom the copyright remains.

93

Thus, the image of and emphasis on Whitman in the two novels differ in regard to the different themes and situations Ngũgĩ depicts in the novels. I will discuss the former novel in more detail because it provides the background information for the political oppression in Kenya, describes how individuals deal with it, and brings into light the basic relevance of Whitman to the Kenyan political situation.

It may, however, seem a far-fetched task to read Whitman as an important "ally" to an African nation struggling for independence because Whitman himself was an enthusiastic believer in the "democratic expansion" of America. Further, in his writings, Whitman sometimes seems to give a valid reason for being read as a "hierarchical" poet.[1] He states that America is the "race of races" (*Whitman*, 7) and "land of lands" (471), that "the greatest poet" (Whitman himself?) is endowed with "the ultimate brain" (9), and, while ranking poems into classes, states that poetry is "the stock of all" (958). Some of his poems, such as "Salut au Monde," also have racist overtones. However, this side of Whitman is at the same time undermined and, I would argue, overpowered by his call to action against oppression and corruption, which is important to the oppressive political situation in Kenya that Ngũgĩ depicts.

My call is the call of battle, I nourish active rebellion,
He going with me must go well arm'd,
He going with me goes often with spare diet, poverty, angry enemies, desertions.
(*Whitman*, 307)

I will here rely most heavily on primary sources: Whitman's *Leaves of Grass* and Ngũgĩ's novels and critical writings. I will also use historical information as I seek to place my argument within a historical context. To the best of my knowledge, no previous studies have been done on this topic. Regarding explicit information about the "contact" and dialogue that Ngũgĩ and Whitman have formed between them, their "relationship" is, of course, best explored in Whitman's poems and Ngũgĩ's novels, which are themselves the most powerful sources. However, Peter Nazareth, professor at the University of Iowa, has also informed me that while he and Ngũgĩ were studying at Makerere University College (1959–1962) in Kampala, Uganda, Ngũgĩ was reading Whitman outside the university curricula. (I have Peter Nazareth's kind permission to record this information here.) Further, in his book *Moving the Centre*, Ngũgĩ points out how Western literature, in spite of humanistic representations of the democratic social struggles of the European peoples, has tended to opt for silence, ambivalence, or collaboration because of the history of European colonialism and the American slave trade. He continues:

Of course there are writers who show great sensitivity to the social evils perpetrated against other peoples: William Blake, Walt Whitman, Brecht, Sartre for instance. But taken as a whole this literature could not avoid being affected by the Eurocentric basis of its world view or global vision, and most of it, even when sympathetic, could not altogether escape from the racism inherent in Western enterprise in the rest of the world.[2]

Thus, instead of reading Whitman as a racist or hierarchical poet, Ngũgĩ realistically takes into consideration the times in which Whitman was living, the openly encouraged racist atmosphere of the period, and the commercial interests at stake. The sometimes racist overtones in Whitman's writings give way to Whitman's democratic and sympathetic political concerns and optimistic attitude toward life.

The relationship and similarities between Ngũgĩ and Whitman reside in their social and political concerns and engagements, as well as in their emphasis on people's unity and maturity. The tone of their voices is one of challenge, resistance, struggle, endurance, optimism. And what lies at the core of their political beliefs is their conviction that a nation's independence has to be built on the nation's own culture and language. Both of them speak out against political corruption and the exploitation of the many by the few. They are concerned with the lives and conditions of workers and peasants—the masses, as Whitman phrases it. Their fight against oppression and subjugation is essentially important, and they both constantly seek to wake up people to their consciousness and capacities. Most important, however, are Ngũgĩ's and Whitman's belief and conviction that the bad must eventually give way to the good, that the positive will prevail. That they are addressing Americans or Kenyans does not matter because, as Ngũgĩ points out,

> [t]he resistance culture and values of the African peasantry and working class have no basic contradiction with the democratic and humanistic cultures and values of the European and American peoples. These can hold a meaningful, fruitful dialogue. This is the dialogue and contact we must continue to aid, encourage and support by every means at our disposal. (*MC*, 45–46)

WHITMAN'S AND NGŨGĨ'S EMPHASIS ON CULTURAL INDEPENDENCE

Ngũgĩ deals with the situation in Kenya as the country was colonized by the British monarchy and portrays people's hopeful anticipation of new and different times after Kenya gained its independence or, in Ngũgĩ's words, regained it, in 1963. Whitman expresses great hopes for America and a belief in people's capacities to make of America an independent, democratic society. At the same time he writes about the political corruption he sees in American society and "democratic" governments that are beginning to resemble monarchical rulers. In his "Collect" he writes: "the sixteenth, seventeenth, and eighteenth terms of the American Presidency have shown that the villainy and shallowness of rulers (back'd by the machinery of great parties) are just as eligible to these States as to any foreign despotism, kingdom, or empire— there is not a bit of difference" (*Whitman*, 1020). Similarly, Ngũgĩ deals with a "democratic" society in newly independent Kenya, a disillusioned independence in which both internal political corruption and foreign exploitation exist. Both Whitman and Ngũgĩ believe that the determination to be self-reliant is crucial for each nation to be independent and the only healthy basis for political and social liberty and rights to exist and flourish. They both emphasize each nation's cultural independence. Whitman criticizes the tendency to bow down to European literature and culture. In his mind the American poets are vitally important because of the role they play in creating, increasing, and strengthening the American people's awareness of their own literary and cultural identity and, ultimately, the independence of the American nation as a whole. Whitman complains in his "Democratic Vistas": "How long it takes to make this American world see that it is, in itself, the final authority and reliance!" (*Whitman*, 980). Although America in Whitman's time was no longer a country ruled by another, he is here pointing to the danger of submitting to mental colonialism. That is why he emphasizes so strongly in his 1855 "Preface" the important role of "the American bards" and "the greatest poet" in the creation of an independent America. There he states: "The Americans of all nations at any time upon the earth have probably the fullest poetical nature. The United States themselves are essentially the greatest poem. . . . The greatest poet does not moralize or make applications of morals. . . . he knows the soul" (*Whitman*, 5, 13). Here, he is neither advocating a supremacist attitude of the American poets nor placing himself on a pedestal. Rather, he is encouraging people to believe in their own literary qualities and capacities—creating America's own identity instead of borrowing it from others. Whitman points out in reference to this national identity: "At all times, perhaps, the central point in any nation, and that whence it is itself really sway'd the most, and whence it sways others, is its national literature. . . . a great original literature is surely to become the justification and reliance . . . of American democracy" (*Whitman*, 956). He emphasizes the importance of the nation creating its own culture and its own values instead of uncritically bowing down to foreign influences. The "Great Poet" can be a workingman or a president, as long as the value of American culture is acknowledged, respected, and perpetuated.

Ngũgĩ criticizes and denounces the domination of European culture in Kenya and sets out to fight for the promotion of Kenyan national culture in all fields of life. In the preface to *Moving the Centre,* he discusses how the cultural aspects cannot be seen in total isolation from the economic and political ones and how dominance over people's culture, particularly language, deepens the economic and political control over them. Both Ngũgĩ and Whitman are thus concerned with independent culture, and essentially language, as the basis for full independence. For both, the struggle can only begin in the resistance against mental control. Ngũgĩ explains how the European languages were entrenched as superior to the African languages and how that was the most effective weapon in oppressing people and alienating them from each other, their own community, and their own sense of identity. He points out that

> [t]here was often not the slightest relationship between the child's written world, which was also the language of his schooling, and the world of his immediate environment in the family and the community. . . . The alienation became reinforced in the teaching of history, geography, music, where bourgeois Europe was always the centre of the universe.[3]

So although studying other languages is good and important, it has to be on a realistic basis; no language can become a substitute for one's own native tongue without disastrous effects. In his preface, Whitman has this to say about American English:

> It is the powerful language of resistance. . . . it is the dialect of common sense. It is the speech of the proud and melancholy races and of all who aspire. It is the chosen tongue to express growth faith self-esteem freedom justice equality friendliness amplitude prudence decision and courage. It is the medium that shall well nigh express the inexpressible. (*Whitman,* 25)

For Whitman, it is the American language and the American culture on which an independent and democratic American society is to be based. For Ngũgĩ, it is the Gikuyu language and culture that is the foundation for Kenya's full independence.

Ngũgĩ scorns the hypocrisy of what he calls the petty-bourgeois intellectuals who are ashamed of their national culture because it is not "refined" enough, not "coming from abroad," not acknowledged and honored by their neocolonial commanders. However, they pretend to be great patriots and "bury their own inaction behind mugs of beer and empty intellectualism about conditions being not yet ripe for action."[4] And Whitman emphasizes the political power and responsibility of both the writer and the reader:

> Books are to be call'd for, and supplied, on the assumption that the process of reading is not a half sleep, but, in highest sense, an exercise, a gymnast's struggle; that the reader is to do something for himself, must be on the alert, must himself or herself construct indeed the poem, argument, history, metaphysical essay—the text furnishing the hints, the clue, the start or frame-work. Not the book needs so much to be the complete thing, but the reader of the book does. (*Whitman,* 1016–17)

Hence both Ngũgĩ and Whitman challenge readers to become mature and critical and evaluate things for themselves. People need to grow up and be able to recognize "patriotism" when used as a tool to conceal something else, to see through those who are "shouting peace while carrying out war against

the people" (*MC,* 116). For Ngũgĩ, the time has come for Kenya to stop seeking solutions from outside because the result is bound to be futile and, ultimately, fatal.

Ngũgĩ's Kenya, as Whitman's America, can only create its own identity,
and thus its ultimate independence, within and from itself. All emancipation
begins from within if the purpose is to throw off shackles, not merely to put
on the stage a self-deceiving show. In an interview done in Limuru in 1979,
Ngũgĩ points out, in reference to postindependence Kenya, that

> [t]he African people must primarily rely on their own resources. . . . the
> strength of a people must come from themselves, or from the homestead. Only
> after this can others find the basis for aiding them. You cannot go to war with
> your eyes on the strength of your friend. That way lies slavery and domina-
> tion.[5]

WEEP NOT, CHILD

Weep Not, Child was published in 1964 but is the second novel Ngũgĩ wrote.
It is important to discuss this novel in some detail to explain the relationship
of Whitman's poem to the novel and to the Kenyan political situation. It is
also necessary to throw some light on the vital role that the mothers play in
Weep Not, Child to show how the hope expressed in the poem is carried out in
the novel. I contend that to understand the tensions and the psychological
pressures people were under during the state of emergency in Kenya, which
Ngũgĩ portrays in this novel, one has to pay attention to the significance of
women in the story and what they stand for. However, to do so within the
context of the story I must first discuss the main male characters in the family
and point out in what way they are failing in the fight against colonialism.
That approach is necessary because although the mothers hold up the story,
their role is modestly portrayed. Ngũgĩ has here placed at the center of the
novel a family that disintegrates, but the novel nevertheless concludes with
an image of hope and unity.

Set in rural Kenya in the turbulent fifties, the novel depicts Kenyan life
under colonial rule, increasing political consciousness and nationalism, and
the rise of Mau Mau, the Kenyan national liberation movement. At this time
tensions were also rising among the African people themselves: between the
proletariat and the African bourgeoisie, between generations, and within
families. The story is seen and told principally from the point of view of
Njoroge, the young protagonist of the novel. Ngũgĩ, in revealing to us this
social crisis and its effects on the individual and the collective lives of the people, shows how this tumultuous period affects Njoroge and his family and
how they all become involved in the crisis.

In this period in Kenyan history, the African soldiers who served in the Second World War are returning home, as is Njoroge's brother, Boro. The war period itself marked a turning point in Kenya's colonial resistance. The African men had fought in a war from whose cause they were alienated, and they were at the same time treated as subhuman by the colonizers. Back home, they see that the situation is not any more "human" than it was before the war. They are supposed to silently submit to the continued oppressive colonial system and accept social and political exploitation, the white supremacy myth, and the division and robbery of their lands. This situation is reflected in Boro's experience: when the war ended he came home, "no longer a boy but a man with experience and ideas, only to find that for him there was no employment. There was no land on which he could settle, even if he had been able to do so."[6] Colonialism here begins to face a more direct threat to its existence. The novel takes off from an epigraph from Whitman's poem "On the Beach at Night." I cite the poem in full, and later cite Whitman's poem referred to in *Petals of Blood,* because I believe it is necessary for the reader to have a fuller perspective and insight into the relationship between Whitman's poems and Ngūgī's novels in relation to the topic of this essay. Just as the whole holographic image is contained in a part of the plate, so here is the whole contained in the part. Citing the whole poems enables the reader to more fully understand and appreciate the epigraphs Ngūgī employed in the novels.

On the beach at night,
Stands a child with her father,
Watching the east, the autumn sky.

Up through the darkness,
While ravening clouds, the burial clouds, in black masses spreading,
Lower sullen and fast, athwart and down the sky,
Amid a transparent clear belt of ether yet left in the east,
Ascends large and calm the lord-star Jupiter,
And nigh at hand, only a very little above,
Swim the delicate sisters the Pleiades.

From the beach the child holding the hand of her father,
Those burial-clouds that lower victorious soon to devour all,
Watching, silently weeps.

Weep not, child
Weep not, my darling
With these kisses let me remove your tears,
The ravening clouds shall not be long victorious,
They shall not long possess the sky, they devour the stars only in apparition,
Jupiter shall emerge, be patient, watch again another night, the Pleiades shall
   emerge

They are immortal, all those stars both silvery and golden shall shine out again,
The great stars and the little ones shall shine out again, they endure,
The vast immortal suns and the long-enduring pensive moons shall again shine.

Then dearest child mournest thou only for Jupiter?
Considerest thou alone the burial of the stars?

Something there is,
(With my lips soothing thee, adding I whisper,
I give thee the first suggestion, the problem and indirection,)
Something there is more immortal even than the stars,
(Many the burials, many the days and night, passing away,)
Something that shall endure longer even than lustrous Jupiter,
Longer than sun or any revolving satellite
Or the radiant sisters the Pleiades.
(Whitman, 398; italics mine, to indicate the epigraph)

The Whitman I see Ngũgĩ responding to here is Whitman the natural-ist, the optimist, the communicator. What is at play here is their emphasis on the idea that dreams and visions can become a reality but only through human relationship. Whitman's poem presents the simple image of a child and father standing on the beach. As he does frequently, Whitman here stresses the importance of personal, physical contact between human beings ("the child holding the hand of her father") as well as the importance of the physical and spiritual relationship between human beings and nature. The child and the father are "reading the sky" as it relates to their own lives—physically in touch with the beach, spiritually in touch with the sky. Their reading is uninhibited by any external influences or oppression, precisely the kind of reading that Whitman encourages in his *Leaves of Grass*. Nothing comes between them and nature, much like nothing can come between you and Whitman as he "spring[s] from the pages into your arms" (*Whitman*, 611). The picturesque simplicity of the poem correlates with the apparent simple writing style Ngũgĩ employs in his novels. And much like the child in the poem, we have in the novel a youthful protagonist who finds himself in a similar situation. Both are watching "ravening clouds, the burial clouds . . . soon to devour all," and both are inclined to cling to what they perceive as the maturity, the protection, of others. But what emerges most powerfully in the novel and in the poem is the belief that evil will eventually have to give way to good, that the clouds "devour the stars only in apparition."

Mother and Son

The novel opens up with the mother, Nyokabi, telling her son Njoroge that he will have the chance to go to school, in spite of their poverty. His reaction is overwhelming: "[f]or a time he contemplated the vision. He lived in it alone. It was just there, for himself, a bright future" (*WNC,* 3). Thus, the novel opens up with the hope presented in the poem. But at the same time, with regard to the poem, the "failure" of Njoroge's vision is suggested: his tendency to remain secluded in an idealistic vision of his own. This is a one-man vision; he is living it alone, even though his dream is to remove the ravening clouds for the benefit of all his people. As Njoroge listens to his father talk about the hardship the African people are facing in the colonized country, and how important it is for his son to get an education, Njoroge begins to be locked up in a world of his own:

> He instinctively knew that an indefinable demand was being made on him, even though he was so young. He knew that for him education would be the fulfilment of a wider and more significant vision—a vision that embraced the demand made on him, not only by his father, but also by his mother, his broth-ers and even the village. He saw himself destined for something big, and this made his heart glow (*WNC,* 39).

But for him to succeed with such a great task, to successfully battle colonial-ism, he needs to communicate his vision to his people and begin with "hold-ing hands" instead of remaining secluded, with an idealistic vision of himself as the hero and the savior. Approaching things with Njoroge's solitary atti-tude while hoping for an achievement on a larger scale will not prove efficient in the actual social situation in which he finds himself. However, his vision and dream of a bright future are at the same time sympathetically explained and justified with regard to the present situation. His family is poor, and Njoroge is aware of the sacrifice his family has made to provide him with an education. He understands when his mother explains that he will not be able to get a midday meal like the other children, and, in spite of his young age, he is grateful for the opportunity to go to school. Thus, we are at the same time introduced to the strength of Njoroge—his potential as a constructive member of the community people have yet to build—and his capable leader-ship in the independence struggle—the people's struggle for a bright future. We also see a reason for the women's interest in and affection for him. Njoroge's dream is sincere and well meant, idealistic but not selfish. He is eager to learn and completely devoted to what he sees as his "mission" to "save" his people through his education. And, in spite of his youth, he is mature enough to be both compassionate and understanding. At the begin-ning, we see hope embodied in both the limited and the capable Njoroge—the harbinger of the hope being his mother.

The Land Issue

In the first pages the narrator explains the crucial land issue, which is the major concern of the people and which, further, becomes a major reason for the conflict within Njoroge's home. People's alienation from the land and the clear-cut division of it is significant for the story:

> The plain, more or less rectangular in shape, had four valleys leading into or out of it at the corners. The first two valleys went into the Country of the Black People. The other two divided the land of the Black People from the land of the White People. This meant that there were four ridges that stood and watched one another. Two of the ridges on the opposite sides of the long sides of the plain were broad and near one another. The other two were narrow and had pointed ends. You could tell the land of Black People because it was red, rough and sickly, while the land of the white settlers was green and was not lacerated into small strips (WNC, 7).

The consequence of this situation was that many African farmers were earning a meager living as an exploited workforce on their former lands, as is Njoroge's father, Ngotho. He is a sharecropper on the land owned by the rich collaborator Jacobo and working on the land now "owned" by the settler Howlands. Further, the war period left Kenya with many more Europeans, besides bestowing them with more political, economic, and executive power[7]—hence, the importance of a vision to struggle for, a vision not of the one but of the many. Therefore, Njoroge's foundation for his dream, that of "saving" his people by entering school and thus "solving the problem," crumbles because he does not want to face the reality of extending the benefits to society by returning. What I mean by "the benefits" is that because he goes to a missionary school, Njoroge has to be careful and seek to resist being "parented" by the colonial mentality; he has to develop an awareness of what deserves to be rejected and fought against and what can be used for the people's struggle against colonialism. His dream must correspond to the image Ngũgĩ gives us in Whitman's poem—the ultimate importance of human relationships and a realistic combination of the ideal and the practical.

Ngotho, Boro, and Njoroge, who, each in their own way, become most intensely involved in and affected by the independence struggle, all lack balance and are extreme in their vision and action. Their extreme and one-sided belief and point of view regarding the whole struggle results in their separation from others, in their removal from reality, and ultimately in failure, pessimism, and hopelessness—if it were not for the women in the story. To Ngotho, the land is everything, and more so than in the practical meaning. Ngũgĩ describes the relationship between him and the land in spiritual terms, like a caring attachment extending the boundaries of life and death: "Ngotho felt responsible for whatever happened to this land. He owed it to the dead, the living and the unborn of his line, to keep guard over this shamba" (WNC, 31). Even the settler Howlands notices this affectionate bond: "He just loved to see Ngotho working in the farm; the way the old man touched the soil, almost fondling, and the way he tended the young tea plants as if they were his own. . . . Ngotho was too much of a part of the farm to be separated from it" (*WNC*, 30). It is clear that Whitman is Ngotho's ally in this respect as he, in "Song of Myself," points out the important ties between people and the earth: "every atom belonging to me as good belongs to you. . . . My tongue, every atom of my blood, form'd from this soil, this air / Born here of parents born here from parents the same (*Whitman*, 188). It is important for the protagonist to keep this attitude in mind because change cannot be effected by clinging to a personal vision that does not allow the space for activation and for others to participate in an all too spiritual vision at the cost of the practical. Although Njoroge's family supports his education, the land is the main thing for them all, not the school he is attending. Therefore he cannot win the battle if he becomes alienated from the very thing for which he is battling. That is particularly true if his dream is one of reconciling the personal with the public, to deal with a difficult situation at home as well as in society at large.

It is relevant and important to address the question of Whitman as a hierarchical poet at this point. Whitman seeks to wake up the reader from passive acceptance into awareness and activism: "I am less the reminder of property or qualities, and more the reminder of life" (*Whitman*, 49). Whitman's statement here does not imply that he himself is endowed with some special qualities above and over others, nor is he inviting hierarchical distinctions and interpretations. On the contrary, he essentially encourages the freedom of everyone to transmit ideas and information. By this remark, he also implies that people cannot be judged by their class in society, or any other distinctions, and that such a prejudiced and hierarchical mentality only hits back the judge by a reduced sense and force of life. Whitman is here set out to wake up the readers to solidarity and the democratic responsibility of communicating important messages among "the masses" and then, as he says, "depart as air." Depart as air, because in Whitman's mind such message, such awakening, has nothing to do with hierarchy or superiority but on the contrary communication and unity, which are like air: invisible but ultimately vital. Whitman's voice and the touch and the drift of his words are, as he says himself, what counts—the words themselves are nothing. His drift is the relevant thing and it is that which has been translated into other tongues, other societies. His concern with his own country and his occasional nationalism only encourage other people to actively engage in all social, political, and other important matters at stake in their own countries. This concern is related and similar to Ngũgĩ's task as a writer. Ngũgĩ's is the voice of challenge and activation, addressed to the Kenyan people but applying to the whole world.

Unfortunately, this voice of challenge, the call to battle, does not seem to successfully reach Ngotho's ears. He believes what the Gikuyu seer of old, Mugo wa Kibiro, has prophesied, that eventually the white man would be driven away and the land returned to its rightful owners. He thus clings to this belief, somehow hoping that the land crisis will solve itself, even though his father waited all his life for the same thing to happen. And when Njoroge, surprised to hear that the land originally belonged to them, asks him: "Where did the land go?" his father's response is, "I've waited for the prophecy. It may not be fulfilled in my life time . . . but, O, Murungu [God], I wish it could" (*WNC*, 25–26). Thus, Ngotho patiently and passively waits for the gods to deliver the land from the colonizers, a waiting that culminates in his inability to unite his forces with the active freedom fighters and devotees in the struggle. And although Ngũgĩ portrays Ngotho's love for the land and his tribal vision with sympathetic understanding, he also criticizes Ngotho. Ngotho needs to go beyond his belief in the prophecy and listen to Whitman in this respect: "I only am he who places over you no master, owner, better, God, beyond what waits intrinsically in yourself" (*Whitman*, 376). Further, Ngotho's problem of noncommunication is also shared by Boro and Njoroge. The three cannot effectively combine their forces in the fight; each is solitary in the struggle. Boro resents his father's belief in the prophecy and regards his father's passiveness as cowardice. They are not able to reconcile with each other, and the tension between them increases. Boro finally leaves home and seeks his fortune in Nairobi, where he becomes involved in politics and joins the Mau Mau guerrilla movement, which began forming around 1950. Boro is an embittered character and disillusioned after his wartime experiences and particularly after having painfully lost his brother in the war:

> Boro thought of his father who had fought in the war only to be dispossessed. He too had gone to war, against Hitler. He had gone to Egypt, Jerusalem and Burma. He had seen things. He had often escaped death narrowly. But the thing he could not forget was the death of his step-brother, Mwangi. For whom or what had *he* died? (*WNC*, 26)

For Boro, the stolen lands will never be regained by passive waiting. In his mind the independence struggle will go nowhere unless fought for with violence. He is extreme in his violent and cynical attitude. He believes in nothing but revenge and states that "[f]reedom is meaningless unless it can bring back a brother I lost. Because it can't do that, the only thing left to me is to fight, to kill and rejoice at any who falls under my sword" (*WNC*, 103). So although he is an active fighter, he is not really a freedom fighter. Thus, with his cynicism and inability to have caring and affectionate relationships, he becomes alienated from the very cause for which he is fighting. For him, "the darkness . . . the ravening clouds" are persistent; he no longer sees the sunshine, the dawn of a new day.

Boro and his political comrades want to fight colonialism through action. They decide to arrange a great strike among the whole African workforce to demand salaries equal to those of the other workers. Ngũgĩ portrays their determination and their effort to fight as an organized group positively.

However, Boro ignores the importance of showing respect and preserving an intimate unity with his own family. Although one can sympathize with him and understand his feelings, he needs to reconcile his hard-line stand with the tribal vision of the older generation. Instead of trying to understand his elders and showing sympathy for his father's point of view, he denounces them thus:

> How could these people have let the white man occupy the land without acting? And what was all this superstitious belief in a prophecy? In a whisper that sounded like a shout, he said, "To hell with the prophecy." Yes, this was nothing more than a whisper. To his father, he said, "How can you continue working for a man who has taken your land? How can you go on serving him?" He walked out, without waiting for an answer. (*WNC, 27*)

Heroism: All I'm Praying For

As Njoroge absorbs this critical situation he begins to visualize himself as a divinely chosen messiah of his people. He begins to develop an extremely unrealistic belief in his missionary education and a heroic "destiny" designed for him, which then results in his drifting further and further from the events of the real world. Throughout the novel, Njoroge avoids coming face to face with himself, asking himself what stand he wants to take in the struggle, and becoming responsible for his own vision and point of view. Instead, he clings to his heroic daydreams and desperately holds on to his education, vainly assuring himself that his missionary schooling and parrotic Christian belief will enable him to successfully battle colonialism, or, rather, will battle it for him: "[he] believed in the righteousness of God. Therefore he thought all this would work out well in the end. And he felt a bit awed to imagine that God may have chosen him to be the instrument of His Divine Service" (*WNC, 94*). And this is the belief he still holds on to, even though the crisis has peaked.

The strike arranged by the freedom fighters fails, and Boro blames his father for causing it to fail. Ngotho, overcome with emotion, had courageously risen to attack Jacobo who appeared there with the white police: "For one single moment Jacobo crystallized into a concrete betrayal of the people. He became the personification of the long years of waiting and suffering— Jacobo was a Traitor" (*WNC, 58*). Ngotho's uncontrolled action had then given the police the opportunity to violently scatter the meeting, with the result that the strike has failed. Consequently, Ngotho and his family are now thrown off Jacobo's land and Ngotho loses his job as a worker on the settled area of Howlands.

After the failed strike a state of emergency is declared and the freedom fighters and their families are arrested and detained. Jacobo has now been made a chief, Howlands is the new district officer, and a curfew has been ordered. Thus, the attempted strike marks the people's downfall and becomes the boiling point of cruelty, violence, and despair. Ngotho is now a broken man, and his home "was a place where stories were no longer told, a place where no young men and women from the village gathered" (*WNC,* 81). Through all this, amazingly enough, Njoroge "was still sustained by his love for and belief in education and his own role when the time came. And the difficulties at home seemed to have sharpened this appetite. Only education could make something out of this wreckage" (*WNC,* 82).

The image of unity Whitman presents in his poem, people standing by each other and holding hands, plays on an important theme in the novel. At the same time, by placing a child and an adult together, Whitman shows that a child becomes an adult—that we need to grow up. Eventually every one of us must be able to face and to take that responsibility. Whitman emphasizes this issue: "Not I, not any one else can travel that road for you / You must travel it for yourself" (*Whitman,* 241). Thus, being united with others is not the same as running away from responsibility, refusing to grow up. This idea is central to Njoroge's experience. He is a child when we are first introduced to him and therefore has a right to cling to others, like the child in the poem. However, as he grows up to become a young man during the course of the novel, he needs to become responsible for his own vision and viewpoint, instead of holding on to his education like a drowning man. This responsibility is particularly important in the context of the real-life situation to which Ngũgĩ refers. Njoroge is attending a foreign missionary school in a colonized Kenya, and in his interview Ngũgĩ explains that education at the missionary schools emphasized "the production of Africans who would later become efficient machines for running a colonial system . . . two diametrically opposed images: the image of the Kenyan patriot as a negative human being and the image of the oppressor and his collaborator as positive human beings."[8] Ngũgĩ further informs us that the curriculum in the schools controlled by foreign powers was entirely European based and, consequently, devoid of Third World literature.

During the course of events the novel depicts, women do not play an apparently big role. Yet Ngũgĩ has given them, however subtly, such a vital role that it demands consideration. The mothers are the ones who symbolize hope, courage, and unity in the story as the Gikuyu society is moving toward independence, and they carry out the hope expressed in the poem. They seek to reconcile the extremes and uphold harmony within the home and to balance the old with the new. And, most importantly, the mothers, as well as Mwihaki, seek to bring Njoroge down from "the clouds" and closer to real life. We are told that the two mothers are "good companions and friends" and that Ngotho's home was "well known for being a place of peace." The foresight and the positive and encouraging atmosphere in the story are centered around the women, and when the young people from the village gather together they meet in either Njeri's or Nyokabi's hut. The mothers' affection is fundamental for Njoroge's psychological well-being, and although he fears his father, still, the worst is "a mother's silence" (*WNC*, 35). Although Nyok-abi presses on with her son's education and encourages him to do well at school, she also warns him not to forget the important ties between the old and the new. She affectionately scolds him: "do your elder mother and myself waste our time telling you all those stories about the tribe?" (*WNC*, 17). And storytelling importantly unites them because it is a part of their cultural her-itage, an important part of their history and identity, and, further, a "com-mon entertainment in their family" (*WNC*, 21).

The mothers also seek to steer Njoroge from the dangerous tendency to select his friends according to their class in society. He is attracted to Mwi-haki, Jacobo's daughter, at least partially because "[i]t was sweet to play with a girl and especially if that girl came from a family higher up the social scale than one's own" (*WNC*, 15). And although we later learn that Mwihaki is a worthy friend, Njoroge's mother only shows that she is fully aware of the social and political situation; she "did not want her son to associate with a family of the rich because it would not be healthy for him" (*WNC*, 15). That is, she does not want him to become a mere pawn of the colonizing world, a blind player in the hierarchy of oppression and false values. The women in the story seek to protect Njoroge from falling prey to his idealistic praying for heroism.

Approaching Earth

Those whose interest the colonial system serves encourage a continued psy-chological and hierarchical division: "Black people had no land because of colour-bar and they could not eat in hotels because of colour-bar. Colour-bar was everywhere. Rich Africans could also practise colour-bar on the poorer Africans" (*WNC*, 64). In this respect, Whitman's naturalism works against systems of hierarchy—that is, it increases one's awareness so as not to accept or fall into such traps. As Whitman points out, it is useful to regularly "re-examine philosophies and religions, / They may prove well in lecture-rooms, yet not prove at all under the spacious clouds and along the landscape and flowing currents" (*Whitman*, 301). Seen in the political context of Kenya, this point is important in that the government may seriously denounce and pro-hibit human rights violations and foreign control over the country in public pronouncements and at the same time practice the opposite. The people therefore need to be able to remove themselves from the lecture rooms and so be able to view and evaluate the real-life situation, without anything or any-one coming in between to obscure and distort reality and intimidate people from thinking for themselves. Looking at things from under "the spacious clouds" suggests that there is no natural space for oppressive and suffocating restrictions of freedoms. And Njoroge is an example of one who unquestionably needs to get out of the lecture rooms. I also agree here with Allen Ginsberg that Whitman poses to us the challenging question of "who actually looks out of their own eyes and sees the revolutions in the trees in the fall or the bursting forth of tiny revolutions with each grass blade?"9 The possibility to change and transform is a real one, and, as Whitman points out, men and and women cannot be seen merely as "dreams or dots" (*Whitman,* 475). And if we protect and preserve our natural and healthy contact with nature, lean and loaf at ease among leaves of grass, we are far more likely to create for ourselves instead of being created by others.

Nyokabi is happy that Njoroge can get an education, but she also views it in a realistic light and estimates it according to the present situation. When the Mau Mau struggle has reached a boiling point and Njoroge's missionary school has been threatened, Nyokabi declares: "My son, you'll not go to that school any more. Education is not life" (*WNC,* 83). Thus, she points out to him that it is impossible to avoid coming face to face with one's own actual social circumstances and try to hide in an illusionary oasis. And Njoroge has in fact become so removed from reality that when Mwihaki, in a moment of passion, suggests that they run away together, he does not like that idea at all because "what would God think if he deserted his mission like this?" (*WNC,* 95). Although in spite of the family's financial and emotional stress he is able to go on with his education, we see by the end of the novel that his reluctance to leave his "oasis" just makes his return to society all the more painful.

Significantly, it is the mother who, with her wisdom and foresight, warns against going on the strike. Nyokabi asks Ngotho not to go on the strike and confronts him with a real possibility: "What if the strike fails?" Ngotho's answer is, "I must be a man in my own house. . . . I have never taken orders from a woman" (*WNC,* 52). However, he tragically finds out that he would have been more of a man to listen to his wife. After the ill-fated strike, Ngotho "had diminished in stature, often assuming a defensive secondary place whenever talking with his sons and their friends," and he "no longer looked anybody straight in the face; not even his wives" (*WNC,* 81). Although the mothers are not able to rescue Ngotho and Boro from a tragic end, their role is vital in that they support and sustain Njoroge, the hero of the novel who carries the hope on his shoulders.

When Ngotho has died after his torture by Howlands (because he confessed to the murder of Jacobo to shield his son) and Boro is waiting to be executed, having killed Jacobo and Howlands, Njoroge still refuses to step out of his daydreams and face reality. Instead, he sentimentally pleads with Mwihaki to run away with him from the situation through a romantic escapade: "You are the one dear thing left to me. I feel bound to you and I know that I can fully depend on you. I have no hope left but for you. . . . we can go away from here." It is she then who, like the mothers, tries to bring him to his senses: "Don't you see that what you suggest is too easy a way out. . . . we have a duty. Our duty to other people is our biggest responsibility as grown men and women." And his "last hope had vanished. For the first time he knew that he was in the world all alone without a soul on whom he could lean" (WNC, 132–34). Although Njoroge is still in the dark and has not yet realized that people can support each other while essentially relying on themselves, he has nevertheless taken an important step forward.

Voices United in Hope and Optimism

Njoroge, now disillusioned and desperate, has to face the painful fact that he has been locked up in a world of his own. He has failed to understand his mothers' implicit advice not to enter school to nurture his daydreams and attempt to escape from reality. Throughout the story the mothers have stood as a symbol for what was the most vital in the Kenyan independence struggle. They do not give up, and they agree with Whitman that it is naturally realistic to expect the light of day—but one also has to make the effort and be willing to hold hands with others. The mothers realize that past, present, and future are to be joined and cannot be severed, whereas Ngotho, Boro, and Njoroge have become imprisoned in the past, present, and future, respectively. They seek to temper and reconcile Boro's cynicism, Ngotho's surrender, and Njoroge's idealism by remaining open to the new while also acknowledging and upholding the old. They know that unity and harmony at home provide the healthy basis for unity in the struggle. And even Mwihaki, Njoroge's youthful love, reminds him of his responsibility, that the time has come for him to grow up. And when Njoroge realizes his failure and the futility of his escape, he attempts the biggest escape: suicide.

In the midst of this social turmoil he has been envisioning himself as a savior and, consequently, failed in his assigned and self-assigned task. He may be a dreamer, an idealist, but if he wants his dream to come true he cannot avoid being politically engaged in a country that is politically oppressed. Throughout, Njoroge has insisted on clinging to the comfort offered him at the missionary school: Christianity. Although the freedom fighters pointed out how "the land had been taken away, through the Bible and the sword" (WNC, 57), education was Njoroge's way of fighting to regain the land for his colonized and landless people:

> he would help all his brothers. Before he went to sleep he prayed, "Lord, let me get learning. I want to help my father and mothers. And Kamau and all my other brothers. I ask you all this through Jesus Christ, our Lord, Amen:" (WNC, 44)

Njoroge's is not quite the right spirit with which to win back the lands that have been taken by the very people hammering and preaching this religious tune. And certainly it is not in accordance with the poem, in which there is a space for supportive human relationships but not for false hopes and escapades. However, as the novel opens up hopefully with the mother, it significantly also concludes with two mothers. They come to rescue their son from a mistakenly understood "escape," and he "saw the light she was carrying and falteringly went towards it. It was a glowing piece of wood which she carried to light the way. . . . And he ran home and opened the door for his two mothers" (WNC, 135–6). The hope is now embodied in Njoroge's renewed energies—atoms belonging to him as good belonging to his people. And, again, the heroic role of the women, who have the ultimate courage not to seek an escape but to deal with things and to light the way into the unknown, is modestly kept in the background. Only now is Njoroge able to honestly examine his own role in the situation. Grimly, he has stepped out of his daydreams and into the world of reality. Yet, however grim and painful, his leap forward has been secured and supported by his mothers, real reminders of life.

PETALS OF BLOOD

Ngũgĩ's fourth novel, *Petals of Blood*, deals with "independent" Kenya and depicts the real problems of neocolonialism. When Kenya gained independence in 1963 and Jomo Kenyatta became president, people were filled with great expectations for the future. In *Detained: A Writer's Prison Diary*, Ngũgĩ's book about his detention for being an independent and an outspoken writer with an independent mind and voice, he discusses Kenyatta's part in the political history of Kenya. As he explains, Kenyatta was known as a leading figure in Kenya's resistance against colonialism and in the independence struggle. So active was he in denouncing the colonial rule that, perceived as a great nationalist and a danger to the system, he was tried in 1952 and detained for 10 years. However, "by 1966, the comprador bourgeois line, led by Kenyatta, Mboya and others, had triumphed. This faction, using the inherited colonial state machinery, ousted the patriotic elements from the party leadership, silencing those who remained and hounding others to death" (*Detained*, 54). Here, then, *independence* and *democratic rights* are only words without meaning

Petals of Blood takes off with an epigraph from Whitman's poem "Europe," and the last part of the novel begins with an epigraph from the same poem. First published in 1850, this poem is about Europe during the year of revolutions, 1848, a celebration of the force of revolution that began in America in 1776 and has spread back to the feudal lands of Europe. However, it is also important to note that at this time Whitman had become disillusioned with his Democratic Party and was writing to attack the corruption he saw taking place in American politics at the time. Thus, the poem may also be taken to imply political corruption in a "democratic" society, a situation in which "frighten'd monarchs" rule, clad in a democratic disguise.

Whitman's poem and Ngũgĩ's novel together give us an important insight into the political concerns and the political bond between the two writers.

Suddenly out of its stale and drowsy lair, the lair of slaves,
Like lightning it lept forth half startled at itself,
Its feet upon the ashes and the rags, its hands tight to the throats of kings.

O hope and faith!
O aching close of exiled patriots' lives!
O many a sicken'd heart!
Turn back unto this day and make yourself afresh.

And you, paid to defile the People—you liars, mark!
Not for numberless agonies, murders, lusts,
For court thieving in its manifold mean forms, worming from his simplicity the poor man's wages,
For many a promise sworn by royal lips and broken and laugh'd at in the breaking,
Then in their power not for all these did the blows strike revenge, or the heads of the nobles fall;
The people scorn'd the ferocity of kings.

But the sweetness of mercy brew'd bitter destruction, and the frighten'd monarchs come back,
Each comes in state, with his train, hangman, priest, tax-gatherer,
Soldier, lawyer, lord, jailer, and sycophant.

Yet behind all lowering stealing, lo, a shape,
Vague as the night, draped interminably, head, front and form, in scarlet folds,
Whose face and eyes none may see,
Out of its robes only this, the red robes lifted by the arm,
One finger crook'd pointed high over the top, like the head of a snake appears.

Meanwhile corpses lie in new-made graves, bloody corpses of young men,
The rope of the gibbet hangs heavily, the bullets of princes are flying, the creatures of power laugh aloud,
And all these things bear fruits, and they are good.

Those corpses of young men,
Those martyrs that hang from the gibbets, those hearts pierc'd by the gray lead,
Cold and motionless as they seem live elsewhere with unslaughter'd vitality.

They live in other young men O kings!
They live in brothers again ready to defy you,
They were purified by death, they were taught and exalted.

Not a grave of the murder'd for freedom but grows seed for freedom, in its turn to bear seed,
Which the winds carry afar and re-sow, and the rains and the snows nourish.

Not a disembodied spirit can the weapons of tyrants let loose,
But it stalks invisibly over the earth, whispering, counseling, cautioning.

Liberty, let others despair of you—I never despair of you.
Is the house shut? is the master away?
Nevertheless, be ready, be not weary of watching, He will soon return, his messen-
    gers come anon.
                     (*Whitman,* 406–407; italics mine, to indicate the epigraphs)

Political Corruption

In the poem, Whitman presents political corruption. People "scorn'd the ferocity of kings." However, "the sweetness of mercy brew'd destruction, and the frighten'd monarchs come back." This is a significant image of the situation with which Ngũgĩ deals in this novel.

This novel takes place in the capital city Nairobi and the fictitious village Ilmorog. It is a spiral work and employs the flashback technique. Thus, at the "beginning" we witness the abrupt arrest of all four protagonists: the teacher Munira, the "corner-shop" merchant Abdulla, the "trade-union agitator" Karega, and the prostitute Wanja. And during the course of the novel we come to know the protagonists, the reasons for their arrest, and the actual social situation of their country. We do so through our encounter with the characters but essentially by observing their own interactions with one another and how they gradually develop a bond as they talk about their experiences with one another. In spite of their differences they, as their political consciousness grows collectively, become united by one common goal, in Munira's words, "to make our independence real."[10]

The manner of their arrest suggests the social situation: no questions allowed and no explanations given. The description of the village itself as a ghastly, barren, slowly dying wasteland symbolizes the situation in the society at large. Under a colonial, neocolonial, or any other system run entirely by privileges of a secluded government, society is prevented from changing and flourishing. In a society that functions by a limited number of people enriching themselves and exploiting the many, the rule will always be characterized by a desperate clinging to the status quo. Where "frighten'd monarchs" rule, hiding behind their train, the government clearly cannot be a healthy one. However, as the second epigraph suggests, the essential spirit of the poem and the novel is not that of acceptance, passiveness, sadness, or self-pity. The cited epigraph from Whitman's poem is in touch with the people's reaction to the arrest of the four protagonists: "disband the tyranny of foreign companies and their local messengers. . . . Workers were waking to their own strength. Such a defiant confrontation with authority had never before happened in Ilmorog" (*PB,* 4). In the poem and the novel we hear the call to battle.

America had carried out a successful revolution, but, if seen in a "democratic" or an "independent" context, the monarchs can signify the "democratic danger" of a popularly elected government—that is, a government that is turned into an "elite" and occupying itself with internal struggles of the "political hierarchy" and worrying about being overthrown by "the enemy." In "The 18th Presidency!" Whitman writes:

> Somebody must make a bold push. The people, credulous, generous, deferential, allow the American government to be managed in many respects as is only proper under the personnel of a king and hereditary lords; or, more truly, not proper under any decent man anywhere. . . . every trustee of the people is a traitor, looking only to his own gain, and to boost up his party. (*Whitman*, 1332)

These words, addressed to the American people in 1856, express much the same political reality Ngũgĩ deals with in *Petals of Blood*, which was first published in 1977. In the novel, one of the local messengers of the neocolonial system we come to know is the paranoid politician Nderi wa Riera, who is the archetype of Whitman's corrupt politician.

The four protagonists of the novel undertake a journey to Nairobi to meet with influential men there and seek help for the village and its inhabitants. They have no other choice than to undertake that task because their village and its inhabitants are fighting for survival; the latest problem is a drought. In Nairobi, they become acquainted with the "frighten'd monarchs" introduced in the poem—frightened because their position is a precarious one. The politician Nderi wa Riera was once perceived as a national hero and a savior of the people, much like Kenyatta was perceived. So the four optimistically seek an appointment with him, deferentially remembering him as the most ardent advocate and fighter for social justice, independence, and improvements in their country. Unfortunately they find out that it is not the case anymore, that was "before he was flooded with offers of directorships in foreign-owned companies" (*PB*, 174). The credulous people find him to be a "traitor, looking only to his own gain."

The member of Parliament is obsessed with the tense suspicion that "the enemy" is plotting against him, and he is immediately filled with such suspicion when the people from Ilmorog come to see him as their trustee. While listening to their concerns he is "racking his brain for a dramatic escape route" (*PB*, 180). However, on the surface he carefully plays the concerned friend of humanity. As the four protagonists explain the situation of the dying Ilmorog and people's struggles, the politician thinks that as the publicly elected representative of the people of Ilmorog he should have known about this situation because "[i]f it became general knowledge, his opponents would make political capital out of the whole mess. It might in fact be too late. It might be his enemies who had learned about the drought and engineered the whole thing to see what he would do about it, certainly to embarrass him" (*PB*, 180). Finally he figures who is the enemy and decides that he must be eliminated—an allusion to the real-life incident (not the only of its kind) Ngũgĩ discusses in *Detained:* "the new Kenyatta relied more and more on those who used to be actively anti–Mau Mau, or on colonial chiefs and sons of colonial chiefs. The sole remaining symbol of Mau Mau militancy to occupy a place of national importance after independence was J. M. Kariuki . . . murdered in 1975" (*Detained,* 89).

Nderi wa Riera, after "racking his brain," speaks to the people as their "humble servant." He appears only too eager to help them solve the problem, while "as if inspired by the crowd and the applause, he saw clearly how he could confound his enemies and turn their machinations to his own advantage." His suggestion to the people is that they just sell the cattle instead of "letting it die," and try to get rich by their "African culture and spiritual values," in his own words: "Dive deep into your pockets" (*PB,* 182). When they tell him that they are starving, he comments "Very important." That is to say, he does not care whether they live or die, since he already has their votes. But if they are starving, they should only feel grateful to him for having the chance to try out his "caring self-help scheme."

Just as Kenyatta was often talked of and perceived as "our man," even when the opposite was only all too obvious, the people of Ilmorog prefer to see their member of Parliament in the same trusting light, as their "democratic hero," without really looking at and examining the reality. Their "sweetness of mercy" holds them in a self-imposed cage of illusions. They hold on to the belief that he is "out there, fighting for them," while at the same time they witness the neglect and the starvation of the village, its transformation into a ghost town, because it is not regarded as a profitable place in which to invest. Eventually, however, necessity forces the four protagonists to face the facts: the frightened monarchs have been raised from the dead and are roaming the country in the disguise of democracy. Whitman's outspoken criticism of "democratic monarchs" who rule by despotism is historically relevant here. The authors of *Independent Kenya* point out that "[f]or all practical purposes, the President, by late 1968 and ever since, has been a kind of 'divine right' monarch—ruling by decree, and often invoking God as his guide and the source of his power."[11] But, as the poem suggests, the monarchs will not be victorious or lasting, as opposed to the dead young men who grow "seed of freedom, in its turn to bear seed" (*Whitman,* 407). Whereas the characteristic of the former is being frightened, the latter "live elsewhere with unslaughter'd vitality."

Christianity and the Question of Values

Neither Ngũgĩ nor Whitman avoid placing the responsibility with the people, "the masses," in Whitman's words, for whom they are primarily writing. By seeking to make people themselves responsible Whitman and Ngũgĩ are thereby making people active instead of passive—demanding action instead of only reaction. Whitman's and Ngũgĩ's concerns and engagement with the theme of religion are important to their purpose of activation and awareness. Christianity was used as a weapon to oppress the colonized people, as Peter Nazareth explains in *The Third World Writer:*

> The Christianity that came from Europe acted in tandem with colonialism, softening the people so that the imperial powers could rule with minimal resistance, both by persuading the colonized people that they were cultural and religious savages before the coming of the White colonizer and by making the people feel that they had to accept the status quo as God's will for man.[12]

Whitman is important in this context. His religious tone is essentially the tone of challenge—in his words "resist much, obey little." This idea is quite contrary to the Christianity the indigenous people, the "savages," were confronted with. As Ngũgĩ tells us in the preface to *Detained,* the purpose of his detention was to "teach him a lesson in submission, silence, and obedience"—the very trinity Whitman is denouncing as he "sound[s his] barbaric yawp over the roofs of the world" (*Whitman,* 247). The way in which Whitman takes on religious matters makes it clear that he is deliberately defying and attacking the old myth of Christianity as the humanized and the civilized salvation of human beings, as the "White Man's Burden" of liberating people from "barbarism." In his "Collect," Whitman describes this element of religion:

> as boundless, joyous, and vital as Nature itself—a germenancy that has too long been unencouraged, unsung, almost unknown. . . . The time has certainly come to begin to discharge the idea of religion, in the United States, from mere ecclesiasticism, and from Sundays and churches and church-going, and assign it to that general position, chiefest, most indispensable, most exhilarating, to which the others are to be adjusted, inside of all human character, and education, and affairs. (*Whitman,*1027)

In religion as in everything else Whitman's message is that "[t]he reader will always have his or her part to do, just as much as I have had mine" (*Whitman,* 667). That is the religion that Ngũgĩ shares and that, as is the case with Whitman, shapes his tone of challenge. Whitman refuses the idea that anything can be more divine than people themselves and points out that priests' work is done, that the time has come for people to be their own priests. Both Whitman and Ngũgĩ seek to "physicalize" religion and oppose its tendency to uphold hierarchy, alienation, and intimidation. In "Song of Myself" Whitman makes an important contribution to the breaking down of religions as hierarchical and intimidating systems:

I have said that the soul is not more than the body,
And I have said that the body is not more than the soul,

And nothing, not God, is greater to one than one's self is . . .
I see something of God each hour of the twenty-four, and
each moment then,
In the faces of men and women I see God, and in my own
face in the glass.

(Whitman, 245)

The "frighten'd monarchs" would be very likely to "put God in a poem or a system of philosophy as contending against some being or influence" (*Whitman*, 16)—that is to say, to contend against the being of defiance, resistance, the seed for freedom, the continuous struggle.

Both Ngũgĩ and Whitman deal with the history of Christianity as various interest groups have employed it effectively in the struggle for power. Both criticize the "humane" action of "feeding" people with "spirituality" while their actual, material, fundamental needs for existence are ignored. At the same time, they also criticize people for not being attentive themselves, as Whitman, in "Europe," points out: "be not weary of watching."

In their journey to Nairobi, Munira, Karega, Wanja, and Abdulla find out that they need to reexamine and reevaluate their ideas about "the servants of God" as their true and real saviors. Seeking a solution in the "Blue Hills" of Nairobi, they become personally acquainted with "the holy man" Reverend Jerrod Brown. When they encounter his signpost they find it disappointing that he is not an African, according to the name. Yet, they are not discouraged because "a man of God under whatever skin was a soul of goodness and mercy and kindness" (*PB*, 145). However, the reverend turns out to be an African who has taken up an English name because it is foreign and thus, he believes, has to be better. But his reception of the people looks promising:

> His voice was filled with pity and understanding. As a Christian he knew wherein lay his duty. . . . He prayed for the poor in spirit; the crippled in soul; for jobless wanderers, and all those who were hungry and thirsty because they had never eaten the bread and drunk the water from the well of Jesus. He prayed for everything and everyone under the sun and his voice touched something, a softness in their hearts. (*PB*, 147–48).

He thus "fills" his guests with merciful preaching and Bible reading. But afterward he tells the starving people to feel free to nourish themselves with "the bread and fish of Jesus," sending them away with it.

Seeds Bearing Seeds

The four protagonists discover that ultimately the solution is not to be sought for and found in the Blue Hills or anywhere else but in themselves. They need to be together in the struggle as independent individuals. At the same time, they need to critically evaluate their supposed "saviors" who seek to advertise themselves as the people's caring and indispensable servants. However, one cannot blame the people for being so credulous and deferential. They certainly want to "make independence real" but have yet to realize that the problem is not essentially about foreign powers exploiting their country but that of their own government's cooperation. As Ngũgĩ says in *Decolonising the Mind: The Politics of Language in African Literature:*

> the point is this: the Mobutus, the Mois and the Eyademas of the neo-colonial world are not being forced to capitulate to imperialism at the point of an American maxim gun. They themselves are of the same mind: they are actually begging for a recolonisation of their own countries with themselves as the neo-colonial governors living in modern fortresses. (80)

Although the people denounce the "local messengers," we see that in their confrontation with the local imperialists, people's attitude is still "credulous and deferential."

But, as Ngũgĩ and Whitman imply, too often people hold on to beliefs that merely sound or should be good, such as Njoroge dreaming of eliminating colonialism through his missionary education, and, here, people credulously believing in the existence of democracy in a country sick from neocolonialism. In both cases, this is a question of looking under the surface, however "glorious" it may seem. Whitman points out the importance of looking under the surface: "the frighten'd monarchs . . . each comes in state with his train," and Ngũgĩ explains this train: "The palace walls of a handful of capitalists are painted with the blood and sweat of a million hands. This handful has an army of intellectuals and artists, journalists, parliamentarians, etc., who rationalize and justify this exploitative relationship."[13] However, the active and the hopeful spirit of the poem correlates with the novel's conclusion as Karega, although behind bars, is visited by a messenger of the people: " 'You'll come back,' she said again in a quiet affirmation of faith in eventual triumph. 'Tomorrow . . .' and he knew he was no longer alone" (*PB,* 345).

Grand Theater: Tickets for Free

Whitman's America and Ngũgĩ's Kenya present us with a political play being acted out on the stage of hierarchy. Some are actors and others directors, depending on where they are situated in the hierarchical ladder. Whitman scorns political hypocrites and how they pretend to be the devoted "protectionists" of the people:

> The profits of "protection" go altogether to a few score select persons—who, by favors of Congress, State legislatures, the banks, and other special advan-

tages, are forming a vulgar aristocracy, full as bad as anything in the British or European castes, of blood, or the dynasties of the past. (*Whitman*, 1092)

This is a "play" in which the players are only occupied with seizing a yet larger "role" in the ongoing "show." For the "audience," there is only one message intended: passiveness. By no means should the audience listen to Whitman as he emphasizes: "Always inform yourself" (*Whitman*, 990). And so much more should they ignore Whitman's and Ngũgĩ's call to battle—for the audience's own good, of course. In *Weep Not, Child*, the "directors" are the colonizers and the white settlers, while Jacobo personifies the "actors," the native ruling class created and controlled by the colonizing nation. And in *Petals of Blood*, Nderi wa Riera and Reverend Jerrod Brown are yet other "players" in the "show," favorite puppets of foreign-owned companies. All are strutting and fretting their hour on the stage in the struggle for power and battling for the biggest piece of the pie, leaving behind them only an echo of destruction.

Whitman's and Ngũgĩ's Challenge to the Audience

But where are the workers, the peasants, the "common man," the masses? Are they just "not in the game," only poor and pitiful objects, feeling sorry for themselves? Not as far as Whitman and Ngũgĩ are concerned. It is true that neither of them envies the life of the frightened monarchs. But it does not mean that these "million hands" should only be content bleeding and sweating for a few. Besides, the numbers are certainly to the million hands' advantage. Following is Ngũgĩ's answer to the question:

> resistance to oppression and exploitation, the strong desire in human beings to overcome the negative aspects of nature and all the things that inhibit the free development of their lives—this is the most important of human qualities. . . . We know that the transformations of the twentieth century have been the results of the struggles of peasants and workers. So how can we say that these two classes, whose labour has changed nature, are weak, naive, stupid, and cowardly?[14]

Both Whitman and Ngũgĩ emphasize the importance of a society being open to both natural and pragmatic change and development. They reject fixity of any kind, such as the traditional Christianity and its employment as a tool, because it prevents people from realistically evaluating the present situation. Here, Njoroge is a case in point, to whom Whitman speaks thus: "We consider bibles and religions divine—I do not say they are not divine, / I say they have all grown out of you, and may grow out of you still, / It is not they who give the life, it is you who give the life" (*Whitman*, 359). Life is essentially the passing moment, and therefore all "truths" can only be examined from the point of view of the present situation. Although Whitman is not always as explicit as Ngũgĩ in his social and political engagements, his importance here should not be overlooked. For example, his poem "When I Heard the Learn'd Astronomer" is a political poem:

When I heard the learn'd astronomer,
When the proofs, the figures, were ranged in columns before me,
When I was shown the charts and diagrams, to add, divide, and measure them,
When I sitting heard the astronomer where he lectured with much applause in the
    lecture-room,
How soon unaccountable I became tired and sick,
Till rising and gliding out I wander'd off by myself,
In the mystical moist night-air, and from time to time,
Look'd up in perfect silence at the stars.   (*Whitman*, 409–410)

Like Ngũgĩ, Whitman seeks to clarify, not obscure, matters, and they both embrace direct confrontation. Further, in their writings, they employ inclusion to work against unconscious mental acceptance of social and political oppression. Whitman, in "Passage to India," claims to be "the true son of God" (*Whitman*, 535) while proudly and loudly shouting his "barbaric yawp" over the world. He insists on being "just as much evil as good," and it is of a little importance whether he develops on the negative or the marginal aspects—that he seeks to bring in the various perspectives is what is important. *Weep Not, Child* provides insight into the different perspectives and beliefs of the main characters. Also, importantly, Howlands and Jacobo are not simply dismissed as evil, but, rather, Ngũgĩ seeks to throw a light on the forces that have created them. And *Petals of Blood,* although explicitly depicting the evils of neocolonialism, also seeks to point out how people can assume certain responsibility and thus become more active in the struggle.

Conclusion

The division and the clear-cut, hierarchical "categorization" of people, education, culture, and, in general, life itself prevent the oppressed and exploited from forming their most powerful tool in the struggle, which is unity. In *Writing against Neocolonialism,* Ngũgĩ explains how important it is for an African writer to write in the indigenous language so that his or her voice can speak to the people. He continues that such a writer must

> above all, learn from [his] great optimism and faith in the capacity of human beings to remake their world and renew themselves. He must be part of the song the people sing as once again they take up arms to smash the neocolonial

state to complete the anti-imperial national democratic revolution they had started in the fifties, and even earlier. A people united can never be defeated.[15]

Ngũgĩ and Whitman set out to fight against all the propaganda of the "humane" justification of the colonization, the oppressing policy, as opposed to the "savage" and "evil" classifications of independence movements. They seek to make clear the policy of hierarchical division and at the same time the psychological obscurity of that division. All were the main obstacles, because people were as much unconscious of them as they were conscious; people had to fight, and continue to fight, on their long walk to freedom. The most difficult thing is often to wake up one's own consciousness and awareness, and I believe that is what Whitman had in mind when he declared himself to be "the remainder of life." For a struggle to take place, regardless of its success, it is necessary to first realize, acknowledge, and identify against whom or what the war is to be waged.

The frightened monarchs as depicted in the novel, the neocolonial servants, are in a place that has been assigned them, or, more accurately, for which they have been created. And although they may find it worthwhile to stay there, because of their wealth and power, they are nonetheless dependent on the fixed and closed social structure to maintain their shallow front. Behind that shallow front they are nothing but a mere tool that serves well the interests of those who profit by investments in the country. And functioning as a tool, their will, power, and capacity to evaluate and examine things for themselves are drastically reduced. Whitman and Ngũgĩ also look at the other side of the coin; the "merciful masses" also need to be aware of "categorization" and seek to be both active and responsible, not see themselves as merely the "recipients of democracy." Whitman points this idea out in his "Thought":

Of obedience, faith, adhesiveness;
As I stand aloof and look there is to me something profoundly affecting in large
    masses of men following the lead of those who do not believe in men.
                                                              (*Whitman*, 413)

That is what Wanja, Karega, Abdulla, and Munira learn on their journey to Nairobi. The time has come for them to stop "following the lead of those who do not believe in men." In their struggle to make independence real, they must wage a war as much against African collaborators as against foreign exploiters. And, within a colonial context, Njoroge has fallen prey to the same misconception. But what use is it anyway to talk about "changes"? Can one talk at all about changes except in an ideal, abstract sense? At least it is certain that, in Ngũgĩ's words, "the struggle continues." Although changes may seem far out of reach and remote from the common people, no God exists to structure society. People, individuals, just as the grass is an ensemble of leaves of grass, structure society. If we decide that things are hopeless and if we, in Whitman's words, refuse to "contribute a verse," then certainly nothing is going to happen. Thus, what we have essentially in Ngũgĩ's novels and Whitman's *Leaves of Grass* is the challenge of the ultimate education, according to Whitman:

> You shall no longer take things at second or third hand, nor look through the eyes of
>   the dead, nor feed on the spectres in books,
> You shall not look through my eyes either, nor take things from me,
> You shall listen to all sides and filter them from your self. (*Whitman,* 189–190)

And although this is an order not to take orders (Whitman's hierarchy?), to never accept without examining, I cannot but confess that in my mind Ngũgĩ's and Whitman's ends justify their means.

I am not going to resist the temptation of letting Ngũgĩ wa Thiong'o and Walt Whitman have the last words here—words symbolizing hope, unity, and optimism. I find these two quotations most telling for them, both as individual writers and as two writers who, in spite of their different time periods, cultures, and whatever else there may be, are significantly related.

These are Ngũgĩ's last words from his acknowledgments at the beginning of *Petals of Blood* as he addresses:

> Many other
> One in the struggle
> With our people
> For total liberation
> Knowing that
> However long and arduous the struggle
> Victory is certain

And these are Whitman's last words in "Song of Myself":

> Failing to fetch me at first keep encouraged,
> Missing me one place search another,
> I stop somewhere waiting for you (*Whitman,* 88)

Notes

1. Walt Whitman, *Whitman: Poetry and Prose* (New York: Library of America, 1996); hereafter cited in the text in this essay.

2. Ngũgĩ wa Thiong'o, *Moving the Centre: The Struggle for Cultural Freedoms* (London: James Currey, 1993), 14; hereafter cited in this essay as *MC*.

3. Ngũgĩ wa Thiong'o, *Decolonising the Mind: The Politics of Language in African Literature* (London: Heinemann, 1989), 17.

4. Ngũgĩ wa Thiong'o, *Detained: A Writer's Prison Diary* (London: Heinemann, 1981), xii; hereafter cited in the text in this essay.

5. Carol Sicherman, *Ngugi wa Thiong'o: The Making of a Rebel. A Source Book in Kenyan Literature and Resistance* (Kent, England: Hans Zell, 1990), 25.

6. James Ngugi, *Weep Not, Child* (Oxford, England: Heinemann, 1987), 26; hereafter cited in this essay as *WNC*.

7. Sorobea N. Bogonko, *Kenya 1945–63: A Study in African National Movements* (Nairobi: Kenya Literature Bureau, 1980), 32.

8. Sicherman, *Ngugi wa Thiong'o*, 20.

9. Allen Ginsberg, "Allen Ginsberg on Walt Whitman: Composed on the Tongue," in *Walt Whitman: The Measure of His Song* (Minneapolis: Holy Cow! Press, 1981), 236.

10. Ngũgĩ wa Thiong'o, *Petals of Blood* (New York: E. P. Dutton, 1978), 10; hereafter cited in this essay as *PB*.

11. *Independent Kenya* (London: Zed Press, 1982), 27–28. Note that the authors of this book must remain anonymous because they are still living in their country.

12. Peter Nazareth, *The Third World Writer: His Social Responsibility* (Nairobi: Kenya Literature Bureau, 1978), 3.

13. Sicherman, *Ngugi wa Thiong'o*, 24.

14. Sicherman, *Ngugi wa Thiong'o*, 24.

15. James Ngugi, *Writing against Neocolonialism* (Middlesex, England: Vita, 1986), 20.

Bibliography

Allen, Gay Wilson, and Ed Folsom, eds. *Walt Whitman and the World.* Iowa City: University of Iowa Press, 1995.

Bogonko, Sorobea N. *Kenya 1945–63: A Study in African National Movements.* Nairobi: Kenya Literature Bureau, 1980.

Cook, David. *African Literature: A Critical View.* London: Longman, 1977.

Erkkila, Betsy, and Jay Grossman, eds. *Breaking Bounds.* New York: Oxford University Press, 1996.

Folsom, Ed, ed. *Walt Whitman: The Centennial Essays.* Iowa City: University of Iowa Press, 1994.

Ginsberg, Allen. "Allen Ginsberg on Walt Whitman: Composed on the Tongue." In *Walt Whitman: The Measure of His Song.* Minneapolis: Holy Cow! Press, 1981.

Independent Kenya. London: Zed Press, 1982. The authors of this book must remain anonymous because they are still living in their country.

Killam, G. D., ed. *The Writing of East and Central Africa.* London: Heinemann, 1984.

Meyer, Herta. *Justice for the Oppressed: The Political Dimension in the Language Use of Ngugi wa Thiong'o.* Essen, Germany: Verlag Die Blaue Eule, 1991.

Nazareth, Peter. *The Third World Writer: His Social Responsibility.* Nairobi: Kenya Literature Bureau, 1978.

Ngugi, James. *A Grain of Wheat.* London: Heinemann, 1967.

———. *Homecoming: Essays on African and Caribbean Literature, Culture, and Politics.* London: Heinemann, 1972.

———. *Petals of Blood.* New York: E. P. Dutton, 1978.

———. *Detained: A Writer's Prison Diary.* London: Heinemann, 1981.

———. *Writing against Neocolonialism.* Middlesex, England: Vita, 1986.

———. *Weep Not, Child.* Oxford, England: Heinemann, 1987.

———. *Decolonising the Mind: The Politics of Language in African Literature.* London: Heinemann, 1989.

———. *Moving the Centre: The Struggle for Cultural Freedoms.* London: James Currey, 1993.

Sicherman, Carol. *Ngugi wa Thiong'o: The Making of a Rebel: A Source Book in Kenyan Literature and Resistance.* Kent, England: Hans Zell, 1990.

Whitman, Walt. *Whitman: Poetry and Prose.* New York: Library of America, 1996.

Prospero and the Land of Calibans:
A Grain of Wheat

HARISH NARANG

The Kenyan national movement—particularly its violent phase—has been the subject of a number of literary works by Kenyans in English. We shall, in this chapter, analyse and evaluate *A Grain of Wheat* (1967) by Ngugi wa Thiong'o. But before we do so, we may like to go into the details of the freedom struggle itself. These details form the pretext of the novel and only in the light of these details can we evaluate the treatment of this aspect of Kenyan history by Ngugi wa Thiong'o.

The covert colonisation of the Kenyan people began towards the end of the 19th century through the granting of a Royal Charter for Trade to the Imperial East African Trading Company within the bounds of what was then known as the East Africa Protectorate. The annexation, however, became overt and formal when the company withdrew for financial reasons and the British government took over the control of the territory in its own hands and appointed a Commissioner for the Protectorate. The resistance against the colonial government began almost simultaneously with the annexation of the region, but such resistance was in the form of isolated incidents involving small groups of people who were immediately affected by the British control of the region. The government decision to bring in foreign settlers from Europe, Asia and South Africa further complicated the situation and made the freedom struggle by Kenyans not only a prolonged one but also a more bitter one. In the words of Nkrumah:

> Kenya under colonial rule, unlike the average colony in West Africa, was plagued with settler problems. Consequently, the liberation struggle in Kenya was bound to be one of the most dramatic in the history of the Continent. (Odinga, 1967: xiv)

The struggle, after decades of peaceful constitutional moves both inside and outside the legislative council, took a violent turn in the early fifties when

Reprinted, with permission, from Harish Narang, "Prospero in the Land of Calibans: *A Grain of Wheat,*" in *Politics as Fiction: The Novels of Ngugi wa Thiong'o* (New Delhi: Creative Books, 1995), 70–92.

the cup of Kenyans' patient suffering and humiliation at the hands of both the settlers and the colonial government began to overflow.

The freedom movement was the result of ills of colonisation affecting almost all tribes in Kenya. Their lands were taken away from them by the Europeans. Their education cut, their freedom curtailed, through forced labour, their wages made miserably low and their pride and dignity trampled through disallowance of observance of tribal customs and rituals and finally through the practice of obnoxious colour bar (MMW:74).

Although, as stated earlier, the struggle against colonisation began almost simultaneously with the act of colonisation, such acts of resistance were both spontaneous and sporadic. These acts obviously did not have much impact because of lack of perspective, proper planning and coordination among various sections of the society.

The most violent phase of the freedom movement occurred between the years 1952 and 1957. It all began "when the most moderate demands made in 1951 were turned down by the British Socialist Government (and) a tougher attitude became apparent in the inner councils of the Africans" (MMD:43). The basic reason had, of course, been the British government's policy of taking over the most fertile land from the Africans and giving it to Europeans to cultivate. This led to a chronic shortage of land in the African reserves. As a result, thousands of unemployed youths were forced to work on European farms at miserably low wages and in appalling conditions.

The post–second world war phase saw a new revolutionary atmosphere in Kenya. The social and economic grievances became plainer as more and more Africans became educated and they began to understand that the social system was not immutable. Moreover, thousands of Kenyan soldiers who had recently returned from war duties abroad had travelled widely and seen Europeans at close quarters in their own homegrounds. As Bildad Kaggia, himself a war-returnee, puts it:

> We could no longer accept the belief that a mzungu was better than an African. This generally pervasive feeling brought about the formation of organisations like the "40 group" which was mainly made up of ex-servicemen. These young-men could not accept the repressive methods in the reserves. (RF:66)

The granting of independence to India and Pakistan also inspired ordinary Kenyans, who were now getting more impatient with each passing day. Their revolt against the colonial masters manifested itself in many ways. They, for instance, resented the patronising attitude of the clergy, who though professing christian brotherhood, regarded the African christians as inferior beings. Kariuki sums up this resentment in the following words:

> When the British came with their missionaries, traders and administrators we felt they had something to teach us which were good. Education, medicine, farming and industrial techniques, these we welcomed. As a tribe the Euro-

peans had certain characteristics which were perhaps, not pleasant. Quick to anger, inhospitable, aloof, boorish and insensitive, they often behaved as if God created Kenya and us for their use. They accepted the dignity of a man as long as his skin was white. (MMD:41)

The trade unions too were clamouring for more rights and better working conditions. There were a number of strikes. This brought an offensive from the settlers and the government in the form of "Kenya Plan." As the details of this notorious move to convert Kenya into "whiteman's country" became known in 1949, the radicals among the Kenyans whose political awareness had been steadily increasing over the years decided to launch a final "do or die" battle for the liberation of Kenya, accepting the alternative of violence "fully realising the suffering it would bring on all of them."

Once the decision was taken to go for militant actions, the first step was to ensure mass support for those who had gone underground. This was achieved through the administration of an "oath" to groups of people. "The unity of numbers was our strongest, indeed almost our only weapon, and plans for cementing that unity with the Movement of the oath were put in train" (MMD:43).

The moment the government came to know about the administration of the oath, it came down heavily on not only those who were involved in it but also on a large number of innocent people. The act of "oath" was condemned in the most derogatory terms. This is how Margery Perham describes it in her Foreword to Kariuki's book:

The movement was fostered and bound together by secret and graded oaths, and the bestiality of the more advanced of these was so revolting to Europeans, and not only to them, that it seemed to many that those who used such methods ceased to be normal human beings (MMD:14).

However, Kariuki himself has the following explanation to offer:

It is easy enough for anyone who knows my people to understand that it was spontaneous decision that they should be bound together in unity by a simple oath. . . . It started slowly, indeed regretfully, and was an oath of unity and brotherhood in the struggle for our land and our independence. (MMD:49)

In the opinion of Bildad Kaggia, "Given the settler's hold on Kenya, the resistance movement had to be secret and underground. The oath ensured the secrecy of membership and activities" (RF:113).

The harsh and brutal measures taken by the government to stop the oath proved to be counterproductive as more and more young people impatient for a change took the oath. The movement became increasingly radical and soon "developed by action and reaction into a full-scale rebellion involving the soul of my people" (MMD:49).

It was during a raid on the oathing ceremonies at Naivasha that the police party is first reported to have heard the term "Mau Mau," a name with which they subsequently tried to damn the entire national freedom movement in Kenya, although as Kaggia says, "we ourselves had no particular name for it in the early days." The word "Mau Mau" has no meaning in either Gikuyu or Swahili and there are interesting speculations about its origin. Some suggest that the expression was arrived at through transposition of the word "Uma-Uma"—out, out—in Gikuyu, which referred to the desire of the Africans that the Europeans leave Kenya. Another explanation offered is that a witness at the Naivasha trial used the expression "mumumumu," referring to the whispered voices at the oathing ceremonies. This was misheard by journalists as "Mau Mau" and so reported in the story. Njama, however, links the expression to the Gikuyu word "Muma" meaning oath, used by a witness at the Naivasha trial and which a police officer was unable to pronounce or spell correctly. He, therefore, created his own pronunciation—Mau Mau.

Whatever the circumstances of origin of the expression, the name "Mau Mau" is "an illustration of how successful propaganda can damn an entire movement to which thousands sacrificed everything, including their lives, by attaching to it an appellation that conjures up all the cliches about the 'dark continent' which still crowd the European mind."[1]

As the movement grew in strength, simultaneous with the most repressive measures used against the Kenyans at large and the Gikuyu in particular, the British government let loose most foul propaganda to paint the entire movement in total black. At the Kapenguria trial, the Deputy Prosecutor, for instance, referred to "Mau Mau" as "a sort of Stern gang." The government tried hard to describe it as primarily a Gikuyu rebellion, lacking any all-Kenya basis and failing to get any support across tribes:

> The Mau Mau movement was in fact a rebellion and in the main, the rebellion of a single tribal group, that of the Kikuyu, with some kindred and neighbouring group, the Kamba, Meru and Embu, affecting in a varying but lesser degree. (MMD:12–13)

Similarly, Margery Perham is of the opinion that "the Mau Mau movement, however, failed to extend beyond the Kikuyu and those groups closely linked with them" (MMD:19).

The entire propaganda machinery of the government swung into action, trying to convince the Kenyans at large that those who had taken to the bush were thirsty for the blood of everyone else. L.B.S. Leakey too in his *Defeating Mau Mau* has painted a one-sided and completely distorted picture of the Kenyan reality:

> . . . the noble whiteman, who fervently engaged in bringing civilisation, christianity, education and the "good life" to Kenya's backward natives, was sud-

denly forced to defend self and property, law and order, peace and morality against the treacherous attack of atavistic savages gone mad with a blood lust.[2]

Again, concerted efforts were made to suppress or underplay the real causes of the movement. Margery Perham, for instance, believed that the Gikuyu had lost only a very small portion of land to European settlers and as such their sense of increasing oppression was "more psychological than reasoned."

The Kenyans, both during the freedom struggle, and after the end of hostilities, have tried to correct this gross distortion of their heroic struggle on each of the above counts:

> The mzungu explanations are not just unconvincing, they are lies which must be corrected. "Mau Mau" must be represented in its true perspective. It must be recognised and praised for the true liberation movement it was, the first of its kind of the continent. (RF:193)

Mau Mau was, therefore, not, as has been sought to be portrayed by the British, a Gikuyu primitive organisation. It was in fact an organisation formed by KAU militants who had lost faith in constitutional methods of fighting for independence. It was, therefore, ready to achieve that end through any means. In fact, this act of putting the movement in its true perspective not only had a welcome effect on the morale of the Kenyans but it also opened the eyes of the common Britishers about the true motives of their government in Africa.

They were surprised and indignant to hear about how their own government was opposing Africans. This was news to them. At that time the majority of English people believed that their government in the African colonies was a benevolent one which "worked very hard to uplift the African." They felt ashamed to hear that the main task of "their" government was to exploit Africa and to do everything possible to keep Africans poor and backward (RF:45).

The freedom movement, contrary to the false propaganda unleashed by both the settlers and the colonial government, was the result of colonisation affecting almost all tribes in Kenya. The forcible "alienation" of land for exclusive European use, the acts of forced labour at miserably low wages, the disallowance of observance of tribal customs and rituals and the observance of colour bar all compounded together led to a situation wherein a solution to all these ills was sought to be achieved through the single demand for national freedom.

As in the case of motives of the movement, so also with respect to the details of the sufferings of Kenyans during the struggle, the colonial government told blatant lies. News of atrocities on common Kenyans in the reserves, on those who had been detained in specially created camps and on those who sought refuge in the jungles was suppressed while details of raids by guerilla fighters were blown out of proportion to malign the movement. But the truth, they say, is like sand held in a closed fist, which always manages to slip out and be revealed. So did the details of gory killings and cruelties perpetrated on Kenyans, particularly during the Emergency:

> A significant sector of the European settler community tended to interpret the emergency declaration and legislation as promulgating a sort of "open season" on Kikuyu, Embu and Meru tribesmen. Forced confessions, beatings, robbery of stock, food and clothing, brutalising of various sorts and outright killings were frequent enough occurrences to arouse a fear in the heart of most Kikuyu that the intent of the whitemen was to eliminate the whole Kikuyu tribe. (MMW:71)

The magnitude of the toll of this "open season" can be gauged from the fact that during the Emergency alone some 10,000 Africans were killed by the security forces and over 80,000 were detained in various camps. Here they were subjected to indescribable brutalities. No detainee was released until he had been passed along a security clearance channel known as "Pipe line." Among the Emergency casualties not recorded are the victims of the "Pipe line" who were injured and permanently disabled by torture to extract confession.

Manyani was the largest and perhaps the most notorious camp. This is what Kariuki, himself a detainee at the camp, has to say about the conditions there:

> "Manyani," the largest camp, capable of holding up to 30,000 of us, is now a word deeply entrenched in the language of every tribe in Kenya, and no one hopes to understand the present temper of Kenya African politics without some awareness of the life led by our 80,000 detainees during those emergency years. (MMD:27)

Conditions in the reserves were no better either, where the chiefs, the homeguards and other such henchmen ruled the roost with the help of local administrative authorities:

> They said that things were very bad there and that the Reserves at this time were no place for young men, who were being chased and arrested on the slightest pretext. Many of them in desperation had already run away into the forest to escape this harrying. (MMD:43)

Even Marjery Perham was forced to concede that the authorities were guilty of acts of torture:

> In the early years some incidents of the torture of prisoners came to light. When I was in Kenya in 1953, I heard stories of harsh treatment and I made my own protest to the Governor. The death of eleven hard-core prisoners at

Hola camp at the hands of African warders in 1959 shocked the British opinion and led to a searching enquiry into the incident.[3] Besides Hola and Manyani, there were many other camps like Lari and Langata where similar massacres of innocent people who had been detained illegally, took place.

With the help of tens of thousands of British troops specially flown for the purpose, the government launched the notorious "Operation Anvil" against both the civilians in cities[4] and the fighters in forests which hardened the attitude of the guerillas who became "desperate men whose souls were filled with the hatred born on both sides in the travail of any war." The intensification of the military operations against them instead of demoralising them had a salutary effect on the fighters. "Out of dire necessity the groups of largely illiterate peasants who went into the forests became under their great generals, experts at guerila warfare, and they defied the might of Britain and Kenya for four years" (MMD:62).

With all their sophisticated weapons and war machinery, as also trained troops, the British government could not crush the freedom movement. Fighting against heavy odds of scarce resources, lack of training, etc., and against superior forces, the guerillas covered themselves with glory by continuing the struggle for more than four years, which earned them universal acclaim. Among them was a British general who advised the government to give up, since the movement could not be stamped out by force. The movement brought to the fore a number of truly great soldiers by any standards of military warfare. To name only a few, Dedan Kimathi, Stanley Mathenge, Gitau Matenjagwo, Ihura Kareri, Manyeki Wangombe, Kago Mboko, Mbaria and Waruhiu Itote were some who were constantly feared by the British government, British soldiers and their helpers.

Apart from the successes in the field, the political achievements of the struggle were also far reaching:

> As to what "Mau Mau" achieved, only blind people could not appreciate the many concessions which the British government granted Kenya. . . . These concessions were what KAU had been demanding for years. During the early months of the Emergency the colonial secretary said no change would be possible until the revolt was quashed. But before the beginning of the struggle, there was no sign of any of them being granted. The British government followed one concession by another, and it was clear that while the British tried on the one hand to discredit "Mau Mau" as a primitive organisation whose only aim was to return the tribe to the past, another part of the government accepted the fact that "Mau Mau" was political and that hostilities would only be ended with political advancement for Africans. (RF:194–195)

In the opinion of Kaggia, the following changes were effected within a short time as a direct result of the armed struggle. These changes eventually paved the way for Kenyan independence:

1. In 1954 a new constitution (the Lyttleton Plan) started giving Africans for the first time in Kenya's history, one Minister in the government.
2. In 1955, the Couts Commission was appointed to work on demarcation of African constituencies and to devise a method of voting for Africans.
3. In the same year the ban on political parties was lifted and Africans were allowed to form district political parties.
4. In 1956, two portfolios were given to Africans.
5. In 1957, limited voting rights were given to Africans and the number of African Members of Parliament increased to eight.
6. In 1958, the number of African Members of Parliament increased to fourteen.
7. In 1959, the Emergency Governor, Sir Evelyn Baring, was removed from office. He had vowed for years to "crush" Mau Mau.
8. Britain agreed to a round table conference with the African members to decide on Kenya's future (RF:195). Let us once again borrow the words of Kaggia to sum up the impact of the "Mau Mau" struggle on not only Kenya but also on the entire African politics:

The Mau Mau struggle, whether one likes it or not, will stand in history as one of the greatest liberation struggles in Africa. It was the first of its kind on the continent. Its heroes will be remembered by generations to come. Kenya would do a great service to future generations by establishing permanent monuments to this noble struggle. The greatness of the "Mau Mau" struggle becomes more striking when one remembers that the fighters had no outside contacts, arms supply or money. "Mau Mau" relied on its own resources. Money was collected from followers and supporters. In addition to capturing arms, the soldiers manufactured their own. It is time to recognise their achievements. Long live "Mau Mau": Long live the freedom of Kenya, which it fought for and brought about. (RF:195–196)

This, in brief, is the history of the "Mau Mau" struggle on various aspects of which many Kenyan writers writing in English including Ngugi wa Thiong'o have based their writings. Each writer has, of course, interpreted this part of Kenyan history in his own way. We will now discuss Ngugi's *A Grain of Wheat*. It will be our endeavour firstly to discover his point of view from his writings and secondly evaluate this first vis-a-vis the views of another major writer on the same theme—Meja Mwangi in his *Carcase for Hounds* (1974)—and then the truth about the struggle as enumerated above by major participant historians like J.M. Kariuki, Karari Njama, Bildad Kaggia and Oginga Odinga.

A Grain of Wheat is a novel about the freedom movement. Through a series of flashbacks in the lives and experiences of his principal characters— Mugo, Gikonyo, Mumbi, Kihika, Karanja and Thompson—all of whom reflect on it on the eve of the Uhuru, Ngugi is able to weave, extremely skillfully, a multi-faced but a powerful picture of the struggle. Both through direct narration and through reflections by his characters, Ngugi creates an atmosphere of hopes and fears, successes and defeats, loyalties and betrayals that were, as we have seen above, typical of the period of the struggle. *A Grain of Wheat* is the story of a group of people from a particular village—Thabai—who are about to celebrate the Uhuru day which is only four days later. This however is also the occasion when each one of them, including the White D.O. Thompson, takes stock of his or her role in the freedom struggle, particularly during the Emergency and the "Mau Mau" phase of the struggle. Mugo, now a village hero, recalls his betrayal of Kihika, the legendary youthful revolutionary who was hanged. Gikonyo recalls his confession of the oath during interrogation in the detention camp. Mumbi recalls the circumstances under which she was forced to submit herself to Karanja, the village Chief and a collaborator of the colonial administration. Karanja recalls his subservience to the D.O., while Thompson and his wife recall their role as a part of the white colonial administration which was trying its best to "civilize" the Africans.

The novel opens with Mugo, a resident of Thabai village in Kamanduru district and a civilian who had suffered extensively at the hands of the government during the freedom struggle, getting up early in the morning for going to cultivate his shamba. Our first impression of him is that he is a strange old man who appears to be seeing phantoms where there are none; one who, like Hester Pryne in Hawthorne's *Scarlet Letter*, seems to be guarding something within him which he feels everyone is out to seek and unravel on this fateful day. Among the first persons he meets is Githua, a fellow victim of the state violence who had not only lost a leg in it but who seems to have gone soft in the head too. "I tell you before the Emergency, I was like you before the white man did this to me with bullets, I could work with both hands" (GW:4).

As we already know from the accounts of Kariuki, Njama, General China and Bildad Kaggia, the story of Githua is the story of thousands who were disabled during the struggle and Githua's remarks put Mugo in a mood for reminiscing about the cruelties of the white man, the utterly senseless killings and tortures that they indulged in. Passing by the hut of an old woman, Mugo recalls how her only son Gitogo, who was both deaf and dumb,[5] was killed by the government troops during one of their raids on the village:

> People were being collected into the town square, the market place, for screening. Gitogo ran to a shop, jumped over the counter and almost fell into the shopkeeper whom he found cowering amongst the empty bags. . . . "Halt!" the whiteman shouted. Gitogo continued running. Something hit him at the back. He raised his arms in the air. He fell on his stomach. Apparently the bullet had touched his heart. The soldier left his place. Another Mau Mau terrorist had been shot dead. (GW:6)

The last sentence—*Another Mau Mau terrorist had been shot dead*—seems to "touch" the readers with the same force as the bullet that had killed

Gitogo. With this one sentence Ngugi had nailed all those lies which talked of "Mau Mau" terrorists being killed in "encounters" with the troops.

Back from the Shamba, Mugo is visited on behalf of the party by a group of village elders: Warui, Wambui and Gikonyo, who want him to lead the celebrations for the Uhuru by making the main speech of the day. Sitting with them and discussing the history of the country, Mugo recalled—". . . the day the whiteman came to the country, clutching the book of God in both hands, a magic witness that whiteman was a messenger from the Lord. His tongue was coated with sugar; his humility was touching" (GW:12). Gradually, however, something else happened which surprised the people around:

> Soon the people saw the whiteman had imperceptibly acquired more land to meet the growing needs of his position. He had already pulled the grass-thatched hut and erected a more permanent building. Elders of the land protested. They looked beyond the laughing face of the whiteman and suddenly saw a long line of other red strangers who carried not the Bible, but the sword. (GW:14)

There could not have been a more precise yet more forthright portrayal of that part of Kenyan history towards the end of the nineteenth century when the British launched a two-pronged attack by the clergy and the soldier to colonise Kenya. It was then, Mugo recalls, that Harry Thuku had appeared on the scene telling them of the discontent with taxation, forced labour on white settlers' land and of uprooting of thousands as a result of resettlement schemes for white soldiers from abroad. It was after he had formed a party and had been arrested that the first protest rally took place. It was 1923, Warui, another elder of the village who was in the crowd, vividly recalls:

> On the fourth day they marched forward, singing. The police who waited for them with guns fixed with bayonets, opened fire. Three men raised their arms in the air. It is said that as they fell down they clutched soil in their fists. Another volley scattered the crowd. A man and a woman fell, their blood spurted out. People ran in all directions. Within a few seconds the big crowd had dispersed; nothing remained but fifteen crooked watchers on the ground, outside the State house.[6]

Mugo then goes on to recall the changing mood of the people—a change from one of defiance to one of militant struggle. Kihika, a fighter who had inspired hundreds of young men, had said in an address: "This is not 1920. What we now want is action, a blow which will tell." Kihika, like many others before, had exposed the game of deceit played by the colonisers in the guise of religion:

> We went to their church. Mubia, in white robes, opened the Bible. He said. Let us kneel down to pray. We knelt down. Mubia said. Let us shut our eyes. We

did. You know his remained open so that he could read the word. When we opened our eyes our land was gone and the Sword of flames stood on guard. As for Mubia, he went on reading the word, beseeching us to lay our treasure in heaven where no moth would corrupt them. But he laid his on earth, our earth. (GW:15)

Once again, the last sentence—*But he laid his on earth, our earth*—exposes the two-pronged attack of the colonial British—through settlers as well as the church—more forcefully then many a long document on the issue.

After the arrest of Kenyatta, Mugo recalls, Kihika disappeared into the forest, later to be followed by a handful of youngmen from Thabai and Rung'ei. Ngugi's message is clear: this is how Mau Mau was born—out of the frustrations of the people to persuade the colonial masters to restore to them what was theirs. It may not be out of place here at this juncture to refer to another novel based on the same theme written by Meja Mwangi— *Carcase for Hounds*—which suggests an altogether different reason for the beginning of Mau Mau activities.[7] General Haraka, the hero of Mwangi's novel, who is the leader of a group of guerillas, recalls how he had become a Mau Mau activist:

Haraka remembered well when the white man struck him. It came as a resounding surprise, right across his face and into his heart. Though he was stunned, his reaction was quick. Spontaneous. He struck back a blow full of hate and distaste and protest against oppression. The D.C. collapsed and lay unmoving on the dusty floor of the office. For a second, a surge of well-being, of selfish revenge flooded him so that he stood rooted to the spot. Then a splinter of fear wedged its way into his mind. Had he killed him? No, the man was only unconscious. Then the magnitude of his crime sank in. Striking a white man was unheard of. Striking a District Commissioner senseless was unthinkable. The other white men would surely take revenge. An affront to the Queen! They might even shoot him. . . . He had to run. Where to? *Naturally* into the forest, to the little terrorist leader. (CH:20, emphasis added)

Thus Maguru, son of Nyaga, is transformed into a freedom fighter by exchanging blows with his boss, the D.C., and by fleeing from punishment. The subtle use of the word *"Naturally"* in the last sentence cleverly suggests that most freedom fighters were such criminals fleeing from the law.

Ngugi, like Mwangi in *Carcase for Hounds,* also recalls through his characters, many raids by the freedom fighters but unlike Mwangi he places these raids in their proper perspective. They raided to obtain rations and ammunition, as also to cripple and destroy the machinery of oppression. Kihika and his fellow fighters were not a gang of terrorists who derived sadistic pleasure out of such raids and killings. As Kihika tells Mugo "We don't just kill anybody. . . . we are not murderers. We are not hangmen like Robson—killing men or women without cause of purpose" (GW:166).

As we know from the accounts by various freedom fighters the torture of civilians had begun on a mass scale simultaneously with the militant struggle, a fact that is borne out by the passing of over a million Kenyans through the concentration camps and the "pipeline" during the four years of the emergency. "Kihika was tortured. Some say that the neck of a bottle was wedged into his body through the anus as the white people in the Special Branch tried to wrest the secrets of the forest from him" (GW:17).

Compared to the stories of atrocities or detainees in Manyani, Hola and Lari camps, Ngugi's above description appears to be an artistic understatement.

Warui, the oldest of those who survived, recalls the role of Wambui: "Wambui was not very old, although she had lost most of her teeth. During the Emergency, she carried secrets from the villagers to the forest and back to the villagers and towns. She knew the underground movements in Nakuru, Njoro, Elburgon and other places in and outside Rift valley" (GW:19).

Several women had played a very heroic role in the freedom movement—the names of Me Kitilili and Mary Nyanjiru spring to the mind immediately—and through Wambui and Mumbi, Ngugi is paying a tribute to those heroic women warriors. He was to do this again through the character of "the woman" in his *The Trial of Dedan Kimathi* (1976). In fact, with *A Grain of Wheat* Ngugi began a conscious attempt to not only create positively powerful women characters but also to make them more "visible" by providing them with greater "space" in his books. This effort culminated in his portrayal of Wariinga as the protagonist in his *Devil on the Cross.*

The suppression of the movement, as observed earlier, had brought untold miseries on a very large section of the civilian population. *A Grain of Wheat,* highlights this through the story of Gikonyo and Mumbi—a very poignant portrayal of their love for each other through the tribulations of detention and physical suffering during the Emergency. Here is Gikonyo on his own and Mugo's detention. "Do you know what it was to live in detention? It was easier, perhaps with those of us not labelled hard-core. But Mugo was. So he was beaten, and yet would not confess the oath" (GW: 26). Being in detention was in many ways worse than being in prison because "in prison you know your crime. You know your terms. So many years, one, ten, thirty—after that you get out." In detention, however, one was in the state of hope and despair simultaneously, the very suspense of being innocent or guilty gnawed at one's vitals every day, every hour, killing something within permanently. Mugo had suffered such a fate for years while in detention. All this the village elders recall while sitting at Mugo's place and waiting for a response from him for their request to him to lead the Uhuru celebrations. However, Mugo refuses to give the delegation a firm commitment about his very participation in the Uhuru celebrations, let alone leading them.

The scene now shifts to the D.O.'s office at nearby Githima and Ngugi presents the whiteman's response to the Uhuru. Thompson, the D.O., a loyal

British bureaucrat, too cannot reconcile himself to this changed new reality and has therefore decided to quit his job as well as the country. He too reminisces. He believes that all that they had built in Kenya with so much of hard work would now be wasted since the blacks are incapable of maintaining it, let alone building on it. "Would these things remain after Thursday? Perhaps for two months: and then—test tubes and beakers would be broken or lie unwashed on the cement, the hot houses and seed beds strewn with wild plants and the outer bush which had been carefully hemmed, would gradually creep into a litter-filled compound" (GW:38).

Thompson also recalls another milestone in his career in Kenya: the strike at the Rira detention camp when he was the officer in charge. "At Rira, the tragedy of his life occurred. A hunger strike, a little beating and eleven detainees died: The fact leaked out. Because he was officer in charge, Thompson's name was bandied about in the House of Commons and in the world press" (GW:42).[8]

His regret is over two things: the leaking of the news and the bandying about of his name. Thompson's regret, like that of most whites at that time, was also because of the realisation that they, the whites, too were dispensable. "Thompson felt that silent pain, almost agony that people feel at the knowledge that they might not be indispensable after all" (GW:42).

His wife too has similar feelings which she too like her husband tries to hide behind her doubts about the capabilities of their African successors: "Was she really using this kitchen for the last time? Would she never, never see Githima again? Would her flowers mean anything to whoever would take her place in this house?" (GW:44).

Thompson is one of those who considered the British colonial expansion to be an act of moral crusade to civilize the world. The British, he believed, were like "Prospero in Africa"—the land of Calibans. Having accepted that position, he goes on to justify the British action against the freedom fighters:

> No government can tolerate anarchy, no civilization can be built on this violence and savagery. Mau Mau is evil: a movement which if not checked will mean complete destruction of all the values on which our civilization has thriven. (GW:72)

However, it was left to Kihika and scores of young men who had heard the stories of whitemen from their elders to discover the real face of Prospero:

> Kihika's interest in politics began when he was a small boy and sat under the feet of Warui listening to stories of how the land was taken from black people. . . . Warui needed only a listener: he recounted the deeds of Waiyaki and other warriors who by 1900 had been killed in the struggle to drive out the whiteman from the land: of young Harry and the fate that befell the 1923 procession; of Muthirigu and the mission schools that forbade circumcision in order to eat, like insects, both the roots and the stems of the Gikuyu society.

Unknown to those around him, Kihika's heart hardened towards "these people," long before he had even encountered a white face. Soldiers came back from the war and told stories of what they had seen in Burma, Egypt, Palestine and India; wasn't Mahatma Gandhi the saint, leading the Indian people against the British rule? Kihika fed on these stories, his imagination and daily observations told him the rest; from early on, he had visions of himself, a saint, leading the Gikuyu people to freedom and power. (GW:72–73)

One has only to contrast this with General Haraka's reminiscences about his youth and the way he became a freedom fighter (CH:20), to know the difference between Meja Mwangi's portrayal of the freedom struggle and Ngugi's:

He thought back to the time when he was not a general, not General Haraka, but simply Maguru son of Nyaga. And the Chief he was no Chief but merely Kahuru son of Wamai. Haraka then thought further back to the time when they first met at the forest station, when it was first started. Their families came from different parts of the country to work for Mr. Jackson, clearing the jungle and planting trees. The two youngmen were no more than fifteen. There was no chief in the village then. The tree men were organised by a foreman under the Forest Officer, Mr. Jackson. As the village grew it knit in the vast family of over thirty families. The younger generation formed a society of their own. This was split in to sections of adolescent gangs, each led by a self-appointed youth able to dominate the others. *They stole green maize from their parents' gardens and raped village maidens in hordes.* (CH:18, emphasis added)

In fact, Mwangi makes General Haraka an ex-accomplice of the colonial government:

He remembered back to the time he headed the village security police before becoming the first chief of Pinewood Forest station; that was before the Emergency and the Curfew and the forest fighters were heard of. (CH:19)

So here is the leader of a group of freedom fighters in the jungles—General Haraka—who was in his youth a juvenile gangster, expert at stealing green maize and raping village maidens in hordes. No wonder the general himself refers to his group as a "gang" and Captain Kingsley considers them to be nothing but "murderer Haraka and his band of cut-throats" (CH:11).

In sharp contrast Ngugi, as we have seen above, has made use of the actual events—the struggle by Waiyaki and the Procession in Nairobi for the release of Harry Thuku in which scores of Africans were killed—as a background for his fictional characters like Kihika.

Ngugi's forest fighter Kihika, incidentally, is dead before the action of the novel begins. Unlike Mwangi's General Haraka, he is a very sensitive youngman who drew inspiration from the Indian National movement, thereby showing a remarkable maturity of approach in recognising the commonness of all such struggles against the colonial British. " 'Do you know,' he told his youthful friends Gikonyo, Mumbi, Karanja and others, 'why Gandhi succeeded? Because he made his people give up their fathers and mothers and serve their one Mother—India. With us Kenya is our mother' " (GW:83).[9] Kihika is an ideal freedom fighter, who realising that christianity had come to have a hold on the minds of many and that the priests were using it as a weapon to damn the freedom struggle, uses the same religious sentiment to arouse the people into action. Referring to the death of Christ, he says:

> In Kenya we want a death which will change things, that is to say, we want a true sacrifice. But first we have to be ready to carry the cross. I die for you, you die for me, we become a sacrifice for one another. So I can say you, Karanja, are Christ. I am Christ. Everybody who takes the oath of unity to change things in Kenya is a Christ. (GW:83)

Kihika is, in fact, a shrewd leader who uses various kinds of arguments to expose the real designs of the colonial masters. "My father's ten acres? That is not the important thing. Kenya belongs to black people. Can't you see that Cain was wrong? I am my brother's keeper. In any case, whether the land was stolen from Gikuyu, Ubabi or Nandi, it does not belong to the whiteman. And even if it did, shouldn't everybody have a share in the common shamba, our Kenya? Take your whiteman, anywhere, in the settled area. He owns hundreds and hundreds of acres of land. What about the black men who squat there, who sweat dry on the farms to grow coffee, tea, sisal, wheat and yet only get ten shillings a month?" (GW:85).

G.D. Killam in his essay on *A Grain of Wheat* in his *An Introduction to the Writings of Ngugi* observes that Ngugi is at "pains . . . to insure that his readers know that the struggle was a just one" (1980:53). He thus considers Kihika's speeches to be laboured. This is uncharitable, to say the least, since Kihika's speeches have a very forceful impact because of their spontaneity and directness, backed as they are by his conviction. Once again, in contrast, are the speeches of General Haraka who had only heard about land and other problems from his little leader and repeated them parrot-like (CH:54) which appear to be contrived completely.

The imposition of the Emergency created a host of other social problems for not only forest fighters like Kihika but for others as well. "More men were rounded up and taken to concentration camps named detention camps for the world outside Kenya. The platform at the railway station was not always empty; girls pined for their lovers behind cold huts and prayed that their young men would come quickly from the forest or from the camps" (GW:90). Unlike Mwangi, who shows General Haraka, Lieutenant Kimamo and others having serious doubts about their cause (CH:102), Ngugi shows them very resolute for their cause. "The detainees had agreed not to confess the oath, or give away details about Mau Mau: how could anybody reveal the binding force of the Agikuyu in their call for African freedom? They bore all the ills of the Whiteman, believing somehow that he who would endure unto the end would receive leaves of victory" (GW:91). The torture grew as the struggle gained strength. "A common game in Rira had been to bury a man, naked, in the hot sand, sometimes leaving him there overnight" (GW:116). Even those who were left behind in villages—mostly women, old people and young children—were not spared such torture. Mumbi, Gikonyo's wife, recalls:

> There were two huts. One belonged to my mother, the other was mine. They told us to remove our bedding and clothes and utensils. They splashed some petrol on the grass thatch of my mother's hut. I then idly thought this was unnecessary as the grass was dry. Anyway, they poured petrol on the dry thatch. The sun burnt hot. My mother sat on a stool by the pile of things from our huts and I stood beside her. I had a Gikoi on my head. The leader of the homeguards struck a match and threw it at the roof. It did not light, and the others laughed at him. They shouted and encouraged him. One of them tried to take the matches from him to demonstrate how it could be done. It became a game between them. At the fourth or fifth attempt the roof caught fire. Dark and blue smoke tossed from the roof, and the flames leaped to the sky. They went to my hut. I could not bear to see the game repeated, so I shut my eyes. (GW:122–123)

Whole villages were forced to dig trenches in most inhuman working conditions. Once again, Mumbi recalls: "They drove us into it, for, you see, there was a time limit. Women were allowed out two hours before sunset to go and look for food. Nobody else was allowed out: even school children had to remain in the village. Within days, the two hours of freedom were reduced to one. And as the time limit neared, even one hour of freedom was taken away. We were prisoners in the village, and the soldiers had built their camps all round to prevent any escape. We went without food. The cry of children was terrible to hear. The new D.O. did not mind the cries. He even permitted soldiers to pick women and carry them to their tents" (GW:166).

It is the perpetration of such atrocities that makes Mugo remark that "a Mzungu is not a man—always remember that—he is a devil."

Neither the fighters, nor the civilians are, however, scared of this naked show of sadistic brutalities. Nor do they turn their other cheek anymore: "We only hit back. You are struck on the left cheek. You turn the right cheek. One, two, three-sixty years. Then suddenly, it is always sudden, you say; I am not turning the other cheek any more. Your back to the wall, you strike back" (GW:126). Throughout the struggle, African collaborators played an important role on behalf of their white masters, not only justifying all that the colonial government did but also emphasising the futility of challenging the invincible might of the mzungu. Thus Karanja:

> The whiteman is strong. Don't ever forget that. I know, because I have tasted his power. Don't you ever deceive yourself that Jomo Kenyatta will ever be

released from Lodwar. And bombs are going to be dropped into the forest as the British did in Japan and Malaya. (GW:130)

Once caught into the logic of surrender and collaboration, Karanja sank deeper into such dependence:

> He sold the party and oath secrets, the price of remaining near Mumbi. Thereafter the wheel of things drove him into greater reliance on the whiteman. That reliance gave him power—power to save, to imprison, to kill. Men cowered before him; he despised and also feared them. Women offered their naked bodies to him; even some of the most respectable came to him by night. (GW:182)

Ngugi, in fact, goes on to show the complete dehumanisation of Karanja by the colonial machinery. When he shot the freedom fighters or innocent citizens, "they seemed less like human beings and more like animals. At first this had merely thrilled Karanja and made him feel a new man, a part of an invisible might whose symbol was the whiteman. Later, this consciousness of power, this ability to dispose of human life by merely pulling a trigger, so obsessed that it became a need" (GW:199).

Here then is Ngugi's portrayal of a traumatic phase in the history of Kenya—the so-called Mau Mau—a phase in which sections of a highly complex society comprised of people belonging to various African tribes, white settlers and Indians acted and reacted to events of violence in a highly emotionally surcharged and often contradictory manner. As P. Ochola-Ojero puts it:

> In A Grain of Wheat the author probes into the psychology of those characters who have undergone serious difficulties and consequent disillusionment but who during the time of emergency have found some meaning and purpose in life in the tough fight for their country's independence.[10]

However, the novel is not as has been stated by both Ochola-Ojero, and David Cook (1983:69) about the theme of betrayal alone, in which "all are guilty." While it may be true that most major characters have during some stage of their respective lives acted in a manner which may be contrary to the behaviour expected from them at that time—Mugo betrays Kihika, Gikonyo confesses the oath and Mumbi sleeps with Karanja—it cannot be held against them as "betrayal," particularly of the cause in question, namely, the freedom struggle. Mugo, for instance, redeemed himself much before his final confession when at Rira detention camp, he was singled out by Thompson for severe beatings. "Sometimes he would have the warders whip Mugo before the other detainees. Sometimes, in naked fury, he would snatch the whip from the warders and apply it himself" (GW:117). Furthermore he had saved a woman—Wambuku—from being beaten in the trenches.

The novel presents a very complex portrayal of the freedom struggle— the role of various sections of the society, their hopes and fears on the threshold of the freedom. The hopes of Warui, Wambui, General R and Lieutenant Koinandu, the fears of Mugo and of Karanja and the conflicting feelings of Gikonyo and Mumbi. Mixing fact with fiction—Kenyatta and Thuku with Kihika and Karanja—Ngugi creates a unique picture of freedom struggle, which is truer than history and more imaginative than ordinary fiction.

The villagers of Thabai represent the ordinary people of Kenya who, with all their human frailties and foibles, were forced to make compromises under terror and torture but still uphold the cause. Kihika represents the revolutionary youth who saw a basic unity in the struggle of the colonial world and who sacrificed everything for freedom. Karanja on the other hand represents the collaborationists who are basically cowards and who put self before society. Gikonyo and Mumbi, once again representing thousands of ordinary people, magnify those personal relationships which went to pieces under the Emergency through sheer physical separation for long periods. While focussing on those traumatic times which the Kenyans faced during their struggle for freedom, Ngugi also hints at the shape of things to come in independent Kenya. Although people danced and sang on the streets on the Uhuru day, showering praise on "Jomo and Kaggia and Oginga" and although they "recalled Waiyaki's heroic deeds," they were not unaware of their dream of independent Kenya as a Shamba for all turning sour. The way their M.P. grabs Mr. Burton's Green Hill Farm, denying Gikonyo and other villagers a chance of starting a cooperative farm, is symbolic of the ensuing struggle between the people and their leaders in new Kenya—a theme which Ngugi was to explore in his next novel, *Petals of Blood*.

Notes

1. B.M. Kaggia, Fred Kubai, J. Murumbi and Achieng Oneko in their Preface to *Mau Mau from Within*, Njama and Barnett, London, Modern Reader Paperback, 1970, p. 9.
2. Cited in his Forword to *Mau Mau from Within* by Njama and Barnett, op. cit., p. 17.
3. Kariuki, *Mau Mau Detainee*, Harmondsworth, Penguin, 1964, p. 12. Incidentally, Wole Soyinka, the Nobel-Laureate Nigerian playwright, poet and novelist, has an interesting story to tell about the killings at Hola being turned into a play called "Eleven Dead at Hola" during a performance of which he refused to go on stage because as an African he felt humiliated at the manner in which Africans were being depicted before a primarily European audience.
4. "In Operation Anvil 25,000 soldiers and police rounded up the entire African population of Nairobi—just over 100,000—and screened and dispatched to specially prepared detention camps all men between the ages of sixteen and thirty-five—the warrior age—from the so-called 'affected tribes'." Oginga Odinga, *Not Yet Uhuru*, London, Heinemann, 1967, p. 118.
5. The episode is based on an actual incident in which a cousin of Ngugi's was killed in similar circumstances.

6.   Ngugi, *A Grain of Wheat,* London, Heinemann, 1967, p. 14. This is a very interesting example of how Ngugi mixes fact with fiction, presenting actual historical events with the help of creative imagination.

7.   For a detailed comparison between Ngugi's *A Grain of Wheat* and Mwangi's *Carcase for Hounds,* see Narang, "Literature as Politics" in H.S. Gill (ed.) *Structures of Signification* vol. 2, New Delhi, Wiley (Eastern) Limited, 1991, pp. 332–343.

8.   As stated earlier, the reference is to an actual incident at Hola detention camp to which Wole Soyinka too has made a reference in his writings.

9.   It may be of interest here to mention that Bildad Kaggia, one of the leaders of the Kenyan national liberation movement like Ngugi's Kihika, mentions Moses and Gandhi as his inspirers: "My greatest 'heroes' became Gandhi and Moses, Moses—because he succeeded in liberating his people and Gandhi as my guide to modern methods of liberation." *Roots of Freedom,* Nairobi, East Africa Publishing House, 1978, p. 55.

10.   P. Ochola-Ojero, "Of Tares and Broken Handles, Ngugi Preaches: Themes of Betrayal in *A Grain of Wheat,*" in *Standpoints on African Literature,* ed. Chris L. Wanjala, Nairobi/Kampala/Dar es Salaam, East African Literature Bureau, 1973, p. 81.

References

Cook, David, and Michael Okenimkpe, *Ngugi wa Thiong'o: An Exploration of His Writings,* London: Longman, 1983.

Kaggia, Bildad, *Roots of Freedom 1921–63,* Nairobi: East African Publishing House, 1978.

Kariuki, J.M., *Mau Mau Detainee,* Harmondsworth: Penguin, 1964.

Mwangi, Meja, *Carcase for Hounds,* London: Heinemann, 1974.

Njama, Karari, and D. Barnett, *Mau Mau from Within,* London: Modern Reader Paperback, 1970.

The Structure of Symbolism in
A Grain of Wheat

BU-BUAKEI JABBI

Symbolism is of considerable functional vitality in the longer narratives of Ngũgĩ wa Thiong'o. His essays on literature, culture, and society may be largely reticent about symbolism as such.[1] And his creative works themselves may be more obviously concerned with political commitment and ideological gropings through diagnoses of power and evolving socioeconomic conditions in Kenya before and since Uhuru. At the same time, however, the texture and structure of his novels often reveal a keen awareness of the active organic relationship between vision and vehicle in much literary art. Ample evidence of such awareness may be seen from a survey of symbolism in any of his major fiction to date. In his fourth novel, *Petals of Blood,* for example, the trenchant socialist vision achieves much of its ideological poignancy and force of social commentary from a fairly varied system of expressive and structuring imagery or symbolism. But Ngũgĩ had already perfected his use of symbolism as a crucial narrative device much earlier in previous novels.[2]

The range of sources and materials he explores for the purposes of symbolic functioning in his narratives is varied and wide. But his fusing of broadly similar elements from disparate sources into cohesive acts or objects of symbolic operation is not so widely acknowledged as yet, many critics being usually content to remark isolated sources of influence at a time. As a beginning novelist, Ngũgĩ seemed fascinated, for instance, by the fact of identical motifs of landscape and of myth in parts of the Bible and Kikuyu folklore. W. J. Howard has accordingly observed in *The River Between* his practice of "blending two separate religious myths—Gikuyu and Christian" in his narrative.[3] Thus the pervasive seer-savior imagery in that novel, like its recurrent hill-ascending motif, is a conflation of parallel elements found in the two traditions. Each of these modes of symbolism thereby becomes a functional correlate to the general themes of syncretism and reconciliation which are central to the story. In *A Grain of Wheat* as well, the art motif which rounds

Reprinted with permission from Indiana University Press from Bu-Buakei Jabbi, "The Structure of Symbolism in *A Grain of Wheat,*" *Research in African Literatures* 16, no. 2 (Summer 1985): 210–42.

off the narrative has been rather exclusively ascribed to the influence of D. H. Lawrence.[4] But that motif is only one element in a general symbolism of creativity sustained from early in the story with the help of allusions to the creation myth of Gikuyu and Mumbi as the primordial parents of the Mugikuyu people. Such fusions and assimilations of cross-cultural parallels and similarities into symbolic moments in Ngūgī's work demand a more balanced critical response, since they are often crucial to the overall vision and message in the works where they occur.

In addition to these symbolic fusions, each tradition may also be a source of discrete allusions, references, and prefigurative motifs in his novels. Furthermore, features of local geography and vegetation, incidents of national history and personal experience, even elements of atmospheric or weather condition and related phenomena like sunshine or the moon may sometimes assume symbolic propensities in certain narrative contexts. But with respect to *The River Between,* when Howard refers to "the elaborate functional geography, the introduction of the double symbolic mythology, the large unifying cosmic image patterns,"[5] he is clearly being more exuberant and enthusiastic than the facts would seem to warrant. However, it is at least true that Ngūgī's major fiction increasingly aspires toward a symbolism that is on the whole at once functional and systemic in the narrative.

I

We may explore at the outset a few concepts that may facilitate our analysis of Ngūgī's literary symbolism, may help to point up some continuities in his use of the device from novel to novel, and perhaps may help to highlight some of its more probable pedigree in certain contexts. A few sets of broad distinctions are hereby proposed between the means or processes by which symbolic import is perceived or crystallized in different cases, between modes of amplifying such significations, and also between patterns of symbolic incidence or recurrence in a work of literature. Some of these concepts may also suggest plausible parallels and affinities with forms of indigenous African symbology outside literature, thereby revealing some of the ways in which forms of traditional expressivity may be utilized in modern literature.

First, two means of perceiving symbolic import or relevance in literature may be contradistinguished as *subjectivist* and *objectivist* symbolism, according to whether or not the symbolic import is mediated to the reader through a recognized fictive subjectivity. In subjectivist symbolism, so-called, there is usually a relatively objectified fictive consciousness who, on his or her own, actively forges the symbolism and perceives its significations invariably prior to or independent of the reader's perceiving of it. That is, the symbolic relevance or suggestiveness is apt to be discernibly induced or invoked by the independent perceptual act of the character; it is forged primarily in the furnace of his/her own intuitions, sensations, introspection, or meditativeness. Objectivist symbolism, on the other hand, tends to inhere in the objective givens of the work without any intervening mediation or sifting through the perceptual act of a fictive being or dramatis persona. That is, the reader perceives it, if at all, by sole dint of his/her own sensitivity.

This distinction is essentially perceptual. But it may be reinforced by the following sociological distinction drawn by Raymond Firth between what he calls "public" and "private" symbols[6]:

> In the study of symbolism by social scientists there are two fairly clearly recognised domains. In one, the province of sociologist and anthropologist, symbols are taken as being characteristic of sets or groups of people, of institutions or of types of situation. . . . [It] is the symbolism of collectivity—of myth, of ritual, of social structure—with which anthropologists are mainly occupied. As against this generalising viewpoint there is the broad psychological domain in which the study is made not exclusively but basically of symbolic forms presented by individuals, often not shared with other people, and corresponding essentially to personal interests, claims, stresses. The symbolism of dream, hallucination, prophetic revelation or drug-induced experience belongs in this domain; and so does much of the initial creativity of poetry and the visual arts. A great deal of this personal symbolism is private in the sense that it is intended to be, or construed to be exclusive to the individual concerned, offering his own particular solution to his problem of adaptation to some aspects of his immediate environment or to his conception of the world.

However, both of Firth's categories are equally capable of subjectivist evocation in literature, so that they do not correspond exactly to the distinctions I have proposed here. Nonetheless, his second category of "personal symbolism" is kith and kin to what I have defined as subjectivist symbolism; it is an effective means of depicting the inner decor and imagining intensity, intuition, and sensations of a character in literature.

There are many effective instances of both subjectivist and objectivist symbolism in Ngũgĩ's novels, sometimes occurring separately but at other times also mixed. A proper assessment of *A Grain of Wheat,* in particular, depends a good deal upon one's appreciation of their respective role and functioning in the narrative. Subjectivist symbolism, for instance, is used extensively to dramatize conditions of stress and distraint, although these uses invariably suggest the impact of Joseph Conrad.[7] Take the scenes in which Conrad's Razumov and Ngũgĩ's Mugo decide to give up Haldin and Kihika to the authorities in the respective stories when the latter revolutionists seek their help. As the inner turmoil incited by the intruding assassin begins to congeal into a decision to betray him, the traitor's inward urge is suddenly projected outward as a hallucinatory vision. Razumov thus sees a phantom of Haldin momentarily stretched flat on the snow, and he decides to trample over it.

> Suddenly on the snow, stretched on his back right across his path, he saw Haldin, solid, distinct, real, with his inverted hands over his eyes. . . . Razumov tackled the phenomenon calmly, [walking right through it]. . . . He made a few steps and muttered through his set teeth—"I shall give him up." (*UWE*, p. 38).

Ngũgĩ's Mugo has a comparable experience as he trudges along toward the local District Office, distractedly turning over in his mind whether to give Kihika up to the authorities.

> After walking a few steps from where he had sat, Mugo saw a strange spectacle. He stared at the corrugated-iron wall. His hair pulled away at the roots. He felt shocked pleasure in his belly. For Kihika's face was there, pinned-framed to the shop, becoming larger and more distorted the longer he gazed at it. The face, clear against a white surface, awakened the same excitement and terror he once experienced, as a boy, the night he wanted to strangle his aunt. There was a price on Kihika's head—a—price—on—Kihika's—head. (*GW*, p. 223)

Moments afterward Mugo informs on where to capture Kihika, who is later crucified on a tree. It must be noted, however, that Ngũgĩ does not use such subjectivist symbolism to depict only pathological conditions like stress, fear, or hallucination; he also uses it in depicting more positive conditions like personal aspirations, hopes, and other visionary sentiments.

Furthermore, the second set of analytical concepts we may explore here concern ways of amplifying symbolic significations. It may be generally instructive for the potential development of modern African fiction to resort here to traditional African ritual symbolism for our next pair of concepts. Victor W. Turner's copious researches and analyses of ritual among the Ndembu of northwestern Zambia highlight symbolism as perhaps its most salient single feature.[8] His collected data contain ample evidence of *polysemy* and *polyphony* as major properties of African ritual symbolism. Of these two concepts, however, Turner's explicit conceptual formulation emphasizes only polysemy, whereas his data and some of his descriptive comments would seem to suggest polyphony as an equally central feature of Ndembu ritual symbolism. Instead of identifying the two as distinct properties of that symbolism, each in its own right, as the evidence seems to suggest, Turner's formulation deceptively collapses them into a single category but with much greater awareness of the polysemous dimension. There is much analytical potency in regarding the two concepts as distinct, one from the other; they may be related, but they are not an inseparable unity.

Turner defines "the 'polysemy' or multivocality" of ritual symbols as "the fact that they possess many significations simultaneously" (*Ritual Process,* p. 37), as the "multiplicity of senses" which a single symbol may be capable of evoking in any one context (*Forest of Symbols,* p. 54). The concept is repeatedly stated in his book on the subject. For example:

> By these terms I mean that a single symbol may stand for many things. This property of individual symbols is true of ritual as a whole. . . . Certain dominant or focal symbols conspicuously possess this property of multivocality which allows for the economic representation of key aspects of culture and belief. Each dominant symbol has a "fan" or "spectrum" of referents, which are interlinked by what is usually a simple mode of association, its very simplicity enabling it to interconnect a wide variety of *significata*. (*Forest of Symbols,* p. 50)

> Such symbols exhibit the properties of condensation, unification of disparate referents, and polarisation of meaning. A single symbol, in fact, represents many things at the same time: it is multivocal, not univocal. (*Ritual Process,* p. 48)

Although Turner uses "multivocality" as synonymous with polysemy, it is clear that his formulation of this concept is confined to the sense of semantic complexity as such, to the multiplicity of significations per single symbol.

Nonetheless, some of his descriptive and analytical accounts of Ndembu ritual tend to infer an additional means of amplifying symbolic signification in the ritual process. For example, the following observations by him would seem to constitute a sufficient basis for a definitive conception of polyphony as a distinct property of Ndembu ritual symbolism and therefore as an intrinsic concept in its own right:

> Each kind of Ndembu ritual contains a multitude of symbols. One might almost say that it consists of symbols or that it is a *system* of symbols. (*Drums of Affliction,* p. 16)

> In an Ndembu ritual context, almost every article used, every gesture employed, every song or prayer, every unit of space and time, by convention stands for something other than itself. It is more than it seems, and often a good deal more. The Ndembu are aware of the expressive or symbolic function of ritual elements. (*Ritual Process,* p. 15)

Polyphony, then, may be said to be the coming together of separate symbols to form one functional chorus within a specific expressive context. So whereas polysemy is perhaps best conceived of as the multiplicity of senses or referents per single symbol, polyphony may be seen instead as the multiplicity of symbols or the combined simultaneous functioning of various symbols within a single expressive act or context. And mere successive recurrence of one or more symbols in an entire sequence of ritual or literary performance would not of itself suffice as polyphony. They must be concomitant and coincident within a relatively identifiable unit of expressive act, scene, episode, or context.

A brief illustration of such concomitant polyphony of ritual symbolism may be taken from Turner's own analysis of the Ndembu *Wubwang'u* ritual of twinship, a ritual sequence performed as a restorative or therapeutic "remedy" of the "overperformance" of a woman "who is expected to bear or who has already borne a set of twins" (*Ritual Process*, pp. 40–79). This specific illustration and Turner's analysis of it refer to only one "episode" or unit-scene from the whole sequence (*Ritual Process*, pp. 56–61). The scene is set as follows:

> The *mudyi* tree (the "milk-tree"), focal symbol of the girls' puberty rites, also appears in the twin ritual. Characteristically, it appears in an episode that portrays the mystical unity of opposites. After the medicines for the basket have been collected, the senior male practitioner cuts a pliant wand of *mudyi*, and another of *muhotuhotu*. These are taken near the source of a stream. The wands are planted on either bank of the stream, opposite one another, their tips are bent over to form an arch [over the stream], and they are bound together. The *muhotuhotu* wand lies on top of the *mudyi* wand. The complete arch is called *mpanza* or *kuhimpa*, a verbal noun meaning "exchanging." (*Ritual Process*, p. 56)

Turner identifies here at least six different symbols or bases of symbolic import in joint interaction. The first set of symbolic bases comprises the three natural elements: the two separate twigs of *muhotuhotu* and *mudyi* plants and the waters of the stream. These three objects are said to derive their respective symbolic significations—each set out in the analysis—from both conventional Ndembu etymologizing and the general natural properties of each object or element. (For the full *mudyi*, or milk tree, symbolism, for example, see especially *Forest of Symbols*, pp. 20–25, 52–58.) The second set of symbolic bases consist in spatial or positional relations established between sets of these three natural objects in the scene. So the placing of the two pliant wands one over the other and tying them together, the arch formed in this way over the flowing stream, and finally the siting of the arch near the source of a stream, are each said to carry certain specified symbolic imports in the overall ritual design. Thus, for instance, "the *mpanza* arch represents fertile, legitimate love between man and woman. The male and female principles 'exchange' their qualities, the opposite banks of the stream are joined by the arch. The water of life flows through it, and coolness and health are the prevailing modes" (*Ritual Process*, p. 60). Turner supports his reading with examples of "indigenous exegesis" by his Ndembu informants. Whatever the specific imports and significations of the symbols, however, the pertinent point for our present purposes is the fact of a variety of symbolic objects and interrelations working together to compose a single cohesive episode of overall symbolic expression. It is such a joint assemblage of separate symbols into one expressive act or episode that we seek here to identify as polyphony, a distinctive concept in its own right.

Our third and final set of analytical concepts to explore for potential application in the analysis of Ngũgĩ's literary symbolism concerns patterns of the incidence or recurrence of symbols throughout an entire sequence of ritual or literary performance. Once again, Turner's descriptive accounts seem to offer in broad outline yet another important aspect of the functioning of Ndembu ritual symbolism, which may found a concept capable of applied use in the analysis of any sustained literary symbolism as well. According to Turner, "the same symbols [may] have varying significance in different contexts" (*Ritual Process,* p. 50).

> Such symbols possess many senses, but contextually it may be necessary to stress one or a few of them only. . . . The same symbol may be reckoned to have different senses at different phases in a ritual performance, or rather, different senses become paramount at different times. Which sense shall become paramount is determined by the ostensible purpose of the phase of the ritual in which it appears. For a ritual, like a space rocket, is phased, and each phase is directed towards a limited end which itself becomes a means to the ultimate end of the total performance. . . . There is a consistent relationship between the end or aim of each phase in a ritual, the kind of symbolic configuration employed in that phase, and the senses that become paramount in multivocal symbols in that configuration. (*Forest of Symbols,* pp. 51–52)

This is a fully characterized account of one pattern of symbolic recurrence in both ritual and literature, and all that is left for us to do is to attach a shorthand name to the basic concept in question. This capacity or tendency of a symbol to vary its significations and suggestiveness in successive dramatic sequence with a course of action or performance may be termed *dynamicism.* Whether in ritual or in literature, then, a symbol may be said to operate dynamically when its connotative imports and significations shift or vary successively in accordance with changing phases or developing transitions in a sequence of action or expressivity. But it may be pointed out here as well that mere recurrence may not necessarily engender dynamicism, since it is possible for a symbol's meaning or even complex of meanings to remain unvarying on its recurrence, notwithstanding ongoing developments or transitions in an action sequence. Such relatively unvarying symbolic signification may thus be contradistinguished as constant or static.

Considerable light can be shed upon the nature and functioning of symbolism in Ngũgĩ's novels with the help of these three sets of analytical concepts. One interesting instance of pure subjectivist symbolism, for example, may be seen in the reverie by Waiyaki immediately prior to his arraignment before the Kiama in *The River Between* (pp. 137–39). This reverie constitutes a structural watershed and a compact encapsulation of the main thematic force of the whole story. Contrapuntal in its overall framework, the reverie comprises in its first half Waiyaki's vision of harmony, unity, and mutual trust among the people of the ridges whom he aspires to lead (p. 137). This half is an idyllic picture of universal love and jollity, embracing even the birds and beasts of the forest, all circling in song and dance round his sweetheart Nyambura as the center of attraction and unity. But by this time in the story, Nyambura had not yet accepted Waiyaki's proposal of marriage since her initial reluctant rejection of it. The first half of his symbolic reverie would thus seem to recapture that tinge of rosy sentimentality and idealistic impulsions which tend to color his public activities and aspirations in the preceding parts of the whole story. The second half of the reverie is a rude reversal of its first half (pp. 138–39), thereby serving to signal Waiyaki's growing apprehension and awareness of the harsher realities and cruder ethos of public life which he would encounter when the people learn of his plans to marry the daughter of their archenemy Joshua. In place of the "perpetual serenity" of collective singing and dancing round Nyambura, the reverie now changes suddenly to the ritual imagery of sacrificial mutilation by a crowd of people, the dismembered victim seeming at first to be Nyambura, then her sister Muthoni in her earlier tragic reversion to circumcision against their father's dictates, and then Nyambura yet again, with the fulfilled throng of ritual participants feeling an oppressive weight of guilt after the event. The imagery of ritual immolation, symbolic of the life of passionate convictions or conscientious resistance to fixed group norms which links Waiyaki and the two sisters in the novel, harks back to Muthoni's fatal revolt earlier in the story and also anticipates the trials and challenges which Waiyaki and his fiancée would face afterward. Symbolism in *A Grain of Wheat,* as well, reveals ample evidence of other properties like the polyphony and dynamicism defined above. For in this latter work, the symbols and motifs tend to coalesce occasionally into crucial definitions of meaning and valuation, and the dominant symbols successively shift and amplify their respective significations at various stages of the developing narrative action.

However, our resort to African ritual in order to highlight such concepts as polyphony and dynamicism does not necessarily suggest that Ngũgĩ's literary symbolism derives these properties directly from, say, Kikuyu ritual and folkloric forms. Indeed, none of the identified properties would seem exclusively peculiar to ritual symbolism, African or otherwise. But if we can analytically authenticate the above claims about Ngũgĩ's use of symbolism, the parallels and affinities to ritual would at least be instructive as to some ways of tapping traditional African forms of expressivity, verbal and nonverbal, to enrich or illuminate modern literary art.

II

Before examining the major symbols in *A Grain of Wheat,* we may give some attention here to secondary instances of symbolism invariably identified with individual personages or confined to discrete episodes in the story. For such minor symbolism, much of which tends to obtain in the subjectivist mode, may often constitute an invaluable key to aspects of character portrayal and plot development, or to shades of tone and response, which could be easily overlooked in critical commentary. Take Karanja's "strange experience" after the race to the train in his youth as he realized that Gikonyo had beaten him to the bosom of Mumbi (*GW*, pp. 108–09). The first half of his distracted vision as the train pulled out of the station underscores his deep sense of loss and disappointment, but the second half also seems to symbolize Karanja's streak of selfishness and indifference to the public welfare which would become pronounced later in his life: "why should I fear to trample on the children, the lame and the weak when others are doing it?" (p. 109). It is also by means of such subjectivist symbolism that the most secret feelings of guilt may be kept alive in a character's mind and ultimately exposed to the reader. Thus the needlessly brutal hacking down of the Reverend Jackson Kigondu during the Mau Mau days becomes entangled in General R's memory with the guilt of having long ago beaten up his own father (pp. 249–50).

A character's hopes, fears, yearnings, or intuitions may also be depicted through the same mode of symbolism. Mugo's secret hopes of public leadership, for example, are thus unearthed in the Moses and Isaac motifs of his habitual reveries (pp. 143, 146, 214, 223–24).

> He had trained himself to enter a twilight calm whenever he lay on his back, in bed, or in the shamba. At such moments his heart dialogued with strange voices. And the voices faded into one voice from God calling out, Moses, Moses! And Mugo was ready with his answer: Here am I, Lord. (*GW*, p. 214)

Similarly, an important aspect of Mumbi's character is initially pointed up through suffering and rescue motifs in her own youthful dreams and reveries. Her brother Kihika's visionary talk, for example, would often arouse in her "dreams of sacrifice to save so many people" (p. 155; see also p. 92). But the best subjectivist key to Mumbi's general character and personality is probably to be found in the following description of her early aspirations and youthful self-conceptions before she got married.

> Her dark eyes had a dreamy look that longed for something the village could not give. She lay in the sun and ardently yearned for a life in which love and heroism, suffering, and martyrdom were possible. She was young. She had fed on stories in which Gikuyu women braved the terrors of the forest to save people, of beautiful girls given to the gods as sacrifice before the rains. In the Old Testament she often saw herself as Esther: so she revelled in that moment when Esther finally answers King Ahasuera's question and dramatically points at Haman, saying: The adversary and enemy is the wicked Haman. (p. 89)

Mumbi does not, of course, go into the forest when the Mau Mau warfare breaks out. But her intuitions of self-sacrifice and of rescue are sufficiently realized in other aspects of her life and conduct, as in her matrimonial devotion despite suffering or her selfless efforts to save the necks of Karanja and Mugo, who had respectively jeopardized both her marriage and her brother's life. The fusion of motifs from Kikuyu and biblical folklore alike may be noted in this passage.

One order of minor symbolism which obtains in both subjectivist and objectivist modes at one and the same time is enacted through motifs of ruin, destruction, havoc, filth, or decay as objective correlatives of an inner moral or emotional condition. What tends to happen here is that a literal scene of ruins, filth, or decay is re-created in its own right, but at a moment when a character on the site is engrossed in the throes of inward stress or emotional rupture; so that either the character or maybe the reader by otherwise unmediated perception apprehends a sort of parallel between the subjective condition and the outward physical circumstance. The character's psychomoral condition is thereby dramatically foregrounded in a flash, as it were. Mugo's rotten sense of desperation as he draws toward a betrayal of Kihika, for example, seems reflected in a mound of decaying rubbish by which he sits for a short rest behind a shop which has its own trail of sordid history; so is his confusion on the same occasion enacted in the dust devil "that so whirled dust and rubbish into a moving cone-shaped pillar" (pp. 221–23). So also when Mumbi's narrative shatters Mugo's emerging hopes of future respite, he is irresistibly drawn to a scene from the past but which is now battered and filled with rubble (pp. 195–96).

Gikonyo is involved in a similar projective experience after his return from detention only to find Mumbi suckling another man's child. As he goes on a dazed survey of the now abandoned site of old Rung'ei, his utter frustration is reflected in the wreckage and ruins of the old village, "ruins that gave only hints of an earlier civilization" (p. 135). One of the more subtle instances of this order of minor symbolism occurs in connection with Wambui, who had sat in judgment over the retributive killing of Mugo in the forest soon after his public confession. Wambui feels sharp pricks of conscience during the couple of days following the execution, an unease reflected in an uncharacteristic personal negligence which Warui is quick to notice on a visit to Wambui's hut.

> . . . They both relapsed into silence, making a picture of bereaved children for whom life has suddenly lost warmth, colour, and excitement. There was no fire in the hearth. Bits of potato peelings, maize-husks and grass lay strewn on the floor as if the hut had not been lived in for a day or two. Under different circumstances, this would have surprised Warui or any visitor, because Wambui's hut was one of the tidiest in the village. She swept the floor at least twice a day and cleaned utensils immediately after use. . . . [They] now conversed, . . . as if they were both ashamed of certain subjects in one another's presence. (pp. 271–72)

It is presumably because of her misgivings about her role in Mugo's execution that Wambui refrains from openly mentioning him by name as they discuss the events of the day of his public confession. "Perhaps we should not have tried him," she mutters to herself when left again on her own. "I must light the fire. First I must sweep the room. How dirt can so quickly collect in a clean hut!" (pp. 275–76).

Some manifestations of subjectivist minor symbolism in *A Grain of Wheat* tend to emanate from personal leitmotivs. Both Mugo's Moses dreams and Mumbi's cure-salvation instincts, for example, are motifs which point to some personal character trait. But sometimes the motif may be the carrier of a hidden guilt which the character is reluctant to face. Such personal leitmotivs of secret guilt would include Mugo's boyhood "fear of galloping hooves," which would change into "the terror of an undesired discovery" during the time that he repressed his remorse for having betrayed Kihika (pp. 194–95), and Karanja's own envisioning of a "hooded self" from the days when he became a home guard during the Emergency (p. 261). But "the steps on the pavement" which haunt Gikonyo throughout the narrative are far more truly leitmotivistic than any of these.

This haunting motif of "steps on the pavement" is a subjectivist index to a hidden guilt in Gikonyo's past and to his secret remorse whenever they resound in his memory's ears. They issue from one of his most despondent moments while he was in detention, when he had confessed the Mau Mau oath at Yala in the vain hope that he might be released to join Mumbi in Thabai.

> His desire to see Mumbi was there. His mind was clear and he knew without guilt, what he was going to do. Word went round. All the detainees of Yala crowded to the walls of their compounds and watched him with chilled hostility. Gikonyo fixed his mind on Mumbi fearing that strength would leave his knees under the silent stare of all the other detainees. He walked on and the sound of his feet on the pavement leading to the office where screening, interrogations and confessions were made, seemed, in the absence of other noise, unnecessarily loud. The door closed behind him. The other detainees walked back to their rooms to wait for another journey to the quarry. . . . The steps had followed him all through the pipe-line, for in spite of the confession, Gikonyo was not released immediately. Screened he had refused to name anybody involved in oath administration. (p. 130)

When he ultimately returns home to find Mumbi with another man's child, the "steps" reecho in his mind's ear with painful irony (pp. 130–36). Even years afterward, they continue to pound into his moments of loneliness and reminiscence, as when he is returning home after the delegation to Mugo's hut only a few nights before Uhuru Day (pp. 33–34). In fact, the "steps" are not finally silenced until the concluding episodes of the narrative, when he reassesses his past and his relationship with Mumbi after hearing of Mugo's confession of his own equally long-suppressed guilt (p. 278).

Even the disputed child he finds with Mumbi soon becomes a sort of existential leitmotiv in its own right, an unfailing reflector of the chilled atmosphere and mutual dilemma engulfing Gikonyo and Mumbi for nearly four years after his return from detention. For Mumbi the child is the indelible evidence of her compromised integrity, while for Gikonyo it is a refractory latch that seldom fails to throw open the floodgates of his sulky jealousy and painful memories of "Karanja on top of Mumbi" (p. 138). The child's presence in the home had thus helped harden Gikonyo's attitude toward Mumbi into an ascetic self-denial, an escapist indulgence of hard work, and a harrowing "valley of silence" (p. 133). As he tells Mugo a couple of days before the latter's catalytic confession:

> "For a moment, a minute, you might say, something rippled in my heart. Mumbi, the woman I knew, could not let Karanja into her bed. She was the same as I had left her. Then I saw the child. And I knew that what I had thought impossible had happened. . . . It was then that I made a decision: I would never talk about the child. I would continue life as if nothing had happened. But I would never enter Mumbi's bed. What more was there for me to do but to give myself wholly to work, hard work?" (pp. 140–41)

Gikonyo's outburst against Mumbi after years of lifeless domestic politeness, although precipitated perhaps by a more recent disappointment with his local parliamentarian over a business matter (pp. 189–94), was again over this child. In the event, he calls her "a whore," an unfair charge which wounds her self-pride so much that she decides to leave Gikonyo's house for good and live on her own (pp. 205–06).

Gikonyo's personal leitmotivs sometimes come together in his consciousness as minor enactments of what we have defined above as polyphonic symbolism. As early as his first arrival home from detention, this phenomenon may be seen at work in his jealous musings over his plight: "The steps in the pavement, the weeping child, and the image of the mother suckling the child, would always haunt him," he would reflect (p. 136). And toward the end, as he contemplates Mugo's confession in the light of his own guilt and his marital dilemma, the "steps" and "child" motifs again come together in his musing, this time to begin the process of his ultimate resolution of conflict. For instance:

> Could he, Gikonyo, gather such courage to tell people about the steps on the pavement? At night he went over his life and his experiences in the seven detention camps. What precisely had all these years brought him? At every thought, he was pricked with guilt. . . . He increasingly longed to speak to [Mumbi] about Mugo and then about his own life in detention. What would she say about the steps that haunted him? Another thought also crept into his mind. He had never seen himself as father to Mumbi's children [i.e., since his return from detention]. Now it crossed his mind: what would his child by Mumbi look like? (p. 278)

At this juncture of nascent change, however, the "child" motif is entering a new phase; it sheds its previous joint subjectivist and objectivist mode of occurrence and begins to assume an exclusively subjectivist recurrence. For, henceforth in the narration, it is primarily an image inside Gikonyo's artistic mind, where it is now being reshaped for imminent merging into the carving motif that would round off Gikonyo's moral resolution in a final polyphonic definition of meaning.

III

The final orders of symbolism to consider are what we may call the symbolism of water and of creativity, which are the novel's two dominant modes of symbolism.[9] In trying to assess the nature and functioning of these symbols in the narrative, an attempt will also be made in each case to determine some of the probable sources of influence as far as that is possible. Meanwhile, a few general remarks may be made here concerning their respective processual patterns throughout the narrative. Each major symbolism is predominantly associated, on the whole, with one main trend of thematic action in the novel, and thereby with different sets of dramatis personae; the interaction between the two sets of thematic areas and characters is also reflected to some extent in the overall operation of the symbolism. As the narrative opens, each dominant symbol initially functions in connection with either one main character or a small group of them at a time, thereby focusing at first on relatively private or personal issues. But as the narrative progresses, each symbolism dynamically tends to amplify or vary its suggestiveness and field of application so as to include other characters or embrace wider issues and other levels or areas of meaning. And in that process, it may finally come to merge with some other symbol or set of motifs for a relatively polyphonic act of expressiveness. The major symbolisms should therefore be regarded as phased, as functioning in stages in accordance with the developing transitions of action and thematic statement, a feature which would also incidentally facilitate the due apportioning of influence or indebtedness.

Accordingly, the water symbolism, for instance, obtains mainly in relation to Mugo's drama of conscience and the general political theme. Initially it is Mugo's dilemma which attracts and sustains the water symbolism in a variety of guises, its relevance to the wider political situation becoming apparent much later on and in yet another guise. As the story draws to a close, this symbolism now tends to merge with others in a process of summative revaluations and interconnecting of various characters. The creativity symbolism, on its part, obtains mainly in connection with the love-jealousy theme in the story, with Gikonyo as the central fount of its expressive force and Mumbi as its joint focus. But Karanja soon comes to be associated with it as well, mainly by virtue of the fact that he commands a "more sure and more finished" handling of the guitar than Gikonyo (pp. 110–11). In fact, Karanja and Mumbi, being crucial unifying bridges between the jealousy and political themes by dint of their forlorn relationship and of Karanja's political opportunism, ultimately come to be involved in varying degrees with both the water and creativity symbolisms, the two symbols actually tending to converge on one or the other as the story winds to a close. It is convenient, however, to survey the two symbolisms separately for a start.

The water symbolism is the appropriate one with which to begin. The first three instances of water symbolism in the novel occur in an exclusively subjectivist mode, and all hinge upon Mugo alone, although each refers to a slightly different phase of his changing inward condition. They cover the period of his painful suppression of his remorse and guilt for betraying Kihika. The opening paragraph of the novel is a subtle enactment of this guilt, or rather, of his inner conflict in grappling with its sustained concealment. It is the record of a dream by Mugo on the Sunday morning preceding Uhuru now only four days away.

> Mugo felt nervous. He was lying on his back and looking at the roof. Sooty locks hung from the fern and grass thatch and all pointed at his heart. A clear drop of water was delicately suspended above him. The drop fattened and grew dirtier as it absorbed grains of soot. Then it started drawing towards him. He tried to shut his eyes. They would not close. He tried to move his head: it was firmly chained to the bed-frame. The drop grew larger and larger as it drew closer and closer to his eyes. He wanted to cover his eyes with his palms; but his hands, his feet, everything refused to obey his will. In despair, Mugo gathered himself for a final heave and woke up. Now he lay under the blanket and remained unsettled fearing, as in the dream, that a drop of cold water would suddenly pierce his eyes. . . . He knew that it was only a dream: yet he kept on chilling at the thought of a cold drop falling into his eyes. (pp. 3–4)

Because of Ngũgĩ's mazy convolutions of time levels in this novel, only much later on in the narrative does it become clearer during a first reading that this dream is the uneasy struggle of repressed guilt and frightened inner conflict which had continually plagued Mugo since the time of Kihika's fateful visit to his hut. The local leader of the forest fighters had mistaken the aloof reticence of Mugo for political dependability and had come to him one night in order to persuade him to organize a new underground movement in the new Thabai around which a trench was being dug by the colonial authorities to isolate the guerrilla fighters of the forest from the civilian population that frequently replenished them. Fearing to be involved in the deadly uncertainties of nationalist politics but also afraid to defy Kihika, Mugo finally decided to give him up to the authorities by informing in advance on the rendezvous where Kihika had arranged to meet him again for further planning. All of Mugo's stratagems to secretly expiate his guilt for the consequent betrayal and execution of Kihika have failed to dissipate turmoil and conflict in his own mind, which is ironically accentuated in the last few days before Uhuru by the people's own mistaken enthusiasm as they clamor afresh that Mugo must be their local leader at the Uhuru celebrations where he must make a speech about the past exploits of Kihika and himself in the freedom struggles. They do not know that it was, in fact, Mugo who had betrayed Kihika and that his life had been ruined by the insistent mental conflict over the secret feelings of guilt for the betrayal. Their renewed efforts to make him their leader for the Uhuru celebrations thus revive Mugo's drama of conscience and fear of being exposed as the traitor. This dream, which takes place some three or four days before Uhuru Day in Thabai, is a subtle enactment of that battle of conscience, with Mugo's better instincts striving to burst the dam of repression and public deception while baser emotions like fear still stand a resolute guard at the behest of his conscious will. His will and his instincts, his mind and body, are thus momentarily locked in symbolic combat over some question of fact or decision, "everything refusing to obey his will" to continued suppression of guilt. The sooty "drop of cold water" threatening to "suddenly pierce his eyes" is akin to the increasingly menacing possibility of his exposure to the people.

The second occurrence of the water symbolism takes place about two days afterward when Mugo goes to Gikonyo's house to report that he had decided to accept the people's offer of leadership (pp. 146, 153). It is on the Tuesday following the Sunday of the "sooty water" dream. He has the chance now to dispel his fears of exposure for good. "He would lead the people and bury his past in their gratitude. Nobody need ever know about Kihika" (p. 146). It is Mumbi alone he finds at home, however, and as they converse she finds it appropriate to tell Mugo about the heady events of the past that had chilled her marital life. But this unwittingly involves her systematic recapitulation to Mugo of the tragic sufferings of the people of Thabai during the Emergency as a direct consequence of Kihika's betrayal, Mumbi having no idea as yet that Mugo had been the traitor. Mugo's guilt feelings are thus intensely reactivated yet again, and his renewed hopes of respite are threatened as Mumbi's narrative proceeds. It seems he cannot now resort to his former life of isolated repressiveness, nor apparently can he now accept the proffered leadership, and he ends up not announcing his recent decision to accept the people's offer. Meanwhile, as Mumbi continues her account (pp. 154–71), Mugo is secretly tormented by the vision of a "silent pool" which he seems to espy in Mumbi's eyes as she recounts her reminiscences.

But this slightly altered reenactment of the water symbolism is rather subtle and elusive, and its contextual signification may be pursued through a habitual "drowning" imagery which used to be Mugo's favorite expression of his desire to be left alone. During the nationalist struggles and before the betrayal, Mugo had always sought to avoid involvement in politics and the life of the community "for fear of being involved in brawls that might ruin his chances of a better future" (p. 221). Such involvement seemed to Mugo akin to plunging into a pit, a pool, or a stream in which he might drown. This was the fear that beset him when Kihika sought to enlist his support in organizing a new underground movement in the rebuilt settlements. " 'Why should Kihika drag me into a struggle and problems I have not created?' he asked himself. 'Why? He is not satisfied with butchering men and women and children. He must call on me to *bathe in the blood*' " (p. 220; emphasis added). Mugo would resort to a related metaphor many years after the betrayal as he explains himself to Kihika's sister (Mumbi) on his first confession to her: "I wanted to live my life. I never wanted to be involved in anything. Then he came into my life . . . and pulled me into the stream. So I killed him" (p. 210). To the prebetrayal Mugo, then, being involved in the turbulent life and politics of his country seemed a fateful stream in which the aloof hermit could easily drown and to avoid it was thus a virtual law of his life. This habitual drowning imagery is subjectively reactivated during Mumbi's story about her past and the sufferings of Thabai after Kihika's arrest.

As Mumbi tells her story, Mugo's feelings of guilt are aroused more intensely, and his recent resolve to accept the offer of leadership begins to recede from his mind.

> [Mugo] saw the light at the bottom of the pool dancing in her eyes. He felt her dark power over him.
> "Yet when they took him [Gikonyo] away, I did nothing, and when he finally came home, tired, I could no longer make him happy."
> She [Mumbi] was still young, vulnerable; but it was he who was scurrying with hands and feet at the bottom of the silent pool. It was terrible for him, this struggle: he did not want to drown. (pp. 155–56)

By the time Mumbi ends her story, with Mugo having apparently changed his mind about openly accepting the people's offer of leadership, his life seems to be threatened afresh with a return to the former state of isolation and secret repression.

> She paused. The light still played in her dark voluptuous eyes. She was young. She was beautiful. A big lump blocked Mugo's throat. Something heaved forth; he trembled; he was at the bottom of the pool, but up there, above the pool, ran the earth; life, struggle, even amidst pain and blood and poverty, seemed beautiful; only for a moment; how dared he believe in such a vision, an illusion? (p. 171)

Is this Mugo's envisioning of an imminent ruin hanging over him? Or is it merely his painful realization that he will forever remain impaled upon the horns of a dilemma that has plagued his life for virtually all the past ten years? Or is it a foreboding of his ultimate submission or confession of guilt, which would only be a version of the "drowning" he had always feared? At any rate, his sense of some crucial juncture of realization seems barely evident in this second enactment of the water symbolism.

An even more lurid enactment of the water symbolism occurs soon afterward as Mugo returns to his hut after hearing Mumbi's story (p. 199). An intense self-questioning as he walks home suddenly erupts into a hallucinatory vision of a lava of blood flowing down the walls of his hut.

> It is not me, he whispered to convince himself. It is not me, it would have happened . . . the murder of women and men in the trench . . . even if . . . even if . . . He was moaning. Mumbi's voice was a knife which had butchered and laid naked his heart to himself. The road from his hut led to the trench. But would it not have happened? Christ would have died on the cross, anyway. Why did they blame Judas, a stone from the hands of a power more than man? Kihika . . . crucified . . . the thought flashed through him, and a curious thing happened. Mugo saw thick blood dripping from the mud walls of his hut. Why had he not seen it earlier, he now wondered, almost calmly, without fear. But he was shaking as he walked to his hut, resolved to find out if the blood was really there. (p. 199; ellipses in original)

This blood-dripping vision, the third recurrence of water symbolism in the narrative, seems to mark or at least presage a slight but dramatic shift in Mugo's hitherto adamant impenitence and concealment of guilt. For it is the very next morning that signs of a possible acceptance of guilt begin to be reflected in Mugo's outward conduct, leading to his first confession the same Wednesday evening (pp. 208–11).

After these three initial subjectivist instances of water symbolism, its subsequent manifestations are each a varying mode of rainfall or threat of rain. But they do not now relate exclusively to Mugo's condition. Three basic tendencies may be seen at work in these later recurrences of the water symbolism: its significations and field of application tend to widen or vary slightly in each successive circumstance, its polyphonic propensity is gradually heightened, and an objectivist mode of occurrence progressively becomes apparent. Henceforth, the signification of the water symbolism on each recurrence tends to transcend the personal plight of Mugo, or refers to some other character in a different context or even merges with another symbolism or motif, and in each case with a relatively different import and suggestiveness. The symbolic significations in these later instances are no longer forged exclusively within the subjectivity of the fictional personage nor may he/she even be aware of them.

These processes seem to set in with the fourth recurrence of the water symbolism, which takes place when Mugo is walking home in the rain on his way from the market on the day following Mumbi's story about her past; it is also the eve of Uhuru Day. It is noteworthy that it is the people watching Mugo exposed in the rain, who first make inferences as to its possible relevance to both his inward condition and their newly won national freedom.

Most of us from Thabai first saw him at the New Rung'ei Market the day the heavy rain fell. You remember the Wednesday, just before Independence? Wind blew and the rain hit the ground at an angle. . . . People said the falling water was a blessing for our hard-won freedom. Murungu on high never slept: he always lets his tears fall to this, our land, from Agu and Agu. . . . It had rained the day Kenyatta returned from England: it had also rained the day Kenyatta returned to Gatundu from Maralal.

We saw the man walking in the rain. . . . The fact that he was the only man in the rain soon attracted the attention of people along the pavements and shop verandahs. Some even forced their way to the front to see him.

"What is he doing, fooling in the rain?" . . .

"Maybe he has a long way to walk, and he fears the night will catch him." . . .

"Or maybe he has something heavy in his heart."

"That's not anything to make him drench himself ill. Which of us does not carry a weight in the heart?"

The man neared the corner at the far end of Rung'ei shops. Women discussed all the risks people ran by exposing themselves to water. Soon the man disappeared, lost behind the shops.

"What prevents him from taking cover?"

"Mugo is a strange man," Wambui said reflectively. (pp. 202–03)

Considering that it is later on this same day that Mugo confesses his guilt for the first time (to Mumbi in his hut), this self-ablution would seem a sort of ritual self-exposure which apparently points to an inward readiness at last to face the need to confess and lift the oppressive burden of secrecy and deception. In place of Mugo's previous "unsettled fearing, as in the dream, that a drop of cold water would suddenly pierce his eyes" (p. 3), he is apparently prepared now to expose his entire body to be drenched in the heavy downpour. And, as the lookers-on are keen to suggest, the rain is apparently also of symbolic relevance for their freedom struggles as well. Later in the night, following Mugo's confession to Mumbi (pp. 207–11, 232, 236), there was an even heavier rainstorm causing a lot of wreckage (pp. 232–33). "The wind and the rain were so strong that some trees were uprooted whole, while others broke by the stems, or lost their branches" (p. 233). Is this later downpour also an evocation of that suffering and destruction of life and limb which the nation had gone through during the struggle for independence, the symbolic reenactment of their Pyrrhic victory in that struggle? Indeed, the birth of the new nation is explicitly likened to birth pangs, "like a woman torn between fear and joy during birth motions" (p. 232), and the people's joy to that of "welcoming a son at birth or at circumcision" (p. 232). However, it is in such minor thickets of possible symbolic functioning that a snare of interpretative excess or trivialism may sometimes lie in wait for the incautious critic.

There would seem to be a clear Conradian influence upon this particular phase of Ngũgĩ's water symbolism. For basically the same imagery of downpour is invoked by Conrad in dramatizing the sudden spate of Razumov's confessions at the height of the narrative in *Under Western Eyes* (*UWE,* pp. 294–306). Ngũgĩ's and Conrad engage the rain image phase of water symbolism in their narratives respectively just before and just after the betrayer's first confession to his victim's sister, sustaining it up until the second confession in public (see also *GW,* p. 269). Razumov walks away from his own first confession under a heavy downpour and rainstorm as he returns to his lodgings.

> Razumov walked straight home on that wet glistening pavement. A heavy shower passed over him; distant lightning played faintly against the fronts of the dumb houses. . . .
> "Yes, I am washed clean," muttered Razumov, who was dripping from head to foot, and passed through the inner door towards the staircase leading to his room.
> He did not change his clothes, but, after lighting the candle, took off his watch and chain, laid them on the table, and sat down at once to write [his confession]. (*UWE,* pp. 294–95)

But the Conradian influence seems to be limited to the phase of the confessions in Ngũgĩ's narrative, and perhaps to the subjectivism of some of the initial three phases of the water symbolism. In order to underscore the overall differences between the treatments of the water symbolism in the two novels, a brief account of its phases in Conrad's novel before the climactic confessions is given here.

In the betrayal episodes of Conrad's narrative, Razumov's choking sense of despondency and imminent ruin is finely evoked and intensified by the falling and thickening snow (*UWE,* pp. 28–62). "Razumov thought: 'I am being crushed—and I can't even run away'" (*UWE,* p. 34). But the vast stretch of snow burying the Russian landscape also enacts the Russian people's oppressed moral and spiritual inertia under what Conrad depicts as a seeming inevitability of perpetual autocracies, "levelling everything under its uniform whiteness, like a monstrous blank page awaiting the record of an inconceivable history" (*UWE,* p. 35). The initial manifestation of water symbolism thus relates mainly to both Razumov's plight and the general political psychology of his country. The subsequent remorse-repression phase of Razumov's condition is symbolically dramatized in his distracted peerings either into the semblance of a pool (*UWE,* pp. 59–60) or into a heady flow of a stream as he hangs over the parapet of a bridge during his later stay in Geneva (*UWE,* pp. 166–69, 235–37). These later symbolic acts of Razumov's distraught condition issue from a momentary but traumatic experience during the original betrayal itself. It is the memory of Haldin descending the stairs from Razumov's room after the latter had already given him up and was sure that a police ambush could be waiting for Haldin at the bottom of the stairs.

Razumov ran forward unsteadily, with parted, voiceless lips. The outer door stood open. Staggering out on the landing, he leaned far over the bannister. Gazing down into the deep black shaft with a tiny glimmering flame at the bottom, he traced by ear the rapid spiral descent of somebody running down the stairs on tiptoe. It was a light, swift, pattering sound, which sank away from him into the depths: a fleeting shadow passed over the glimmer—a wink of the tiny flame. Then stillness.

Razumov hung over, breathing the cold raw air tainted by the evil smells of the unclean staircase. All quiet. (*UWE,* pp. 59–60)

This stifling and acute awareness of guilt on Razumov's part is what he reen-acts in his repeated peerings into the stream in Geneva when he is confronted once more with people who remind him incessantly of the man he had betrayed. It is possible that this phase of Conrad's water symbolism might have influenced the second recurrence of water symbolism in Ngũgĩ's *A Grain of Wheat,* that is, Mugo's imaginary "light at the bottom of the pool dancing in [Mumbi's] eyes" which is analyzed above. If this conjecture is true, however, Ngũgĩ's complete change of the texture of the symbolism is patent in that phase. Another major difference between Ngũgĩ's use of water sym-bolism in his third novel and that in *Under Western Eyes,* which undoubtedly influenced his molding of symbolism as a narrative device, is that after the central confessions Ngũgĩ still reengages the rain imagery in a slightly differ-ent form and for a slightly different symbolic purpose toward the close of his narrative. Conrad's water symbolism, on the other hand, reaches its climax and conclusion in Razumov's spate of confessions and punishment.

Ngũgĩ's narrative in *A Grain of Wheat,* it may be noted, carefully demar-cates two phases of rain imagery, one corresponding with the confessions and the other emerging soon afterward. After Mugo's public confession, the nar-rative continuously insists on characterizing the rainfall as a drizzle, sharply distinguishing it from the early downpour and rainstorm: "the rain when later it fell, did not break into violence. It drizzled continuously, varying nei-ther in speed nor in volume. The country, it seemed, was going to plunge into one of those stinging drizzles that went on endlessly" (*GW,* p. 254). A couple of days afterward, when Warui visits Wambui in her hut (pp. 271 ff.), the incessant drizzle is still a pointed subject of conversation. It is reengaged henceforth to help in the summative reassessments of certain characters as the story winds to a close. The other dominant symbolism is also reengaged toward the end for a similar purpose in connection with another set of charac-ters. Meanwhile, this latter creativity symbolism may now be examined from its earliest occurrences in the narrative.

It has been indicated above that the creativity symbolism in *A Grain of Wheat* is connected mainly with the relationship between Gikonyo and Mumbi. Ebele Obumselu has suggested that this relationship and its associated creativity or art motifs are "modelled" on parallel factors in D. H. Lawrence's novel *The Rainbow*[10]:

> In particular the treatment of the marriage between Gikonyo and Mumbi seems to be modelled on that between Will and Anna. Will and Gikonyo are carpenter-artists and musicians. Both, meeting the woman they marry, plan a carving in which the rapture of first love will be expressed. But Will's tribute to Woman is soon held up, and Gikonyo does not even begin.

Obumselu has unearthed here a significant source of influence on Ngũgĩ's portrayal of the Gikonyo-Mumbi relationship, but seems to exaggerate, by implication, the extent of the influence and the parallel with the Will-Anna relationship in Lawrence's book. For whereas Lawrence uses the art motifs to point up a radical disharmony of sensibility or modes of perception between the newlywed Will and his wife, Anna, Ngũgĩ's art motifs operate to underscore the natural rapport and affinity between Gikonyo and Mumbi. And whereas the artistic instinct in Will seems atrophied through marital interaction with Anna,[11] only detention and alienation from Mumbi in a sustained bout of jealousy after his return from detention seem to hold up Gikonyo's carving, and a restoration of harmony between the two Ngũgĩ characters is ultimately effected mainly through a promised revival of the creative instinct in Gikonyo. The general idea of having an emotional relationship symbolically pointed up through references to a set of art motifs may have been more or less directly taken by Ngũgĩ from Lawrence, but his treatment of the technique and the actual relationship it helps portray would be misrepresented somewhat by the inference of a closer or more extensive parallel in this respect.

More credence may be gained for these suggestions if further attention is given to another source of influence upon the Gikonyo-Mumbi relationship and its associated creativity symbolism. As Obumselu himself briefly notes, "in Gikonyo and Mumbi we probably have the ancestors of the Kikuyu in whose lives the fortunes of the tribe are shown" (Obumselu, p. 88). The Kikuyu creation myth of Gikuyu and Mumbi is utilized in a variety of ways in almost all of Ngũgĩ's novels, perhaps most subtly of all in this novel, *A Grain of Wheat*. The case can be founded mainly on a speculative critical reconstruction, supported not only by the obvious parallels between the names of the mythical parents and Ngũgĩ's two figures but also by a pointed fictional attempt by Mumbi in the novel to underscore such an allusion (*GW,* pp. 92–93). Viewed hermeneutically, the tribal legend in question may be taken as embodying in the mythical parents the active principle of creative essence, since these ancestral figures are usually represented as primal creators and molders.[12] If creativity is the defining essence of the mythical figures, it could well be that Ngũgĩ has sought to infuse the same principle into his Gikonyo and Mumbi and that the idea of portraying their relationship with the help of their own artistic or creative acts and gestures would only be a natural correlate of what they embody. But to what extent may this be verified or endorsed from the novel itself?

Gikonyo and Mumbi are depicted in the novel each as an artist of a sort; their mutual attraction and feelings of love are portrayed from the beginning through their reciprocal appreciation of their own joint creativity or of each other's artistic performance in some respect (pp. 90–92, 94–96). Gikonyo is a reputable carpenter and carver, a natural artist in wood capable of a deep and almost mystical communion with wood as his material medium (pp. 85–87, 94–96). He is also fond of and quite skillful with his guitar and has a fairly good singing voice. Mumbi, on her part, seems especially fond of knitting and has an even better voice for singing, a trait inherited from her mother, Wanjiku (pp. 88, 90–92). Just before the consummation of their love in the woods, Gikonyo and Mumbi underscore this affinity of creative spirit between them almost as an efficient cause of their union.

"I am sure," she went on, "it must be wonderful to be a carpenter, to work in wood. Out of broken pieces of timber, you make something."

"You knit pullovers, too."

"It is not the same. I once watched you in your workshop and it seemed—it just seemed to me you were talking with the tools." (pp. 105–06)

A mutual creative instinct or artistic sensitivity thus seems a significant element in the compelling rapport and affinity between them.

The symbolic functioning of the creativity instinct is transmuted into a carving motif when the national Emergency takes Gikonyo away from his Mumbi for some six years of detention. It should be noted that, henceforth and in inverse relation to the water symbolism, the carving motifs which now sustain the creativity symbolism progressively become exclusively subjectivist as the narrative draws to an end. For, unlike the joint music or Gikonyo's entranced making of a *panga* handle for Mumbi at the inception of love between them (pp. 90–96), the symbolic relevance of the carving motif is now forged entirely within Gikonyo's changing meditative consciousness in accordance with successive transitions in his outward circumstances. Although entirely subjectivist in its final stages, however, the creativity symbolism still musters a good deal of dynamicism, and on occasion it draws together the personal leitmotivs of the Gikonyo-Mumbi relationship in some eloquent moments of expressivity.

Before his detention, Gikonyo had planned to carve a wedding gift for Mumbi, a domestic stool, which he had not been able to start. His artistic sensibility in connection with this projected stool becomes for him throughout his detention a sensitive barometer of his feelings and his relation to his environment. The desire to carve the stool is revived in his mind in moments of acute nostalgia and despondency during detention. While Gikonyo was at

Yala camp, for instance, suffering and a deep nostalgia for Mumbi revive pensive thoughts of the uncarved stool (pp. 126–27), leading in a short while to his confession of the Mau Mau oath in the vain hope of being released to rejoin his Mumbi (pp. 121–30). Again, as he and other detainees worked on the Mweya irrigation site during his final year in detention, the motif recurs in similar circumstances as an index to a similar set of moods.

> It was at Mweya . . . that he again seriously thought of carving a stool from wood, a wedding gift for Mumbi. The idea gradually took concrete shape as he worked in the sun amidst the river-decay and the muddy earth. He would carve the stool from a Muiri stem, a hardwood that grew around Kirinyaga and Nyandarwa hills. The seat would rest on three legs curved into three grim-faced figures, sweating under a weight. On the seat he would bead a pattern, representing a river and a canal. A jembe or spade would lie beside the canal. For days afterwards, Gikonyo thought about the carving. The men's faces kept changing; he altered the position of their shoulders, their hands or heads. How could he work a river in beads? Shouldn't he replace a jembe with a panga? He puzzled over little details and this kept his mind and heart away from the physical drudgery. He hoped to work on the stool as soon as he left detention. (pp. 277–78).

Although the carving is intended for Mumbi, the artist is seeking here to make it reflect his own condition and circumstances in a particular period of his life. Thus, at this stage, the seat of the stool would carry motifs which would reflect the great suffering endured by Gikonyo and the other detainees as they went through "the pipeline" of detention through the years. On his release, however, a prolonged bout of jealousy prevents Gikonyo from effecting his plan. And when years later he reconsiders carving the stool, it is the altered circumstances and feelings of that future time he seeks to transfuse into the various motifs of the stool. The symbolic significations would thus vary again, attesting to the dynamicism of the creativity symbolism. These concluding recurrences of the creativity symbolism would depict the crowning moral recovery of the narrative, first resolving the inner conflicts signaled by Gikonyo's various personal leitmotivs (p. 278) and finally reconciling him to Mumbi once more in a happy marriage (pp. 279–80).

Before then, however, the other dominant symbolism in the novel helps in the final revaluations of a few other major characters. We have already noted that this new phase of the water symbolism is in the form of "one of those stinging drizzles that went on endlessly." The drizzle in which Karanja makes his "narrow escape" back to Githima after the independence ceremony in Thabai seems to coalesce with a fine cluster of dirt and breakage motifs and with a suitably varied aspect of the creativity or artistic motifs to help evoke the sense of frustration, failure, and futility which seem to constitute Karanja's own final impression of the life he has always led (pp. 254–62). At least two fine instances of such polyphonic symbolism light up Karanja's last appearance: the moment of his final departure from Thabai after the public confession (p. 257) and that of his arrival at the fly-ridden eating house at Githima (pp. 259–60). The first instance, when he goes to collect his guitar from his mother's hut and bid her farewell, will suffice here.

> Karanja had forgotten his guitar until now. During the Emergency he had stopped playing it altogether. He rummaged through a pile of broken pots and calabashes until he fished out the instrument from the bottom. The wood was cracked, was covered with dust and soot, and smelt of smoke. The strings were loose and two were broken. He tried to dust off the layer of dust and soot, then gave up the effort. He fastened one or two of the loose strings. He strummed a little; the instrument produced a rumbling noise as dust fell into the hole. He walked to the door. Outside, it was still drizzling. . . .
> The drizzle tapped, drummed the guitar and the bag. Soon the dust and the soot soaked and started to slug down. He walked towards the bus stop at Thabai Trading Centre, through the greying mist, looking neither to the right nor to the left. (p. 257)

The sense of futility, emptiness, and waste evoked here is kept up throughout this chapter on Karanja which seems to be summing up his role in the whole story: "Life was empty like the dark and the mist that enclosed the earth," Karanja finally muses as he absentmindedly recovers his change at the Githima eating house after having "paid for the meal he had not eaten" (p. 261).

A similar exposure to rain has an entirely different kind of symbolic texture and complexion in the case of Mugo after his public confession. After this traumatic act which threatened his very life, Mugo is initially minded to flee Thabai, "his body aflame with a desire to escape" (p. 268). But taking shelter from the rain, he goes into the Old Woman's hut, where he changes his mind about fleeing and decides to return to his own hut, even if his avengers are to catch up with him.

> Later, he shut the door behind him and went into the drizzling rain. He did not continue with his earlier plans. Instead, he walked back to his hut. In the hut, he lit the oil-lamp and sat on the bed. He did not remove his wet clothes. He stared at the wall, opposite. There was nothing on the walls: no visions of blood, no galloping footsteps behind him, no detention camps, and Mumbi seemed a vague thing in a remote past. Occasionally he tapped the bed frame, almost irritably. . . . Water dripped from his coat, again in broken lines, down his legs and on to the ground. A drop was caught in his right eye lashes and the light from the lamp was split into many tiny lashes. Then the drop entered his eye, melted inside, and ran down his face like a tear.
> He did not rub the eye, or do anything.
> There was a knock at the door. Mugo did not answer it.
> The door opened and General R., followed by Lt. Koinandu, came in.
> "I am ready," Mugo said, and stood up, without looking at his visitors.

> "The trial will be held tonight," General R. pronounced, gravely. "Wambui will be the judge. Koinandu and I will be the only elders present at the hearing."
> Mugo said nothing. (pp. 269–70)

This marks the height of Mugo's reconciliation to the ugly reality engendered by his sordid past; it signifies his readiness at last to face its consequences squarely. The leitmotivs or memories of his former suppression of guilt and remorse are now evoked only to show that they have been dispelled. The drop of cold water that he previously feared may now enter his eye and melt there without his doing anything defensive or deceptive about it. His readiness to face any punishment for his past is manifest in his calm, unruffled greeting to his vengeful executioners: "I am ready." Later the same evening, they sentence him and immediately execute him in a ritual murder in the forest, completely indifferent to the spiritual dimension of the great courage he had shown in confessing at a time when, as Gikonyo puts it later on, "he stood before much honour, praises were heaped on him [and] he would have become chief" (p. 265).

Indeed, Mugo's "courage to face his guilt and lose everything" is to have a catalytic effect upon Gikonyo in his own attempt to resolve the dilemma of his marriage (pp. 278–80). He is profoundly touched by Mugo's confessing at a time of being well insulated against discovery. This catalytic relationship between the plights of Mugo and the Mumbi-Gikonyo pair had started when the two had trusted Mugo enough to tell him the problems of their marriage on separate occasions. Mumbi's story, in particular, had deeply touched Mugo: "She had trusted him, and confided in him. This simple trust had forced him to tell her the truth" (p. 266). This reciprocal catalysis between the dilemmas and crowning resolutions of the conflicts in the two main thematic areas of the narrative is another means of its unified cohesiveness. Accordingly, Mugo's confession now helps to quicken Gikonyo's resolution of conflict as the ultimate climax of the novel's scheme of moral discoveries.

Gikonyo now begins to reconsider his relationship with Mumbi and the question of the disputed child. The stool he had long ago wanted to carve for her, with all the other leitmotivs of his past, now becomes the natural idiom of a reawakened but resolutive drama of conscience.

> Lying in hospital, Gikonyo was again possessed by a desire to carve the stool. He had been in Timoro for four days. For the last three days he thought of Mugo and the confession. Could he, Gikonyo, gather such courage to tell people about the steps on the pavement? . . . Another thought also crept into his mind. He had never seen himself as father to Mumbi's children. Now it crossed his mind: what would his child by Mumbi look like?
> It was on the fifth day that he recalled Mweya and his desire to carve a stool. . . . He would carve the stool now, after the hospital, before he resumed his business, or in-between the business hours. He worked the motif in detail. He changed the figures. He would now carve a thin man, with hard lines on

the face, shoulders and head bent, supporting the weight. His right hand would stretch to link with that of a woman, also with hard lines on the face. The third figure would be that of a child on whose head or shoulders the other two hands of the man and woman would meet. Into what image would he work the beads on the seat? A field needing clearance and cultivation? A jembe? A bean flower? He would settle this when the time came. (pp. 278–79)

Gikonyo's personal leitmotivs of "the child" and "the steps on the pavement" now merge with the art motif of the stool, which also consistently occurs in an exclusively subjectivist mode, in order to enact the inward process of his moral recovery or resolution of conflict. The gradual process of this inward change is thus systematically reflected in the series of changes Gikonyo now plans to make on the stool when he comes to carve it in the future. In musingly feeling his way back to Mumbi's bosom, he learns here to accept the disputed child, reconcile himself with Mumbi as she is, and with the renewed prospect of a meaningful marital life. Instead of the faces of three "men" as in the Mweya motif, the figures supporting the stool are now to be altered into a man and woman (obviously himself and Mumbi), each of them "with hard lines on the face" to portray the suffering they have gone through, with a child between them over whom their hands would link. Mumbi and the disputed child are presumably being notionally received into Gikonyo's fold of responsibility and loving care for the first time since his return from detention.

This conciliatory development is outwardly reflected in Gikonyo's uneasiness when Mumbi, having taken the child to the clinic, is unable to visit Gikonyo in hospital the next day. And when she comes on the following day, it shows again in his coaxing concern about both the sick child and the possibility of Mumbi's return to the matrimonial home. "Let us talk about the child," he now implores. "Will you go back to the house, light the fire, and see things don't decay?" (p. 280). But Mumbi's self-respecting sense of realism asserts itself in her response to this unexpected request, "as if she was now really aware of her independence" (p. 280). According to her, too much had happened between them to be glossed over so blandly: they would need to discuss it properly, examine their hearts, "and then together plan the future we want" (p. 280). The new Gikonyo is quick to concede the point to her.

> He knew, at once, that in future he would reckon with her feelings, her thoughts, her desires—a new Mumbi. . . . Then he sank back to bed. He thought about the wedding gift, a stool carved from Muiri wood. "I'll change the woman's figure. I shall curve a woman big—big with child." (p. 280)[13]

To all intents and purposes, Gikonyo's moral recovery and his reconciliation with Mumbi as his wife have now come full circle with this last change of one motif into a pregnant woman. Not only has he presumably forgiven Mumbi's affair with Karanja; Gikonyo has apparently resolved at long last to commit himself once again to a happy and fruitful marital life with her.

Notes

1. Ngugi wa Thiong'o, *Homecoming: Essays* (London: Heinemann, 1972).
2. Especially in *The River Between* (1965) and *A Grain of Wheat* (1967), both published by Heinemann, like *Petals of Blood* (1977).
3. W. J. Howard, "Themes and Development in the Novels of Ngugi," in *The Critical Evaluation of African Literature,* ed. Edgar Wright (London, Ibadan, and Nairobi: Heinemann, 1973), p. 98.
4. Ebele Obumselu, "*A Grain of Wheat:* Ngugi's Debts to Conrad," *Benin Review,* 1 (June 1974), 89.
5. Howard, pp. 97–107. See also Charles E. Nnolim, "Background Setting: Key to the Structure of Ngugi's *The River Between*," *Obsidian,* 2 (Summer 1976), 20–29.
6. Raymond Firth, *Symbols: Public and Private* (London: Allen & Unwin, 1973), p. 207.
7. The symbolism of *A Grain of Wheat* is less influenced than its plot-thematic structure by Conrad's fiction (mainly *Under Western Eyes {UWE}*). For the latter, see B. Jabbi, "Conrad's Influence on Betrayal in *A Grain of Wheat*," *Research in African Literatures,* 11 (Spring 1980), 50–83.
8. See especially Victor Turner, *The Forest of Symbols: Aspects of Ndembu Ritual* (Ithaca: Cornell University Press, 1967); *The Drums of Affliction: A Study of Religious Processes among the Ndembu of Zambia* (Oxford: Clarendon Press, 1968); and *The Ritual Process: Structure and Anti-Structure* (Harmondsworth: Penguin, 1974).
9. A detailed analysis of these dominant symbols was first undertaken by me in chapter 3 of "The African Narrative Tradition: Folktale and Novel," B.A. dissertation presented to the English Department in Fourah Bay College, Freetown, in May 1968.
10. Obumselu, p. 89.
11. For the relevant corroborative evidence, see, for example, the following episodes in Lawrence's *The Rainbow* (Harmondsworth: Penguin, 1966): Anna's responses to Will's church singing (pp. 110–14) and to the phoenix butter-stamper he carved for her (pp. 116–17); the unfortunate history of his "Creation of Eve" panel carving (pp. 120–21, 174–75); their survey of cathedrals and church paintings (pp. 158–67, 200–06); and Will's withered return twenty years on to artistic work (pp. 355–56).
12. Jomo Kenyatta, for example, recounts the same "Gokoyo-Moombi" creation myth in *Facing Mount Kenya* (London: Secker & Warburg, 1938), pp. 3–8, and *My People of Kikuyu* (London: Lutterworth Press, 1942), pp. 6–7. In the latter he glosses the name "Moombi" as "the creator or the moulder." Josiah Mwangi Kariuki, in *Mau Mau Detainee* (London: Oxford University Press, 1963), also glosses "Gikonyo" as meaning "navel," which may be suggestive of the tree at the navel of the world in the same Kikuyu tribal myth.
13. Editor's Note: In subsequent editions, "curve" was changed to "carve."

Ngũgĩ wa Thiong'o's *A Grain of Wheat:*
Season of Irony

KENNETH HARROW

I should have been a pair of ragged claws
Scuttling across the floors of silent seas

—The Love Song of J. Alfred Prufrock

Between the idea
and the reality
Between the motion
and the act
Falls the Shadow

—The Hollow Men

With the publication of Ngũgĩ wa Thiong'o's *A Grain of Wheat* in 1967,[1] the African viewpoint on the struggle for independence in Kenya was given its fullest, most complex, and most moving expression. East African literature appeared also to have finally come into its own with this novel which capped Ngũgĩ's burgeoning career. Two prior works, *Weep Not, Child* and *The River Between,* had established Ngũgĩ's sensitivity to the crisis engendered by colonialism and to the conflicts and brutality Kenyans had experienced in their revolt against British rule. But with the fuller scope accorded the movement for independence and the questionable consequences of Uhuru, Ngũgĩ emerged as one of the major voices of the new wave of postindependence writers.

In many ways Ngũgĩ utilized the elements of fiction in *A Grain of Wheat* in a distinctively African way. War and its nightmarish consequences form much of the substance of the novel's themes, all of which are grounded in the specifically Kenyan experiences of the violent times that led to independence. The imagery draws upon the African environment, geography, and seasons in accordance with fundamental patterns that have little correlation to the archetypal values attached to them by European traditions, as so well cata-

Reprinted with permission from Indiana University Press from Kenneth Harrow, "Ngũgĩ wa Thiong'o's *A Grain of Wheat:* Season of Irony," *Research in African Literatures* (Indiana University Press) 16, no. 2 (Summer 1985): 343–63.

loged by Frye. The mode of irony as employed by Ngũgĩ is not original, but as in the writings of Ngũgĩ's Nigerian contemporary Soyinka and many other African writers, it is particularly responsive to current conditions and sensibilities in Africa. An emergent body of literature written in this mode has recently developed across the continent.

Structurally, *A Grain of Wheat* is built on a series of character studies in which, looking back from the perspective of Kenya on the eve of independence, Ngũgĩ gradually reveals the complicated past in each of the characters' lives. The novel is panoramic, in that we are presented with the full spectrum of heroes, traitors, oppressed and oppressors, and particularly with those who do not fit comfortably into any such easily defined categories. The fuller treatment is reserved for those moments of moral uncertainty, often experienced as betrayal and relived as excruciating guilt, and which define the boundaries of the characters' lives and their sphere of moral action. The principal characters experience more of doubt than certainty in their lives—they are the conquered, apparently victims of something larger than an unfortunate immediate circumstance, something closer to being a malevolent condition that engulfs all of life itself. The critical issue of establishing the novel's mode, here viewed as the form of irony defined by Frye, is heightened by its relationship to the constricting universe in which the characters move.

In order to build an adequate complexity into his vision, Ngũgĩ employed devices that refuse absolutist solutions. His use of imagery most clearly conveys this: the seasons and their elements, the sun, the rain, light and dark, appear repeatedly, almost insidiously insisting upon interpretations that are nonreductionist. Similarly, conventions of comedy and tragedy seem inadequate to explain the horrors of a nightmarish universe: failures in communication and in self-understanding are ultimately more characteristic of irony than of any other mode, and Ngũgĩ expands upon this sense of loss, of a gap, until it seems that the cosmos itself is in complicity.

Though Ngũgĩ was undoubtedly influenced by such authors as Conrad and Eliot, we must seek in his original use of the elements of fiction indications of how the African sensibility is responding to the realities of its time. Since independence, that vision, among the major authors of African fiction, has not been a complacent one. To many it has seemed that "mere anarchy" has been set loose upon the world, and to borrow the phrase from the title of Soyinka's second novel, the seasons of anomy have been visited upon the continent. Irony is the final expression of that anarchy, and Ngũgĩ's *A Grain of Wheat* stands as the strongest example of the ironic mode in East African fiction.

I

The central point of reference of the narrative is established at the beginning by having the action located in a typical Kikuyu village, Thabai, on the eve of the Uhuru celebrations. We are quickly thrust into the network of personal relationships that cross the lives of those taken for heroes in the long struggle for freedom, such as Mugo, General R, and the martyred Kihika, along with the traitors, such as Karanja. Those whom we initially sense to be less obviously morally charged with positive or negative qualities then emerge— Mumbi and Gikonyo, whose names echo the primeval Adam and Eve couple in Kikuyu mythology, and finally the equally unheroic, undifferentiated mass of villagers, mostly peasant farmers, traders, or craftsmen, whose passivity or suffering throws into relief the main dynamics of action involving the protagonists.

This most auspicious of moments in Kenyan history, with which Ngũgĩ chooses to open the novel, is presented to us in a singularly undramatic fashion at the outset: we find ourselves in Mugo's hut where he dreams that rainwater is dripping on him through the worn thatched roof. Indeed, the season cannot escape our notice: independence came to Kenya in December, during the rainy season. On the night before the Uhuru celebrations, we learn there was a rainstorm of such proportions that "some trees were uprooted whole, while others broke by the stems, or lost their branches" (p. 233). This dampened augury of the elements was not without its precedents. Earlier that same evening the villagers of Thabai had sung and danced, praising the heroes of the freedom struggle, Kihika and Mugo:

> Somewhere a woman suggested we go and sing to Mugo, the hermit, at his hut. The cry was taken up by the crowd, who, even before the decision was taken, had already started tearing through the drizzle and the dark to Mugo's hut. For more than an hour Mugo's hut was taken prisoner. His name was on everybody's lips. We wove new legends around his name and imagined deeds. We hoped that Mugo would come out and join us, but he did not open the door to our knocks. (p. 232)

The rain which waters the preindependence celebration and the darkness through which the villagers pass figure in Ngũgĩ's broader schematic use of the elements which functions to give coherence to the ironic tone and mode of the novel. According to Frye's well-known formulation, each of the four seasons is linked to its own mode: spring-comedy, summer-romance, autumn-tragedy, and winter-irony and satire. In Africa, however, these four seasons do not occur as in the regions with a temperate climate (except in the extreme north and south); almost everywhere the alternation of rainy and dry seasons is known. Kenya is no exception. The landscape and elements of weather continually appear in *A Grain of Wheat,* functioning as a backdrop to the main action.

The Kikuyu living around Thabai and Rung'ei in the Gikuyu Reserves people a land of ridges and valleys. When Gikonyo is exiled to the concentration camp at Yala, the sun, dust, and heat combine with the flatness of the terrain to complete the feeling of exile. "They were abandoned in a desert where not even a straying voice from the world of men could reach them. This frightened Gikonyo, for, who, then, would come to rescue them? The sun would scorch them dead and they would be buried in the hot sand where the traces of their graves would be lost forever" (p. 123). Likened to the burning plains of hell, Rira camp "was in a remote part of Kenya, near the coast where no rain fell and nothing grew except sand, sand, and rocks." There men abandoned the seeds of their common humanity and resorted to desperate measures: "A common game in Rira had been to bury a man naked, in the hot sand, sometimes leaving him there overnight" (p. 150). Gikonyo's vision of home and inspiration is Kerinyaga—Mount Kenya, the sacred symbol for the Kikuyu—the sight of whose snow-capped tops "moved him to tears" (p. 277) in his last detention camp. His dreams of salvation, as it were, are shaped by the Kikuyu attachment to their land, so that when he returns to find Mumbi the mother of another man's child, his despair is figured in terms of the landscape: "Life had no colour. It was one endless blank sheet, so flat. There were no valleys, no mountains, no streams, no trees—nothing" (p. 132). The sign of victory with which he had hoped to have his return graced was "green leaves" (p. 130); clearly the sterility of the desert plain is the antithesis of the green rolling hills.

Exile and concentration camp are consistently marked by extreme heat, sun, a desert landscape, sand, and dust, presaging the elements of Gikonyo's unhappy return: "Some of the dust entered Gikonyo's eyes and throat; he rubbed his eyes with the back of his hand (water streamed from his eyes) and he coughed with irritation" (p. 130). Likewise, the suffering of the people is seen in the ravages visited on the countryside by the relentless sun: "The battered bumpy land sloped on either side; sickly crops just recovering from a recent drought, one more scourge which had afflicted the country in this period leaving the anxious faces of mothers dry and cracked, were scattered on the strips of shamba on either side of the road" (pp. 120–21). Mugo also experiences the sun and dryness as complements to his hidden despair. At the very beginning of the novel, he is driven by guilt—a guilt compounded by the mistaken praise heaped on him by his fellow villagers. Despite their illusions, he suffers: "In the shamba, he felt hollow. There were no crops on the land and what with the dried-up weeds, Gakaraku, micege, mikengeria, bangi—and the sun, the country appeared sick and dull" (pp. 8–9). Mugo works the soil, but without enthusiasm, and like Gikonyo finds his mood reflected in the uncongenial dust: "He could hear the soil, dry and hollow, tumble down. Dust flew into the sky, enveloped him, then settled into his hair and clothes. Once a grain of dust went into his left eye. He quickly dropped the jembe in anger and rubbed his eye which smarted with pain as water tossed out from both eyes" (p. 9).

Indeed the dry season appears as a "drought"—the term used to describe the two months without rain during which Gikonyo hoarded his sacks of beans and maize so as to sell them later at a higher price during the rainy times. But the irony of the seasons is such that during the season of drought and heat the granaries are full from the previous harvest and the work demanded by the fields is less extensive, while the period of rain, which brings green leaves and cooler weather, is a time of hard work and scarcity: it is then that the food and seeds in the granaries must be stretched and made to last until the end of the growing period when once again food can be harvested.

This ambiguity is developed in the symbolism of the sun and rain as sharing both good and bad attributes. One day in May 1955, at the height of the Emergency, before his imbroglio in the affair of Kihika, Mugo finds utter contentment in working his fields in the sun: "The sun burnt the bare black torso pleasantly." Working his crops, Mugo reveled in the verdant fullness of the earth: "The air was fresh and clear and sharp. The fields around, all covered with green things—long, wide leaves hiding the dark earth—appeared beautiful to look at." Yet, in practically the same moment that it blesses, the sun also curses with its force: "The sun became increasingly hotter; the moisture on leaves evaporated; leaves drooped, so that at noon the greenness had waned, slightly ashy, and the fields appeared tired" (p. 143). Mugo's subsequent vision of the Lord calling on him to be a Moses leading the people reveals the same ambivalence: as a false prophet his role is to become a Judas rather than a redeemer. Others share the same Janus-headed fate. Gikonyo and Mumbi first discover their love for each other under the benevolent eye of the sun. As Gikonyo pulls Mumbi down onto the rich ground in the long grasses, "her body gleamed in the sun" (p. 106). Ironically, both Gikonyo and Mugo are sent to the same sun-beaten concentration camp, Muhia, away from the ridges and the dark earth and green grasses, in a place where the sun always burned down.

The instances of horror visited on Kenya were multiplied repeatedly throughout the days of the Emergency. Villagers were forced to burn their huts and relocate in new "protected" locations. As the huts in the old Thabai are fired and the soldiers pour petrol on the thatched roofs, "[t]he sun burnt hot" (p. 159), and Mumbi and Wangari stand helplessly by, watching in despair the destruction of their homes. Blood is shed in the building of the trenches, in the beatings in the camps, in the punishment of the freedom fighters, in the slaying of collaborators, in the torturing of prisoners; blood, rubbish, garbage, excrement, as well as dust and sand, give sterility its features under the glaring eye of the burning sun. The white man's gaze paralyzes, and Mugo and Karanja quail before Thompson; the queen's "protective" arm falls on her trembling subjects; a universe best described as that of a concentration camp, a scene from a holocaust, is evoked in these images of a war-torn and oppressed Kenya. The symbol for this is a sun of brutal intensity which wreaks destruction upon the land, transforming its fertile and life-giving properties into the sterility of a desert.

Yet life is not associated, purely and simply, with rain either. On the one hand, freedom and all God's blessings are "rained" down: as the Reverend Kingori put it at his invocation for the Independence Day celebration, " '[L]et your tears stream down upon us, for your tears, oh Lord, are eternal blessings' " (p. 247). Others said that "the falling water was a blessing for our hard-won freedom. Murungu on high never slept: he always let his tears fall to this, our land, from Agu to Agu" (p. 202). At its most beneficial, rain is associated with growing plants and the greenness of the earth. The first gift from Ngai, about which the children sing, is the land: "Ngai has given Gikuyu a beautiful country" (p. 202), and the morning after the violent storm that breaks on the eve of Independence, Ngũgĩ gives us his most beautiful picture of a new land, a new country, a new life breathed into the soil by the life-giving showers: "But the rain had stopped. The air was soft and fresh, and an intimate warmth oozed from the pregnant earth to our hearts" (p. 233). The counterpoint to Mugo's and Gikonyo's alienation and exile is this vision of fructification—the "pregnant earth"—echoed later in the novel in Gikonyo's project of carving a stool for Mumbi which would be decorated with the images of a family, including a pregnant woman.

Yet the description of rain on the Wednesday before Independence sends more mixed signals: "Water dripped down the sack and the pieces of clothing with which [people] covered their heads; little pools formed on the cement floor" (p. 202), the latter phrase echoing less happy circumstances. When Mugo was first arrested and beaten, what he remembered most vividly was not "the hobnailed shoes [that] dug into his flesh, but . . . the water on the cement floor" (p. 197). If rain ushers in Independence and hope for the new days of freedom, it also reminds Mugo of his guilt and symbolizes that hidden, haunted, and guilt-ridden past. This is the image, in fact, with which Ngũgĩ begins the novel:

> Mugo felt nervous. He was lying on his back and looking at the roof. Sooty locks hung from the fern and grass thatch and all pointed at his heart. A clear drop of water was delicately suspended above him. The drop fattened and grew dirtier as it absorbed grains of soot. Then it started drawing towards him. He tried to shut his eyes. They would not close. He tried to move his head: it was firmly chained to the bed frame. The drop grew larger and larger as it grew closer and closer to his eyes. (p. 3)

The image of the sooty drop recurs in other forms later as dirt and water mix to form mud and filth, another facet of Ngũgĩ's vision of hell.

Mugo's guilt is presented from the beginning as the hidden wellspring of all his actions. A similar conjunction of guilt, water, and dirt is linked to others, with Karanja's final departure from Rung'ei painted thus: "The drizzle tapped, drummed the guitar and bag. Soon the dust and the soot soaked and started to slug down" (p. 257), and as he, like Mugo earlier, walks out of the falling water, he is apparently indifferent to the fact that he is being soaked: "His head and clothes were drenched with water" (p. 259). When Mugo trudges home in the downpour, he calls attention to himself, occasioning comments from all those at the New Rung'ei Market who, like the novel's narrator, take cover: "What is he doing fooling in the rain? . . . It is a dumb and deaf man he is. . . . Maybe he has a long way to walk, and he fears the night will catch him. . . . Or maybe he has something heavy in his heart" (p. 203). Both Karanja and Mugo are guilt-ridden characters whose eventual isolation is a consequence of their antisocial or amoral character. The remarks occasioned by Mugo's exposure to the rain reflect society's response to that which sets him apart from the others.

Moods of joy or elation momentarily illuminate and lighten the heavy burdens of existence borne by most of the characters, but pain and despair follow quickly, as rain, cold, and darkness follow intimations of release from oppression. After Mugo passes the market—in a rain that is again likened to Ngai's tears, or to that which fell when Kenyatta was released from prison—a rapid change for the worse occurs: "Then suddenly the sun seemed to die prematurely, the country and sky turned dull and grey" (p. 203). Death follows life, in this scene and throughout the novel, and indeed couched within the symbolism of this and almost all scenes is to be found the same paradox given as the oxymoron of life in death and death in life. The same tears of blessing that Ngai sends to waken the green buds of new life form pools of water on hard cement. The horror of men being tortured by having bottles driven up their anuses is so nightmarish that only psychological correlates can match its intensity, as in the mental pain man inflicts upon himself in the guilt of betrayal: yet the spilled blood is likened to the agony of the seed which must crack and die before a new life can be created—the Christian theme evoked in the novel's title taken from the Epistles of Paul and John.

The seasons in Africa do not flow as with the gentle rhythms of European weather. They come with violence and are considerably more extreme, if not in temperature, at least in rainfall and sunlight. The two months or more of drought that precede the rains bake the soil and turn it to a dust that covers the traveler from head to foot, penetrates every crevice and recess. The heavy rains, when they come, create muddy roads and paths leaving their mark on the walls and dirtying the clothes of all who venture out. The weather is always strong, always dominant, visible, aggressive even, and it brings life and death to the strong and weak alike: its force is irresistible, inescapable, as in the violent storm that came on the eve of Independence:

Later in the night, the drizzle changed into a heavy downpour. Lightning, followed by thunder, would for a second or two red-white-light our huts, even though it only came through the cracks in the walls. The wind increased with the rain. A moaning sound, together with a continuous booming which went on all night, came from swaying and breaking trees and hedges as the wind and the rain beat the leaves and the branches. Some decaying thatched roofs freely let in rain, so that pools collected on the floor. To avoid being drenched, people kept shifting their beds from spot to spot, only to be followed by a new leakage. (pp. 232–33)

As in David Rubadiri's "An African Thunderstorm," the storm aptly suggests the pervasive destruction caused by the white man's arrival and invasion, the breaking of those who resisted, the necessity to bend, to shift, to move continually so as to survive. The devastation appears to be wrought on the whole social fabric, but there are also intimations for the future, for the time when the storm will have passed and the new age dawned. After the uprooting of the crops, the laceration of the plants, the land still lies there, pregnant with possibilities for another day, another life. Death and life are the yin and yang of the rainy and dry seasons: they are polar opposites which follow upon each other so automatically that neither can be thought of in isolation from the other as embracing totally positive or negative values. The seasons bring relief, and life is present in both—but so is death, oppression, and guilt. The appearance of a storm of destruction quickly yields to images of resurrection; Ngai's tears pass into premature death; the sun burns, gives life, and withers the green leaves. Both are necessary. Mugo's confession to the crowd of celebrants at Rung'ei lightens his heart and frees him from guilt, but it is immediately followed by fear, the desire to escape, and death. Judas had very little time in which to enjoy his thirty shekels—Mugo had even less.

The rain and the sun are the necessary ingredients for life, but they are also harbingers and carriers of death. The paradox of a dry season, a season of "drought," marked by full granaries and harvest celebrations, and a wet season marked by green fields and growth, by new life, and yet by stretched, empty stomachs, perhaps explains the difficulty in assigning simple qualities of mode to their literary equivalents. Life in death or death in life is paradoxical, and such paradox is revealed in the characters' lives themselves, and in their psychological burdens. Here the consistent use of irony is apparent, and it seems appropriate to attach the label of irony to the seasons as well, since in this novel appearance is so often belied by hidden truth.

II

Irony presupposes contradiction. In speech, it arises when there is a contradiction between an ostensible meaning and one that is implicit. In events, the contradiction lies in an occurrence that is apparent belied by one that is hidden, but actual or real. In characterization the *eiron* is "the man who deprecates himself."[2] When Mugo says he is not worthy to give the Independence Day speech, his self-deprecation is doubly ironic: he is unworthy, but not humble as his supplicants think. The deepening of irony, however, leads to characterization in which a victim or scapegoat—a *pharmakos*—appears, again frequently seeming to be other than what he is. As irony moves in a universe in which the objective truth is hidden behind a screen of apparent reality, the depiction of life often entails the interplay between the forces that reveal truth and those that conceal it. The victim of these forces does not master his fate: indeed it is fate itself that should be called into question, though to do so in such a universe would be meaningless: who could play such a role? In the end Job backs down; and Mugo lacks the imagination to push his daring so far. It is the size of the universe that shrinks characters in irony. If Sophocles' Oedipus is a victim of fate, nonetheless he acts and feels the weight of responsibility as Cocteau's modern counterpart, caught in the *engrenage,* cannot do. Thus all the characters in *A Grain of Wheat* may be said to be victims in that, like the *pharmakos,* each is "innocent in the sense that what happens to him is far greater than anything he has done provokes, like the mountaineer whose shout brings down an avalanche. He is guilty in the sense that he is a member of a guilty society, or living in a world where such injustices are an inescapable part of existence."[3] This description of guilt seems particularly appropriate for characters whose lives are governed by the mechanism of a concentration camp in which the condition of survival is the complicity of executioner and victim alike. The poor Gikonyos who confess, Mugos who betray, Karanjas who collaborate, or even Mumbis who slip just once, all survive and bear the evil fruits of guilt or a burdened past. Only Kihika, who dies, may be said to have avoided such a fate.

If irony is the proper mode for such fiction, then death and chaos or destruction are the signs of its seasonal attributes. We have seen how the sun and rain have Janus-like faces of death and life. When they follow with the natural rhythms of order, life flourishes. But when chaos, or, as Soyinka aptly terms it, anomy prevails, death takes the ascendant. For both Soyinka and Ngũgĩ, internal uncertainty and obsession are indissolubly linked to social and political disintegration: the dark downward spiral of events that resulted in the Biafran conflict is captured by Soyinka in the nightmarish vision of his second novel, *Season of Anomy;* and the dark, narrow confines of a solitary cell form much of the boundaries of his autobiographical account of prison life in *The Man Died.* For Ngũgĩ, darkness is often used to convey this same negative side. Though the elements of guilt, rain, cold, and the darkness are all present in the opening scene in Mugo's hut, the movement in the novel generally proceeds from light to darkness. The progression is not a simple and direct one; like the seasons, light and darkness are not presented as purely diametrical opposites. Further, they are linked to the sun or to cloudy weather which are also dualistic in nature. The brightness of the sun is mentioned at times of discomfiture or even betrayal, as when Mugo decides to betray Kihika: "And his mind was a white blank dazzling the eye like the sun at midday" (p. 222). However, generally the light does not last; its pleasantness fades; and in this striking passage Ngũgĩ rapidly encapsulates Mugo's vertiginous descent into the obscurity of a personal hell: "Kihika's face was indelibly engraved in his mind; . . . Mugo shiver[ed] in spite of the *daylight*. Imagine a man who has been walking through a *twilight* and feels security in his isolation. Then suddenly *darkness* descends" (p. 220; emphasis added).

At times the coolness and darkness of the forest are favorably evoked, although the couples who seek refuge there for their lovemaking invariably find a clearing, a place in the sun. But the dark, cold, wet night sets the scene for most of the dramatic action of the last half of the novel as we have seen in the storm that precedes Independence Day and in the misty cold weather that follows it. The dark conveys the feeling of solitude, and both Karanja's and Mugo's isolation (as well as Gatu's solitary confinement in Yala camp) are framed in terms of darkness. In powerful terms Ngũgĩ sets the stage for Mugo's self-deluded plan to conceal his guilt and to lead the people on Independence Day. Leaving the bar where he encounters Githua and General R, Mugo marches out into the night: "Mugo was now alone in the darkness" (p. 146). Except for the one magic moment when Mumbi reaches out and touches him, this small phrase might best describe Mugo's entire life. Mugo's betrayal of Kihika, through which he thought to free himself and at least momentarily find solidarity with the whites, is marked as a passage from self-deception to despair; again it is darkness which lies at the end of this trajectory: "He thrust his arms into the air. The bottom was so far away he could see only darkness" (p. 227).

Likewise, the conjunction of the dark and of cold rain, a dismal picture of hell awaiting those who flee from commitment, or those who betray their own people, faces Karanja at the end. Dante's image of a descent is that of a path that leads downward into the cold, frozen ice, to a place devoid of all light. Karanja is surely headed there at the end, for like the figure of Judas in *The Inferno,* or like Mugo, he is a traitor whose life has lost all meaning: "He sipped another mouthful of tea. It had gone cold, and he pushed it aside. Life was empty like the dark and the mist that enclosed the earth" (p. 261). Our last image of Karanja, soaked, standing on the platform "like a ghost," close enough to the train to recall the earlier suggestion that suicide and death were attached to it, is one of utter emptiness and isolation: ". . . the darkness around him deepened; the night seemed to have grown darker" (p. 262).

We should not, however, think that Ngũgĩ appropriates a simple dualism of light-dark, good-evil. Light has its negative sides, as I have shown above, and the darkness is not all bad. Kihika and the freedom fighters emerge from the darkness and disappear back into it. It affords relief from the oppressive sun, as we indicated for the couples in the forest. The earth is dark, and most significantly Mumbi's beauty is portrayed as joining the light to the darkness. In Mugo's perception of her, the two seem mixed in confusing fashion: "He saw light at the bottom of the pool dancing in her eyes. He felt her dark power over him" (p. 155). The confusion, however, is only temporary. As she continues to make her confession to him, and as that confession shows him the possibility of a life he had not imagined, Ngũgĩ recasts the image with greater clarity and beauty: "The light still played in her dark voluptuous eyes" (p. 171). In thus portraying Mumbi as a symbol of hope, Ngũgĩ suggests that pure absolutes do not exist in real life. Further, he dismisses the illusions of Gikonyo, who dreamed of her in detention: "He raised his head and saw her angel's smile and her hands carried a flaming torch that dispelled the darkness in front of her. She wanted to lift him up, she who appeared so pure, an incorruptible reality in a world of changing shadows" (p. 129). Here Gikonyo's vision of Mumbi has the uncomfortable ring of Thompson's visionary idealizing of his queen and his mission.

What gives Ngũgĩ's use of light and dark imagery its particular ironic quality is the self-conscious manner in which it is linked to other conventional European images of alienation. The most obvious example is T. S. Eliot's portrait of J. Alfred Prufrock, whose vision of himself as a lost sea crab is echoed in Mugo's words. Immediately after referring to the "light at the bottom of the pool dancing in [Mumbi's] eyes," Mugo sees himself in that very pool, evoking Prufrock's figure: "He . . . was scurrying with hands and feet at the bottom of the silent pool. It was terrible for him this struggle: he did not want to drown" (pp. 155–56). The struggle is desperate, not noble, that of a creature fighting for its life, not a man whose dignity is at stake. The silence in the pool complements the two principal qualities of alienation shared by Mugo and the others in this novel—their isolation or sense of being alone, and their failure to communicate—qualities doubly inimical in the African context in which, as Mbiti puts it, "I am because we are."[4]

What lifts Mumbi above this level is not her purity—this being Gikonyo's illusion of her—but her honesty and especially her insistence upon communicating, on telling her story without hiding it. Ironically, again, it is the male survivors who have a past to hide or which they would like to forget: Lieutenant Koinandu his rape of Dr. Lynd; General R his "patricide"; Mugo his betrayal of Kihika; Gikonyo his breaking of the oath; Thompson the beatings at Rira; and Karanja his abuse of power and betrayal of his people, as well as his exploitation of Mumbi's moment of weakness, which in this case is too flagrant to be hidden. If Mumbi hides less, it might be said that a child is harder to conceal than an act of betrayal, but also that a child of whatever parentage symbolizes hope and fertility, a new life. Mumbi's life-giving properties are the answer to Mugo's alienation, and the use of Eliot's symbolism is not complete until this positive vision of Mumbi is seen to inspire Mugo. Eventually Mugo perceives the light in Mumbi's eyes, and thus sees more clearly his own situation: "he was at the bottom of the pool, but up there, above the pool, ran the earth; life, struggle, even amidst pain and blood and poverty seemed beautiful" (p. 171).

As the symbolism of darkness deepens, the sense of bitter irony increases, and the darkness is now tied to death. For Joseph Conrad, man's brutality can be seen buried in the soul of Kurtz. As Marlow pursues his voyage inland, he sees the veneer of civilization gradually being stripped off, revealing a vision of savagery at the heart of the bestiality. Marlow discovers the darkness, figured metaphorically within Kurtz and voiced with his dying words, "The horror. The horror." Robson—the embodiment of death, the white man as killer—wears that same visage of destruction: "He was a man-eater, walking in the night and day. He was death" (p. 212). Appropriately his demise parallels that of Kurtz: Robson dies uttering the one word "Brutes" (p. 212). Like Achebe, in the ironic ending of *Things Fall Apart,* Ngũgĩ here uses European referents to refute imperialist claims to European superiority—employing Conrad's terms to his own purposes of transvaluation.

Mugo's reaction to the torture and the camps, to the rule of Robson and Thompson, highlights this use of darkness as an ironic recasting of the "light" of the "civilizing mission." The conventional imagery functions as the shell or surface which is needed if the irony is to burst the illusion, and it is provided in Thompson's dream of the British Empire which originally inspired him to come to Africa: "For me, a great light had shone in the darkness" (p. 63). When the Reverend Jackson preaches about salvation, he uses the same symbolism: "One God . . . sent Christ, the son, to come and lead the way from darkness into light" (p. 97). However, when Mugo has to learn the painful truth of this same "light," he sees only darkness. On first coming across a white man, he tells Mumbi, "I did not know who he was or where he came from." After the experience of torture at Rira, ironically the same camp run by the formerly idealistic Thompson, he learns more: "Now I know that Mzungu is not a man—always remember that—he is a devil—devil. . . . I saw a man whose manhood was broken with pincers. . . . For me I only looked into an abyss and deep inside I only saw a darkness I could not penetrate" (p. 209). Total light, like total darkness, is an infernal counterpart to the season of anomy—unnatural and ultimately life negating.

The essence of irony is disjuncture. Between the rhetoric of the "white man's burden" and the black man's oppression lies a valley of contradiction. Between Gikonyo's private dream of Mumbi and the reality which greets him upon his return lies another gulf. And when he finds that Mumbi has not been faithful, not only is he lost once again in the darkness—"Gikonyo lay on his back and stared into the darkness" (p. 133)—he now experiences his separation from Mumbi as a disjunction: "Could the valley of silence between him and the woman now be crossed?" (p. 133). One of the recurrent motifs of the novel is the failure of couples to communicate with each other: Wambuku is deluded by Kihika's response to her request that he stay with her, and for a brief moment they each think they have found happiness, but only "in their separate delusions" (p. 114). When Thompson thinks of opening up his heart to Margery on the eve of their departure, he finds her asleep, and like Gikonyo earlier in the novel, who paused in front of Mumbi's door as if to go in to her, he retires without a word. Both couples do not communicate: "There is nothing to talk about," says Gikonyo, "with acid emphasis" (p. 35), and when he does speak it is to accuse, to berate: "Have you no ears? It's to you that I'm speaking" (p. 189).

Speech is used as a weapon, but so is silence, and Mugo's refusal to confess to an oath he did not take is the only way he has to deal with the whites. The silence on the part of the truly brave, like Kihika, goes down to the grave with them. Mugo's silence, of course, is mistaken for courage—another irony, since it is actually his sense of guilt which drives him to accept the punishments. In *A Grain of Wheat,* silence is rarely heroic, or when it is, it is tied to death, as in the tragic killing of the deaf-mute son of the old woman. Rather, it is more often the case that silence, like ironic speech, is the manifestation of missed or failed communication—a phenomenon so frequently portrayed in the novel as to lead one back to speculation on the universe in which the silence is set. The pervasive expression of irony here signifies what the seasons of anomy, what the total blankness of darkness or light connote—a universe of the concentration camp.

Frye's depiction of irony as a mode in which the hero is "inferior in power or intelligence to ourselves, so that we have the sense of looking down on a scene of bondage, frustration, or absurdity,"[5] is particularly apt when one considers the frustrations generated by Gikonyo's failure to listen to Mumbi, Mugo's semiarticulate ruminations, or even the Thompsons' and Karanja's aborted or gauche attempts to speak to each other. None of the characters, and especially none of the surviving male characters, is treated heroically. In every case their lives are marked by some failure, some hidden flaw, some guilty past. But in a sense, ultimately the burden does not fall entirely upon them because, as Frye observes in the case of tragic irony, "human nature [is] under sentence of death."[6] The ironic hero, the *pharmakos,* is a victim *despite* his guilt, his sins, because the overwhelming oppression of the universe bears down upon him with ferocious intensity: "The incongruous irony of human life," in this vision, is such that "all attempts to transfer guilt to a victim give that victim something of the dignity of innocence."[7] This description is most fittingly applied to Mugo at the end, though in a fuller sense it applies to all those characters' lives for whom there is no absolute truth to be found, no pure light or darkness.

It is the pervasiveness of this irony that is shed on every character, every relationship, and every perception that gives one the impression of a total universe burdened by lacunae, frustration, failure, and deception. The villagers singing Mugo's praises on the eve of Independence deepen the irony by accentuating his complex emotions of guilt and escapism, while at the same time naively dancing to the pipes of some malevolent spirit. Every day that starts out with a fresh morning and ends with such overcast gloom that the darkness at noon melds unperceived into the fall of night is an expression of irony. The "protecting shadow" of the "christian woman" (p. 15), the white man's "benevolence and protection" (p. 16) that hang over the land like a "sword" (p. 5), only form part of the larger irony of history for which the appearance of changing events is belied by the recurrence of oppression: "What happened yesterday could happen today. The same thing, over and over again, through history" (p. 122). The repeated statements of the various dreams of each character—of Kihika's desire to be a Jesus or a Moses, of Mugo's to be the same, of Mumbi to be an Esther, of Thompson, of the Christians and born-again Christians and missionaries, the redeemers, the saviors, of the whites and of the warriors in the forest—all end in ironic disillusionment: "We fought for freedom. And yet now!" (p. 145). The terrible irony of Mugo's submission to punishment being taken as an act of resistance or courage; his elevation, ironically, to the status of a hero; the gap of irony which glares at the reader who sees Mugo's name linked to that of the man he betrayed; all are too huge to arise from any single human will. The irony pervades all, encompasses all, so that even the words unintentionally express meanings unbeknown to the speaker: Warui commenting on Mugo's famous speech, which he and all the others misinterpreted: "Those were words from no ordinary heart" (p. 77). Like the flat, sterile, burning desert or the dreary expanses of mist and darkness, irony is life denying when it embraces all actions, all hopes. Finally, irony denies freedom, and with it responsibility, by incorporating guilt into the fabric of the universe. Thus it is all the more compelling that the most terrible irony occurs in the very heart of the novel—in the relationship between past and present.

We have seen above how totalitarian force and terror operate to deny time itself: the ultimate ironic commentary on life: "The same thing over and over." Those who live in isolation, under illusion, or with guilt also deny time by either refusing responsibility for the past, refusing to accept the responsibility for present actions, or refusing responsibility toward others. But if irony is life denying, life itself seems to refuse such negation: the past returns to haunt our heroes—footsteps in the dark follow Gikonyo and Karanja, blood dripping on walls obsesses Mugo. The Independence Day footrace brings to a climax the futile attempt of each of the men to escape himself, his past: "He did not want to think about the past" (p. 243). The return of the ghost of the dead Gitogo is a ghoulish reminder to all that the past cannot be escaped: Mugo's childhood with his aunt persistently returns in his encounters with the old woman; the crimes committed by Thompson, the General's brutal slaying of Reverend Jackson, and all the other events that shaped the lives of the characters return and insist on being confronted until they are exorcised. There is no flight from one's past: it is carried with each in all that he or she says and does. If the failure to deal with the past gives rise to irony, the inevitable resurgence of the past suggests the limitations of irony—and the need to go beyond it. Mumbi is the key to this going beyond, this overreaching of the frustrated condition of life in death.

Before hearing Mumbi's account of her life, Mugo had decided to lead the people at the Independence Day celebration. Her confession to him, as well as General R's words about Githua's real past, had the effect of breaking his illusions, of reinforcing his sense of isolation: "He was again alone, his vision disrupted by Mumbi and General R" (p. 172). Gradually her words, and her confidence in him, play on his guilt. If she represents the light at the end of the dark passage, he can reach her only by following her example. More than any other character, Mugo tries to seek isolation from others, from the past and from responsibility. Mumbi makes this impossible:

> He felt pursued from behind, and he could not escape. He wanted to return to his hut. . . . But he was irrevocably drawn to the lives of the villagers. He tried to think of something else—himself, his aunt—but he could not escape from his knowledge of Gikonyo's and Mumbi's lives. . . . Yesterday, this morning, before Mumbi told her story, the huts had run by him, and never sang a thing of the past. Now they were different: the huts, the dust, the trench, Wambuku, Kihika, Karanja, detention-camps, the white face, barbed-wire, death. (p. 195)

Forced to come face to face with himself, Mugo begins to experience the effects of Mumbi's painful revelations as well as her openness, her faith. He is compelled by her—not by General R or Gikonyo, each of whom reserves some measure of guilt, of a private past for which they attempt to compensate—because, though not without illusions or weaknesses of her own, Mumbi most successfully gives voice to the life-giving qualities within. She addresses her tasks with both hands, rejecting absolute solutions to human problems. She regrets not having accepted Karanja's offer of food earlier: so what if it gives the appearance of misconduct—purity has a price to pay which life cannot afford. She accepts the need to suffer because she senses the truth that is repeated throughout the novel, "that which thou sowest is not quickened except it die." The transvalued Christian message is that suffering in life need not be life denying, need not be ironic—indeed, no seed can grow without cracking open its case, no life can continue and develop without dealing with suffering and pain, and especially with the agony of guilt over one's past.

Nowhere is this message conveyed with more force than at this moment of *anagnorisis* to which Mugo is driven: "How was it that Mumbi's story had *cracked open* his dulled inside and released imprisoned thoughts and feelings" (p. 195; emphasis added). The sense of isolation, of fleeing before his past, crumbles before this pressure:

> Previously he liked to see events in his life as isolated. . . . One had no choice in anything as surely as one had no choice in one's birth. He did not, then, tire his mind by trying to connect what went before with what followed after. . . . Incidents tumbled on him. . . . He was again drawn to the trench and seemed impotent to resist this return to yesterday. (p. 195)

Confronted with the image of his past, his punishment, and his deception—the trench where the first impressions of his heroism were born—he relives what has gone by despite his best efforts to evade it.

When Gitogo's ghost subsequently reappears, Warui weakly attempts to repudiate it: "Those buried in the earth should remain in the earth. Things of yesterday should remain with yesterday" (p. 198). However, Mugo can no longer find solace in this philosophy. Vainly he attempts to flee the apparition, the judgment of the past: "Life itself seemed a meaningless wandering. There was surely no connection between sunrise and sunset, between today and tomorrow" (p. 198). But the ghost will not be laid, and Mumbi's words continue to act upon him: "Why was he troubled by what was dead, he thought, remembering the old woman. And immediately he heard Mumbi's voice in his heart" (p. 199). As Mugo then collapses, writhing and moaning as the white man's whips could not make him moan, he attempts to flee the burden of responsibility: "He was moaning. Mumbi's voice was a knife which had butchered and laid naked his heart to himself. The road from his hut led to the trench. But would it not have happened. Christ would have died on the cross anyway" (p. 199). With this extraordinary rationalization, the irony here takes its most bitter turn: the disjuncture laid bare is located within Mugo himself—in the form of bad faith.

Though his final confession and death have something of Judas's fate, Mugo does not then go out and commit suicide. The point of his suffering will be lost if he does, and the ultimately ironic conclusion—that life is a "meaningless wandering"—will paint the universe in unbearably absurd terms, in unrelieved and dreary colors. More important, the suffering and Mumbi's actions will have no meaning. But just as she symbolizes life, the effect of her inspiration is to give Mugo a "glimpse of a new earth" (p. 266). The irony of Mugo's fate now "cracks" before the pressure of her openness and faith: "Every word of praise carried for [Mugo] a piercing irony. What had he done for the village? What had he done for anybody? Yet now he saw this undeserved trust in a new light, as the sweetest thing in the world" (p. 266). The image of Mumbi does not leave him, and with the arrival of Independence Day, Mugo dismisses the temptation to let Karanja take his punishment and decides to confess: "How else could he ever look Mumbi in the face? . . . It was the clarity of this vision which gave him courage as he stood before the microphone and the sudden silence. As soon as the first words were out, Mugo felt light. A load of many years was lifted from his shoulders. He was free, sure, confident" (p. 267). Though he holds to this feeling for only a minute, it is enough time for the truth to dawn upon him: "So he was responsible for whatever he had done in the past, for whatever he would do in the future" (p. 267). It was a difficult truth in light of the price of suffering it cost him, and, indeed, the price of living by it cost him his life.

The novel does not end on this triumphant note; Mugo does not ride to heaven on a fiery chariot. The vision of life here evoked in existential terms is stripped of all glamour and glory, just as Independence in Kenya failed to usher in the golden age. Mugo experiences something of the anguish and the fear that Sartre said we feel when aware of the burden of our freedom, or our responsibility—only now the weight of this is felt as hostility projected onto all those in society whom he has betrayed in turning in Kihika: "Suppose all those people had risen and dug their nails and teeth into his body?" (p. 267). He considers flight, but the dawning of new consciousness obviates old solutions: his hut no longer provides safety; the roads to escape are all blocked. The past must be confronted. He returns to the old woman's hut for the last time, seeking refuge from the weight of the newly perceived freedom, from the rain, only to see the illusions of the past recast into one last hideous scene. Thinking to see her son return, the old woman rises to greet him, emerging literally from the ashes: "You—you have come back!" (p. 268). Mugo enters into the delusion and, enraged, mistakes her ghostly form for that of his aunt. The past rises to mock him, and his response is to negate it and to strike it out: "For suddenly her face had changed. Mugo looked straight into the eyes of his aunt. A new rage moved him. Life was only a constant repetition of what happened yesterday and the day before that. Only this time she would not escape" (p. 269). But before he can put his impulse to murder the ghost out of his past into effect, the old woman falls back and dies, the final ironic comment on his existence: "And suddenly he knew: the only person who had ever claimed him was dead" (p. 269).

With Mugo's return to his hut, where he awaits General R and the final judgment, Ngũgĩ calls forth the imagery with which the novel begins, that associated with the guilt-ridden Mugo. Here the symbolism of water as representing an ineluctably guilty past is completed: "Water dripped from his coat, again in broken lines, down his legs and on to the ground. A drop was caught in his right eyelashes and the light from the lamp was split into many tiny lashes. Then the drop entered his eye, melted inside, and ran down his face like a tear" (p. 269). The subsequent appearance of General R ends the ironic and tragic fate of Mugo, but it does not give us the sense of triumph with which tragedy concludes because the larger irony of history in Kenya does not then—and does not now, for Ngũgĩ—conclude in triumph and in freedom.

The muted and bleak tones that bring this chapter of history and the characters' lives to a close sound a note of stubborn persistence, too unoptimistic to be hopeful, too attached to life's forces to be entirely, tragically ironic. The image of a pregnant woman with which the novel concludes takes hold of Gikonyo's imagination, and we realize that if the condition of life in this universe is guilt, that guilt need not destroy us if we are willing to come to grips with it. On the level of personal responsibility, this credo bears the imprimatur of existential doctrine. But this is a novel of historical proportions in which the weight of past and private responsibility cannot be divorced from public accountability. When General R confronts Mugo at the end so as to deliver the final sentence, the judgment—"You—No one will ever escape from his own action" (p. 270—he is also expounding the larger ideological conviction that events in history, as well as in our lives, have meaning and that the flight from personal responsibility has broader implications for society. The ultimate effects of negating personal responsibility are not felt just in one's private life; if they were, Mugo's acts would concern only himself, his conscience, and the law. The connection between past and present upon which this novel insists is the necessary condition for life to acquire meaning, but also and especially for historical process to occur. Gikonyo's failure to find in his commitment to Mumbi the key to his existence is not due to her betrayal, but to his mistaken faith in a totally private commitment. Between the extremes of his failure to understand the need for a larger fidelity to society—to life in the public realm—and Kihika's failure to understand Wambuku's private needs lies the ideological middle ground which this novel occupies, in which to be human is to meet the demands of both private and public commitments and in which the sense of coherence and of meaning which the actions of the past confer on the present belongs to our individual lives and to history alike. The role Mumbi plays is to inspire the protagonists to find the courage to face their responsibility, reminding us that confronting our past in both the public and private realm is part of the condition of life.

Notes

1.   James Ngugi (now known as Ngũgĩ wa Thiong'o), *A Grain of Wheat* (London: Heinemann Educational Books, 1967). Subsequent references will be annotated in the text.
2.   Northrop Frye, *Anatomy of Criticism* (Princeton: Princeton University Press, 1973), p. 40.
3.   Ibid., p. 41.
4.   John Mbiti, *African Religions and Philosophy* (New York: Doubleday, 1970), p. 141.
5.   Frye, p. 34.
6.   Ibid., p. 42.
7.   Ibid.

Ideology and Form:
The Critical Reception of *Petals of Blood*

JOSEPH MCLAREN

The literary contribution of Ngũgĩ wa Thiong'o is substantially represented in his large body of fiction. As a successful and controversial author, Ngũgĩ has generated a considerable amount of critical commentary. His six novels have been particularly suited to critical analysis because of the strong political and historical dimensions which they present. Literary critics in the West and Africa have produced a counter-text, a body of interpretations which attempt to explain, evaluate and judge the merits of Ngũgĩ's fictional corpus.[1] This large body of critical commentary is a sign of the "preeminence of Ngũgĩ wa Thiong'o as a writer articulating central issues for African literary culture" (Sicherman iv).

From the onset of its publication in 1977 to the early 1990s, critics have approached *Petals of Blood* with particular attention to its ideological message, which reflects Ngũgĩ's support of a Marxist interpretation of history. Critics of the novel have addressed narrative perspective, presentation of characters, and plot techniques in relation to the novel's ideological framework. The immediate international reaction to the novel considered the viability of characterization in conjunction with authorial political intention. Although the bulk of support for the novel came from African critics, there was no uniform acceptance by African reviewers and literary scholars of Ngũgĩ's politicizing of certain characters. The essential criteria of assessment concerned the devices of "realistic" fiction and their validity in voicing political imperatives.

The variety of critical responses by critics in Europe, the United States, Canada, and Africa point to the far reaching effects of Ngũgĩ's forceful political assertions. The responses of Kenyan critics show both support and disapproval, revealing the controversial nature of the political novel and the continued debate regarding art as ideology.

Petals of Blood, one of the more complex and extended works of post-Independence African fiction, provoked a much stronger critical reaction than did earlier novels by Ngũgĩ, such as *Weep Not, Child* (1964), *The River Between*

First appeared in *Paintbrush: A Journal of Poetry and Translation,* Vol. XX (Nos. 39 & 40), Spring/ Autumn 1993.

(1965) and *A Grain of Wheat* (1967). As Ngũgĩ's fourth novel, *Petals of Blood* was a turning point in his conception of novelistic form and his presentation of political ideology of the left. The publication of the novel preceded Ngũgĩ's year-long detention, which began with his arrest on December 30, 1977, and, along with the staging of his play *Ngaahika Ndeenda (I Will Marry When I Want)* in Limuru, was part of the literary-political background of his incarceration. After *Petals of Blood,* Ngũgĩ's works of fiction were written in Gĩkũyũ and were based more explicitly on devices of orature.

Petals of Blood showed Ngũgĩ's interest in historical memory through his retelling the interrelated stories of four main characters, Munira, Karega, Wanja and Abdulla, who, at the beginning of the novel, are suspected of having committed the murder of a number of wealthy businessmen. Using flashbacks and multiple narrative perspectives, Ngũgĩ details the metamorphosis of Ilmorog, a fictional village, as it is transformed by influences of neo-colonialism and the seduction of Western capital to the New Ilmorog in which the masses of the population are marginalized. The novel closes with the possibility of political organization by the working classes.

THE EUROPEAN AND NORTH AMERICAN RECEPTION

With the release of *Petals of Blood,* critics in the West began to review the work with particular attention to political ideology and novelistic form, often raising questions regarding the role of literary art. One of the first reviews to appear was Christopher Ricks's "Power Without Glory in Kenya," published in the June 26, 1977, issue of the London *Sunday Times.* Ricks was complimentary of Ngũgĩ's achievement and used the metaphor of power to explain the literary effects of the novel. *Petals* was hailed as a "remarkable" and "compelling" novel which was successful because of the way in which it presented political issues within the context of "other things" (Ricks 41). In using the metaphor of power, Ricks suggested the inherent power of art to transform: "art at work upon the old and the new to create something which is at once new and old . . ." (41). Furthermore, *Petals of Blood* was innovative in its use of language despite its being written in traditional English prose.

Another response in the British press was offered by Homi Bhabha in the August 1977 issue of the *Times Literary Supplement.* The main critique was that traditional novelistic form was not an appropriate vehicle for a political message. Bhabha suggested that Ngũgĩ "seems not to be embarrassed by the very sound of his most potent political message" (Bhabha 989). Bhabha investigated the principal conflict of the novel, the transformation of Ilmorog from a primarily agricultural village to an industrialized one. He also recognized the use of traditional story telling modes of African orature. It was, however, the question of literary form which most troubled Bhabha. Ngũgĩ's stylistic form, identified as the social realistic, was seen as contrary to the revolutionary socialism which was inherent in the novel's development (Bhabha 989). This critique related ideology to novelistic form, one of the overriding critical issues surrounding the novel.

In January of 1978, Hugh Dinwiddy in *African Affairs* connected Ngũgĩ's political ideas to those of Sekou Touré and Frantz Fanon (Dinwiddy 127). For Dinwiddy, Ngũgĩ was able to achieve a successful marriage of artistic form and political content. "It is a masterly book of long gestation: the tone is messianic" (128). Dinwiddy, however, suggested that in the ending of the novel, the "message, delivered with conviction, comes across: the points made for the detached observer, perhaps too simplistically" (129).

Françoise Albrecht's contribution to *Échos du Commonwealth* (1980–81), a French journal, explored the development of imagery. "Blood and Fire in *Petals of Blood*" traced the use of "blood" as image and metaphor, "the blood of life, the blood of the men and women who are the life-force of a village, the blood that flows away towards the town, putting the village in jeopardy." "Fire" is also a traceable motif in the novel, presented as an "ambivalent image" because it is sometimes a destroyer and other times "illuminates and purifies" (85–86).

Reviews in American publications also addressed the issue of political ideology. In the February 1978 *New York Times Book Review,* Charles Larson, who had published *The Emergence of African Fiction* (1971), commented sympathetically on Ngũgĩ's detention but saw *Petals* as weakened by the introduction of what he called "the author's somewhat dated Marxism: revolt of the masses; elimination of the black bourgeois; capitalism to be replaced by African socialism" (Larson, "Afric. Diss." 22). Nevertheless, Larson was especially praiseworthy regarding Ngũgĩ's treatment of Wanja and her relationships with her lovers.

Larson also reviewed *Petals* for *World Literature Today.* He complimented Ngũgĩ on certain aspects of the novel but again negatively viewed the use of political ideology (Larson, "Anglophone" 245–47). Unlike Homi Bhabha's review, Larson's did not comment on the use of form generated from a Western realistic tradition which had influenced Ngũgĩ's fictional style.

Later in 1978, *World Literature Today* continued its discussion of *Petals of Blood* in Andrew Salkey's review, which was essentially positive, acknowledging that the novel "satisfies both the novelist's political intent" as well as his artistic "obligation" (Salkey 681). However, Salkey did suggest that the story line was somewhat "crudely" presented and ironically "too compact." Other critics had commented on what they thought was the rambling nature of the novel. By January of 1979, shortly after Ngũgĩ's release from detention on December 12, 1978, the *New Republic* presented its review written by Paul Berman. Similar to the form of other reviews, it offered some explication of the text, suggesting that the plot "leans heavily on coincidence," the "Zola-esque" qualities viewed as positive. Ironically, this review ended with the comment, "This is an anti-imperialist novel, but it is not, properly speaking, anti-American" (40).

Well-known American novelist and short story writer John Updike reviewed *Petals* for *New Yorker* magazine in July of 1979. In a satirical manner, Updike suggested that Ngũgĩ's use of political issues detracted from his writing style. Updike remarked, "Whatever else political fervor has done for Ngũgĩ, it has not helped his ear for English; the fine calm style of 'A Grain of Wheat' . . . has here come unhinged" (92). Was Updike suggesting that the novel was totally flawed stylistically or just the particular passage he chose to cite? Updike must certainly have been aware that Ngũgĩ's "political fervor" had resulted in Ngũgĩ's detention and that his own comment would ring with a facetious tone. Updike's remarks reflected a critical position which was insensitive to the larger political context surrounding Ngũgĩ's conscious ideological statements. The allusion to the "calm style" of Ngũgĩ's earlier fiction implied that strident narrative perspectives somehow weakened the fictional work.

Critical interest in *Petals of Blood* continued to be expressed into the mid-1980s by American journals.[2] *Research in African Literatures* devoted its Summer 1985 issue solely to Ngũgĩ. The issue contained Christine Pagnoulle's "Ngũgĩ wa Thiong'o's 'Journey of the Magi': Part 2 of *Petals of Blood*," which pursued a close reading of the journey of the Ilmorog villagers to the "Big City," Nairobi, in search of social justice. Pagnoulle offered parallels to the Yeatsian theme inherent in the larger title of the section, "Toward Bethlehem." A mostly formalist reading, Pagnoulle's piece did contribute to the explication of *Petals* (Pagnoulle 264).

After 1985, the importance of *Petals of Blood* as a political novel resulted in its inclusion in works dealing specifically with ideological issues. Georg M. Gugelberger's *Marxism and African Literature* (1986), an edited collection, offered a variety of perspectives on a range of African writings. Included in the collection was "The Second Homecoming: Multiple Ngũgĩs in *Petals of Blood*," contributed by the Ugandan writer and critic Peter Nazareth. Nazareth's article summarized the essential structure of the novel and critiqued its form by posing a theory of authorial voices. For Nazareth, Ngũgĩ had presented three differing voices: the Ngũgĩ of "the village," who is "in pursuit of a deeper Christianity," the Ngũgĩ of secular "radical political ideas," (122) and the Ngũgĩ who is "struggling to be born but being resisted by the first two" (124). These "multiple Ngũgĩs" often rivaled one another within the narrative structure. Nazareth also questioned Ngũgĩ's political intentions, accusing him of using clichés, especially in the closing of the novel. Ngũgĩ's plotting was also critiqued by Nazareth who suggested that the original plot intention of the novel, to discover the killer of Mzigo, Chui, and Kimeria, was not fulfilled. Nazareth cited examples which he thought showed a "failure of organic technique, an arbitrariness in the movement through time" (126). On the other hand, Nazareth recognized the effectiveness of the novel in conveying the results of colonialism and neocolonialism despite Ngũgĩ's lack of recognition of his multiple selves.

Published the same year as Gugelberger's work, Carol Boyce Davies and Anne Adams Graves's *Ngambika: Studies of Women in African Literature* (1986) also considered a specific critical issue, the presentation of women by African writers and the parameters of African feminist theory. A collaborative work by a Caribbean and an African-American critic, *Ngambika* included remarks on the broader issue of Ngũgĩ's treatment of female characters. Davies suggested that Ngũgĩ saw the "woman's struggle as inextricably intertwined with the total struggle" (Davies and Graves 11).

Ngũgĩ's commitment to political struggle in *Petals of Blood* continued to be a concern for Western critics of the 1980s. In 1986, in "The Politics of the Signifier: Ngũgĩ wa Thiong'o's *Petals of Blood*," which appeared in *World Literature Written in English,* a Canadian journal which published other commentaries on the novel, Stewart Crehan questioned the role of the literary critic who avoided considering the literary merits of *Petals of Blood*. He remarked, "Could it be that the moralistic urgency of *Petals of Blood* is so infectious that the resultant spiritual heat has led otherwise level-headed critics to throw certain critical criteria out of the window?" Crehan also suggested that Ngũgĩ's political status might have influenced critics to avoid negative appraisals of certain issues so as not to be labeled "agents of neo-colonialism" (Crehan 2). Crehan's comments indicated a critical perspective which challenged a reading of the novel that placed its political correctness above its literary accomplishments.

In contrast, one evaluative critique after 1985 contained little mention of political positions and was primarily a reader's guide to the novel. The appearance of K. B. Rao's *"Petals of Blood"* summary in *Masterplots II: British and Commonwealth Series* (1987) is an example of a critical context which offered a non-judgmental analysis, explicating the narrative as evidence of its standing in the canon of Commonwealth literature (Rao 1320–1324).

The interest in *Petals of Blood* by Commonwealth journals such as *World Literature Written in English* has been reflected in a variety of critical statements. In 1988, Joyce Johnson's "A Note on 'Theng'eta' in Ngũgĩ wa Thiong'o's *Petals of Blood*" emphasized the symbolic significance of "Theng'eta," the drink which is consumed by the four main characters, and its multiple effects of both unity and fragmentation, serving as a representation of "the revolutionary impulse" (Johnson 15) but also as an indicator of the abuses of commercialism.

Ngũgĩ's use of indigenous symbols such as "Theng'eta" interestingly contrasted with his employing of Christian symbolism, a theme which Hugh Dinwiddy developed in "Biblical Usage and Abusage in Kenyan Writing," which appeared in the *Journal of Religion in Africa* in 1989. Dinwiddy, who had reviewed the novel in 1978, thought that *Petals of Blood* was to a great extent "structured on Biblical associations" (Dinwiddy 42).

By 1990, Western critics had begun to link the work to other texts which bore ideological similarities. In "The Untruths of the Nation: *Petals of Blood* and Fuentes's *The Death of Artemio Cruz,*" published in *Research in African Literatures,* Edna Aizenberg approached both novels in terms of the colonial struggle and independence movements. She considered *Petals of Blood* as part of a "shift" in "novelistic discourse" which paralleled historical time. *Petals of Blood* reflected this transition in its "anguished vision" (Aizenberg 85–86). Aizenberg observed that both novels were received with mixed appreciation by their respective critics. She emphasized that the critical responses pointed to the characteristics of modernism in fiction which included the "breakup of the straight line of narrative, splintering of the authorial voice, fissuring of time and character," all of which reflected "the crisis of language" (Aizenberg 95).

The comparative interpretation of *Petals of Blood* in relation to other works of literature was also addressed in a 1991 article in the *Journal of Black Studies,* the African-American publication edited by Molefi Asante. In the issue edited by Abu Shardow Abarry, Leonard A. Podis and Yakubu Saaka argued in "*Anthills of the Savannah* and *Petals of Blood:* The Creation of a Usable Past" that Achebe's 1987 novel had "narrowed" the "ideological gap" between Achebe and Ngũgĩ. Just as *Petals of Blood* had been viewed as a major turning point in the ideological and literary direction of Ngũgĩ, Podis and Saaka suggested that *Anthills of the Savannah* represented a similar decisive "watershed" (Podis and Saaka 105–106). In assessing the differences in characterization, they noted that Ngũgĩ's more expansive work contained characters who were often "drawn more one dimensionally" as opposed to the portrayal of characters in Achebe's novel in which the government officials were "generally not the absolute incarnations of evil that their counterparts tend to be in *Petals*" (106–107). Further parallels were drawn between the novels in terms of plot development and characterization as well as in the common theme of "the regeneration of community based indigenous roots" (110).

THE AFRICAN RECEPTION

The novel's reception in Africa also revealed patterns of critical assessment involving ideology, form and characterization. Certain Western critics had been concerned with Ngũgĩ's presentation of Marxist ideological themes; a good number of African critics were equally interested in this issue from the onset of their responses to *Petals.* Kenya's the *Weekly Review* of June 27, 1977, provided a thorough review titled "Ngũgĩ's Bombshell." Focusing on the complex of characters, the anonymous reviewer discussed Ngũgĩ's interweaving of plot and characters to produce a novel which would have a particular impact on Kenyan readers. Described as Ngũgĩ's "crowning literary achievement," the novel was presented as a pinnacle in Ngũgĩ's fictional technique. It was also noted that a Kenyan reader might get the effect that Ngũgĩ has been "walking all over your soul" because of the way the novel questioned the results of independence. Another issue was the absence of humor in the text which was thought to be a shortcoming: " . . . laughter is totally lacking and it seems to take laughter out of an African's life is to misread him" ("Ngũgĩ's Bombshell" 40). For the reviewer, Ngũgĩ "overestimates the secularism of the people" and their absorption of Marxist philosophy.

> People don't walk into the Hilton Hotel from their cardboard dwellings in Kawangare and turn into roaring Trotskytes. Neither is it possible that the workers of Ilmorog could shout the slogans of Che Guevera! (40)

Ngũgĩ's politicizing of his characters was brought to question, echoing the remarks of Bhabha and Larson regarding Ngũgĩ's movement to the left.

A few weeks after the *Weekly Review* assessed *Petals,* another Kenyan publication, the *Daily Nation,* reviewed the novel. Joe Kadhi recognized the impact of the work in terms of its political assault. The novel was "without doubt, the most hard-hitting novel criticising contemporary Kenyan society written since independence" (Kadhi 14). Similar to the previous review, Kadhi's remarks considered the reactions of the insider, of the Kenyan citizen who might read the novel as a historical and political assessment of his country's transformation from colonialism to independence. Among the Kenyan writers who have criticized the "system," Ngũgĩ had achieved the most successful rendering of the issues in fiction. According to Kadhi, "No writer has yet been able to expose the evils of such a system in as bold and fearless a manner as Ngũgĩ has done in his present book" (14). One irony observed by Kadhi was that the novel was published by Heinemann, a company based in London and which could be seen as a "foreign company." *Petals of Blood* often focused on the negative influences of foreign investment; the novel's discussion of an "Anglo-American international combine" would be evidence of this concern (Ngũgĩ 281). Furthermore, those Kenyans who were painted in a negative light could possibly accuse Ngũgĩ of "committing a sin of omission" by "failing to portray the good society of contemporary Kenyan society" (14). Kadhi did not consider the difference between Ngũgĩ's status as a writer as opposed to the entrepreneurial governing class presented in the novel.

Another popular Kenyan publication, the *Standard,* reviewed *Petals* in its July 15, 1977 issue. Chris Wanjala, a prominent Kenyan literary scholar, recognized the ground breaking nature of *Petals* and Ngũgĩ's departure from previous novelistic issues.

> Ngũgĩ has written a novel which at once rates him very highly amongst writers of the Third World and marks a welcome *tour de force* from the narrow concerns of Gĩkũyũ nationalism of his early novels. (Wanjala 12)

In Wanjala's view, Ngũgĩ had also achieved a level of literary critique which surpassed popular Kenyan writers of the "post-Mangua" period in Kenya. Many of these writers had focused on "cheap sex, prostitution, brothel life, wanton lust for intoxicating liquor" without making connections to the "materiality of life in Africa." Ngũgĩ's novel, on the other hand, was a critique of various segments of the Kenyan population which had "betrayed the masses." Wanjala saw the central focus of the work in the portrayal of Karega, a Dedan Kimathi figure and "the embodiment of every Kenyan critical force against the *status quo*." Another observation underscored the visual portrayals and the possibility of Ngũgĩ's having conceived the novel in cinematic terms because of the "vivid manner that would be even more lucid on the screen." Despite Wanjala's mostly praiseworthy remarks, he did fault Ngũgĩ's use of doctrinaire Marxism, a view held by certain critics in the Western press as well. Wanjala's projection that the novel would be widely read in the West was prophetic.

Petals of Blood and Ngũgĩ's earlier novels were given continued critical attention as a result of his detention and support by various international organizations. Often African writers expressed their views of the novel in magazines and journals published in the West but which were focused primarily on African concerns. *West Africa,* published in London, is a prime example of this kind of publication. Less than two months after Ngũgĩ's detention, Lewis Nkosi, the well-known South African writer and critic, assessed *Petals of Blood* in the February 20, 1978 issue of *West Africa*. Aptly titled "A Voice from Detention," Nkosi's article raised a number of issues concerning Ngũgĩ's prior novels and Ngũgĩ's ideological shift in *Petals*.[3]

Nkosi's interpretation of *Petals of Blood* began with the recognition that the novel's thematic content would offend those in "higher places" in Kenyan society. From a formal perspective, the work suggested characteristics of the fable rather than a novel and was evidence of Ngũgĩ's "attempt to think aloud about the problems of modern Kenya" (334). Nkosi saw the elements of satire, parody and especially fable as contradictory in terms of the conventional fictional goals and Ngũgĩ's translation of socialist thought to novelistic structures.

> I think Ngũgĩ's latest fiction fails because the author is so conscious of not having written a "socialist novel" before that he gives up concrete observation, which is the correct starting point of all true materialists, in favor of a fable-cum-satire-cum-realist fiction in order to illustrate class formations in modern Kenya. (Nkosi 335)

Ngũgĩ's ability to portray the contrasting and often conflicting emotions of Wanja were, for Nkosi, the measure of his literary skill. Certain segments of dialogue spoken by Wanja to Karega revealed "how well Ngũgĩ can dramatise these contradictions." The essence of fictional success might rest in the "concrete" depiction of characters and the writer's willingness to "delve into his characters" (335). This argument for depth of portrayal and concreteness is the measure of the traditional realistic novel. As many critics such as Nkosi observed, Ngũgĩ had clearly departed from the requirements of this tradition.

During Ngũgĩ's detention in 1978, other evaluations of *Petals* were published by African writers. The recognition of Ngũgĩ's ideological movement to the left was addressed by Marxist critics. Ngethe Kamau's " 'Petals of Blood' as a Mirror of the African Revolution," published in *African Communist,* a London-based journal, in 1978, was an example of a straightforward Marxist interpretation of the novel.[4] Kamau's approach to the novel linked the ideological intentions of *Petals* with Leninist philosophy. Kamau asserted, "Ngũgĩ's novel is a demonstration of the truth and validity of Lenin's penetrating analysis as applied to the post-independence state, not only in Kenya but in Africa as a whole" (74). By quoting various passages from the novel, Kamau demonstrated Ngũgĩ's similarity of intention to specific ideological statements of Lenin. In a close example, Kamau demonstrated the way Lenin's remarks on infrastructure and road building could be paralleled to Ngũgĩ's portrayal of the Trans-African highway in *Petals.* Kamau saw the relationships between Leninist views and *Petals* as a positive representation of political ideology in fiction. Unlike those who saw Ngũgĩ's politicizing of the masses as unrealistic, Kamau discussed this element of the novel as the "proletarianization of the African peasantry and the rest of the working masses" without attention to its feasibility within the "realistic" context.

Critics continued to offer a variety of interpretations of *Petals* in 1978. In *Ufahamu,* Ntongela Masilela approached *Petals* with a summary of Marxist interpretations of the relationship between literature and history. Using the ideas of Walter Benjamin and Lukács, Masilela suggested that "Ngũgĩ's profound understanding of the complex relation between history and literature" could best be understood after a grounding in literary historical relationships from the Marxist perspective. The connection between realism and history was also addressed through the use of numerous references which punctuated the general discussion of Ngũgĩ's historical schematic design. The essential meaning of realism, so important to the critical assessment of Ngũgĩ's novel, was also addressed when Masilela used Brecht's definition as the "most succinct and lucid": "revealing causal connections in society, unmasking dominant points of view as the points of view of the dominators, writing from the point of view of the class which is ready with the widest solutions to the most pressing difficulties in which human society is enmeshed" (Masilela 16). Of equal importance was the larger question of critical reception and the need to examine the way literary works have been received.

Also in 1978, Kelwyn Sole in "Art and Activism in Kenya," published in *Africa Perspective,* a South African journal, discussed the range of political and artistic issues surrounding *Petals of Blood* as well as *The Trial of Dedan Kimathi.* Acknowledging that Kenyan written literature of the day was concerned with "political, social and economic problems," Sole questioned the links between political ideology and artistic achievement. Again, Ngũgĩ's use of ideological messages was addressed in terms of the Western tradition of the novel. For Sole, both works of Ngũgĩ "fall prey at times to a doughy social realism which recalls the unhappy days of Russian literature under Zhdanov" (Sole 27). After citing a passage from *Petals* which contained clear Marxist language, Sole claimed that "form and language" were "stylized and vague" and that some of the characters in the novel were rendered in a "two-dimensional" fashion. However, Sole realized that Ngũgĩ's choice in overtly presenting political ideology was important because it revealed the dilemma of African authors in general and the stance of Western critics.

> The Western-trained critic, then, should perhaps not be too quick in condemning his [Ngũgĩ's] lack of subtlety. The fact of the matter is that a discussion of Ngũgĩ's consciously chosen position as regards literature relates to the problem of the position of the African writer in his or her society and connected problems of criticism. (Sole 28)

Ultimately, Sole recognized the problems of analyzing "high art" and "political art" and the importance of measuring African literature by "fresh critical concepts" which reconsider the intentions of Eurocentric critical ideas.

The following year, F. Odun Balogun's "Ngũgĩ's *Petals of Blood*: A Novel of the People" appeared in a 1979 issue of *Ba Shiru*. Unlike certain critics who questioned the balancing of message and art, Balogun argued positively for the unity of form and ideology. He compared *Petals* to achievements attained by other African writers of the period such as Achebe in *Things Fall Apart* and *A Man of the People* and Armah in *The Beautyful Ones Are Not Yet Born*. The importance of *Petals of Blood* was that Ngũgĩ had "gone beyond most African writers in creating a 'novel of the people' " (50).

In 1980, *Petals of Blood* was reexamined in John Chileshe's "*Petals of Blood*: Ideology and Imaginative Expression," published in the *Journal of Commonwealth Literature*. As with the majority of African critics, Chileshe grappled with the question of ideological message and the "work of art." For Chileshe, the artistic success of *A Grain of Wheat* was not duplicated in *Petals of Blood* because *Petals* was "weakened somewhat by the conflict between authorial ideology and the literary mode of expression used" (Chileshe 133). Chileshe saw Ngũgĩ as an artist involved in a "nationalistic struggle against imperialist hegemony," an activity which suggested certain contradictions because artists engaged in this struggle were often waging battle from "*within* the imperialist hegemonic structure" (134). This issue was complicated by the medium and artistic form which were "weapons" which had been "inherited from the culture at which the struggle was directed." However, Ngũgĩ had achieved a narrative structure for his multiple and collective narration by using elements of the traditional African story-telling mode which demonstrated one of the "potential strengths of the novel" (134).

Contrary to Chileshe's assertions regarding inconsistency of ideology and characterization, the review by Ugandan writer S. K. Wasswa, which appeared in a 1981 issue of *Forward,* a Ugandan journal, supported the consistency of form and ideology by suggesting the significance of Ngũgĩ's message to Ugandan society. Unlike those critics who took issue with Ngũgĩ's projection of ideology and form, Wasswa held that Ngũgĩ had "displayed a mastery of content and form" as Ngũgĩ had done in his earlier works. The political significance of *Petals* was expressed in terms of its "crucial relevance to Uganda's present situation" (Wasswa 13–14).

Angela Smith's commentary in a 1983 issue of *Outlook,* published in Malawi, showed that the critical appraisals of the work had begun to generate their own text against which critics such as Smith began to present their assessments. Smith identified four prominent critics, Gerald Moore, Eustace Palmer, G.D. Killam and Clifford Robson, all of whom had given the novel "a good deal of space in their studies" (Smith 12). Smith's contention was that the four critical appraisals had identified Munira as the central character of the work. She thought that it was a "misreading of both *A Grain of Wheat* and *Petals of Blood* to ferret about for one central character or hero" (24).

One of the last review-type appraisals of *Petals of Blood* appeared in a 1984 issue of *The Native.* Kenyan Gĩtahi Gĩtĩtĩ's "*Petals of Blood* as a Stage in Ngũgĩ wa Thiong'o's Evolving Social Perspective" examined the novel in relation to *The River Between* and Ngũgĩ's works to 1984. Gĩtahi Gĩtĩtĩ observed a crucial transition in the novels of Ngũgĩ from critical realism to social realism. In a positive view, Ngũgĩ's achievement was based on his linking of "all the major preoccupations of the anti-colonial and ideologically sound African novel from its beginning to the present day" (26–27). *Petals,* however, suggested a point of contention for Gĩtahi Gĩtĩtĩ because the novel did not "conform" to Ngũgĩ's statements concerning African literature expressed in African languages. This post-*Petals of Blood* stance of Ngũgĩ's could be used to address his work following *Petals.* If *Petals* is viewed as the transitional novel in Ngũgĩ's use of indigenous language, then one might expect to view the seeds of this new direction rather than a fully formed representation.

During the 1980s, the rise of literary criticism which focused on the portrayal of African women expanded the critical debate concerning form and ideology. Kavetsa Adagala's "Wanja of *Petals of Blood:* The Woman Question and Imperialism in Kenya," published in 1985, placed *Petals* within a historical and ideological framework. One of the goals of her critique was to "criticize Wanja from a historical standpoint employing the dialectical approach" (Adagala 1). Wanja was explored as a character who represented multiple characteristics as a result of her transformation from "schoolgirl, unwed mother, barmaid, destitute prostitute and poor peasant" to "a woman who is determined to acquire riches, never marry and prepared to sell her body to wealthy men and tourists" (Adagala 22). Wanja, then, represented the choices which were available to the symbolic Kenyan or African woman in the transitional neo-colonial state. At the same time, these choices or options were to a degree defined by the forces which led Wanja toward the negative extremes of her actions.

According to Adagala, Ngũgĩ was not offering a character who was either stereotype of the African woman—mother or prostitute. Ngũgĩ was suggesting that prostitution was not confined to women but was part of the larger issue of bartering away the promise of Independence. Wanja eventually triumphed over these forces and in the end remained an image of the reemerging consciousness which for Ngũgĩ was bound to the political ascendancy of the workers.

In 1986, a year following the publication of Adagala's critique, Peter Amuka's doctoral dissertation, "Kenyan Oral Literature, Ngũgĩ's Fiction and His Search for a Voice," examined the relationship between Ngũgĩ's use of the novel form and "the social effects of Ngũgĩ's written ideas on a predominantly oral audience" (Amuka vii). Like other Kenyan critics, Amuka's argument grew out of his first-hand contact with Kenyan cultural issues. Amuka's conclusion considered the applicability of the novel form to a coalescing of "art and action." In tracing the development of Ngũgĩ's fiction, Amuka viewed *Petals of Blood* and *Devil on the Cross* as transitional works which established a more "visible" and unsuppressed authorial voice (Amuka 160). The dilemma for Amuka was that the written mode of discourse suggested a "passive" application of art and action (217).

Most African critics of *Petals of Blood* were willing to approach the novel as written discourse which could be discussed in terms of plot structure and narrative perspective. Ayo Mamudu's "Tracing a Winding Stair: Ngũgĩ's Narrative Methods in *Petals of Blood*," which appeared in *World Literature Written in English* in 1987, considered the narrative structure and Ngũgĩ's "revelatory approach" which involved the "interlacing of past and present" to create a kind of circular effect which has meaning in the future as well (Mamudu 18). Mamudu did not object to the political characterizations but rather saw the "integration of form and content" rather than a "cleavage" (Mamudu 25).

The debate among African critics of *Petals of Blood* continued to address political and formal issues. One of the emerging Kenyan critics of the 1980s, Simon Gikandi, had written a major critical work on the African novel, *Reading the African Novel* (1987). Gikandi, who responded to the implications of Chinweizu's approach to African literature, explored *Petals of Blood* in a chapter titled "The Political Novel," which included discussions of Ousmane's *God's Bits of Wood* and La Guma's *In the Fog of the Season's End*. Gikandi showed an appreciation of Ngũgĩ's development of his quartet of characters in *Petals of Blood*. Gikandi, who explored the novel principally in terms of Ngũgĩ's presentation of Munira, Abdullah, Wanja and especially Karega, considered the relationship between "character and consciousness." The "problem," as Gikandi viewed it, was in Ngũgĩ's using character to "reflect society"; this approach of Ngũgĩ's had flaws because of the limitations of "one man's vision" (Gikandi 134). The difficulty of balancing a realistic depiction of society with the "logical development of the interaction of characters" represented the challenge of *Petals of Blood* and other African novels with clear political intentions. Gikandi examined Ngũgĩ's portrayal of each of his central characters by focusing on the various narrative perspectives and reliability of certain personas. Gikandi was particularly concerned with the way Ngũgĩ as author served as critic of his various narrators, subjecting many of them to "authorial censure" (135). Unlike Gĩtahi Gĩtĩtĩ, Gikandi objected to the reduction of the novel to a fundamental conclusion which underscored Ngũgĩ's political intention.

Like Gikandi, Chidi Amuta also produced a substantial critical work on African literature. Amuta's *The Theory of African Literature* (1989) opened with remarks concerning Chinweizu's *Toward the Decolonization of African Literature*. Gikandi had also used Chinweizu's ideas as a starting point in *Reading the African Novel*. Amuta responded to what he called the "kind of reductionism and romantic simplification represented by the Chinweizu formation." In Amuta's substantial remarks on *Petals of Blood* in the section titled "Class Struggle and the Socialist Vision: Ngũgĩ's *Petals of Blood*," part of a larger section on "History and Dialectics of Narrative," Amuta challenged the opposing critics who objected to the ideological intentions of the novel.

> Against the timid imputations of bourgeois critics, the decisive ideological thrust of *Petals of Blood* does not weaken its artistic identity. On the contrary, the strength of the novel derives from the sheer aesthetic force of its informing and objectified ideology. (Amuta, *The Theory* 148)

Amuta stressed the close interrelationship of the "dialectic of content and form" which he considered central to understanding the symbolic nature of the novel's structure (*The Theory* 148). Amuta also addressed *Petals of Blood* a year following the publication of his theoretical work. In another of Amuta's writings on *Petals of Blood*, "The Revolutionary Imperative in the Contemporary African Novel: Ngũgĩ's *Petals of Blood* and Armah's *The Healers*," published in *Commonwealth Novel in English,* Amuta observed the close relationship between history and modern African writing. Both novels represented a presentation of "revolutionary consciousness" (Amuta, "Revolutionary" 132) and, when viewed together, showed the "dynamism and rapid change which are perhaps the most dominant characteristics of modern socio-political experience." These characteristics can be observed particularly in the African novel (Amuta, "The Revolutionary" 141).

CONCLUSION

Because *Petals of Blood* represented a major transitional period in Ngũgĩ's literary career, its critical reception has been central to understanding Ngũgĩ's use of ideology of the left in conjunction with novelistic form which derived from Western aesthetics but which contained strong elements of the African oral tradition. As the critical discussion moved beyond the initial years of the novel's publication, observers still questioned the validity of straightforward ideology imbedded in characterization and expressed in undisguised narrative commentaries. On the whole, critics could not deny that much of what Ngũgĩ had achieved in the novel was based on his infusing the work with complexity of plot and characterization, the layering of the work with political dimensions which ultimately generated the most controversial critical attack.

The success or failure of *Petals of Blood* for a particular critic was not necessarily a function of the critic's national origin but was rather based on his or her aesthetic and political criteria. Critics of both the West and Africa who saw ideology as a weakening element were most often exponents of a kind of realism which eschewed bold political character representations. On the other hand, certain African critics supported Ngũgĩ's use of the novel form to present political issues and ideology regardless of their effects on characterization.

The critical discussion which has surrounded *Petals of Blood* not only demonstrates the potency of political issues in African literature but the complexity of literary concepts of form in modern African writing. Although African writers such as Ngũgĩ initially patterned their works on Western fiction, they were not bound to continue that particular tradition. In *Petals of Blood*, Ngũgĩ's notion of "realism" was based more on authorial purpose than on a supposed believability of action. Ngũgĩ's assumption of a narrative voice which projected historical interpretation indicated his breaking the boundaries of any proscribed notion of authorial distance. In so doing, many of the characters in *Petals of Blood* take on larger-than-life significance which might be seen as "unrealistic" within the novel's context of characterization.

Petals of Blood showed Ngũgĩ's willingness to risk a conception of novelistic form which had earned him his initial successes in order to assert political ideas which he considered crucial to the righting of Kenya's social dilemmas. Despite the often strong critique of this intention in *Petals of Blood*, Ngũgĩ continued to infuse his subsequent novels with a political imperative directed toward both revaluation and rectification.

Notes

1. The wealth of critical materials on Ngũgĩ's works have been compiled in the very useful work of Carol Sicherman, *Ngugi wa Thiong'o: A Bibliography of Primary and Secondary Sources, 1957–1987* (New York: Hans Zell, 1989). Furthermore, *Petals of Blood* has been treated

in a variety of book-length studies of African literature, including Eustace Palmer's *The Growth of the African Novel* (London: Heinemann, 1979), Emmanuel Ngara's *Stylistic Criticism and the African Novel* (London: Heinemann, 1982), Chinweizu, Onwuchekwa Jemie and Ihechukwu Madubuike's *Toward the Decolonization of African Literature,* Vol. 1 (Washington, D.C.: Howard University Press, 1983) and Simon Gikandi's *Reading the African Novel* (Portsmouth, N.H.: Heinemann, 1987).

Sicherman served as a great help and resource in tracking down a number of the reviews in African journals and other relevant sources.

2. Although critiques in periodical literature would continue to appear after 1980, the growth of post-Independence African literature led to the increased production of book-length studies devoted to authors such as Ngũgĩ. By 1980, Ngũgĩ's development as a novelist led to the first full-length treatment of his works. G.D. Killam's *An Introduction to the Writings of Ngũgĩ* (1980) contained a section devoted to *Petals of Blood.* Three years later, Cook and Okenimkpe's *Ngũgĩ wa Thiong'o: An Exploration of His Writings* (1983) furthered the extensive scholarly interpretation of *Petals of Blood,* followed in the subsequent year by the publication of Killam's edited collection, *Critical Perspectives on the Writings of Ngũgĩ wa Thiong'o* (1984), which included commentaries by African as well as Western critics. The collaborative work of Cook and Okenimkpe represented a fusion of Western and African critical perspectives. These book-length treatments offered extensive critical treatments of *Petals of Blood.*

3. In February, groups such as the African Students Union of the United Kingdom, the London-based Pan African Association of Writers and Journalists, and PEN had all begun to mount protests against Ngũgĩ's imprisonment. This kind of concern for Ngũgĩ's detention was expected to achieve the end result of his release. At that time, Nkosi observed, "Unless the Kenyatta Government sees fit to free its famous novelist or at the very least to bring him to trial, it is likely that the international campaign for his release will acquire more passion and nerve" (Nkosi 334). Ngũgĩ's detention was based on his alleged violation of the Public Security Laws, but, in fact, his activities were primarily literary and creative in his involvement with the production of *Ngaahika Ndeenda.*

4. Although credited to Ngethe Kamau, this article was later published under the name Grant Kamenju in Georg M. Gugelberger, ed., *Marxism and African Literature* (Trenton, NJ: Africa World Press, 1986), 130–35.

Works Cited

Adagala, Kavetsa. "Wanja of *Petals of Blood:* The Woman Question and Imperialism in Kenya." Nairobi: Derika Associates, 1985. Orig. Univ. of Nairobi Department of Literature Staff Seminar Paper. 1981.

Aizenberg, Edna. "The Untruths of the Nation: *Petals of Blood* and Fuentes's *The Death of Artemio Cruz.*" *Research in African Literatures* 21.4 (1990): 85–103.

Albrecht, Françoise. "Blood and Fire in *Petals of Blood.*" *Échos du Commonwealth* 6 (1980–81): 85–97.

Amuka, Peter. "Kenyan Oral Literature: Ngũgĩ's Fiction and His Search for a Voice." Dissertation. University of California at Los Angeles, 1986.

Amuta, Chidi. "The Revolutionary Imperative in the Contemporary African Novel: Ngũgĩ's *Petals of Blood* and Armah's *The Healers.*" *Commonwealth Novel in English* 3.2 (1990): 130–142.

———. *The Theory of African Literature: Implications for Practical Criticism.* London: Zed Books, 1989.

Balogun, F. Odun. "Ngũgĩ's *Petals of Blood:* A Novel of the People." *Ba Shiru* 10:2 (1979) 49–57.

Berman, Paul. Rev. of *Petals of Blood. New Republic* 20 Jan. 1979: 40.

Bhabha, Homi. "African Praxis." Rev. of *Petals of Blood. Times Literary Supplement* 12 Aug. 1977: 989.

Chileshe, John. "*Petals of Blood:* Ideology and Imaginative Expression." *Journal of Commonwealth Literature* 15.1 (1980): 133–137.

Crehan, Stewart. "The Politics of the Signifier: Ngũgĩ wa Thiong'o's *Petals of Blood." World Literature Written in English* 26.1 (1986): 1–24.

Davies, Carol Boyce, and Anne Adams Graves, eds. *Ngambika: Studies of Women in African Literature.* Trenton, N.J.: Africa World Press, 1986.

Dinwiddy, Hugh. "Biblical Usage and Abusage in Kenyan Writing." *Journal of Religion in Africa* 19.1 (1989): 27–47.

———. Rev. of *Petals of Blood. African Affairs* 78.1 (Jan. 1978): 127–29.

Gikandi, Simon. *Reading the African Novel.* London: James Currey, Nairobi: Heinemann Kenya, 1987.

Gĩtahi Gĩtĩtĩ [Victor L.]. "*Petals of Blood* as a Stage in Ngũgĩ wa Thiong'o's Evolving Social Perspective." *The Native* 1.1 (1984): 26–33.

Gugelberger, Georg M., ed. *Marxism and African Literature.* Trenton, N.J.: Africa World Press, 1986.

Johnson, Joyce. "A Note on Theng'eta in Ngũgĩ wa Thiong'o's *Petals of Blood." World Literature Written in English* 28.1 (1988): 12–15.

Kadhi, Joe. " 'Petals' Will Land with a Thud." Rev. of *Petals of Blood. Daily Nation* 15 July 1977: 14.

Kamau, Ngethe. " 'Petals of Blood' as a Mirror of the African Revolution." *African Communist* 80 (1978): 73–79.

Larson, Charles. "African Dissenters." Rev. of *Petals of Blood. New York Times Book Review* 19 Feb. 1978: 3, 22.

———. "Anglophone Writing from Africa and Asia." *World Literature Today* 52.2 (1978): 245–47.

Mamudu, Ayo. "Tracing a Winding Stair: Ngũgĩ's Narrative Methods in *Petals of Blood." World Literature Written in English* 28.1 (1988): 16–25.

Masilela, Ntongela. "Ngũgĩ wa Thiong'o's *Petals of Blood." Ufahamu* 9.2 (1978): 9–28.

Nazareth, Peter. "The Second Homecoming: Multiple Ngũgĩ s in *Petals of Blood." Marxism and African Literature.* Ed. Georg M. Gugelberger. Trenton, N.J.; Africa World Press, 1986: 119–129.

"Ngũgĩ's Bombshell." *Weekly Review* 27 June 1977: 39–40.

Ngũgĩ wa Thiong'o. *Petals of Blood.* 1977. New York: E.P. Dutton, 1978.

Nkosi, Lewis. "A Voice from Detention." *West Africa* 20 Feb. 1978: 334–335.

Pagnoulle, Christine. "Ngũgĩ wa Thiong'o's 'Journey of the Magi': Part 2 of *Petals of Blood." Research in African Literatures* 16.2 (1985): 264–75.

Podis, Leonard A, and Yakubu Saaka. "*Anthills of the Savannah and Petals of Blood:* The Creation of a Usable Past." *Journal of Black Studies* 22.1 (1991): 104–122.

Rao, K.B. "*Petals of Blood." Masterplots II: British and Commonwealth Fiction Series 3.* Ed. Frank N. Magill. Pasadena: Salem Press, 1987: 1320–1324.

Ricks, Christopher. "Power Without Glory in Kenya," *Sunday Times* 26 June 1977: 41.

Salkey, Andrew. "Kenya." Rev. of *Petals of Blood. World Literature Today* 52.4 (1978): 681–682.

Sicherman, Carol. *Ngugi wa Thiong'o: A Bibliography of Primary and Secondary Sources, 1957–1987.* New York: Hans Zell Publishers, 1989.

Smith, Angela "*Petals of Blood." Outlook* 1.1 (1983): 12–31.

Sole, Kelwyn. "Art and Activism in Kenya." *Africa Perspective* 8 (1978): 26–31.

Updike, John. "Books: Mixed Reports from the Interior." Rev. of *Petals of Blood. New Yorker* 2 July 1979: 89–94.

Wanjala, Chris. "New Novel by Ngũgĩ Keeps Him at Top." *Standard* 15 July 1977: 12.

Wasswa, S.K. "Literature: A Tool in the Struggle." Rev. of *Petals of Blood. Forward* 3.2 (1981): 13–16.

Ngũgĩ wa Thiong'o's "Journey of the Magi": Part 2 of *Petals of Blood*

CHRISTINE PAGNOULLE

The structure of Ngũgĩ wa Thiong'o's fourth novel, *Petals of Blood,*[1] has attracted a considerable amount of critical attention: the shaping of the plot by way of carefully delayed revelations, the complex shifts in time, the subtle use of several viewpoints, the interweaving not only of different stories but of different narrative levels—all these aspects have been explored and dia-gramed.[2] In this paper I wish to examine the particular position allotted to the second of the four parts of which the novel consists.

Even at the most immediate level, there are some arresting differences between part 2 and the three others. There are six chapters in the first part, and the first chapter in part 3 is chapter 7. Part 2 thus stands apart from the succession of numbered chapters. This particular status is corroborated by the exceptional use of a second title, "The Journey," beside the title that seals for-mally the continuity with the other parts: "Toward Bethlehem." The titles of the first three parts—"Walking," "Toward Bethlehem," "To Be Born"—echo the last lines of W. B. Yeats's "The Second Coming": "What rough beast / Slouches toward Bethlehem to be born?" though with a notable difference, for the words apply here, not to some "rough beast," but to the people of Ilmorog; hence the substitution of the purposeful "walking" for the ignoble and repulsive "slouches."[3]

A third indication that part 2 stands on a special footing is its position in relation to Munira's report, this "mixture of an autobiographical confessional and some kind of prison notes" (p. 190) written during the eleven days he spends in jail after the arson of Wanja's place and the consequent triple mur-der. This report provides one of the structural frames of the novel. Its main function, I suggest, is occasionally to remind the reader of the police inquiry in the context of which twelve crucial years in the history of Ilmorog are reconstituted. In the six sections of part 2, there is not one single reference to those feverish pages by the schoolmaster, and it is obvious that part 2 cannot belong to the report either: apart from inconsistencies of tone between the

Reprinted with permission from Indiana University Press from Christine Pagnoulle, " 'Journey of the Magi': Part 2 of *Petals of Blood,*" *Research in African Literatures* 16, no. 2 (Summer 1985): 264–75.

two, how could Munira know what happens at Mr. Hawkins's house, or what takes place between Wanja and Karega when they go to the lawyer, or what thoughts occur to their MP as he ruminates upon his humiliation and the course of his vengeance?[4]

This complete separation from Munira's report is all the more striking as the last lines of part 1 as well as the first line of part 3 belong to the schoolmaster's statement. In chapter 6 he writes: "It was the journey, . . . it was the exodus across the plains to the Big Big City that started me on that slow, almost ten-year, inward journey to a position where I can now see that man's estate is rotten at heart" (pp. 117–18). His words there point to another journey of the soul toward understanding, albeit in his case an understanding utterly distorted by his religious fanaticism: "man's estate is rotten at heart," he says, echoing Hamlet, and all we can do is turn to God and obey His orders. The last words on that page—"The journey. The exodus toward the kingdom of knowledge"—have to be similarly interpreted as referring more to that inner journey than to the actual trekking across the plains. While these passages refer to changes in Munira himself, the first words of part 3 stress the importance of the expedition as a turning point in the fortunes of Ilmorog: "Yes, Ilmorog was never quite the same after the journey" (p. 190).

But part 2, the account of the journey itself, is removed from the limiting viewpoint of Munira's report. It exists on its own and is soon to become a legend, part of the running mythical history of the Ilmorog community as it is remembered and sung by the elders. "Nyakinyua, mother of men" (p. 123) is the one who takes upon herself the task of commemoration. At the harvest festival a year after the expedition, they all listen to her singing:

> She was singing their recent history. She sang of two years of failing rains; of the arrival of daughters and teachers; of the exodus to the city. . . .
> And now it was no longer the drought of a year ago that she was singing about. It was all the droughts of the centuries and the journey was the many journeys travelled by the people even in the mythical lands of two-mouthed Marimus and struggling humans. (pp. 209–10)

It was Nyakinyua too whose eloquent support had won the adhesion of the group to the idea of going as a community to the capital: "We must sing our tune and dance to it. Those out there can also, for a change, dance to the actions and words of us that sweat, of us that feel the pain of bearing. . . . But Ilmorog must go as one voice" (p. 116). Once they were on their way, she was "the spirit that guided and held them together" (p. 123).

After two years without proper rains, famine threatened Ilmorog, and Karega proposed to go tell their MP about their plight as an alternative to the killing of Abdulla's donkey, charged with the crime of being an impenitent grass eater. Clearly, though, the journey is more than an errand for outside help, it is also a quest for some deeper source of life. And for all main characters involved, as well as for the community as a whole, it turns out to be the starting point of changes far deeper than what they had expected.

There is at least one other famous "Journey" "Toward Bethlehem" in contemporary English literature: T. S. Eliot's "Journey of the Magi."[5] While parallels can be traced between the two (very dissimilar) situations, the reference works mainly by contrast. Christianity is an imported commodity in Kenya, and mostly a cover-up for exploitation: "Christianity, Commerce, Civilisation: the Bible, the Coin, the Gun: Holy Trinity" (p. 88). The god the Magi came upon in a manger can thus hardly be a source of regeneration, and there is more loss than gain in the change of dispensation that followed upon the journey to Nairobi. But the journey does bring out the strength of collective concerted action and will indirectly result in an assertion of life that counters and defeats the "harlot's curse."

Unlike Eliot's Magi, they leave behind not a place filled with decadent comfort ("the summer palaces on slopes, the terraces / And the silken girls bringing sherbet") but a wasteland, a place of starvation. The hardships they have to endure, however, are comparable. In both cases they travel at "the worst time of the year / For a journey." Lancelot Andrewes spoke of the snow and the sharp weather. Our pilgrims have to face the heat of the sun and the severity of the drought; as Munira is to write:

> I can once again feel the dryness of the skin, the blazing sun, the dying animals that provided us with meat, and above us, soaring in the clear sky, the hawks and vultures which, satiated with meat of dead antelopes, wart-hogs and elands, waited for time and sun to deliver them human skin and blood. (p. 118)

Indeed for some days they find themselves "without food and without water" (p. 143), and "hawks and vultures [fly] high above them" (p. 144). But this they can meet almost to the end with communal courage springing from the awareness newly revived by Abdulla that they are all capable of heroism:

> despite the sun which had struck earlier and more fiercely than in the other days, as if to test their capacity for endurance to the very end, despite indeed the evidence of the acacia bush, the ashy-furred beleshwa bush, the prickly pears, all of which seemed to have given in to the bitter sun, they walked with brisk steps as if they too knew this secret desire of the sun and were resolved to come out on top. (p. 143)

Much worse still than those natural calamities is the hostility they meet when they eventually reach Blue Hills, an affluent, polished, and policed suburb of Nairobi. "And the cities hostile and the towns unfriendly," the Magi also remembered. But in Ngũgĩ's novel, lack of charity is not left general and anonymous. Three people are branded with patent heartlessness or worse, and all three are Africans, that is, traitors. One is the Reverend Jerrod Brown, who stands for a hateful hypocritical mission Christianity; then come Chui, the famous headmaster of the famous Siriana High School, and Mr. Hawkins, otherwise known in the novel under the name of Kimeria, the man who seduced Wanja and left her with child, the former homeguard who betrayed Abdulla and Karega's elder brother.[6]

What the Magi find at the end of their journey will forever remain ambiguous: "were we led all that way for / Birth or Death?" While to a Christian believer, the ambivalence of this birth that also signifies death points to the presence of the Passion within the Nativity; and while those balanced lines recall the truth that birth is necessary to death and conversely death to birth, the words have yet another specific meaning to those kings from pagan countries. They say "this Birth was / Hard and bitter agony for us, like Death, our death," and they explain two lines further that what has been shaken and ruptured is the "old dispensation," an order in which there is no place for the Resurrection. They feel stranded between two worlds—"no longer at ease," which, significantly, is the title of Achebe's second novel—and thus wish for "another death."

In *Petals of Blood* too, the journey marks the beginning of a complete disruption in the "old dispensation" and contains the elements of a possible rebirth. The one is an ironical result of their mission; the other has not been found in Nairobi, but has germinated, as it were, in the process of the expedition.

There is something altogether wrong about the end of the journey. Not that it is mistaken to go to claim one's rights when the situation is desperate. But the people of Ilmorog set out, not toward a village, much less toward a stable by the wayside, but to "the Big Big City," reminiscent more of Babylon than of Bethlehem, toward a place which some of them at least, among whom the originator of the idea, know to be a trap. Yet as long as they toil on, the capital-city shines in their hearts, even in the hearts of those who know better, like a promise of salvation; and when they can at last distinguish the buildings down in the valley, they feel the same elation as Christian and his companions do when they behold the Celestial City: "But for Joseph's illness, they would all have felt immeasurable happiness at the sight. For they could now see the city below them" (p. 145). But the next sentence points to the rot that eats Kenya as the worm eats the flower with petals of blood (p. 22). The proud symbol of Kenyan political independence has been erected, with Western money, next to an international symbol of tourism as big business. Their experience of the town—first, the heartlessness of the inhabitants of Blue Hills; then, the crawling misery of those who try to sell themselves, their work power or their bodies, in order to survive—accounts for the two bleak epigraphs by William Blake: the terrible "harlot's curse" from the last verse of "London" and the chilling exposure of the falsehood that lurks in pity from "The Human Abstract."

In the city, however, they also find the lawyer,[7] and it is that dedicated man who expresses most clearly, about the middle of the novel, how the beast goes to work, how the monster-god money eats the seed of African freedom and turns it into a parody:

> . . . the whole world, motivated by different reasons and expectations, waited, saying: they who showed Africa and the world the path of manliness and of black redemption, what are they going to do with the beast? They who washed the warriors' spears in the blood of the white profiteers, of all those who had enslaved them to the ministry of the molten beast of silver and gold, what dance are they now going to dance in the arena? . . . But we, the leaders, chose to flirt with the molten god, a blind, deaf monster who has plagued us for hundreds of years. (p. 163)[8]

Ilmorog had not been quite forgotten by the beast. There are in part 1 clear indications that the land was drained dry of resources and men by colonial exploitation: "The road had once been a railway line joining Ilmorog to Ruwa-ini. The line had carried wood and charcoal and wattle barks from Ilmorog forests to feed machines and men at Ruwa-ini" (p. 11); "the only thing that pained them was this youth running away from the land. . . . even this had always been so since European colonists came into their midst, these ghosts from another world" (p. 19). Yet on the whole, an ancient economic balance had been maintained, largely because the place was far removed from any developing project. Their market, for instance, "was more of a social gathering of friends than a place for exchanging commodities and haggling over prices. . . . One could more or less do without hard cash except when one went to Abdulla's shop or to Ruwa-ini. Money or food or an item of clothing: any of these would do as a basis of exchange" (p. 17). Everything in "both Ilmorog ridge and Ilmorog plains" (p. 17) is regulated by Mwathi wa Mugo, an invisible but all-powerful wise man and sorcerer, who knows when to plant and when to harvest, when the cattle should be moved to higher grounds, what to do when it does not rain, and how fecundity can be restored to a woman's womb. Significantly, weapons can only be beaten at his place, so that the ironmonger is "protected from the power of evil and curious eyes" (p. 17).

The most spectacular consequence of the journey is to bring the beast down to Ilmorog and blast what survived of the old dispensation: "He would soon launch a giant financial project—Ilmorog (KCO) Investment and Holdings Ltd—as a quick means of developing the area. Ilmorog would never be the same" (p. 187).

These are the thoughts of Nderi at the end of part 2. While part 3 does show a kind of rebirth (which I shall discuss presently), the bitter comments by Munira with which it begins, disclosing as they do most of what is going to happen to that rural community, cast a black pall over what frail light may seem to emerge:

after that journey . . . a devil came into our midst and things were never quite the same. (p. 190)

We went on a journey to the city to save Ilmorog from the drought. We brought back spiritual drought from the city! (p. 195)

Such statements are qualified by the narrator as being inspired by Munira's later-day fanaticism, yet also partly sanctioned:

There was an element of truth in Munira's interpretation of events that followed their journey to the city. An administrative office for a government chief and a police post were the first things to be set up in the area. Next had come the church. (p. 195)

After those "outposts of progress" came the road:

And so the road was built, not to give content and reality to the vision of a continent, but to show our readiness and faith in the practical recommendations of a realist from abroad. . . . And so, abstracted from the vision of oneness, of a collective struggle of the African peoples, the road brought only the unity of earth's surface; every corner of the continent was now within easy reach of international capitalist robbery and exploitation. (p. 262)

The effects of this shattering advent are presented in part 4. A climax in the uprooting and leveling process is the destruction of Mwathi's place:

So we stood and watched as the machines roared toward Mwathi's place. We said: it cannot be. But they still moved toward it. We said: they will be destroyed by Mwathi's fire. Just you wait, just you wait. But the machine uprooted the hedge and then hit the first hut and it fell and we were all hush-hush, waiting for it to be blown up. . . . The two huts were pulled down. But where was Mwathi? There was no Mwathi. (pp. 265–66)

Appropriately then part 2 moves from Ndemi to Nderi. It begins with the glorious story of Ndemi "who tamed the forest," "who wrestled with God" (p. 121), of Ndemi the mythical founder of the agricultural community of Ilmorog. It ends with the petty political plotting of Ilmorog's MP, Nderi wa Riera. Absorbed in his selfish and greedy calculations, he is unable to understand that people may be disinterested and ready to help a community which is not their own without harboring some further motives or being manipulated by some other ill-intentioned politician:

Then he remembered his enemies. . . . Who were they? Could it be that boy Karega and that teacher and the crippled fellow? [Karega, Munira, and Abdulla are from Limuru.] No, these were only front men: they were working for somebody else. Who could it be? And suddenly he knew. The lawyer of course! (p. 187)

For a time it does seem as though the beast and its ministers—whether they hid their greed behind some respectable pretense like Nderi, the "man of the people," or Jerrod, the "man of God," or do not even bother to disguise their selfish appetite for more and more profit like Kimeria—would crush those who dare to rebel and to claim a right to live and not to starve, as though the quest for rebirth was to end in the victory of universal prostitution and in the final denial of hope: "this Africa knows only one law. You eat somebody or you are eaten," Wanja tells Karega after he has been away for five years (p. 291).

Yet the journey has also initiated different changes whose fruits will grow only later. One is a definite heightening of communal militant awareness. The expedition acts as an element of cohesion: "The trek to the city had attracted many people carried on the waves of hope and promises, and had awoken a feeling that the crisis was a community crisis needing a communal response" (p. 123). This sense of community is fed by Nyakinyua's tale of the distant past in the first section and further sharpened by Abdulla's story of heroic defeat in the second:

They had a feast that night. Even long afterwards they were to remember it and talk about it as the highest point in their journey to the city. (p. 139)

Abdulla's feast, as they called it, had leased them new life and determination. (p. 143)

The third section of part 2 presents the people's several ordeals on entering the city. But the fourth takes them to the temporary haven of the lawyer's place. As we have seen above, he provides a thorough theoretical exposition of what went wrong at the Independence, as well as a possible remedy:

here is our hope . . . in the new children, who have nothing to prove to the white man . . . and therefore can see the collective humiliation clearly and hence are ready to strike out for the true kingdom of the black god within us all. (p. 167)

This, however, is partly lost on his listeners: "They were all captivated by the parable, although they did not always understand it" (p. 166). When they face Nderi wa Riera in the next section, only Abdulla has the right answer to the politician's apologetic lies and dilatory argumentation. He tells how Hare made use of Antelope to get out of the hole into which they had both fallen, then not only failed to help him but lectured him instead. Afterward he walks out without another word. His response, however, is prompted not by anything the lawyer may have said, but by an innate intuition of Nderi's treacherous cunning.

The awareness they gain results in a more rational organization of labor on the fields once they have come back:

> Munira could not understand the new motion of things, the new mood of the village after the journey. Wanja and the other women on the ridge had formed what they called Ndemi-Nyakinyua Group to cultivate and weed the land and earth the crops, working in common, one on another's fields in turn. (p. 200)

This cohesion too may seem wholly lost when the money monster steps in and divides. But it emerges again at the end of the novel on a larger scale and fraught with wider promises.

The journey is also loaded with Wanja's quest for love and need for a child. In the first section of part 2, Nyakinyua's tale brings Wanja and Karega close to each other and helps establish a complicity between them. Together perhaps they can exorcise the past. Perhaps, without even mentioning anything, each can absolve the other of the death for which they feel responsible: Karega for that of his beloved Mukami, who jumped from a cliff because she loved him; Wanja for that of her newborn child.[9] This complicity is completed in physical communion in the night of *theng'eta* drinking, an almost mystical ceremony presided over by Nyakinyua:

> Then they started slowly, almost uncertainly, groping toward one another, gradually working together in rhythmic search for a lost kingdom, for a lost innocence and hope. . . . And she clung to him, she too desiring the memories washed away in the deluge of a new beginning, and he now felt this power in him, power to heal, power over death, power, power . . . and suddenly it was she who carried him high on ocean waves of new horizons and possibilities in a single moment of lightning illumination, oh the power of united flesh, before exploding and swooning into darkness and sleep without words. (p. 230)

There is no irony in this beautiful rendering of the act of love. But the passage may point to one reason for which their union will not be strong enough to detain Karega when he is dismissed by Munira, or indeed to give Wanja the child she so much wants. Both look for oblivion in their embrace; that is, they are not yet ready to face the complexity of their predicament. Moreover, at this stage, Wanja has not yet fully disclosed what happened to the child she had by Kimeria. Besides Karega is still a very young man who has to find himself. He goes away, and when he comes back he is unable to help her, although she pleads with him: " '. . . and I am only sorry, really sorry, that you are on their side. KCO and Imperialism stand for the rich against the poor. They take from the poor and that's why they hate to see the poor organise and you are helping them' " (p. 327). Karega has all the right ideas; by the end of the novel he knows how they should proceed in order to bring about "the kingdom of man and woman . . . joying and loving in creative labour" (p. 344). But he is too self-righteous to understand Wanja's plight and to admit that he is partly responsible for it. Not Karega but Abdulla, the forgotten hero, will be the father of Wanja's child. Abdulla does not judge. Once he refuses the money she offers because it comes from the man he ought to kill. But he knows he is wrong: "But later he felt ashamed of the action. He knew very well that it was her who was now paying school fees for Joseph. In any case, he did not blame her: she was turning the way the world was tilting" (p. 313). He has weaknesses and shortcomings, and he is aware of them—for instance, of the way he treats young Joseph until Wanja insists that he go to school, or of the wish for private property:

> the question had always troubled him . . . . : is it right that that which had been bought by the collective blood of a people should go to a few hands just because they had money and bank loans? Was it bank and money that had fought for it? But he had never found an answer because it was true that black hands were owning it. And he would have liked to own one of those farms himself. (p. 166)

But he is also capable of selfless dedication. Because of this very human mixture of weakness and strength, he is the one who plants the seed of life between the thirsting lips of Wanja's womb.[10]

The seed of future harvest is not to be found in some imported myth, but within the past of the people. As the lawyer says, " 'Our people had said: Let's not be slaves to the monster: let us only pray and wrestle with the true god within us. We want to control all this land, all these industries, to serve the one god within us' " (p. 164). The regeneration proposed in Ngũgĩ's novel has to feed on their indigenous past. It is not, however, the impossible dream of some return to precolonial time. In spite of his direct reference to Yeats, Ngũgĩ's vision of time is not cyclical: things never come back to their beginning; they move on to new beginnings.[11] While Eliot's poem ends in a mood of somber resignation, part 2 of *Petals of Blood* ends with ominous threats of destruction and death that will materialize in part 4, but it also outlines promises of life that find a tentative development in part 3 and blossom in the last pages of the novel.

Notes

1. Ngugi wa Thiong'o, *Petals of Blood* (London: Heinemann, 1977). All page references in the text are to this edition.

2. See in particular the first two papers in the issue of *Echos du Commonwealth* devoted to *Petals of Blood:* René Richard, "History and Literature: Narration and Time in *Petals of Blood,*" *Echos du Commonwealth,* 6 (1980–81), 1–36, and Christine Abdelkrim, "*Petals of Blood:* Story, Narrative, Discourse," *Echos du Commonwealth,* 6 (1980–81), 37–51.

3.   See Christine Abdelkrim, p. 45, and Florence Stratton, "Cyclical Patterns in *Petals of Blood*," *Journal of Commonwealth Literature,* 15 (1980), 115–24, esp. p. 123.

4.   The distinction I make between part 2 and Munira's report is in contradiction with the view held by René Richard: "As the reader might at times forget it, the novelist frequently takes pains to remind him that *all episodes* are related by Munira in the statement, that everything (or practically everything) is seen through the prism of the narrator" (pp. 8–9; emphasis added).

5.   There are other references to T. S. Eliot in the novel, for instance, Ngũgĩ's characterization of Munira with phrases that echo the spiritual emptiness of J. Alfred Prufrock: "the burnt-out cigarette-ends of his life" (p. 269); "why should I dare?" (p. 30).

6.   Wanja tells the story of her seduction in chap. 2, pt. 1, pp. 38–41. Abdulla relates how Kimeria decoyed him and Nding'uri in chap. 7, pt. 3, pp. 221–24. They recognize that they have been betrayed by one and the same man in chap. 10, p. 256.

7.   Contrary to what Françoise Albrecht believes ("Blood and Fire in *Petals of Blood*," *Echos du Commonwealth,* 6 [1980–81], 87), the lawyer is not an Indian, although he lives in an area "formerly and exclusively reserved for Indians" (p. 160). It is clear that he is an African from Wanja's reaction when she first meets him ("I have never been so grateful for the sight of another black skin," p. 134) and from the education he received in the United States ("While I was at a black college in Baton Rouge," p. 165), as well as from his commitment to the cause of black people.

8.   This recalls an image used by Abdulla in one of the very last sections of the novel: "maybe, he thought, history was a dance in a huge arena of God. You played your part, whatever your chosen part, and then you left the arena, swept aside by the waves of a new step, a new movement in the dance" (p. 340).

9.   Karega tells about his ill-fated love for Mukami in chap. 7, pp. 219–20. Wanja eventually blurts out the long repressed truth about her child several years later, in chap. 11, p. 291.

10.   See also Jacqueline Bardolph, "Fertility in *Petals of Blood*," *Echos du Commonwealth,* 6 (1980–81), 75.

11.   There is, of course, a cyclical recurrence of similar patterns of events. But history, unlike nature in its seasonal cycle, never comes full circle. This is in contradistinction with what Florence Stratton claims (p. 121). The way modifications are effected within an apparent repetition is perhaps most explicitly illustrated by the four strikes that take place at Siriana High School. The pattern of events is roughly the same: pupils rebel, go on strike, and are eventually defeated. But each strike has a different aim and the level of awareness is gradually higher. This point is neatly developed by Christine Abdelkrim, p. 47. The novel in no way warrants the assumption that Wanja, whom Stratton chooses to illustrate her point, is unable to break the circle of guilt and money and that the sense of rebirth she experiences toward the end will not take her "anywhere but full circle" (p. 121). The novel is wholly open-ended, which also means that, while we may entertain doubts, based on sad historical observation, as to the future of the workers' movement, social renewal too is suggested as a possibility on the last pages of the book.

Recuperating a "Disappearing" Art Form: Resonances of "Gĩcaandĩ" in Ngũgĩ wa Thiong'o's *Devil on the Cross*[1]

Gĩtahi Gĩtĩtĩ

I

For all its limitations as political activity, writing has been an essential component of the process of decolonization in Africa, as well as in the rest of the formerly colonized world. If the imperial-colonial enterprise had relied on writing as a strategy of fixing reality, anti-colonial struggles at the cultural and political levels took recourse to writing as one of the means of countering the suppression and misrepresentation inherent in colonial discourse.

That the burden of emancipatory writing would be taken up by an easily recognizable élite from among the colonized or formerly colonized does not require much demonstration. In his *The Wretched of the Earth* (1961, 1965), especially in the chapters entitled "The Pitfalls of National Consciousness" and "On National Culture," Frantz Fanon wrote fairly prophetically about the tumultuous events that would characterize the period between insurrection and nominal independence in the formerly colonized world. Fanon's insight into the nature and character of the "national bourgeoisies" to emerge out of this maelstrom is particularly keen. While he vilified this "profiteering caste" as the bane of the post-independence moment, Fanon also recognized that this class would partly have enhanced the nationalist momentum. In their hands, writing, in one form or another, had played, and would continue to play, a central role in the process of colonial struggle and in the move toward self-determination.

It is not necessary here to demonstrate the influence of Fanon's thought on African (and other "Third World") ideological/political formations. Suffice it to say that there is ample evidence that Ngũgĩ wa Thiong'o would be familiar with Fanon's politics of culture, language and autonomy. Indeed, Ngũgĩ affirms that "it is impossible to understand what informs African writ-

First appeared in *Paintbrush: A Journal of Poetry and Translation*, Vol. XX (Nos. 39 & 40), Spring/ Autumn 1993.

213

ing, particularly novels written by Africans" (Ngũgĩ, 1986: 63), without reading Fanon's *The Wretched of the Earth,* among other books. Evidently, this observation is no less applicable to Ngũgĩ's own writings, creative as well as critical. Fanon's thesis on the (re)deployment of oral literature is a fitting point of departure for an examination of Ngũgĩ's language practice in the novel *Devil on the Cross* (1982), a practice further amplified in his aptly titled *Decolonizing the Mind* (1986).

Fanon postulated that, in the colonies, national(ist) literature is born at the juncture when the native intellectual moves away from addressing the colonizer and creates a completely new public—his own people:

> It is only from that moment on that we can speak of a national literature. Here there is, at the level of literary creation, the taking up and clarification of themes which are typically nationalist. This may be properly called a literature of combat, in the sense that it calls on the whole people to fight for their existence as a nation. It is a literature of combat, because it molds the national consciousness, giving it form and contours and flinging open before it new and boundless horizons; it is a literature of combat because it assumes responsibility, and because it is the will to liberty expressed in terms of time and space. (Fanon, 1968: 240)

According to Fanon, the nations arising out of the colonial project of territorial and cultural domination incorporate the oral tradition into the liberatory textual praxis that is part of the process of decolonization:

> On another level, the oral tradition—stories, epics and songs of the people—which formerly were filed away as set pieces are now beginning to change. The storytellers who used to relate inert episodes now bring them alive and introduce into them modifications which are increasingly fundamental. There is a tendency to bring conflicts up to date and to modernize the kinds of struggle which the stories evoke, together with the names of heroes and the types of weapons. The method of allusion is more and more widely used. (Fanon, 1968: 240)

Ngũgĩ wa Thiong'o's writings, particularly those composed in the Gĩkũyũ language, fall within the ambit of Fanon's vision. There is a sense in which *Petals of Blood* (1977) can be seen to have aspired to be the post-independence *magnus opus* sufficient to the task outlined above. But *Petals of Blood* was written in English. Beginning in 1977, Ngũgĩ's involvement with the Kamĩrĩĩthũ "phenomenon" would be largely responsible for his determination to write in the Gĩkũyũ language, starting with *Ngaahika Ndeenda* (1977) and leading on to *Devil on the Cross* and its successor, *Matigari* (1989), among others. The themes which Ngũgĩ's Gĩkũyũ-language texts revisit and re-elaborate are very like the motifs in a *gĩcaandĩ* performance which are characterized less by their lack of resolution than by a dialectical indeterminacy.

II

Ngũgĩ has consistently written and spoken openly about "the history of Kenyan people creating a resistance culture, a revolutionary culture of courage and patriotic heroism. . . . A fight-back, creative culture, unleashing tremendous energies among the Kenyan people" (Ngũgĩ, 1981: 64). This history of resistance takes place at many levels—politically, economically, and in the realm of culture or socially creative labour. In literature, writes Ngũgĩ,

> the energy found creative expression in the many patriotic songs, poems, plays and dances over the years, giving rise to a great patriotic literary tradition of Kenyan poetry and theatre. There was for instance the Ituĩka, a revolutionary cultural festival among the Aagĩkũyũ which was enacted every twenty-five years both as a ceremony transferring power from one generation to the other; and as a communal renewal of their commitment to a struggle against tyrants, as their forefathers the Iregi generation had done. (1981: 65)

Devil on the Cross is obviously Ngũgĩ's test case for the adequacy of the Gĩkũyũ language to articulate political, economic, linguistic, religious, philosophical, and scientific concepts. Ngũgĩ also wanted to give central place to the oral tradition as an efficient conveyor of collective experience. Especially acute is Ngũgĩ's awareness of the sweeping colonial disparagement of non-European modalities of local expression. With reference to *gĩcaandĩ*,[2] W. Scoresby Routledge and Katherine Routledge had written in 1910 that

> Occasionally a boy is seen going about by himself, dancing, singing, and accompanying the song by shaking a gourd which he holds in his hand, and which has been formed into a rattle. This proceeding he continues for a month or six weeks, and is termed ku-i'-nya ki-shan'-di (sic).
> The words of the song are traditional; they are apparently gibberish, and convey nothing even to the performer. The gourd is scoured by him with signs which constitute a record of his travel. Instruction in the art of this singing and writing is given to the boy who wishes to learn it, by a "warrior" or young man. (Routledge and Routledge, 1910: 109)

There is a schizophrenic twist to the Routledge account at this point: are a people who indulge this "gibberish" capable of the following accomplishments?

> The Akikũyu as a race (sic) are gifted with the musical ear. Their songs are almost always improvised solos with a chorus sung to a well-known air. Some hundreds of persons, strangers to one another, will join in a song with the dash and precision of a trained choir.
> The rhythmical movements of their dances, too, show their marked sense of musical time.

> By song and dance they give expression to their emotions with a spontaneity
> that is quite foreign to us. (Routledge and Routledge, 1910: 111)

It is also rather difficult to imagine that the Routledges did not witness
an adult performance of *gĩcaandĩ*, or that they could have failed to see that the
"boy" in question was undergoing the apprenticeship which would prepare
him for his later years among his poetic peers.

Nor is it difficult to understand the reasons for the devaluation of
African literary artefacts. Colonial description (which served also as a mode of
containment and control) vacillated between the total dismissal and the *reduc-
tio ad absurdum* of the cultural production of the Other. In her *Oral Literature
in Africa* (1970), Ruth Finnegan points out that the main characteristic of
European study of African oral literature was the reduction of the latter to
raw ethnographic material. Until the mid-1850s, European collections and
translations

> ... contain narratives of various kinds (including stories about both animals
> and humans), historical texts, proverbs, riddles, vernacular texts describing
> local customs, and very occasionally songs or poems. (Finnegan, 1970: 28)

Early European academic, freelance, and missionary "interest" in African
oral material is remarkable for its fragmentary and fragmenting nature, with
a tendency to deny or obscure indigenous African literary traditions:

> The main emphasis in these collections was, it is true, linguistic (or, in some
> cases, religio-educational, preoccupied with what it was thought fitting for
> children to know). There was little attempt to relate the texts to their social
> context, elucidate their literary significance, or describe the normal circum-
> stances of their recitation. There are many questions, therefore, which these
> texts cannot answer. (Finnegan, 1970: 28)

Scant attention seems to have been paid to sung poetry: even when it was collected, its study was less rigorous:

> Prose narrative was more often referred to than sung poetry, since it was easier
> to make a quick record of it and since it was more suitable, particularly in the
> form of "myths," for use in functional analysis. Altogether the emphasis was on
> brief synopsis or paraphrase rather than a detailed recording of literary forms as
> actually recorded. (Finnegan, 1970: 38)

Finnegan further notes that obsession with primitivism and the "folkloristic"
bias in European scholarship had the effect of relativizing and therefore
devaluing the object of scholarship:

Because primitive tribes were supposed to be preoccupied with tradition rather than innovation, "traditional" tales were sought and "new" ones ignored or explained away. Because interest was focused on broad evolutionary stages, few questions were asked about the idiosyncratic history, culture, or literary conventions of a particular people. Finally because origins and early history assumed such importance in people's minds, there was little emphasis on the *contemporary* relevance of a piece of literature, so there seemed every excuse for collecting and publishing bits and pieces without attempting to relate them to their particular social and literary context. (Finnegan, 1970: 37)

It is precisely the contemporary relevance of the diverse indigenous African (or Kenyan) literary forms that Ngũgĩ is at pains to demonstrate and concretize. "The quest for relevance" is not only a chapter in *Decolonizing the Mind* but also Ngũgĩ's entire literary *modus vivendi*. However incomplete the task, the rendering of *Devil on the Cross* as a "gĩcaandĩ" novel represents an effort to contemporize *gĩcaandĩ*. There is ample evidence of Ngũgĩ's determination to attempt to repair, or at least arrest, the damage occasioned to the Kenyan (and by extension, African) political, cultural and spiritual body by decades of colonial and neocolonial activity.

In a prefatory note to *Decolonizing the Mind* (1986), dedicated to "all those who write in African languages, and to all those who over the years have maintained the dignity of the literature, culture, philosophy, and other treasures carried by African languages," Ngũgĩ declared that he was bidding "farewell to English as a vehicle for any of my writings. From now on it is Gĩkũyũ and Kiswahili all the way." Time and necessity have already impinged on Ngũgĩ's pledge; nevertheless, Ngũgĩ has steadfastly blazed what is more than a symbolic trail in the campaign to foreground the question of the material and historical conditions of collective expression. Subsequent to the publication of *Petals of Blood* (1977), Ngũgĩ has written, published and lectured predominantly in Gĩkũyũ, relying on the medium of translation to bridge the linguistic gap.

Ngũgĩ's advocacy of writing in African languages is perhaps best summarized in his assertion that

We African writers are bound by our calling to do for our languages what Spencer, Milton and Shakespeare did for English; what Pushkin and Tolstoy did for Russian; indeed what all writers in world history have done for their languages by meeting the challenge of creating a literature in them, which process later opens the languages for philosophy, science, technology and all the other areas of human creative endeavours. (Ngũgĩ, 1986: 29)

Ngũgĩ is careful not to fetishize the mere gesture of writing in an African language, being conscious that

[W]riting in our languages per se—although a necessary first step in the correct direction—will not in itself bring about the renaissance in African cultures if that literature does not carry the content of our people's anti-imperialist struggles to liberate their productive forces from foreign control. . . . (Ngũgĩ, 1986: 29)

Ngũgĩ has borrowed and made extensions to Amilcar Cabral's ideological concept of a "return to the source"[3] as a means of re-inventing a set of enabling, transformative modalities for social change. Proceeding from the truism that "the struggle of Kenyan national languages against domination by foreign languages is part of the wider historical struggle of the Kenyan national culture against imperialist domination" (1981: 61), Ngũgĩ urges Kenyan writers to remember that

[N]o foreigners can ever develop our languages, our literatures, our theatre for us: that we in turn cannot develop our cultures and literatures through borrowed tongues and imitations.
Only by a return to the roots of our being in the languages and cultures and heroic histories of the Kenyan people can we rise up to the challenge of helping in the creation of a Kenyan patriotic national literature and culture that will be the envy of many foreigners and the pride of Kenyans. (Ngũgĩ, 1981: 64–65)

In *Devil on the Cross,* Gatuĩria is Ngũgĩ's perfect example of the erstwhile "assimilated" intellectual groping his/her way back to a nativist or progressive consciousness, tripping over the syllables of his/her native language and despairing of ever regaining a coherent centredness:

Let us now look about us. Where are our national languages now? Where are the books written in the alphabets of our national languages? Where is our own literature now? Where is the wisdom and knowledge of our fathers now? Where is the philosophy of our fathers now? The centres of wisdom that used to guard the entrance to our national homestead have been demolished; the fire of wisdom has been allowed to die; the seats around the fireside have been thrown on to a rubbish heap; the guard posts have been destroyed; and the youth of the nation has hung up its shields and spears. It is a tragedy that there is nowhere we can go to learn the history of our country. . . . (1982: 58)

Gatuĩria, the seeker-searcher-researcher who is also in part Ngũgĩ's *alter ego,* recounts that he and "some people at the university, students and teachers, are now attempting to unearth the roots of our culture. The roots of Kenyan national culture can be sought only in the traditions of all the nationalities of Kenya" (1982: 59). His dream is to compose "a piece of music for many human voices accompanied by an orchestra made up of all kinds of national instruments: skin, wind, string and brass . . ." (1982: 59). Towards the end of the novel, Gatuĩria has completed the score (it will never be played, it turns out) which is nothing short of the majestic harmony of a new and changed Kenya:

> In his mind, of course, Gatuīria can reconstruct the whole process of mixing the various voices and the various sounds in harmony: how and where all the voices meet; how and where they part, each voice taking its own separate path, and finally how and where they come together again, the various voices floating in harmony like the Thīrīrīka River flowing through flat plains towards the sea, all the voices blending into each other like the colours of the rainbow. (1982: 226)

The *gīcaandī* instrument ranks high on the grand score that Gatuīria is composing. Significantly, its inclusion in the First Movement ("Voices from the past, before the coming of British imperialism") connotes a pre-colonial, pre-European knowledge-of-the-self. *Gīcaandī* as a questing (dialogic), multi-voiced text seems to have provided Gatuīria with a partial solution to the nagging question he has been wrestling with:

> Our stories, our riddles, our songs, our customs, our traditions, everything about our national heritage has been lost to us.
> Who can play the gīcaandī for us today and read and interpret the verses written on the gourd? (1982: 59)

And music as an inseparable component of the enactment (performance) of contemporary Kenyan history must reflect the vicissitudes of resistance and struggle as well as the desired triumph of the peasant-worker coalition against international monopoly capital. When Warīīnga wonders why it has taken Gatuīria two whole years to compose a national oratorio, the latter replies:

> Music that tells the story of one's country? Music to be played by an orchestra of hundreds of instruments and sung by hundreds of human voices? And remember, you have to indicate where each instrument comes in. My friend, there is music and *the* music; there is song and *the* song! (1982: 226)

Like his own not-so-fictional creation, Gatuīria, Ngũgĩ is engaged in a search for suitable containers and conveyors of the various facets of individual African cultures—literature, philosophy, technology, politics, musicology, and so on. Ngũgĩ questions the role of research institutes at African universities (such as institutes of African Studies: what else should they be, Ngũgĩ has once asked). It is not Gatuīria's voice so much as Ngũgĩ's that we hear in the exploration of cultural ways and means:

> Gatuīria is trying to explain to Warīīnga the movement of the different voices and sounds. He is trying to explain to Warīīnga the kinds of instruments that

might be made to represent the workers and peasants as they rescue the soul of the nation from imperialist slavery. He is trying to explain the difficulties of writing down African music, for the notation of African music has not yet been sufficiently developed and differentiated from that of European music. (1982: 230)

As we shall see later, the narrative structure of *Devil on the Cross* is undergirded by an interlacing network of genres—riddles, proverbs, songs, "tales," myths and legends, and so forth. Though no single genre is predominant, the proverb as a "condensing" narrative form (especially in the stacking so consciously conducted at the novel's opening) is worth some attention. The urgency to "reveal all that is hidden" is already forcefully articulated in the Gĩkũyũ proverb: *Kwa mwaria gũkĩhĩa, kwa mũkĩri kwahĩĩre tene.* (The house of the person who does not call out for help is more likely to burn down than the house of the person who calls for help.)

The narrative burden in *Devil on the Cross* is carried by the Prophet of Justice who is simultaneously/interchangeably the Gĩcaandĩ Player. The history of infamy of post-independence Kenya—the "story" of the reign of the devil of capital after he has been resuscitated by his local acolytes at the urging of and with the active support of international monopoly capital—is the burden weighing heavily upon the Prophet of Justice, inhibiting him from telling "this story [which] was too disgraceful, too shameful [and therefore] should be concealed in the depths of everlasting darkness" (1982: 1). But then

> Warĩĩnga's mother came to me when dawn was breaking, and in tears she beseeched me: Gĩcaandĩ Player, tell the story of the child I loved so dearly. Cast light upon all that happened, so that each may pass judgement only when he knows the whole truth. Gĩcaandĩ Player, reveal all that is hidden. (1982: 1)

It is demanded of the Prophet of Justice that he constitute himself into an oracle, in the best sense of the word. The task cannot ultimately remain an individual one: prophecy, the projection of what is (likely) to come to pass—which involves what has come to pass as well—is a collective concern. The Prophet of Justice is at first diffident, but after a ritual fast of seven days he is empowered to speak. A voice "like a great clap of thunder" admonishes him: "Who has told you that prophecy is yours alone, to keep to yourself?" It is the voice of the people, which is the voice of God, which mandates and authorizes the Gĩcaandĩ Player's complex narrative. The moment of the initiation of the many-layered *gĩcaandĩ* narrative is the beginning of an extended divination of the ills of the nation. The Prophet of Justice will henceforth discharge the office of diviner/priest, investigator, philosopher, counsellor, comforter, the voice of conscience, validating once again the multi-purpose function of *gĩcaandĩ* as formulated in the coded utterance which comes at the beginning of virtually every *gĩcaandĩ* performance:

Gĩcaandĩ to ũgo kana ciira,
Kana ũthamaki wa riika;
Ti kũragũra matua kũragũra,
Na ti ciira. (Vittorio Merlo Pick, 1973: 167)

Gĩcaandĩ is not only magical divination [or medicine];
nor is it just the government of the extant age-set;
it is more than diagnosing the cause of illness and
prescribing a remedial ceremony;
gĩcaandĩ is not a law-suit. (My translation)

Although it is the form he most wants to rediscover and refashion as a powerful dramatic-narrative form in *Devil on the Cross,* Ngũgĩ had, by 1979, referred only obliquely to the *gĩcaandĩ* tradition of the Aagĩkũyũ. In *Writers in Politics,* Ngũgĩ describes how "the oppression of Kenyan languages during colonial and postcolonial times went hand in hand with the suppression of the cultures of the various nationalities" (1981: 63). He offers as examples the banning in Central Province of "the big Ituĩka cultural festival of dances, songs, and poems, and instrumental music." In the period of British colonial rule, Ngũgĩ tells us, "the only poems and songs ever banned were those composed in Kenyan languages." Among these, Ngũgĩ enumerates the provocative mũthĩrĩgũ dance and song in the 1930s and the Mau Mau patriotic songs in the 1950s. Curiously, Ngũgĩ makes no specific reference to *gĩcaandĩ*. It is reasonable to speculate that the performance of *gĩcaandĩ* was banned sometime between 1900 and the 1930s; there is, for all practical purposes, no official mention of this banning. The mystery is further deepened by the relative paucity of publishing, indigenous or otherwise, on the subject of what now persists as a severely endangered art form.

III

The *Kikuyu-English Dictionary* defines *gĩcaandĩ* as follows:

n. (III), picture rattle shaken rhythmically as an accompaniment; a kind of dance, the song to which the rattle is an accompaniment; *ina˜*, sing the rattle-song which consists of riddles and conundrums in which two persons compete; cf. irebeta. (1964: 46)

The *Dictionary* further defines *irebeta* as follows:

irebeta, ma-, n. (III), song with cryptic phrasing sung to the accompaniment of the picture rattle; see gĩcandĩ. 2. wise witty saying, epigram; wise-cracking indulged in between young people in conversation as well as in song.... (1964: 374)

Clearly, then, *gĩcaandĩ* and poetry are intricately linked, and their field of application is very broad.

The most extensive written *gĩcaandĩ* text is Vittorio Merlo Pick's *Ndaĩ na Gĩcandĩ: Kikuyu Enigmas/Enigmi Kikuyu,* first published in 1973. Part Two of the book contains 127 stanzas of a *gĩcaandĩ* performance (out of an original 150). Merlo Pick, who after V. Ghilardi categorizes *gĩcandĩ* as "traditional poetry sung in the moonlight," is drawn to this particular genre for its ethnological value. He writes:

> The GICANDI is a poem which in the thirties [1930s] was still known to a few initiates, and is now almost forgotten. It is made up of elegantly elaborated enigmas which were sung by two people in competition. The song was accompanied by the shaking of a kind of rattle, itself called gĩcandĩ, which was prepared specially and blessed by a medicine-man who had inherited the secret. This instrument is particularly interesting, because it bears, carved on its side, writings in the mnemonic-pictorial system, the only specimen of this kind, as far as I know, to be found among Bantu tribes. (Merlo Pick, 1973: 18)

It is necessary to state that *gĩcaandĩ,* while it is a trade plied by the initiated (much like "poetry" which is still "read" to us by "poets" who are "better" than we are) is by no means a dead art form. At least in the 1970s and '80s, the Gĩkũyũ Service of The Voice of Kenya regularly aired *gĩcaandĩ* performances and interviews with living *gĩcaandĩ* poets. What is curious indeed is the silence in Kenyan official circles surrounding the life and future of *gĩcaandĩ* as a representative of dialogue poetry in its myriad forms in Kenya. It is remarkable, too, that Jomo Kenyatta, in his *Facing Mount Kenya* (1938), his pioneering work on the life of the Aagĩkũyũ, wrote not a word about *gĩcaandĩ*.

Contrary to Merlo Pick's assertion, it is not at all probable that in the 1930s *gĩcaandĩ* was "known to a few initiates," given the numbers of performers whose texts have been recorded in the last few decades—for The Voice of Kenya radio and by researchers such as Wanjikũ Mũkabi Kabĩra (with Karega Mũtahi), Lee K. Kaguongo and Kĩmani Njogu, among others.

Merlo Pick's *Ndaĩ na Gĩcandĩ* presumes a total separation of genres such as riddles, proverbs, story and poetry. The reductive, ethnographic impulse is evident in this description of *ndaĩ* ("riddles"):

> The ndaĩ have as a subject, in most cases, matters and objects which belong to the environment in which the Kikuyu live and which they know in all details and circumstances: the hut and the homestead, the village, the members of the family, the domestic animals and their habits, the birds, the field, the crops, the forest, the different kinds of trees, the waste plains,—the whole nature with which a Kikuyu is unendingly in contact, observing its phenomena during the long hours spent over the grazing animals, in loneliness. (Merlo Pick, 1973: 26)

"Riddling," however, is creative activity, requiring the ability to metaphorize across time, space and event. In Merlo Pick's introduction, the literary value of *ndaī* is dismissed amid claims of the cultural exoticism of the Aagĭkũyũ whose intellectual faculties are *intrinsically* different from those of Europeans:

> [Riddles] often play on a double meaning, figures of speech, comparisons, metaphorical meanings, exaggerations of speech. The likeness between the object described and the one meant is very varied: the Kikuyu often space with their imagination in the realm of strangely grand representations, and we Europeans feel lost; very often we would find ourselves under obligation to «pay» in order to be told the solutions to the riddles; and even then we would be unable to see the connection. (Merlo Pick, 1973: 26)

Even a cursory reading of a *gĭcaandĭ* text reveals the complex interplay of genres—riddles, proverbs, biographical "information," history, commentary—and a performance dramatic quality which invests in voice, gesture and attention to the audience. Merlo Pick violently separates *ndaī* from *gĭcaandĭ*, genres that are traditionally interdependent and integrated. He thus does violence to a discourse/tradition that recognises no such dichotomy.

The narrative tenor of *Devil on the Cross* is saturated with a "conversational," oral/aural dimension that demonstrates the dramatic sequence of challenge, response, conflict/tension, and reconciliation typical of *gĭcaandĭ* performances. *Devil on the Cross* is Ngũgĭ's own translation of *Caitaani Mũtharaba-inĭ*. Ngũgĭ's profound interest in theatre is well demonstrated by *The Trial of Dedan Kimathi* (with Mĭcere Mũgo), *Ngaahika Ndeenda* (with Ngũgĭ wa Mĭriĭ) and *Maitũ Njugĭra*, to name but a few. Yet Ngũgĭ translates the original *mũini wa gĭcaandĭ* as "Gĭcaandĭ Player." In Gĭkũyũ the verb *kũina* means to sing, to dance, to perform a dance. In the Gĭkũyũ cultural milieu song and dance are, generally speaking, not separable, so even the phrase *kũina rwĭmbo* translates as both to sing (a song) *and* to perform a dance. There is an important dimension of performance which is omitted in the move from *mũini wa gĭcaandĭ* (one who performs the *gĭcaandĭ*) to "Gĭcaandĭ Player." The oral/aural dimension of *gĭcaandĭ* is part of its inscription/creation. Performance is conveyed through the act of *kũina gĭcaandĭ*—both "singing" and extemporaneous (but not haphazard) creation of verse. *Uini* (performance in its entirety) consists of "rhythming," "poetry-making" (dependent on a sense of movement, balance, structure) and prosody.

As Merlo Pick had noted, the object referred to in a *ndaī* is called *mũũndũ* (man), unlike the gĭcaandĭ in which it is called *ngeithi* (greeting). While this is true enough, *ngeithi* can also mean subject, message, address, debate, point of view, discourse (or a variety of discourses). The pictographic inscriptions on the *gĭcaandĭ* instrument itself are also called *ngeithi*. A typical *gĭcaandĭ* "line" states:

> Ngeithi nĭ hĭrĭrĭ nyiingĭ
> Kũrĭ irũũngiĭ, kũrĭ ikĭĭgiĭ
> Na kũrĭ ituramĭire iria ingĭ

Ngeithi are of many stripes
There are those which stand upright; others are horizontal
And others which face each other. (My translation)

The *gĩcaandĩ* instrument is made from a gourd which grows from a gourd vine, *rũũngũ*, which is an annual plant. The gourd is easily broken, and in times of drought there may be no vines to produce gourds to be made into *gĩcaandĩ* instruments. The latter scenario is enacted in an excerpt of the *gĩcaandĩ* text recorded by Merlo Pick, where one participant poses the crucial question:

Q. Ngũũria kũrĩa mwarutire nyũngũ cia kũhaanda nĩguo mware gĩcandĩ: mwarutire kũ? Na Gĩkũyũ gĩothe kĩagĩte na Ikamba na Ukabi. (Merlo Pick, 1973: 199)

I wonder where you obtained the seeds for planting, that you might start *gĩcaandĩ*,
when none could be found in the land of the Gĩkũyũ and Ikaamba and Ukabi.

A. Uigue: kaheti cũcũ gakĩruta tũgoto twĩrĩ: tũgoto twohete mbegũ ya nyũngũ, rĩrĩa gũkoira ahande.

Listen: My old grandmother took them out of a purse made of banana-bark, and planted them when the rains started. (My translation)

Besides, a performer can always lose his instrument to a competitor. What would happen to *gĩcaandĩ* as an art form or tradition if its very source were destroyed or lost? Seeds of the gourd vine must always be saved, so that a future planting can be insured. *Gĩcaandĩ* is, ultimately, about self-generation and continuity: the storing of the seed for future planting involves a selection of the best. The continuity of *gĩcaandĩ* as a productive text requires discursive strategies that accommodate diverse interpretations and points of view. Hence the call to be adaptable: *Garũrĩra mbeũ, ti ya kĩnya kĩmwe.* (Change, for the seeds in the gourd are not all of one kind.)

Kĩnya is the generic name for a gourd or calabash in the Gĩkũyũ language. The proverb refers to the practice of storing seeds in gourds. There is an important parallel to be drawn between the gourd used as a seed store and the *gĩcaandĩ* gourd as an emblem of a people's cultural "wisdom." This self-signifying gesture demonstrates not only the consciousness of the danger posed by the vagaries of the natural world on community survival, but also the literary encoding of the requisite strategies for the continuance of *gĩcaandĩ* as a cultural artistic form. In this regard, *gĩcaandĩ* is the equivalent of *kĩgĩĩna* (treasury). Besides, as the Aagĩkũyũ are fond of saying, {*Mũũndũ*} *Utamerithũũtie ndaigaga kĩgĩĩna thĩ.* (S/he whose seeds have not germinated does not put away the seed-hoard.)

As an event that takes place in the public square, *gĩcaandĩ* is not only a performance but a site of performance, providing a model for interpersonal and public discourse. Practically every *gĩcaandĩ* performance concludes with the formula: *Hau twacemania ũmũũthĩ, no ho tũgaacemania rũũciũ.* (We will meet again tomorrow in the same place where we met today.) Far from signifying changelessness, this formulaic line promises future encounters between performers in which new themes will be introduced and old ones re-examined. The public, let it not be forgotten, will be in attendance.

Incidentally, the instrument of divination, the *mwano,* is also made from a gourd/calabash and contains rattling seeds. The *gĩcaandĩ* and the *mwano* are both means of discerning the nature of that which is not always clearly understood. The "answers" in a *gĩcaandĩ* contest and the prognosis given by a "medicine-man" are almost never the same, even for the same "seeker" or quest(ion). Herein lies the value of the implied connection between *kũina gĩcaandĩ* and *gũthiĩ ũgo-inĩ* (to go to a diviner).

The relationship between individual *perform*-ance and collective participation is cogently dramatized in the exchange where one *mũini wa gĩcaandĩ* enjoins the other to

Nyambĩkĩra ngeithi, amu ndingĩhota ũtambĩkĩte.

Start the weaving of the *ngeithi* for me, for I cannot begin without your collaboration. (My translation)

The fellow *mũini* responds with a most complex formulation of the communal ethos within which *gĩcaandĩ* is performed:

Mũtumi wa kĩondo. Mwambĩrĩria wa ũhandi. Mũgo agĩkunũrwo ambĩrĩrie ũgo akĩambĩrĩria na ndawoine. (Merlo Pick, 1973: 297)

The weaver of a string basket. The young girl who ritually initiates the season's planting of the seed. The diviner/medicine man, when he is first "initiated," has no prior experience. (My translation)

Throughout most of his writing, Ngũgĩ pays homage to the enormous contribution of peasants and workers to the Kenyan economy and culture. The Kenya Land and Freedom Army (or "Mau Mau") figures prominently in Ngũgĩ's musings on Kenyan history. The metaphor of the weaving of the *kĩondo* finds its ultimate articulation in a stanza of a "Mau Mau" song of the 1950s and '60s in which what was apparently started by an individual or a small group matures and is borne to its conclusion by collaborative enterprise:

Kĩondo kĩambirwo nĩ Kenyatta wa Mũigai
Mũingĩ ũkĩogothera ndigi

Mau Mau ĩgĩtiriha
Kamũingĩ kooyaga ndĩrĩ
Kĩondo kĩambirwo

The *kĩondo* was "started" by Kenyatta son of Mũigai
The patriotic collective spun the uprights and the cross strings
"Mau Mau" put the finishing touches
The *kĩondo* was thus woven. (My translation)

In *Matigari*, Ngũgĩ pays particular attention to the lessons to be gleaned
from the Mau Mau struggle and how those lessons might be applied to the
continuing engagement between the producers and the parasites in contemporary Kenya. Change and innovation are key words in both *Matigari* and
Devil on the Cross; both ideas proceed from the construction of "the other
heart," a humanity motivated by the collective good:

> That humanity is in turn born of many hands working together, for, as Gĩkũyũ
> once said, a single finger cannot kill a louse; a single log cannot make a fire last
> through the night; a single man, however strong, cannot build a bridge across
> a river; and many hands can lift a weight, however heavy. The unity of our
> sweat is what makes us able to change the laws of nature, able to harness them
> to the needs of our lives, instead of our lives remaining slaves of the laws of
> nature. That's why Gĩkũyũ also said: Change, for the seeds in the gourd are not
> all of one kind. (Ngũgĩ, 1982: 52)

In Ngũgĩ's reckoning, Mau Mau and their ideological offspring, *matigari ma
njirũũngi* (those who survived the bullets), become the logical descendants of
the Iregi generation, that

> . . . generation of revolutionary rebels, who had overthrown the corrupt dicta-
> torial regime of King Gĩkũyũ, established ruling councils and established (sic)
> the procedure for handing over power, an event commemorated in the Ituĩka
> festival of music, dance, poetry and theatre. The last such festival was held
> towards the end of the nineteenth century. The next, due in about 1930, was
> banned by the colonial overlords as a threat to public peace and order. (Ngũgĩ,
> 1981: 65)

Gĩcaandĩ celebrates this long history of resistance, throwing its weight behind
the party of Iregi (the ones who said "NO!") and their descendants:

Kuuma Wanyahoro gũũka
Gũtirĩ kĩama giũkĩĩte
No kĩrĩa kĩa Iregi na Mũũriũ (Mũkabi Kabĩra and Karega Mũtahi, 1988: 167)

Since the arrival of Wanyahoro
No [new] party has arisen
Except that of Iregi and his descendants.[4] (My translation)

The "open endings" of both *Devil on the Cross* ("Warĩĩnga walked on, without once looking back. But she knew with all her heart that the hardest struggles of her life's journey lay ahead . . ." [1982: 254]) and *Matigari* ("And suddenly he seemed to hear the workers' voices, the voices of the peasants, the voices of the students and of other patriots of all the different nationalities of the land, singing in harmony: Victory shall be ours . . ." [1987: 175]) no doubt reweave a *gĩcaandĩ* theme:

> *Hau twacemania ũmũũthĩ,*
> *No ho tũgaacemania rũũciũ . . .*

Notes

1. This is an abbreviated version of a work-in-progress on the subject of *gĩcaandĩ* as dialogue/dialogic poetry.

2. My orthography, including the spelling of *gĩcaandĩ,* is in accordance with the recommendations of the Gĩkũyũ Language Committee of 1980/81 (not to be mistaken for the colonial United Kikuyu Language Committee [1949]). Merlo Pick's orthography follows the latter.

3. See especially "National Liberation and Culture," in *Return to the Source: Selected Speeches of Amilcar Cabral.* (New York: Monthly Review Press, 1973).

4. Wanyahoro is the "corrupted" name of Francis Hall, an early colonial administrator in the Mũrang'a district of Central Kenya. The implication of the statement: We hold steadfastly to the tradition of resistance of the Iregi generation. Our embrace of other political "parties" is merely strategic.

Works Cited

Benson, T. G. *Kikuyu-English Dictionary.* Oxford: The Clarendon Press, 1964.

Fanon, Frantz. *The Wretched of the Earth.* New York: Grove Press, 1968.

Finnegan, Ruth. *Oral Literature in Africa.* Oxford: The Clarendon Press, 1970.

Merlo Pick, Vittorio. *Ndaĩ na Gĩcandĩ.* Bologna: Editrice Missionaria Italiana, 1973.

Mũkabi Kabĩra, Wanjikũ, and Mũtahi, Karega. *Gĩkũyũ Oral Literature.* Nairobi: Heinemann, 1988.

Ngũgĩ wa Thiong'o. *Decolonizing the Mind.* London: James Currey, 1986.

———. *Detained: A Writer's Prison Diary.* Nairobi: Heinemann, 1981.

———. *Devil on the Cross.* Nairobi: Heinemann, 1982.

———. *Matigari.* Trans. by Wangũi wa Goro. Nairobi/London: Heinemann, 1989.

———. *Writers in Politics.* Nairobi/London: Heinemann, 1981.

Routledge, W. Scoresby, and Routledge, Katherine. *With a Prehistoric People: The Akikuyu of British East Africa.* London: Frank Cass & Co. Ltd., 1910 (1968).

Orality and the Literature of Combat: The Legacy of Fanon

ALAMIN MAZRUI AND LUPENGA MPHANDE

1.

Prior to the inception of European colonial rule in Africa many of the societies on the continent had modes of communication that tended to preclude the medium of writing. Such societies have sometimes been described as belonging to the "oral tradition" in the wider sense of the term that includes not only expression in speech form, but also in its "complimentaries" like the drum, the dance, the performance and other paralinguistic practices. But even in societies, like that of the Amhara in Ethiopia, which had indigenous scripts centuries before their encounter with European invaders, the production of texts continued to be primarily a function of the oral domain. Writing can, and does often, take a life of its own. But in these precolonial, scripted African societies, writing was not only relatively restricted in its functions, but it also remained, to a large extent, a mere expression of the oral word.

This particular configuration of orality, writing and literacy is, of course, a product of certain material and social conditions obtaining in specific societies, and indeed globally, at a certain historical juncture. But there has often been a tendency to regard writing as an exclusive preserve of the Western mind, and orality as a peculiarly African predisposition. In colonial scholarship, in particular, this supposedly Western orientation towards writing and the supposedly African orientation towards orality often assumed the form of the grand racialist divide between "civilization" and "primitivity." Oral literature, for instance, was seen as nothing more than a manifestation of an earlier stage in the historical evolution of society towards a more advanced state of a writing "culture." It is this colonial legacy that led Ama Ata Aidoo to state:

> One doesn't have to really assume that all literature has to be written. I mean one doesn't have to be so patronizing about oral literature. There is present validity to oral literary communication. I totally disagree with people who feel that literature is one stage in the development of man's artistic genius. (1972: 23–24)

First appeared in *Paintbrush: A Journal of Poetry and Translation,* Vol. XX (Nos. 39 & 40), Spring/ Autumn 1993.

But even when orality has been freed from negative associations, the tendency to regard it as something peculiarly African has remained strong. It is not uncommon to find claims that the distinction between the oral and the written underlie the entire relationship between sub-Saharan Africa and the West (1990: 69).

Partly as a result of this ahistorical dichotomy between the writing West and "oralizing" Africa, many Africans came to see the advance of writing in the Roman script in Africa as an aspect of the continent's capitulation to European imperialist designs. The colonial conception of "African" orality as an undeveloped form of expression that does not do justice to the human creative potential was now met with an anti-colonial view of "Western" writing as a pervasive form of cultural tyranny.

This juxtaposition of the Western-African divide on a dichotomous view of the orality-literacy continuum expectedly led to the emergence of a neonationalist school which sought to "reclaim" orality as one of the many glories of the indigenous heritage of Africa. Oral literature came to be regarded as a hallmark, *sui generis,* of the African creative mind which needed to be "conserved" and protected against the imperialist onslaught of the written word. Orality now came to be romanticized. It came to carry the entire weight of African civilization and its historical longevity. In some instances it came to help define the very soul of a preconceived Africanity. In Negritudist circles, for example, the supposed oralness of African societies came to be a mark of their humanism (Leopold Senghor, 1965: 84–85), in contrast to the supposedly detached and impersonal character of writing.

But the neonationalist cultural struggle was by no means restricted to the revalorization of orality as an independent mode of discourse and literary creativity. Evidence of orality in written texts, and especially in the novel, became part of the quest for an authentically African literature. According to Mbye Baboucar Cham, the process of conflating the oral with the written is seen by some as "an act of literary authenticity clearly meant to put an imprint of legitimate Africanness on the work" (1982: 24).

Some have acknowledged that the novel in Africa is indeed part of the Western legacy. Nonetheless, they have proceeded to argue that the indigenous force of orality managed to Africanize it to a point where we can now talk of a novel that is peculiarly African in style. Phanuel Egejuru has described how elements from the oral tradition are sometimes inserted in contemporary African novels to "add a specific African flavor to the work" (1990: 1–2).

Others have sought a complete break with the West, seeking instead to place the origins of the novel in Africa in a progressive path of development from Africa's own heritage, rather than in a more recent history of Western imposition. Chinweizu, Jemie and Madubuike, for example, have contended:

> Since there are these pre-European narratives, both oral and written, some of which are comparable to European novels, and others which have contributed

> to the development of the African novel, there is no reason why they should not be considered African antecedents to the African novel, antecedents out of which the African novel might entirely have evolved, without hybridization by the European novel. (1985: 22)

Similarly, Harold Scheub criticizes the common assumption that the novel evolved first in the West only to be later transported to the rest of the world. Describing this view as blind as it is arrogant Scheub concludes that "the early literary traditions were beneficiaries of the oral genres, and there is no doubt that the epic and its hero are the predecessors of the African novel and its central characters" (1985: 1).

But the ahistorical opposition between orality as African and writing as Western, and the undialectical relegation of orality to Africa's precolonial heritage have combined to make the oral literature of African intellectuals and academia frozen in time and virtually closed to organic growth. Contrary to its dynamic, growing, and creative character, oral literature is often regarded as a static heritage that can only be passed on "intact" from one generation to another. Many African writers come to see their role as one of digging into this "past" to uncover material for display in their writing as an affirmation of their Africanness. It is precisely this kind of orientation that led Christopher Miller to suggest that,

> Orality in its broadest sense thus has a clear political connotation in Africa, representing the authenticity of the precolonial world: "tradition" and orality are synonymous. The traditional African verbal arts, however, while extant, are fast disappearing or becoming something else. It is said that every time an old African dies another museum disappears. (1990: 70–71)

The very terminology used in placing oral literature within a historical time-frame betrays the extent to which the tradition has become fossilized in our imagination.

All these tendencies described above are products of a particular phase of a more general phenomenon that Frantz Fanon described as alienation or estrangement from one's existential and cultural being. This phenomenon begins with a stage of attempted assimilation into the culture of the oppressor, in which the writer is virtually completely inspired by the aesthetics of European creative writing. His or her works can easily be linked up "with definite trends in the literature of the mother country" (Fanon, 1967: 179).

The "native" writer is soon shaken into a rude awakening that the desperately sought doors of Europeanness are, in fact, completely closed. At this point the writer is forced to remember and to express his or her Africanity. But with lost cultural roots, the writer is no longer

> a part of his people, since he has only exterior relations with his people, he is content to recall their life only. Past happenings of the bygone days of his child-

hood will be brought up out of the depth of his memory; old legends will be reinterpreted in the light of a borrowed aestheticism and of a conception of the world which was discovered under other skies. (Fanon, 1967: 179)

Precisely because the African writer or intellectual now seeks to be attached to the people without actually being an integral part of them, he or she only manages "to catch hold of their garments." Yet these garments are merely the reflection of a hidden life, teeming and perpetually in motion. As Fanon observes, "The man of culture, instead of setting out to find this substance, will let himself be hypnotized by these mummified fragments which, because they are static, are in fact symbols of negation and outworn contrivances" (1967: 180).

Operating within the boundaries of this particular psychology of culture, the early Ngũgĩ as well as many other African writers, incorporate into their works fragments from the oral tradition in a manner that is mummified, exotic and usually unrelated to the dynamics and realities of the lives of their people. However, the fossilization of oral literature reminiscent, to some extent, in Ngũgĩ's early works, is a tendency which he manages to overcome in his later writings. After *Petals of Blood* in particular Ngũgĩ begins to use oral literature in a way that maintains its life and vibrancy. Whether drawn from a pre-existing pool or newly created, and whether its presence is substantive or stylistic, orality in Ngũgĩ's writing comes to have an existence that is in an organic and rhythmic communion with the dynamics and counter-dynamics of life at present.

This development in Ngũgĩ's writing is partly a product of a maturation of national consciousness on his part. A manifestation of this national consciousness is described by Frantz Fanon as that habit of the "native" writer, acquired progressively over time, to turn away from addressing the audience defined by the oppressor, and seeking to address, instead, his or her own people. Ngũgĩ's increasing use of his native language, Gĩkũyũ, and his campaign for the promotion of African indigenous languages in African writing, is partly a product of this attempt to redefine the audience of African literature. Precisely at this point, in Fanon's view, when the focus on a new audience has taken root, can national literature be said to have come into being (1967: 193).

This redefinition of the audience, this creation of a completely new public, necessarily disrupts the entire vocation of literary creation. In the process new forms, new styles and new themes may emerge to characterize the emergent national literature. In Fanon's conception a national literature may properly be called a literature of combat, in the sense that

it calls on the whole people to fight for their existence as a nation. It is a literature of combat, because it moulds the national consciousness, giving it form and contours and flinging open before it new and boundless horizons; it is a lit-

erature of combat because it assumes responsibility, and because it is the will to
liberty expressed in terms of time and space. (1967: 193)

The revolutionary nature of this literature, its fighting spirit, comes to
provide oral literature with a new value and a new orientation altogether.
Again, in the words of Fanon:

> the oral tradition—stories, epics and songs of the people—which formerly
> were filed away as set pieces are now beginning to change. The storytellers
> who used to relate inert episodes now bring them alive and introduce into
> them modifications which are increasingly fundamental. There is a tendency to
> bring conflicts up to date and to modernize the kinds of struggle which the
> stories evoke, together with the names of heroes and the types of weapons.
> (1967: 193)

It is these attributes of national literature, which Fanon saw as developing
independently in oral literature, that came to manifest themselves in substance and style in Ngũgĩ's creative writing. In the area of literature, Ngũgĩ
can rightly be described as a follower of the legacy of the literature of combat
that was described by Frantz Fanon over thirty years ago. The multifarious
utilitarian potential of orality particularly vitalizes Ngũgĩ's own literature of
combat.

2.

The history of the Mau Mau movement against British colonialism in Kenya
has been a central feature of virtually all of Ngũgĩ's creative works. Furthermore as Ngũgĩ has moved more and more to the political left, and as he has
increasingly come to espouse the quasi-Marxist view of history as a potential
weapon of revolution, the more his own conception of Mau Mau has changed.
Ultimately Mau Mau has assumed a more radical character with greater
emphasis being placed on issues like class alliances, the trans-ethnic quality of
the movement, the active role of women in the war front, the primacy of local
over foreign factors as immediate causes of the revolutionary upsurge, and the
collective nature of its leadership. All this has had a certain impact on
Ngũgĩ's literary style. Employing history as a kind of weapon to transcend
the boundaries of mere description of reality and negate the notion of individual consciousness, he has broken away from the traditional conception of the
novel. As he has revolutionized his perspective of African history, his mode of
creative discourse about that history has molded a new kind of novel.

Ngũgĩ's political radicalization seems to have affected his views not only
in relation to the substance and nature of the Mau Mau movement, but also

in terms of what should be considered the more "authentic" and more "reliable" source of the history of the movement. And it is here that the question of orality versus writing comes into prominence once again.

By the time Kenya attained its independence in 1963, virtually all records on the Mau Mau movement that existed in writing could be described as colonial in perspective. The Mau Mau combatants were described as bloodthirsty terrorists and some of their leaders, like Kīmaathi, as lunatics. Partly because most written sources were colonial, and partly because of the mental colonization precipitated by both colonial and neocolonial education, the history written by Kenyans in the postcolonial period continued to assume a colonial character. Because of these twin factors, Ngũgĩ came to regard most written sources on Mau Mau as highly unreliable, and the resort to oral sources became a compelling quest.

The opposition between written and oral sources of history has centered around the fundamental question of whose history we seek to represent. Is it the history of the colonial and neocolonial bourgeoisie and their ideologues, or is it the history of the mass of the exploited people from whose ranks the Mau Mau emerged? It is against this background that Ngũgĩ and Mīcere Gīthae Mūgo found it necessary to make the following remarks as they were preparing to compose their play on Kīmaathi:

> There was no single historical work by a Kenyan telling of the grandeur of the heroic resistance of Kenyan people fighting foreign forces of exploitation and domination, a resistance movement whose history goes back to the 15th and 16th centuries when Kenyans and other East African people first took up arms against European colonial power. . . . Our historians, our political scientists, and even some of our literary figures were too busy spewing out, elaborating and trying to document the same colonial myths. . . . For whose benefit were these intellectuals writing? (1976: ii)

Maina wa Kīnyattī went even further by describing leading Kenyan historians like B.A. Ogot, William Ochieng, E.S. Atieno Odhiambo and B.E. Kipkorir as essentially anti-Mau Mau in their intellectual orientation (1980: 9, fn.70). The oral versus the written, posed not only the question of whose history were we drawing from, but also whose history were we documenting for posterity.

Consequently, Ngũgĩ and Mīcere Mūgo decided, for the first time, to turn to the oral tradition, and to elicit a first hand oral account of Kīmaathi directly "from the people who had known him as a child, a villager and a guerilla hero" (1976: iii). In the process they discovered a history of Kīmaathi, and a history of Mau Mau, that was in direct contra-distinction to the one they had read in most written texts. Historians trained in the Eurocentric tradition that put primacy on written records, and on the fetish of "objectivity," were quick to condemn Ngũgĩ and Mūgo's play, *The Trial of*

Dedan Kīmathi, as lacking in historical veracity. The two writers were condemned for "creating" a Kīmaathi who was not in conformity with the "historical" Kīmaathi (See, for example, E.S. Atieno Odhiambo, 1977). Apart from the fact that *The Trial of Dedan Kīmathi* was essentially a work of fiction, Ngũgĩ and Mũgo were not interested in producing anybody's "objective history" of the Mau Mau. Their aim was to present an aspect of Kenyan history as seen by the people, from their point of view and in conformity with their class interests. That people's history, emanating from the womb of the oral tradition, necessarily entailed an element of myth-making as a way of empowering it and hightening its liberative essence. Yet such history, both in its factual and mythological dimensions, was a genuine product of the people's oral tradition on which Ngũgĩ and Mũgo had come to rely. *The Trial of Dedan Kīmathi* recreated it, albeit in a fictionalized manner.

While oral tradition as a source of information influences all of Ngũgĩ's subsequent creative writing, *Matigari* attains a new level of involvement. The novel can be seen as a reincarnation of the collective Mau Mau, yet the main character can also be regarded as a return of Kīmaathi who survived the colonial bullets. This is in conformity with the oral account in which Ngũgĩ and Mũgo were told by a woman: "Kīmaathi will never die. . . . But of course if you people have killed him, go and show us his grave!" (1976: iii).

Matigari can be considered a rekindling of the spirit of the people's oral history of Mau Mau not only in its substance but also in its orientation. The thematic development of the novel is, at the same time, a process of creating a myth of the Mau Mau character that is Matigari. This process of myth creation is both a product of the oral tradition and a revalidation of a people's oral history in the politics of power.

The critical achievement of *Matigari* notwithstanding, important to remember is that at the early stages of Ngũgĩ's quest for information directly from "the people," Ngũgĩ was drawn to the oral tradition more by default than by design. He was forced to turn to the oral tradition only because the history he sought to represent existed primarily in the oral mold. At first, Ngũgĩ had difficulty transcending the "museum" conception of the oral tradition. His use of orality in *Petals of Blood,* which was published at more or less the same time as *The Trial of Dedan Kīmathi,* did not show much progress from its use in his early novels. Nevertheless, these efforts to seek a non-colonial interpretation of Kenyan history from the people who were a part of it, also brought him directly into contact with them. He forced himself to submit, almost as a student, to the wisdom of peasants and workers of Kenya, a phenomenon that was later extended to his work at the Kamĩrĩĩthũ Center. In this process, Ngũgĩ came to discover the wider dimensions of orality and its utilitarian potential as an instrument of combat, which ultimately led him to accord orality a different kind of treatment altogether in his writings after *Petals of Blood.*

3.

One of the earliest uses of orality to be found in Ngũgĩ's works is as a component of his writing. In his first two novels, Ngũgĩ delves into the themes of colonialism, alienation from Gĩkũyũ land, and peoples' resistance to the politics of occupation. In this connection, Ngũgĩ uses orality in the form of the myth of Mũũmbi and Gĩkũyũ as the progenitors of the displaced Gĩkũyũ people. At the beginning of things, it is reported in *The River Between,* "there was only one man (Gĩkũyũ) and one woman (Mũũmbi)." God, the myth continues, brought these two progenitors to Kĩrĩnyaga hill and "showed them the whole vastness of the land. He gave the country to them and their children and the children of their children, tene na tene, world without end" (1965: 18). Inserted into the text, the myth legitimizes the Gĩkũyũ peoples' claim to the land in their conflict with European settler forces and establishes how and why life in Gĩkũyũ land comes to be the way it is.

Prophecy is another oral strand that Ngũgĩ uses in the early works to legitimize the Gĩkũyũ's claims to the land, justify their political protest, and give credence to its leadership. In *Weep Not, Child,* for example, after making huge sacrifices to fight the white man's war, the Gĩkũyũ come home to find that "The land was gone":

> My father and many others had been moved from our ancestral lands. He died lonely, a poor man waiting for the white man to go. Mugo had said this would come to be. The white man did not go and he died a Muhoi on this very land. It then belonged to Chahira before he sold it to Jacobo. I grew up here, but working. . . . (1969: 48)

The old seer, Mugo wa Kibiro, had prophesied, "There shall come a people with clothes like butterflies," and the people did not believe him: "They would not listen to his voice, which warned them: 'Beware!' " The people of the ridges "gave him no clothes and no food. He became bitter and hid himself, refusing to tell them more." The nationalists triumphantly claim association with Gĩkũyũ seers and prophets of long ago from whom they purposefully derive their authority: "We are his offspring. His blood flows in your veins" (1965: 18–19). Being a descendant of the great Gĩkũyũ seer, Mugo wa Kibiro, for example, gives Chege a greater claim to Gĩkũyũ religious leadership, and Waiyaki to the Kenyan political leadership. Similarly, the name "Mugo" gives the character with that name in *A Grain of Wheat* a greater claim to heroism in the Mau Mau movement in the eyes of the people than his actual role, and helps to depict the movement as the natural heir to the prophecy.

Exemplifying Ngũgĩ's use of the oral tradition, these Mau Mau myths were used by the movement itself to validate its military campaign and its claim to the land. They can also be found in Mau Mau songs (Maina wa Kĩnyattĩ, 1980). In other words, these myths and prophecies come as part of the Mau Mau "baggage," and Ngũgĩ uses them within the boundaries of a realistic rendering of the Mau Mau oral history. The Mau Mau used them not only to fire up nationalistic sentiment and resolve against colonial oppression and land alienation in Kenya, but also to project their nationalist leaders in the form of biblical seers, prophets who had come to remind the people that this lush land now in European settlers' hands was once given to them by God. Furthermore, the approach of these modern seers resembled that of the prophets of old who had warned their fellow countrymen against the impending doom with the arrival of the white man.

In Ngũgĩ's early works, the tragic seer/nationalist heroes like Mugo wa Kibiro and Chege in the *River Between* only preach at their people: "Now, listen my son. Listen carefully, for this is the ancient prophecy. . . . I could do no more. When the white man came and fixed himself in Siriana, I warned all the people. But they laughed at me . . ." (1965: 20). In his later works, however, Ngũgĩ transforms this type of tragic hero to a more combative hero like Dedan Kĩmaathi in *The Trial of Dedan Kĩmathi,* and Matigari, who works with the people instead of preaching at them. Through this transformation Matigari becomes the reincarnation of the old prophets, going from community to community seeking for truth and justice. However, instead of his words ringing in the wilderness they are now repeated again and again at workers' rallies, in prison, and everywhere where people dwell. Ngũgĩ makes it explicit that Matigari is in fact to be understood as the re-incarnation of the old prophets when the farmers, unaware that they were talking to Matigari, say: "Go back . . . and look for a man called Matigari ma Njirũũngi. He is the one who now beats the rhythm to the tune, 'truth and again truth' " (1987: 79).

Yet the impression we get at the end is that Matigari is much more than just the incarnation of the old prophets. To the people he is the messiah, the redeemer, the one who survives the bullets to fulfill the prophecy the way Jesus survives the nails on the cross. Ngũgĩ also uses the oral tradition of prophecy to universalize his themes by unifying the traditional Gĩkũyũ prophecy of old with the biblical prophecy into one. Thus to the question "Who is Matigari?" at the court scene, another person answers "Don't you know that the Bible says he shall come back again?" "Do you mean to say," the other persists, "he's the One prophesied about? The Son of Man?" (1987: 81).

Ngũgĩ's later works remold the old inherited myths and prophecies into new forms to serve his own ideological purposes rather than merely to describe the ideological foundations of Mau Mau. He begins to explore orality as a creative process rather than as a received tradition. Even biblical myths are re-assessed and re-created. The very title of *Devil on the Cross,* for example, is an ironic twist of the original story of the crucifixion: The Devil, the ruthless genius of capitalism, is crucified by workers and peasants. The myth of the resurrection is also re-moulded so that now it is Satan who is rescued from the cross and nurtured back to life by the rich and powerful who adhere to His creed. Thus, instead of accepting the biblical myth as received from the Bible, Ngũgĩ re-creates it and inverts its meaning to sharpen the contrasts in the abstract concept of good and evil within a capitalist setting.

The myth of the hereafter too, with its provision of heaven and hell, is re-created in a new way and made relevant to the present living conditions of the people. As Mũturi puts it, "Heaven and Hell? . . . Both exist . . . Listen. Our lives are a battlefield on which is fought a continuous war between the forces that are pledged to confirm our humanity and those determined to dismantle it" (1982: 53).

In *Matigari,* too, there is a creative rather than merely traditional use of the biblical myth. In the prison scene, for example, in a re-enactment of the Last Supper and the Christian Communion service, Matigari shares with other prisoners his food and beer—items that miraculously evade the stringent prison security checks. Matigari, we are told, "took the food, broke it and gave it to them. . . . Then he took the bottle of beer, opened it with his teeth, poured a little of it on the floor in libation and gave them to drink and pass round" (1987: 57). The collective capitalist oppressor, who acts as the Devil in the *Devil on the Cross,* is pitted against the collective revolutionary patriot who acts like Jesus in *Matigari.* The title of the Minister of Truth and Justice in *Matigari* is a similar inversion for the same purpose.

Orality is similarly transformed in the realm of song and ritual. In his early novels, Ngũgĩ often introduces songs and ritual with sometimes elaborate explanations: Waiyaki's initiation and Muthoni's decision to undergo circumcision in *The River Between,* for example, are introduced by lengthy preambles about their intentions and reasons for wanting to undergo the rituals. Circumcision, in fact, generates a heated argument between Muthoni and her sister, Nyambura. To the charge of being demonically possessed and that "Every man of God knew that this was a pagan rite against which, time and time again, the white missionaries had warned," Muthoni answers: "Look, please, I—I want to be a woman. I want to be a real girl, a real woman, knowing all the ways of the hills and ridges" (1965: 25–26). This example highlights Ngũgĩ's reaction to the overzealous anthropologists who condemned Africa's cultures and practices, including its ritual and songs. In the early novels, partly because of his focus on a Western defined audience, Ngũgĩ is inclined to use his writing to answer the charge that African customs were barbaric and a sign of backwardness.

Similarly, songs and chants are sometimes accompanied with elaborative explanation, and if they are in Gĩkũyũ they are usually accompanied by an English translation. This becomes necessary partly because the songs themselves as a tradition of the oral are detached from the central narrative. At this stage Ngũgĩ's inclination to throw in chunks from the oral tradition into his writing within the specifications of the Western concept of the novel leaves such oral forms undigested.

After *Petals of Blood* and in the process of redefining his audience, Ngũgĩ integrates song, dance and formal patterns of celebration into his writing without feeling the need to explain or justify. In the *Devil on the Cross,* for example, Mũturi constantly describes himself as talking into song:

> They have been taught new songs, new hymns that celebrate the acquisition of money. That's why today Nairobi teaches:
> Crooked to the upright,
> Meanness to the loving
> Civil to the good. . . . (1982: 15–16)

Warĩĩnga also employs song simultaneously in a semi-autobiographical narrative:

> For today Kareendi has decided that she does not know the difference between
> To straighten and to bend,
> To swallow and to spit out,
> To ascend and to descend
> To go and to return.
>
> Yes, for from today she'll never be able to distinguish between
> The crooked and the straight,
> The foolish and the wise. . . . (1982: 25)

In *Matigari,* Matigari confronts the cowardly priest by asking him: "You, wise man, did you say that this world is not upside-down? A world in which

> The builder sleeps in the open,
> The worker is left empty-handed,
> The tailor goes naked,
> And the tiller goes to sleep on an empty stomach?

Tell me! Where are the truth and justice in all this? Where in the world can one find justice? (1987: 98)

As Ngũgĩ modifies his use of song and ritual so that they relate more directly to the kinds of struggle which they evoke, he starts to use song and ritual as media of communication in their own right, and in the process transforms the singer and ritual performer into a Brechtian type of collective agents. In this transformation Ngũgĩ's central intention is to present ideas, and not just to entertain. In his early novels, Ngũgĩ draws his audience into his descriptions emotionally; but now he wants his audience to comprehend the action intellectually as well. The singer-as-chorus technique keeps the audience captivated yet alert. In his early novels, Ngũgĩ uses orality to argue (for example, about the validity of the peoples' claim to their land). The use of singer as chorus in the later novels enables him more subtly to suggest. In this way, the creative employment of song and ritual with their own rhythms, call and response technique, and borrowings from the Bible, all directed at a new audience, give his narrative style a combative thrust that goes beyond the traditional use of orality for mere authentication.

There is, therefore, a transformation in Ngũgĩ's use of orality in his writing. In the early works, he uses orality in a "chunking" fashion partly to reproduce the Mau Mau narrative and partly to authenticate his work. Orality is treated as a pristine, static and unchangeable phenomenon, employed within the Western concept of the novel, and necessitating, in Fanon's words, a "borrowed aesthetics" for its interpretation. In his later works, however, Ngũgĩ uses orality as a dynamic vibrant reality, and as part of the call and response pattern that brings out its collective power. As his own creative development leads him to re-define his audience, Ngũgĩ modifies his use of the most identifiable oral forms by enlivening them to maximize their revolutionary potential. Nevertheless, to accomplish this Ngũgĩ had first to totally identify himself with the people, and see history from their point of view.

4.

The adoption of orality in its Brechtian didactic form is most apparent in Ngũgĩ's later works. He uses different oral features to establish an oral form and style that help him to deliver his moral lessons and to clarify the issues on which those moral decisions are based. In his early novels, Ngũgĩ tends to restrict his use of oral style to epithets or stock phrases, starting with names, such as Joshua (Christian), or Livingston (Colonial), or mythological names, such as Mũũmbi, Mugo, Chege, and others. Such names and phrases become easy to remember, both for the narrator and for the audience, and handy to exaggerate certain characteristics that the writer wants to emphasize. This epic narrative style gives the reader a vivid and concrete impression of what the issues are and how the characters contrast with each other. Even when he reverts to mythology, Ngũgĩ is quick to create a contrast of mythological figures:

> Kameno threw up more heroes and leaders than any other ridge. Mugo wa Kibiro, that great Gĩkũyũ seer of old. . . . Or there was that great witch, Kamiri, whose witchery bewildered even the white men at Muranga. Another was Wachiori, a great warrior, who had led the whole tribe against Ukabi, Masai. As a young man he had killed a lion, by himself. . . . (1965: 2)

Effective as this narrative style is in his early novels, its scope remains constrained by Ngũgĩ's use of orality as a received tradition rather than as a creative process.

Ngũgĩ's later work continues to employ epithets in a kind of epic style, yet it powerfully exploits additional epic and oral techniques like fantasy, exaggeration, and prophesying to impart specific moral lessons to his audience. For instance, *Matigari* contains many stock phrases to describe characters and situations that the author wants to render familiar to the audience: "His eyes shone brightly" describes Matigari; "those-who-reap-where-they-never-sowed" describes the capitalists. To articulate and characterize the central theme of "truth and justice" that runs throughout the novel, certain phrases are repeated again and again: "a seeker of justice never tires"; "A farmer whose seeds have not germinated does not give up planting"; "girded with a belt of peace"; and "too much fear breeds misery." Like epithets or stock phrases, songs, too, are repeated throughout the novel; as are episodes such as the one about the hunter-and-hunted confrontation between Matigari and Settler Williams. Also typical of oral tradition, these episodes, which are told over and over again, are never repeated in exactly the same way. Each version differs from the others, depending on the particular audience, much like the repeated news broadcasts.

Simultaneously redefining his style and his audience, Ngũgĩ also bases his transformation of oral narrative on prophesying, gospel preaching, and public address. To take an early example, when Mugo wa Kibiro, the great Gĩkũyũ seer, says, " 'There shall come a people with clothes like butterflies,' " the reader can practically hear the voice. A similar oral power enlivens the preaching and debating encounters between adversaries like Waiyaki and Joshua in the church, or Waiyaki and Kabonyi at the Kiama in *The River Between,* or Mugo's public address at the independence anniversary rally in *A Grain of Wheat.* However, the settings in these early novels are formalistic, their rhetorical style stilted, the characters warped in their individualistic psychological impotence, and their speeches like the muffled voices of hermits preaching disjointedly to an empty space. Prophets are neither met nor heard. There are only reports about them. Similarly, there is a mere description of what Waiyaki and Kabonyi say at the Kiama rally. Even Chege appears as somebody beyond this world: a recluse isolated from his people and forced into hiding and talking in riddles. In Fanon's terms, the use of preaching, prophesying, and public address in Ngũgĩ's early narratives cannot be considered an example of national literature because it is not of the people and from the people!

When Matigari goes to an old woman hermit in the wilderness in the fashion of the old prophets to seek for truth and justice, he is told: "My dear wanderer, you cannot find answers here where nobody lives. Truth and justice are to be found in people's actions" (1987: 87). This statement corresponds to Ngũgĩ's own re-assessment of his early use of the prophesying narrative style. Ngũgĩ radically modifies the narrative style of his later works to become more informal and more combative. In both the gathering of thieves in *Devil on the Cross* and the political assembly by the Minister of Truth and Justice in

Matigari, Ngũgĩ uses the oral narrative style of prophesying and public address to portray his characters as persuasive verbal combatants. Furthermore, he punctuates the text with songs of praises from the hymn-book entitled *Songs of a Parrot!*

Transforming a biblical type of prophesying instead of preaching from the wilderness, Matigari stamps through the country to confront his enemies on country-roads, farms, political rallies, churches, courtyards and prisons. He cries, "You breed of parasites! Give back the keys to these houses and these lands which you took away from the people. . . . This country has its owners" (1987: 78–79). The tone is messianic. Yet when asked whether he is the Second Coming of Jesus prophesied long ago, Matigari replies: "The God who is prophesied is in you, in me and in other human beings. He has always been there inside us since the beginning of time" (1987: 156).

The beginning of *Matigari* sounds thoroughly oral: "So say yes, and I'll tell you a story! Once upon a time, in a country with no name . . ." (1987: ix). The story of Matigari also ends as it begins: "This day, rumour has it that the torrential rain that fell was what put out the fires that had earlier consumed the houses. Across the land children came out to sing" (1987: 174). In *Matigari* Ngũgĩ warns us from the outset that "This novel is based partly on an oral story. . . . The story is simple and direct, and it dispenses with fixed time and place" (1987: vii). In Matigari, the character, we are confronted with a phantom: someone belonging to no particular time and space, someone we never actually see. Later he warns the policeman who attempts to arrest him: "Don't you dare touch me! I am as old as this country" (1987: 112).

Ngũgĩ uses oral narrative style to characterize Matigari as a folk character, a form of Everyman. He is alleged to be "there at the time of the Portuguese, and the time of the Arabs, and the time of the British." Nobody knows if Matigari is a man or woman, adult or child, solitary as the old prophets or part of a group—in fact he is sometimes addressed in the plural: "Can't you guess who Matigari ma Njirũũngi are?" (1987: 72). Nobody knows either his nationality or his size. The woman returning from the river describes him as "a tiny, ordinary-looking man," and yet other people describe him as "a giant who could almost touch the sky above" with smoke gushing out of his nose, mouth and ears (1987: 75–77). Matigari suddenly appears wherever he wants to go; and he instantly meets the person he is looking for. He does not eat, yet he is described as supernaturally strong. Even the weather around him, in a typical fairy tales style, is constantly described as "neither hot nor cold," at least in the earlier part of the novel, to characterize a form of lifelessness in the country arising from the oppressive atmosphere in which "nothing was clear." Yet when Matigari eventually leads an insurrection against that oppression, the weather suddenly changes, and we are told that "The sun was blazing hotter than the hottest coals" (1987: 137).

Transforming the conventional, individualistic and hermitic prophet trapped in the impotency of his own stream of consciousness, Ngũgĩ's oral narrative style reveals an enigmatic voice that is truly collective in character. While in early works like *A Grain of Wheat* combatants are usually portrayed as brave individuals displaying their bravery against overwhelming odds, Matigari faces the Minister of Truth and Justice, who is flanked by an awesome paramilitary force, by standing right in the middle of the crowd. Yet he is the crowd, too. In a typically collective style, the individual stands for the whole. Wherever he is, Matigari is surrounded by other people, reinforcing his own adage: "Those who eat alone die alone."

In a typical Western novel, character portrayal is individualized. Emphasis is placed on the psychological predisposition of the individual character and the various dimensions of his or her life. In Ngũgĩ's later works, however, there is a tendency, typical of the oral tradition, to use archetypal characters, who are often flat, as a way of reinforcing the social and collective voice rather than the individual voice. In the *Devil on the Cross* and *Matigari*, Ngũgĩ even "exaggerates" the very use of the oral style of exaggeration. In the former, when he uses the biblical parable of the citizens given talents to suggest its capitalist implication of the exploitation of the masses, he presents the whole issue of international capitalism in a graphically exaggerated way:

> And now before I sit down, I shall call upon the leader of the foreign delegation from the International Organization of Thieves and Robbers (IOTR), whose headquarters are in New York, USA, to talk to you. I think you all know that we have already applied to become full members of IOTR. There are many tricks we can learn from them. We should never be afraid to acknowledge the fact that we don't know as much as foreigners do, and we should not feel ashamed to drink from foreign fountains of knowledge. (1982: 87)

The cave scene in general reminds one of names like "Chief Rat" in primary school folklore, "Mr. All of You" in Achebe's folk tales, or even Dickensian satirical names like Mr. Pumblechook and Mr. Magwitch. They provide a kind of visual symbolism, right down to physical appearance and mode of dress. The characters are over-portrayed. Their characteristic mannerisms and activities are over-emphasized. The final item on the agenda of the Devil's Feast is a scheme to market human organs for transplants so that the elite will be able to purchase physical immortality and leave death to the workers!

To represent the collective voice rather than the individualistic in *Matigari*, Ngũgĩ avoids naming characters. Matigari's "real" name is not known. The name "Matigari" simply stands for those who survived the guerrilla war against the European settlers. The Minister's name is not known; nor are those of his VIPs. We see the diplomats from America, Japan and Europe through their parroty mannerisms: "All the guests on the platform took their handkerchiefs out of their pockets at about the same time" (1987: 115). None of the characters are named. The only way to identify them is through such exaggerated description of their actions or appearance. The MP is identified as the one "who wore a silk suit, a KKK tie and thick-rimmed sunglasses" (1987: 119).

This narrative style of exaggeration reveals dexterity with language and culture on the part of the narrator. Ngũgĩ's role in the composition of his tales can be taken as really that of the griot or *imbongi* of the oral tradition. He is "a master of words," versatile, and willing to engage all shades of his audience. A griot takes a tale, a trait or character and embellishes it by exaggerating, extolling, praising, or parodying. Both in his writing and in his profession as a teacher Ngũgĩ wa Thiong'o could be compared to a griot or an *imbongi* on several different levels. A griot has different functions in society, but as a teller of tales and a chronicler of the people's history, he may, as did the griot in the epic of Sundiata, describe himself as follows:

> I am a griot. It is I, Djeli Mamoudou Kouyate, son of Bintou Kouyate and Djeli Kedian Kouyate, master in the art of eloquence. Since time immemorial the Kouyates have been in the service of the Keita princes of Mali; we are vehicles of speech, we are the repositories which harbour secrets many centuries old. . . . I derive my knowledge from my father Djeli Kedian, who also got it from his father. . . . I teach kings the history of their ancestors so that the lives of the ancients might serve them as an example. (Okpehwo, 1992: 26)

Ngũgĩ's use of the griot tradition is present in his early writings, too. In *The River Between,* for example, Ngũgĩ describes Chege as knowing "more than any other person, the ways of the land and the hidden things of the tribe. He knew the meaning of every ritual and every sign. So, he was all the head of every important ceremony" (1965: 7). In adopting the oral style of a griot, Ngũgĩ, like Chege, wants to "guard this knowledge and divulge it to none but the right one(s)." Yet Ngũgĩ's "right ones" become the children, students, farmers, and workers that he eventually discovers in his later works. As a "master of eloquence" in his early novels, Ngũgĩ chronicles Gĩkũyũ genealogy and Kenyan history as portrayed by the deeds of the Mau Mau movement. This use of orality serves the purpose primarily of a master of the spoken word who also has the power to charm, to heal, to divine. Narrating the troubled history of his people, Ngũgĩ offers a healing remedy for those wounded and betrayed by the Mau Mau war. Nevertheless, in these early works Ngũgĩ "divulges" this knowledge primarily within the confines of the realistic form of the novel.

The griot oral narrative style of Ngũgĩ's later works transcends realism to chronicle his own interpretation of that knowledge and history. Matigari says that for people to seize their own history, "one had to have the right words; but these words had to be strengthened by the force of arms. In pursuit of truth and justice," he continues, "one had to be armed with armed words" (1987: 131). In typical Fanonian fashion, the only way a griot can fashion a new language and a new aesthetics that can enable him to interpret the people's heritage in accordance with the people's interests is to become an active participant in their struggle.

As a griot, Ngũgĩ is very methodical with his use of orality as a style of delivery. Even the prison reminiscences in *Detained* demonstrate that Ngũgĩ does not choose his literary strategies lightly, but carefully selects those oral devices that not only enable him to tell a story, or give information, but also to give moral counsel (1981: 8). In a typical griot tradition, Ngũgĩ employs oral tradition in the form of fable, fantasy, exaggeration, and song to bring issues for public debate, with himself acting as a moderator: in other words, not only praising but also criticizing. By the time he writes *Devil on the Cross,* Ngũgĩ abandons his earlier attempts to act as an omnipotent author indicting his characters and describing their deeds, and now uses orality to create a satiric world in which villains themselves assert their own villainy. Ngũgĩ transforms the narrative style of exaggeration deliberately to blur the boundary between reality and fantasy: a device he employs effectively in the cave scene shifting from the real to the unreal. Ngũgĩ's newly developed skills in oral narrative succeed in creating stereotypical characters which enable him to present more clear-cut contrasts between social classes which these characters represent: more adequately expressing the horrors created by class antagonism in a capitalistic world. Ngũgĩ's adoption of a bolder oral tradition style leads not to a cruder technique but to a brilliantly new and more appropriate kind of literary tool.

Ngũgĩ's development of an oral narrative style is crucial to his own auctorial identity as a committed writer activist. Yet orality itself is the product of the griot tradition that comes from the people's voice and assures that the linkage between the griot and the people is immediate. Thus works like *Devil on the Cross* and *Matigari* go beyond the Western boundaries set by Ngũgĩ's early novels, and instead become unique events in language based on the imperatives of an immediate and direct communion with peasants and workers. Ironically, it is a double tragedy for Ngũgĩ that just at a time when his work is becoming orally "accessible" to the people of Kenya, since he turns to writing in Gĩkũyũ language and adopts a more dynamic oral form and style, that his primary audience will not "read" his books until the political and literary conditions in Kenya make reading possible. Yet Ngũgĩ's active participation in Kenyan politics re-directs his work from its early tendencies of being a mere product of the colonial discourse of domination and neo-colonialism towards becoming a very important event in Gĩkũyũ language and the struggle of the Kenyan people against oppression. His works become a clear organizational project intended to create a popular narrative style that is of the people, yet simultaneously the Kenyan people are changing themselves and the world around them. In the project, Ngũgĩ re-invents the Gĩkũyũ language in a new context as an oral granary of symbolic traditions, and in the process he also re-invents the novel. As a new griot in a new political situation, Ngũgĩ reclaims oral tradition and liberates it from its traditional, relatively passive use as a vehicle for authentication and passing messages from generation to generation.

5.

The question of orality in Ngũgĩ's writing relates to the audience for whom he writes. As indicated earlier, Fanon describes a national literature as a literature of combat partly because it appeals to the potential revolutionary consciousness of a non-elitist local audience, rather than to the sentiments of a more elitist trans-local audience that is defined by its proficiency in a shared European language. But in many instances the decision to "go local" in Africa entails, in linguistic terms, composing in languages that are predominantly ethnic bound: which is precisely the linguistic path that Ngũgĩ takes in his quest for a truly national literature of the Kenyan people.

Is Ngũgĩ's decision to write in Gĩkũyũ merely a manifestation of his ethnic chauvinism?[1] According to a section of Kenyan writers and scholars, a "modern, secular" education partly functions to transform people into "intellectuals" who would have, as some of their characteristics, a trans-ethnic world outlook and a commitment to a trans-ethnic community.[2] Responsibility and allegiance to such a community demands, of necessity, the use of an international medium of intellectual exchange like English and French. Nevertheless, this group does not find objectionable the idea of an Oromo, for example, who has not had any schooling, composing in his or her native Orominya. They would contend that such an individual has not acquired an international medium of exchange; and lacking in "education"—the "intellectualizing" agent—he or she cannot be expected to conceive of an individual's responsibility and commitment in relation to a community wider than the ethnic one. However, to them, for an educated intellectual like Ngũgĩ to write in a language that is ethnic bound is seen as an act of betrayal of the international community and the universal value of ideas, and a capitulation to a merely parochial melody of ethnicity.

To counter this argument, Ngũgĩ asks if the children of Kenya have been educated by their peasant and proletarian parents, often under very strenuous and almost unbearable financial hardships, only to come and express the knowledge they have acquired over the years in foreign language? Furthermore, do such oppressed peasants and proletarians finance the education of their children for the benefit of foreigners?[3] According to Ngũgĩ, to write in European languages demonstrates precisely such a socio-political orientation towards an audience that has been defined by "foreigners." In an attempt to break away from this sociolinguistic prison-house of imperialism, he writes in his mother tongue, Gĩkũyũ.

This language of Ngũgĩ's new writing, however, like many other African languages, exists primarily as an oral medium. There is, as yet, very little that has been written in Gĩkũyũ. Furthermore, written Gĩkũyũ has not yet assumed a life of its own apart from the "linguistic culture" of orality. The Gĩkũyũ language has yet to develop discernible features that can be considered to belong primarily to its written mode of discourse. In a sense, the very act of writing in Gĩkũyũ necessarily demands from Ngũgĩ's works a certain degree of orality. Both *Devil on the Cross* and *Matigari,* Ngũgĩ's two novels composed originally in Gĩkũyũ, are replete with linguistic conventions of orality rather than those of writing. That the oral aspect of the Gĩkũyũ language would have a certain impact on his novels is, of course, a matter that Ngũgĩ himself was fully conscious of from the very beginning (1986: 77–78).

To turn to Ngũgĩ's audience in Gĩkũyũ, the majority of Gĩkũyũ peasants and workers have not had the opportunity to attend the formal institutions within which precincts the skills of reading and writing are often imparted. Those who have acquired literacy in local languages through the efforts of church and other literacy societies usually belong to a class of people who cannot afford to buy published materials in those languages. Also, the pedagogic approach used in many literacy classes produces learners that are less than functionally literate. Reading in local languages in Kenya seems to have remained a relatively undeveloped activity.[4] Therefore, Ngũgĩ writes in Gĩkũyũ for an audience that is predominantly oral in that language.

A result of this incongruence between written works and an oral audience is the transformation of Ngũgĩ's works in Gĩkũyũ into orally transmitted extended stories. Just as children once used to sit around their parents and grandparents to listen to stories from the oral tradition, adults may now be seen sitting with members of their own generation or younger, listening to narrations from Ngũgĩ's novels. Commenting on the transmission of his *Caitaani Mũtharaba-inĩ,* Ngũgĩ writes: "A family would get together every evening and one of their literate members would read it for them. Workers would also sit in groups, particularly during the lunch break, and would get one of them to read the book. It was read in buses; it was read in taxis; it was read in public bars" (1986: 83). Ngũgĩ formally identifies this process as "the appropriation of the novel into the oral tradition." Through oral transmission *The Devil on the Cross* and *Matigari* are embellished and enriched, both substantively and aesthetically, by the immediate, collective and participatory response of the listening audience, both in their linguistic and para-linguistic reactions.

6.

Orality serves a variety of functions and assumes a variety of forms in Ngũgĩ's creative writing, especially after *Petals of Blood.* Orality features at the levels of inspiration, composition, narration, and transmission,[5] each feeding into the other to produce a cohesive product that is at once conventional and revolutionary, old and new. Furthermore, orality in Ngũgĩ's post-*Petals'* novels takes an even more creative, dynamic and natural character that distinguishes it, to a large extent, from the more static and "museum-type" of orality found in his early novels and in the novels of many other African writers.

Developing a literary style informed by the powers of orality, Ngũgĩ creates a literature that represents the interests of the "masses" and, in the process, a literature of combat that is both national and anti-imperialist in character. Radical as *Petals of Blood* may be in its theme and message, the book is bound by the imperialist terms of reference of an audience that served the ends of neocolonialism at the expense of the national interest. *Devil on the Cross* and *Matigari* are a radical attempt to depart from this tradition and chart out a new course towards a national literature, specifically, and a national culture in general. But the growth, maturation and consolidation of a national culture ultimately depend on the presence of politico-economic conditions necessary to support and sustain that new culture. Attempts at creating a national culture must go hand-in-hand with efforts to create a new political environment altogether. As Fanon states: "To fight for a national culture means in the first place to fight for the liberation of the nation, that material keystone which makes the building of a culture possible. There is no other fight for culture which can develop apart from the popular struggle" (1967: 187). No person can purport to be contributing to the creation of a national culture and yet distance himself or herself from the popular struggle for liberation. In the words of Fanon: "No one can truly wish for the spread of African culture if he does not give practical support to the creation of the conditions necessary to the existence of that culture; in other words to the liberation of the whole continent" (1967: 189).

Precisely this Fanonian legacy requires the national artist to be, at the same time, a political activist, and this distinguishes Ngũgĩ from many other creative writers in Africa. In addition to being a producer of elements of a national culture, Ngũgĩ is a staunch political activist who has earned the wrath of the successive neocolonial regimes of his home-country, Kenya. Through his political involvement, orality emerges as an organic dimension of Ngũgĩ's later works.

Notes

1. Much of this discussion took place informally within the corridors of Kenya's universities.

2. Of course the reality in Africa has been quite different. While there has indeed been a trend towards declining ethnic behavior, there seems to have been a rise in ethnic consciousness which has been most pronounced precisely among the "educated" elite.

3. This argument is contained in the introduction of the Gĩkũyũ original, *Caitaani Mũtharaba-inĩ* (1980).

4. According to Onyango Ogutu, Marketing Manager of East African Publishing House (formerly, Heinemann (kenya) Ltd.), there has been very little demand for their publications in local languages other than Kiswahili. Among these Ngũgĩ's two novels in Gĩkũyũ have shown the highest sales.

5. In his two plays originally written in Gĩkũyũ, *I Will Marry When I Want* and *Mother Sing for Me*, Ngũgĩ also experimented with orality as a method of composition. Actors and actresses among the Gĩkũyũ peasants and workers affiliated with the Kamĩrĩĩthũ Center were provided only with outlines of the plays, and collectively developed them into complete scripts. Through this process, Kamĩrĩĩthũ Center became a venue for producing a Kenyan "participatory literature."

Works Cited

Aidoo, Ama Ata. Interview. *African Writers Talking*. Ed. C. Pieterse and D. Duerden. New York: Africana, 1973.

Atieno-Odhiambo, E.S. "Rebutting "Theory" with Correct Theory: A Comment on *The Trial of Dedan Kĩmathi* by Ngũgĩ wa Thiong'o and Micere Githae Mugo." *Kenya Historical Review* 5. 2. 1977: 385–88.

Cham, Mbye Baboucar. "Ousmane Sembene and the Aesthetics of African Oral Traditions." *Africana Journal* 13. 1–4. 1982: 24–40.

Chinweizu, Onwuchekwa Jemie, and Ikechukwu Madubuike. *Toward the Decolonization of African Literature*. London: KPI Ltd., 1985.

Egejuru, Phanuel. "Traditional Oral Aesthetics in Modern African Literature: Oka Okwu in Theme and Character Exploration in *The Lands Lord*." *The Literary Griot* 2.2. Fall 1990: 1–22.

Fanon, Frantz. *The Wretched of the Earth*. Harmondsworth: Penguin, 1967.

Maina wa Kĩnyattĩ. Ed. *Thunder from the Mountains*. London: Zed Press, 1980.

Miller, Christopher L. *Theories of Africans: Francophone Literature and Anthropology in Africa*. Chicago: University of Chicago Press, 1990.

Ngũgĩ wa Thiong'o. *The River Between*. London: Heinemann, 1965.

———. *A Grain of Wheat*. London: Heinemann, 1967.

———. *Weep Not, Child*. New York: Collier Books, 1969.

———. (With Micere Githae Mugo). *The Trial of Dedan Kĩmathi*. London: Heinemann, 1976.

———. *Petals of Blood*. London: Heinemann, 1977.

———. Introduction. *Caitaani Mũtharaba-inĩ*. Nairobi: Heinemann, 1980.

———. *Detained: A Writer's Prison Diary*. London: Heinemann, 1981.

———. *Devil on the Cross*. London: Heinemann, 1982.

———. (With Ngũgĩ wa Mirii). *I Will Marry When I Want*. London: Heinemann, 1982.

———. *Decolonizing the Mind: The Politics of Language in African Literature*. London: James Currey, 1986.

———. *Matigari*. Oxford: Heinemann, 1987.

Okpewho, I. *African Oral Literature*. Bloomington: Indiana University Press, 1992.

Scheub, Harold. "A Review of African Oral Traditions and Literature." *African Studies Review* 28.2/3. June/September 1985: 1–72.

Senghor, Leopold Sedar. *Senghor: Prose and Poetry*. (selected and translated by John Reed and Clive Wake). London: Oxford University Press, 1965.

Chanting Down the Culture of Fear: Transformation and Redemption in the Literature of Ngũgĩ wa Thiong'o and the Orature of Robert Nesta Marley

David G. Hulm

The well-known decision by Ngũgĩ wa Thiong'o to create his texts exclusively in the Gikuyu and Kiswahili languages was an affirmation of his African culture and a revolutionary response to the colonial and neocolonial imposition of the English language. Ngũgĩ sees language as the carrier of culture, and culture, "particularly through orature and literature," carries "the entire body of values by which we come to perceive ourselves and our place in the world."[1] For Ngũgĩ, language is a tool used by colonial and neocolonial forces to manipulate "the mental universe" of Africans and others to subordinate their culture to European culture. Through this process, the primary goal of colonialism, the control of a people's wealth, can be achieved.

Ngũgĩ's texts seek to rouse the colonized from "mental slavery"[2] to expose and undermine the agents of colonialism. The process of decolonizing the mind, through the restoration and advocacy of African culture, will empower the oppressed to seek the means for their own liberation and self-determination. Colonialism and neocolonialism have created what Ngũgĩ calls a "culture of fear"[3] which keeps the oppressed silent. Their silence keeps the bars of colonialism in place.

In Ngũgĩ's novel (written while he was in political detention and published originally in Gikuyu) *Caitaani Mũtharaba-inĩ* or *Devil on the Cross,* he likens those who impose the "culture of fear" to parasites who by drinking the human blood and eating the human flesh of the oppressed weaken them so they cannot possibly rebel. His text suggests that the unification of the clan of workers, peasants, and students would create a body large enough to destroy the "culture of fear." Collective action is necessary because "a single finger cannot kill a louse."[4]

This essay is published here for the first time by permission of the author, with whom the copyright remains.

Perhaps the most notable proponent of the culture of fear and one of the most complex characters of *Devil on the Cross* is the Devil, most horrific in his role of "the Voice" that questions Waríínga, the protagonist. The Voice reveals both truth and lies to Waríínga, but seemingly unforeseen by the "Liar" the simple truths are most beneficial to her. He tells her as clearly as possible the reasons why she can be exploited. She learns from him the possibility of a revolutionary "Third World" whereby the cannibalistic system of living off the sweat and blood of others is overthrown by those who reject the notion of an eternal dualistic reality, the eater and the eaten; the oppressors will use "intellectual and spiritual and cultural brain-washing poisons" to make the clan of workers and students believe that they must remain subordinate to the exploiter/oppressor clan.[5] This imposed culture will reinforce their sacrosanct relationship to God and God's will.

Most importantly, the Voice reveals the lack of self-faith Waríínga possesses: "The trouble with you, Waríínga, is that you have no faith in yourself. You have never known who you are!"[6] In this way, it reveals that she has been culturally brainwashed, that her African identity has been displaced by the colonial and neocolonial imposition of culture, which has rendered her impotent against the forces oppressing her. The Voice then attempts to seduce her, but Waríínga, in fear and the beginning of self-knowledge, uses the Voice's knowledge against it. She does not really know who she is; that is, she does not possess a clear identity. But she now knows whom she is addressing. The Voice's identity is quite clear, truthfully spoken by Waríínga, "Leave me alone, Satan!"[7] Waríínga has used her voice to protect herself. Ironically, the Devil provides a significant part of the text for Waríínga's liberation.

Waríínga's lack of self-knowledge, as Ngũgĩ explicitly states in *Devil on the Cross,* is the fruit of the colonial and neocolonial brainwashing; her self-hatred is most outwardly expressed by her desire to appear more European— she uses skin-bleaching creams, straightens her hair, and wears European-style clothes. Yet "that which was born black will never be white."[8] So Waríínga despairs because it is impossible for her to meet the European standard of beauty. She recognizes only her own suffering and cannot identify with anyone beyond herself. Little wonder, then, as alienated as she feels, that she would attempt suicide twice. Unbeknownst to her, she is redeemed by members of the clan of producers who save her life.

By the conclusion of the text, Waríínga has transformed (physically, mentally, and spiritually) into a revolutionary, one who is willing and able to use "a single finger" to kill a louse,[9] a parasite, the father of her daughter, and her financé's father—one of many oppressors. Her action both defies and reinforces the Gikuyu saying "a single finger cannot kill a louse." Her single finger on the trigger of a pistol kills the Rich Old Man. Yet the memory of those "who had roused her from mental slavery"[10] initiates a repetition of the action of her finger when she shoots two more oppressors. Her hands are no longer sacrificed to the whims of the Boss. They are hers to be used as needed, in self-defense[11] and proactive response. She uses her hands in the service of the collective.

Essentially, Warĩĩnga receives energy from the efforts of the clan of producers (the collective) to destroy or debilitate the clan of parasites. Her finger symbolizes the collective efforts and conviction of the clan of producers. She, as a living example of the third revolutionary world, is now able to silence the silencers. Her culture, African culture, becomes a means to redemption and change. In this sense, the "real music" has sounded in her soul.[12] This notion of "real music" is at the heart[13] of Ngũgĩ's revolutionary message in *Devil on the Cross*. We not only witness the redemption of Warĩĩnga but we also struggle with Gatuĩria as he fails to recognize and make crucial choices regarding his role in the transformation to the "revolutionary third world."

Warĩĩnga's fiancé explicitly rejects the oppression of the Kenyan people, yet ironically he cannot decide which path to take. Gatuĩria is like the hyena who tries to walk both paths at the same time. Gatuĩria rejects his father's world and wealth to pursue his artistic vision, a composition that would be truly Kenyan:

My ambition and dream is to compose a piece of music for many human voices . . . made up of all kinds of national instruments: skin, wind, string and brass. I have composed a number of songs. But I have not yet found the tune or the theme of the music of my dreams. Day and night I have searched for the tune and the theme, but in vain. You can't know the pain I carry about in my heart.[14]

Gatuĩria's ambition is noble (much like the use of music in the work by the two Ngũgĩs, *I Will Marry When I Want*), and his "pain" reflects the alienation of his upbringing. By the end of the text, Gatuĩria stands as witness to Warĩĩnga's proactive response, but he hears in his mind music that leads him nowhere.

In this way, Gatuĩria is dehumanized. He recognizes the power and necessity of the collective but cannot commit himself to the struggle. "Cultural brainwashing" has rendered him impotent. This impotence, based on the corruption caused by the imposition of foreign culture and the subjugation/devaluation of natural culture, renders haves (Gatuĩria will inherit his father's money) and have-nots alike powerless to stop their own exploitation. The recognition of this state leads the oppressed to either action or despair. His love for Warĩĩnga, his lack of cultural contact with the masses, and his alienation prevent him from creating a redemption song.

As we witness the decolonization of Warĩĩnga's mind in *Devil on the Cross* and her redemption, we must remember Ngũgĩ's personal struggle with despair and awakenings as recorded in *Detained*. Ngũgĩ's detention was a direct result of his action, a revolutionary use of Kenyan theater, Kenyan music, Kenyan language—essentially Kenyan culture.

In creating *Ngaahika Ndeena* or *I Will Marry When I Want,* Ngũgĩ with Ngũgĩ wa Mĩrĩĩ celebrated the language of the common person. *I Will Marry When I Want* is a play about the tribulations of the Kiguunda family when a multinational corporation wants to purchase the one and a half acres they survive on in order to build an insecticide factory. Written and performed in Gikuyu, the play also focuses on the social conditions of the working class in Kenya. The question of land and land ownership plays a significant role in the history of colonial and neocolonial Kenya; this question underscores the play. According to Ngũgĩ, the creation and production of the play was entirely a communal effort. The people of Kamĩrĩĩthu participated in all levels of its creation and its performance. Ngũgĩ says:

> Because the play was written in a language they could understand the people could participate in all subsequent discussions on the script. They discussed its content, its language and even the form. The process, particularly for Ngugi wa Mirii, Kimani Gecau, and myself was one of continuous learning . . . [l]earning our language, for peasants were essentially the guardians of the language.[15]

Ngũgĩ discovered the significance of song in the daily life of the common person: "Even daily speech among peasants is interspersed with song. . . . What's important is that song and dance are not just decorations; they are an integral part of that conversation, that drinking session, that ritual, that ceremony."[16] He had tapped into the creative force of the people.

The play became a musical drama, one that extended into their daily lives. They identified with the characters; they used phrases of the text in their conversations; they sang the songs of resistance; they were creating a "culture of revolutionary courage and optimistic determination."[17] And for this, *Ngaahika Ndeenda* was perceived as a threat by the culture of fear and stopped by the Kenyan government. Because he helped to give voice to those whom the culture of fear would rather keep silent and servile, Ngũgĩ was arrested and placed in detention—without trial, without hope of release. Ngũgĩ's own awakening to the power of the collective and the process of creation within the collective led to his imprisonment: "The reception of a given work of art is part of the work itself; or rather, the reception (or consumption!) of the work completes the whole creative process involving that particular artistic object."[18] Part of the reception of *I Will Marry When I Want* meant a one-year loss of freedom (detention) and the loss of his homeland (exile).

Near the time of Ngũgĩ's release, December 1978, the Jamaican reggae artist and revolutionary Robert Nesta Marley was in Kenya, fulfilling his dream of seeing Africa and Ethiopia in particular. Earlier that year in February, Marley had returned home to Jamaica after 13 months of "self-imposed" exile, the result of a 1976 assassination attempt that left four people, including Marley, wounded.[19] His commitment as an artist-revolutionary was seen as a political threat, particularly because Marley spoke in the language of the people.

Four hundred years of colonial oppression had nearly destroyed any significant retention of African languages in the Caribbean, but it could not destroy the rhythms completely. Bob Marley spoke and sang in the language of the *sufferahs,* Jamaica's so-called underclass. He used the power of language to "chant down Babylon."[20] Babylon, for Bob Marley, referred not only to the Old Testament city of false pride and corruption but also to its present incarnation—the economic and political systems that have exploited and still exploit the "Third World" for material gain. The "Babylon system"[21] is supported by, and promotes, the culture of fear. Marley encourages those who are oppressed to "Get Up, stand up, stand up for your rights / Get up, stand up, don't give up the fight."[22] Like Ngũgĩ, Marley's "Redemption Song" rouses the colonized to "Emancipate yourselves from mental slavery / None but ourselves can free our minds."[23] Marley's Rastafari way of life was an affirmation of African culture and a rejection of the colonial and neocolonial imposition of European culture and language.

The Rastafari way of life preserves and encourages the dignity of African heritage in a culture of fear that is determined to keep those of African ancestry in an underclass position. The Rastafari concept of language is a rejection of the language vibration of the oppressor. One of the primary goals of the Rastafari movement is repatriation to Africa. The knowledge of an African language is crucial for a full physical, mental, and spiritual return to Africa. Many Rastas seek literacy in Amharic, the language of Ras Tafari. Others study a language and culture of West Africa, because they identify strongly with that part of Africa. But before such time as this *homecoming* is possible, the Rastafari use language based on the concept of word, sound, and power: every sound carries a vibration, and that vibration can have positive or negative power.

The "Queen's English" carries the negative vibrations of the "Babylon system" and creates a culture based on this vibration. The Rastafari transform words to carry a positive vibration—hence, a more life-affirming culture. One example is the word *deadline.* The negative vibration is carried through *dead.* The Rastafari would never rush to meet a *deadline;* instead, they would meet a *lifeline.* Another example is the word *dedicate.* In truth, when dedication takes place, a life force of a person or persons is celebrated; in Rastafari language, one *livicates.* Language is also used to reveal the true nature of things—language is part of the force of creation. As Marley would introduce his song "Positive Vibration" live in concert, "The Rastaman vibration is positive!" and the lyrics would continue, "If you get down and you quarrel everyday / You're saying prayers to the devil, I say / Why not help one another on the way?"[24] He also used the language of "the street people talking / we the people struggling."[25] It was to the common person Marley addressed many of his songs; he used their language, because it was his language, too. Marley said that reggae music comes from "the masses of the people" who struggle and suffer and that reggae music and lyrics carry "earth force . . . people riddim. . . . It is the rhythm of people workin', people movin'."[26]

Though on the surface it may not seem that Marley—as a Jamaican reggae and Rasta musician—and Ngũgĩ—as a Kenyan writer and patriot—have much in common, they do. Both were born and raised in a British colony and experienced similar imposition of British culture and subsequent subordination and degradation of their African culture. And though their nations became independent (Jamaica in 1962 and Kenya in 1963), both witnessed the broken promise of independence and suffered under neocolonialism. Ngũgĩ describes the state of "artificial rivalry"[27] promoted by the divisive forces of the cultural parasites colonialism and neocolonialism. In Kenya, this rivalry is seen in the material and capitalistic concerns of the ruling elite; they impose their cultural values on those whose land and culture have been stolen by international imperialists and Kenyan traitors.

In Jamaica, the procapitalist Jamaican Labour Party (JLP) headed by Edward Seaga and the "democratic socialist" People's National Party (PNP) once headed by Michael Manley promote artificial rivalry. In the seventies and early eighties elections in Jamaica triggered violence against the *sufferahs*. Both parties co-opted the have-nots into political violence for the crumbs of capitalist exploitation. The oppressed are coerced in a situation in which they battle among themselves for petty material gain in support of political ideology. It was in this atmosphere that Marley, vis-à-vis his criticism of the divisive nature of politics (in Marley's terms, *-isms* and *schisms*), was the target of an assassination attempt in 1976. His lyrics called for revolution: "It takes a revolution / To make a solution."[28]

The Smile Jamaica concert was an attempt by the government of Michael Manley to curb violence before the December elections. Marley expressed publicly that his performance at the concert was not a commitment to either political party but rather a gesture of his "love of de people."[29] Marley created the song "Smile Jamaica" to reinforce his commitment to the people, and it was one of the few Marley songs allowed to be radio broadcast during his lifetime.[30] During an evening rehearsal session two days before the concert, Marley's home was surrounded by gunmen who intended to kill him. They fired dozens of rounds, and one gunman announced, "I got him." The assassins then fled the scene.

After being treated for his injuries and released from the hospital much later that evening, Marley went into seclusion to decide if playing the concert was too dangerous. After nearly 36 hours of deliberation, Marley was taken by police escort to Heroes Stadium in Kingston. A makeshift Wailers band supported Marley, as did Rita Marley, who was still dressed in her hospital gown. At the end of the concert, Marley ripped open his shirt to show where the assassins had failed. He threw back his head, shaking his dreadlocks, and with a smile on his face, imitated a Western gunslinger drawing his guns on the forces, visible and invisible, that tried to silence him.[31]

As with Ngũgĩ's art, the "reception" of Marley's art nearly got him killed, and it separated him from his birthplace on more than one occasion.

The assassination attempt was an effort by the culture of fear to remove Marley from society. Marley survived, and the reception of his music would again influence not only Jamaican politics but also African politics. A key to survival, Marley warns, is to "Never let a politician grant you a favor / They will always want to control you forever."[32] They will want to keep you silent.

Ngũgĩ's detention was a means of control by the culture of fear. By placing him in isolation and silence, they meant to weaken his "mental universe," to make him feel abandoned by his family, his friends, his colleagues at the university, and the people. His first visitor was the prison chaplain, who urged Ngũgĩ to confess his sins. And Ngũgĩ admits that by this time, he was weakening and beginning to question: "Isn't it easier, for me, for everybody, but mostly for me, to buy peace with silence?"[33] Though the chaplain urged his confession, Ngũgĩ realized it was not meant for God but for the state:

> Then suddenly, from somewhere in the depths of my being, rose a strong rebellious voice. 'Wake up from your spiritual lethargy and intellectual torpor. Don't let them drug you with this opium, don't let them poison your system with it. . . . If you let him get away with this, you are going to be his prisoner for the rest of your stay here and possibly for the rest of your life.'[34]

Ngũgĩ refused the enslavement of his mental universe as much as he resisted physical enslavement when the guards demanded he wear chains to seek medical attention and to visit his family. Ngũgĩ's resistance carries into the voices and visions of his characters in *Devil on the Cross.*

Resistance and redemption both come for Wariinga when she learns how to resist the culture of fear both in language and in action. We follow her progress through three journeys (though the third, Wariinga's most difficult, is only alluded to at the completion of the novel). The first is to Ilmorog in a matatu taxi from Nairobi, and the second is in a red Toyota from Nairobi to Nakuru; the passengers common to both journeys are Wariinga and Gatuiria. In the two years between the first journey and the second, they have fallen in love and are engaged to be married. Both have risen in political consciousness, but Wariinga has experienced a more profound change. She has passed from the state of being an unwilling victim, in despair, to being in control of her destiny. Gatuiria has completed a lifelong ambition—creating a truly Kenyan music; he hopes "above all that his music will inspire people with patriotic love for Kenya."[35]

Music and song are critical elements in *Caitaani Mũtharaba-inĩ;* it follows that Ngũgĩ, as a writer, is recognizing the revolutionary potential of music in literature and society and its significance as a means of cultural resistance to colonialism and neocolonialism. As he says in *Detained,* "But even behind the barbed wire and stone walls of the colonial Jericho, they went on composing new songs and singing out a collective patriotic defiance that finally brought those walls tumbling down."[36] At the competition/feast of the thieves and robbers (organized by the devil), the clan of producers uses songs to combat the negative energy of the system of exploitation. The devil's feast is broken by the cooperative efforts of the workers, peasants, and students who sing a song of rebellion:

> Come one and all,
> And behold the wonderful sight
> Of us chasing away the Devil
> And all his disciples!
> Come one and all![37]

Wariinga and Gatuiria are captivated by this song, and it is then that Wariinga commits to the collective struggle. But they are both mistaken when describing it as "a new song,"[38] for it is the same song Wangari sang in the matatu on the road to Ilmorog.[39] Wangari identifies it as a song of the patriots of the Land and Freedom Army of Kenya. Her songs are the songs of Kenyan patriots:

> Great love I found there
> Among women and children.
> A bean fell to the ground—
> We split it among ourselves.[40]

The songs of the patriots glorify freedom and the struggle for freedom; they glorify patriots who do not sell out their culture and the creators of that culture. Cooperation and patriotic action are encouraged in the lyrics, as are songs sung to soothe the troubled soul.

By the end of the text, we learn that Wariinga and Gatuiria have different opinions of the music that will move their hearts. "Real music will sound" in Wariinga's "soul"[41] when political prisoners are released. In the dramatic conclusion when Wariinga shoots and kills the Rich Old Man, Gatuiria is struck speechless and motionless "hearing in his mind music that leads him nowhere."[42] Rich Old Man was a capitalist exploiter who after seducing Wariinga and making her pregnant abandoned her; Rich Old Man is Gatuiria's father. Wariinga has gained her independence by destroying the parasites who feed on the flesh and blood of others. Gatuiria has no song for this action.

Regardless, the Kenyan people heard the song; *Caitaani Mūtharaba-inī* was appropriated by the people into the oral tradition.[43] The text was created in Gikuyu using the cultural traditions of Gikuyu storytelling. It was read aloud in private and public places, from living rooms to bars. "The isolation imposed by poverty and illiteracy"[44] was overcome by the public consumption and sharing of the text. Those who could not afford to buy a copy read a friend's copy; those who could not read found someone who could. The audience for whom Ngũgĩ created the text received the text, and the "whole creative process" was complete.

The seeds of Ngũgĩ's revolutionary art, though planted sporadically throughout his earlier works, broke soil through his tending the germination of his African heritage, celebrated in the music and the whole creative, generative process of *I Will Marry When I Want*. The fruit, however, was detention and subsequent inspiration for *Devil on the Cross* and *Detained*. The end result, for Ngũgĩ, was exile. Because his desire for an independent Kenya was so strong, he was forced to leave his home indefinitely.

Bob Marley's return to Jamaica had been arranged by the PNP and the JLP, when members of both parties met with him on neutral ground in London. A representative from the JLP admitted responsibility for the assassination attempt in 1976.[45] The JLP could then guarantee Marley and his family safety in Jamaica. Their primary reason for contacting Marley was to ask for a "homecoming" performance at the One Love Peace concert. The concert was a celebration of a mutually arranged peace treaty between the warring factions of the JLP and PNP. Marley returned to Jamaica.

The concert featured some of the best reggae artists and groups in Jamaica, but the return of Bob Marley and the Wailers was the main attraction.[46] During an emotional performance of "Jammin'" Marley achieved what some believed an impossible task. He asked for the presence of Michael Manley and Edward Seaga onstage. With Manley and Seaga flanking him on either side, Marley joined their hands and prayed for peace in Jamaica. The political ideology of these two men was responsible for thousands of deaths; it was generally known that their animosity was mutual. The crowd did not miss the political significance of the act.

Marley's visit to Africa, prior to this concert, inspired his revolutionary artistic impulse. While he was in Kenya, he listened to the Kenyans' stories about the liberation struggle in Zimbabwe. He traveled to Ethiopia and heard about a different Haile Selassie from the peasants who suffered under his autocratic rule. The extent to which this information affected Marley is unclear, although sources close to Marley say he was disappointed by what he saw and heard in Africa.

In Jamaica, there was some current information describing the political state of nations in Africa (apartheid in South Africa was widely discussed and protested), but the myth of Africa as an Eden held great sway, especially among the Rastafarl. In Africa, specifically in Kenya and Ethiopia, Marley witnessed the same kind of oppression he had experienced in Jamaica. When a person's vision is shattered by reality, there are, seemingly, few options. Marley returned to Jamaica and began an intense period of recording music. In all likelihood, he was already aware that the cancer, which had started in his foot, had spread. His conviction toward the notion of liberation of all before repatriation intensified his commitment to the struggle.

In 1980, Marley received an invitation from Robert Mugabe and Edgar Tekere to perform at the official independence celebration in Zimbabwe on April 18. Though Marley had some knowledge of the impact of his 1979 release, *Survival,* he was unaware that the song "Zimbabwe" had been adopted by the freedom fighters and was sung as they went into battle. The lyrics to this song are indeed revolutionary, and they speak openly of the need to fight for independence:

> Every man got a right to decide his own destiny.
> And in this judgment, there is no partiality.
> So arm in arm, with arms
> We'll fight this little struggle.

Marley was there, significantly, at the request of the people, and he was the only performer who was not from Zimbabwe. Because he had been there, through his music, with them in battle, the people felt he should be there in celebration of their liberation and freedom.

Marley paid the entire expenses for the Wailers to perform at the Zimbabwe independence celebration. When thousands of peasants and freedom fighters were turned away at the gates of the stadium, Marley decided to perform a free concert for them the next evening. To the crowd of 40,000, Marley expressed his wish of playing in a free Azania (South Africa) the next time he performed in Africa.

But he was on his final tour. On May 11, 1981, Bob Marley flew home to Zion: "One bright morning, when my work is over / Man will fly away home." The reception of Marley's work, his orature, included receiving the Order of Merit from the government of Jamaica, a United Nations Peace Medal nomination, the National Association for the Advancement of Colored People (NAACP) Image Award, and the respect of millions of fans across the world. His music directly affected the politics of Jamaica and Zimbabwe. Eusi Kwayana described the political and social effects of Marley's work:

Such is the power of art that Bob Marley's music has done more to popularise the real issues of the African liberation movement than several decades of back-breaking work of Pan-Africanists and international revolutionaries.[47]

Bob Marley's music and lyrics should be included in any study of the literature of the African peoples. His lyrics embody what Ngũgĩ calls "the struggle for a cultural identity" as they speak "the language of struggle."[48] The texts of selected Marley songs are precisely the music Gatuĩria was trying to create in Ngũgĩ's *Devil on the Cross.* The most profound relationship between the literature of Ngũgĩ wa Thiong'o and the orature of Robert Nesta Marley occurs in their use of the language of struggle: both seek to chant down the culture of fear.

Notes

1. Ngũgĩ wa Thiong'o, *Decolonising the Mind* (London: Heinemann, 1986), 16.
2. Ngũgĩ wa Thiong'o, *Devil on the Cross* (London: Heinemann, 1982), 254.
3. Ngũgĩ uses this phrase in several texts.
4. Ngũgĩ, *Devil on the Cross,* 52 and elsewhere.
5. Ngũgĩ, *Devil on the Cross,* 189.
6. Ngũgĩ, *Devil on the Cross,* 190.
7. Ngũgĩ, *Devil on the Cross,* 193 and repeated on 194 as "Get thee behind me, Satan." The repetition here is like a call and response pattern. Different aspects of Warĩĩnga's identity are revealed in such repetitions. On p. 194, she relies on a prototypical King James Bible version, reflecting her Christian school background.
8. Ngũgĩ, *Devil on the Cross,* 11.
9. Warĩĩnga learned how to use a gun, at the insistence of the Rich Old Man, so that they could "play" the game of the Hunter and the Hunted. Like the Voice, the Rich Old Man provides Warĩĩnga, albeit unknowingly, the tools for her own liberation.
10. Ngũgĩ, *Devil on the Cross,* 254.
11. Warĩĩnga shoots the Rich Old Man from Ngorika in self-defense; he threatens her life: "Right now, I would only have to open my mouth, and you would not reach Gilgil" (252).
12. Ngũgĩ, *Devil on the Cross,* 232.
13. As Ngũgĩ reminds us in *Devil on the Cross,* heart in Gikuyu can refer to the soul.
14. Ngũgĩ, *Devil on the Cross,* 59.
15. Ngũgĩ, *Decolonising the Mind,* 45.
16. Ngũgĩ, *Decolonising the Mind,* 45.
17. Ngũgĩ, *Decolonising the Mind,* 69.
18. Ngũgĩ, *Decolonising the Mind,* 82.
19. During a rehearsal session for the Smile Jamaica concert, a peace concert, several gunmen surrounded Marley's home and rehearsal space. They opened fire on the house where the Wailers, spouses, and children were. Bob Marley was shot in the arm; the bullet went through and bounced off his chest, causing injury. Rita Marley, a singer and Bob's wife, was shot in the head, where the bullet lodged between her scalp and skull. Lewis Griffiths, a close friend, was also shot. Marley's manager, Don Taylor, received several wounds in his back and groin; he had stepped in front of Marley as a gunman came in the back door, shooting at Bob. None of the victims died.
20. Bob Marley, "Chant Down Babylon," *Confrontation,* Island Records, 79005-1, 1983. The phrase "chant down Babylon" is central in Rastafarĩ language and refers to the process of deconstructing negative language vibration by using positive vibration.
21. In his song "Babylon System," Marley describes the system as being a vampire "sucking the blood of the sufferahs"; he urges them to "rebel."
22. Bob Marley and Peter Tosh, "Get Up, Stand Up," *Burnin',* Island Records, ILPS 9256, 1973.
23. Bob Marley, "Redemption Song," *Uprising,* Island Records, ILPS 9596, 1980.
24. Bob Marley, "Positive Vibration," *Rastaman Vibration,* Island Records, ILPS 9383, 1976.
25. Bob Marley, "So Much Trouble in the World," *Survival,* Island Records, ILPS 9542, 1979.
26. Marley, interview from *Time Will Tell,* Tuff Gong, 440 084 059-3, 1992, Polygram videotape.
27. Ngũgĩ wa Thiong'o, *Detained: A Writer's Prison Diary* (London: Heinemann, 1981), 82.
28. Bob Marley, "Revolution," *Natty Dread,* Island Records, ILPS 9281, 1974.

29. Bob Marley, quoted by Timothy White, in *Catch A Fire: The Life of Bob Marley* (New York: Henry Holt and Co., 1983), 292.

30. Some of the music of the Wailers and most of the songs of Bob Marley and the Wailers were too political to broadcast. The "Babylon System" had already decided that reggae music, in general, was too crude for the radio. The Jamaican tourism industry has now recognized the capitalist benefits from reggae; one can hear reggae on the radio, though this has been a difficult struggle, and much of the reggae allowed is not significantly political. Exceptions exist, however.

31. This dramatic stance parallels Wariinga's shooting of the Rich Old Man and other parasites at the conclusion of *Devil on the Cross.*

32. Bob Marley, "Revolution," *Natty Dread,* Island Records, ILPS 9281, 1974.

33. Ngũgĩ, *Detained,* 24.

34. Ngũgĩ, *Detained,* 24. Bob Marley, paraphrasing Marcus Garvey, expresses a very similar message in his song "Wake Up and Live": "Rise ye mighty people / There's work to be done / So let's do it a little by little." The inference is that those oppressed must rise from a "sleepless slumber."

35. Ngũgĩ, *Devil on the Cross,* 227.

36. Ngũgĩ, *Detained,* 66.

37. Ngũgĩ, *Devil on the Cross,* 39. Bob Marley created a song, "Crazy Baldhead," which says that those who have built the penitentiaries and the schools, the *sufferahs,* receive an education of propaganda to make them look foolish and are hated by those in power, the baldheads. After the oppressed become aware, they want to "Chase those crazy baldheads out of town."

38. Ngũgĩ, *Devil on the Cross,* 200.

39. Ngũgĩ, *Devil on the Cross,* 74–75.

40. Ngũgĩ, *Devil on the Cross,* 39. In "No Woman, No Cry," Bob Marley sings, "And we would cook cornmeal porridge / Of which I'll share with you." The common ground here is that in the context of both songs, the have-nots share what little they have with each other. Marley's song "Rat Race" espouses "Collective security, for surety."

41. Ngũgĩ, *Devil on the Cross,* 232.

42. Ngũgĩ, *Devil on the Cross,* 254.

43. Ngũgĩ, *Decolonising the Mind,* 83.

44. Ngũgĩ, *Decolonising the Mind,* 83.

45. Stephen Davis, *Bob Marley* (New York: Doubleday, 1985), 195.

46. The concert was also boycotted by some of the best reggae artists, including Bunny Wailer, who had grown cynical about these so-called treaties. It should be mentioned that Peter Tosh's performance at this concert held great political and social importance. Tosh leveled frank criticism at the political leaders of Jamaica (who were in the audience) and called for revolutionary change in Jamaica. Less than three months after the concert, Tosh was arrested for possessing a small amount of ganja. He was taken to a police station and beaten nearly to death. Many feel that Tosh's arrest and subsequent brutalization were a direct result of his performance at the One Love concert.

47. Quoted in Horace Campbell, *Rasta and Resistance: From Marcus Garvey to Walter Rodney* (Trenton, N.J.: Africa World Press, 1987), xii.

48. Ngũgĩ, *Decolonising the Mind,* 98, 108.

Ngũgĩ wa Thiong'o's Visions of Africa

Christine Loflin

I was living in a village and also in a colonial situation.

—Ngũgĩ, *Homecoming* (48)

Landscape as an aspect of fiction has tended to be underrated: less interesting than narrative, rhetoric, or tropology. Yet through landscape the author creates the horizons of the novel, establishing it in a historical (or an ahistorical) space. The landscape is not merely the setting of the story: it is a shifting, expanding territory, where the boundaries of public/private, fictional/real overlap. It has been said that African writers are particularly uninterested in landscape description (Roscoe 177–78). If, however, landscape is understood as the description of the land and its role in the cultural, economic, and spiritual life of the community, it immediately becomes clear that landscape is an essential part of African literature. Throughout the African novel, concerns about land use, ownership, spiritual values, nationalism, and pan-Africanism are reflected in the description of the land. In their descriptions of Africa, their mapping of boundaries, their choice of features and background, of what matters in the landscape of Africa, African writers challenge Western visions of Africa and reclaim the landscape for themselves. In Ngũgĩ wa Thiong'o's novels, the importance of the landscape is paramount, as the landscape of Kenya is intimately related to the community's spiritual, social, and political identity.

Ngũgĩ's descriptions of landscape are shaped by some specific circumstances of Kenyan history: the centrality of land in the Gikuyu worldview, the forced removals of the Gikuyu from the White Highlands, the Mau Mau independence war, and post-independence disillusionment in Kenya. Ngũgĩ himself has insisted on the connection between particular historical events and literature:

Literature does not grow or develop in a vacuum; it is given impetus, shape, direction and even area of concern by social, political and economic forces in a particular society. (*Homecoming* xv)

Reprinted, with permission, from Christine Loflin, "Ngũgĩ wa Thiong'o's Visions of Africa," *Research in African Literatures* (Indiana University Press) 26, no. 4 (Winter 1995): 76–93.

In analyzing the description of landscape in Ngũgĩ's novels, I want to do more than show his mastery of a Western technique; Ngũgĩ's works re-evaluate the importance of landscape, integrating geography with his people's cultural environment, religious beliefs, and economic system.

For the Gikuyu people, land is central to their spiritual, cultural and economic practices:

> to anyone who wants to understand Gikuyu problems, nothing is more important than a correct grasp of the question of land tenure. For it is the key to the people's life; it secures for them that peaceful tillage of the soil which supplies their material needs and enables them to perform their magic and traditional ceremonies in undisturbed serenity, facing Mount Kenya. (Kenyatta xxi)

Jomo Kenyatta's study of Gikuyu culture shows that the Gikuyu see land as connecting them to God and to their ancestors, as well as to the village community. In the Gikuyu myth of creation, the land was given to them by God; in addition, "Communion with the ancestral spirits is perpetuated through contact with the soil in which the ancestors of the tribe lie buried. The Gikuyu consider the earth as the 'mother' of the tribe. . . . Thus the earth is the most sacred thing above all that dwell in or on it" (Kenyatta 21). Ngũgĩ's descriptions of land in his early novels incorporate these traditional Gikuyu beliefs about their land.

Colonialism caused catastrophic disruption in Gikuyu society. Not only were the Gikuyu forcibly brought under British colonial rule; the Gikuyu lands, particularly the area known as the White Highlands, were seen as especially suited for Europeans, because of the similarity between their climate and Europe's:

> [A] point which is often overlooked is that regions most favoured by Europeans may be those least suited to Africans. Europeans instinctively select a country where the climate, vegetation and temperature most resemble those of the cold north. Natives, on the whole, thrive best in hotter, lower, wetter places. (Huxley, *White Man's Country* 1: 72)

In addition to this suggestion that there was a kind of racial affinity that justified the annexation of the Highlands, Elspeth Huxley and others also claimed that the Gikuyu were not doing anything with the land: "To us that was remarkable: they had not aspired to recreate or tame the country and to bring it under their control" (Huxley, *Flame Trees of Thika* 45). Throughout colonial African literature, there runs the theme that the land belongs to the people who would develop it, based loosely on the Biblical notion of the good steward. The good stewardship of the Gikuyu, and the environmental value of fallow land, was not yet appreciated by the British.

The British colonists then developed a legal argument justifying the appropriation of land:

the Europeans [misinterpreted Gikuyu land tenure] by saying that the land was under the communal or tribal ownership, and as such the land must be *mali ya serikali,* which means Government property. Having coined this new terminology of land tenure, the British Government began to drive away the original owners of the land. (Kenyatta 26)

Thus by a sleight of hand, communal land became the property of the Crown. In actuality the open land the Europeans saw in the Highlands was used as pasture-land and woodlands, and also represented future village sites, as populations expanded and farming plots became exhausted. By relocating whole villages as the soil gave out, the Gikuyu were able to design a sustainable agriculture; with the coming of permanent ownership of the land and a growing population, however, they were no longer able to move to open land, and their plots became poor and subdivided.

The Mau Mau uprising in Kenya in the 1950s was a crucial event not only in Kenyan history but also in Ngũgĩ's personal development. His older brother, Wallace Mwangi, was a freedom fighter (Gurr 101). While Mau Mau was strongest among the Gikuyu, it was a national movement that united the Kenyan people: "Through Mau Mau, they organized themselves, in the villages, and in the towns, their vision going beyond the narrow confines of the tribe" (Ngũgĩ, *Homecoming* 12). Ngũgĩ's political philosophy was strongly influenced by Marxism, but at the same time he felt that he was articulating a nationalist and socialist vision that was essentially African, not Western:

My thesis, when we come to today's Africa, is then very simple: a completely socialized economy, collectively owned and controlled by the people, is necessary for a national culture. (*Homecoming* 13)

Although Ngũgĩ's early novels emphasize the relation of a specifically Gikuyu culture to the land, all his works also articulate a national and socialist vision of Kenya.

Ngũgĩ grew up in a small village; his father had four wives and twenty-eight children. He was sent to boarding school to get a British-style education and later studied at Makerere and Leeds Universities. His first three novels, *The River Between, Weep Not, Child,* and *A Grain of Wheat,* were written in Uganda and England; *Petals of Blood* "was drafted in the USA and completed in the USSR" (Gurr 17). The traces of this history are apparent in the Western form and techniques used in these early novels. By examining the changes in the description of landscape in Ngũgĩ's novels, and considering them as a response to colonial literature about Kenya and in connection with Ngũgĩ's critique of the economic and political situation in Kenya, we can trace the development of his fiction from a limited acceptance of Western techniques of description to a rejection of these techniques as implying a view of nature that Ngũgĩ no longer shares.

Ngũgĩ's earliest written novel (although it was published after *Weep Not, Child*) is *The River Between*. This novel opens with a sweeping description of the landscape:

> The two ridges lay side by side. One was Kameno, the other was Makuyu. Between them was a valley. It was called the valley of life. Behind Kameno and Makuyu were many more valleys and ridges, lying without any discernable plan. They were like many sleeping lions which never woke. They just slept, the big deep sleep of their Creator.
>
> A river flowed through the valley of life. If there had been no bush and no forest trees covering the slopes, you could have seen the river when you stood on top of either Kameno or Makuyu. Now you had to come down. Even then you could not see the whole extent of the river as it gracefully, and without any apparent haste, wound its way down the valley, like a snake. The river was called Honia, which meant cure, or bring-back-to-life. Honia river never dried: it seemed to possess a strong will to live, scorning droughts and weather changes. And it went on in the same way, never hurrying, never hesitating. People saw this and were happy. (1)

This opening paragraph can be compared to Western descriptions of landscape. The omniscient narrator supplies a bird's eye view of the landscape and names the prominent features for us. The description is organized along the lines of a landscape painting: first we see the most prominent features, the two ridges, then the valley, and finally the background features are filled in. As in a novel by Dickens, Hardy, or Lawrence, the landscape is used to foreshadow the conflicts in the novel: the river divides the two ridges, but it could also be seen as a uniting force. Ngũgĩ's use of the ambivalent term "between" in "Between them was a valley" (and in the title of the novel) offers at least two interpretations; if people have something between them, it can be joining or dividing them. Ngũgĩ's use of personification in this passage stays within the limits of traditional realism: although the river is described as "possessing a strong will to live, scorning droughts and weather changes," the narrator distances himself from this description through the phrase "it seemed." As a final touch, Ngũgĩ ends the paragraph with a reference to people, like the small figures, sometimes including a figure of the artist himself, included in a landscape painting to provide a sense of scale. An important difference here is that the figures are not of the artist, but of the community itself as collective onlookers: "People saw this and were happy."

When the landscape is looked at from inside the valley rather than from the air the foreshadowing of conflict is intensified:

> When you stood in the valley, the two ridges . . . became antagonists . . . they faced each other, like two rivals ready to come to blows in a life and death struggle for the leadership of this isolated region. (1)

The river divides rather than unites, marking the boundary between the two opposing sides (Christian and traditional villages). By placing these descriptions side by side, Ngũgĩ leaves the "correctness" of either vision open; Waiyaki, the protagonist, must decide whether the Gikuyu are ready to be united or are destined to be split into two camps. The choice of action is linked to the choice of perspective; if Waiyaki can persuade the villages to see themselves as united—part of the same community, the same valley—they will be able to overcome their differences, but if the river is seen as a boundary between the two rather than a unifying force, the social rift will be unbreachable.

Ngũgĩ's description of the landscape is integrated with his development of action and character. Waiyaki's father, Chege, takes him to visit a place sacred to his clan, pointing out medicinal herbs along the way. Here, "the landscape, the forests and hills, are conspiring to unite father and son as they have united the Gikuyu nation for generations. We cannot understand the individual, social, and spiritual significance of either character outside their relation to the landscape" (Roscoe 178). Through this scene, we see how Waiyaki is being educated in the connections between the Gikuyu community and nature, and specifically in the connections to this particular landscape, where medicinal herbs grow, and where there are sacred sites. Ngũgĩ's description of the community's relation to the land at the moment when colonialism, through the arrival of Christian missionaries, was just beginning to make itself felt, echoes Kenyatta's claims about the importance of land to the Gikuyu people: "These ancient hills and ridges were the heart and soul of the land. They kept the tribes' magic and rituals, pure and intact" (*The River Between* 3).

Throughout the novel, the conflict between Christianity and traditionalism is seen as threatening the people's connection to the land. In one scene, Muthoni, the daughter of a minister, reveals to her sister Nyambura that she wants to be circumcised and become "a real woman, knowing all the ways of the hills and ridges" (29). Nyambura is shocked by Muthoni's decision, as it is against the principles of their church:

For a second Nyambura sat as if her thoughts, her feelings, her very being had been paralysed. She could not speak. The announcement was too sudden and too stupefying. How could she believe what she had heard came from Muthoni's mouth? She looked at the river, at the slightly swaying bulrushes lining the banks, and then beyond. Nothing moved on the huge cattle road that wound through the forest towards Kameno. The yellowish streaks of morning light diffused through the forest, producing long shadows on the cattle path. The insects in the forest kept up an incessant sound which mingled with the noise of falling water farther down the valley. They helped to intensify the silence, created by Muthoni's statement. (28)

Female circumcision was (and continues to be) one of the crucial conflicts between Christians and traditionalists: to Christians it is barbaric; but without it, a woman cannot be initiated into her clan. That Muthoni, the daughter of a minister, would choose to be circumcised is extremely shocking, and it has stunned her sister into silence. Yet Muthoni's description of her decision shows that she sees this action as the only way to have an authentic connection to the hills and ridges. On the other hand, when Nyambura reaches out to the landscape to reassure herself and support her Christian beliefs, she receives nothing: the insects' noise "helped to intensify the silence" and "nothing moved." Ngũgĩ's description clearly shows that Christianity detaches the individual from the landscape, both through the loss of traditional initiation rites which would connect the individual to the clan and to the land, and through the loss of traditional interpretations of the landscape—for Nyambura, the symbolic significance of the land in the Gikuyu culture has been lost. The land is silent.

Adrian Roscoe quotes this passage and comments:

> Muthoni's announcement is heard by "the river" which neatly divides the landscape and the human community of the book. . . . Even "the slightly swaying bulrushes" have their place in this scene, repeating a reed-in-the-tide image which J. P. Clark popularized as a symbol of cultural hesitation. Muthoni so far has been weak like this plant; but now by the waters of the Honia she has made a decision which will restore her to strength. (177)

Thus Ngũgĩ shows Muthoni's choice to be in harmony with the landscape of the valley.

In *The River Between,* the colonialists have not yet moved into the hills. Their influence is felt through the Christian school in a nearby town, and their political and economic power is known only through descriptions of their houses and through the tax gatherers. Yet Waiyaki, the protagonist, senses what is to come:

> And still it rained, with the little streams gathering and joining together. He saw what they were doing—
> > Carrying away the soil.
> > Corroding, eating away the earth.
> > Stealing the land.
> And that was the cry, the cry on every ridge. Perhaps the sleeping lions would sleep no more, for they were all crying, crying for the soil. The earth was important to the tribe. (76)

Waiyaki explicitly connects this irresistible erosion with the white settlers: "That was why Kinuthia and others like him feared the encroachment of the white man" (76). This coming threat emphasizes the importance of Waiyaki's quest to unify the two villages; without unification, both villages will be washed away by the erosion caused by the white settlers.

Near the end of the novel, Ngũgĩ foreshadows the coming of Mau Mau: "suddenly the people who stood on the hills or up the slope saw big yellow flames emanated by the setting sun. The flames seemed near and far and the trees and the country were caught in the flames. They feared" (166). Ngũgĩ's image of the flames of the sunset here suggests that the Mau Mau uprising was a natural, even inevitable, phenomenon.

Throughout the novel, the river Honia is a symbol of life, power and unification. In this image, Ngũgĩ draws on the importance of the river in traditional life, as a source of water, and as a source of spiritual renewal. Even Christianity is included in the landscape through the Biblical language of the river's song: "And Honia river went on flowing through the valley of life, throbbing, murmuring an unknown song. *They shall not hurt nor destroy in all my holy mountains, for the earth shall be full of the knowledge of the Lord, as the waters cover the sea*" (173). The river's warning is unheeded by the people of Kameno: they reject their teacher because he preaches unification with the Christians of Makuyu. With the betrayal of Waiyaki by the people of Kameno, it would seem that the hope of unification has been lost forever, but Ngũgĩ closes the novel with a final image of the river: "Honia river went on flowing between them, down through the valley of life, its beat rising above the dark stillness, reaching into the heart of the people of Makuyu and Kameno" (175). Charles Nnolim, in his essay "Background Setting: Key to the Structure of Ngũgĩ's *The River Between*," sees this as a tragic ending: "Ngũgĩ seems to look on Honia River as symbolizing the continued and eternal strife between the Makuyu and Kameno tribesmen" (138). However, in "Kenya: The Two Rifts" Ngũgĩ uses a similar image: "Kenya is potentially a great country. . . . the different springs in every tribe and race can and should be channelled to flow together in a national stream from which all may draw" (*Homecoming* 24). In opposition to the eroding forces of colonialism, Ngũgĩ claims that nationalism and socialism are life-giving, unifying forces. Thus, although Waiyaki, the "middle figure" in between the two ridges, is unable to find a resolution, the Honia River's ability to reach into the heart of the people in both villages implies that there is still the possibility of unification and social change in Kenya.

Early critics of Ngũgĩ's fiction noted his use of landscape as an integral part of *The River Between*. Ime Ikiddeh saw the Honia River as a symbol of the inherent unity of the two communities: the division between them is an "unnatural struggle" (5). In some Western interpretations of the novel, however, the description of landscape became a point of contention as to whether the novel was borrowing Western conventions of description or was revealing a uniquely African consciousness. In the first group was C. B. Robson, who linked Ngũgĩ's description of landscape with D. H. Lawrence's and universal-ized the Kenyan struggle for independence in the novel: "Even his attempt to form a 'new retrospect,' of the clash with Europe, is conveyed as part of man's struggle to come to terms with the implications of his own momentum" (Robson 129). On the other side was Gerald Moore, who saw African writers in general as expressing a unity of nature that was lost to the West:

> What seems to be involved is a complete identification of the poet with the constituent features of the landscape around him. He does not so much inhabit this landscape as become inhabited by it. . . . Western man simply cannot fuse himself back into a nature which he has deliberately set apart from himself in order to master it. (Moore 151)

Yet either way, whether these Western critics praise African writers for their continuity with Western traditions or for their alterity, the center of the discourse is the use of these literatures for a Western audience. Chris Wanjala, in *The Season of Harvest: A Literary Discussion,* criticizes Moore's position, which "implies a homeliness of a writer in an environment of primeval innocence (Garden of Eden?) and bliss":

> Such a society does not exist here in East Africa today. He [Moore] refers the writer's consciousness only to place and disregards the history of the forming nations of East Africa, and the connection of Ngũgĩ's writings to the pre-independence nationalism in Kenya. (53–54)

The same criticism can be made of Robson's interpretation of the novel: by "elevating" the issue in the novel to a universal crisis of modern man, Robson elides the significance of the novel as a critique of Western colonialism and capitalism. Wanjala asserts that Ngũgĩ's purpose is to portray "the destruction that inhered in colonialism and to evoke the need for a renewal and a rebirth of African cultural and economic institutions that help the African to be at home in his society and in his physical environment" (70). Thus in *The River Between,* Honia River is a representation of the potential for renewal in the two communities.

Ngũgĩ's use of landscape in *The River Between* does share similarities with early works by other African authors, such as Chinua Achebe's *Things Fall Apart.* In each of these, the author uses some Western techniques and has an orientation towards a Western audience. Ngũgĩ, writing about the "scandalous allegation" that Africans have no culture, has said, "Because he knew that this 'scandalous allegation' was also embodied in European books, especially fiction, on Africa, the African writer tried to answer by asserting in the books he wrote that Africa had a culture as good as any" (*Homecoming* 11). After their early novels, the careers of Ngũgĩ and Achebe moved in different directions, as Achebe continued to claim that English can be African, while Ngũgĩ began to write in Gikuyu. Ngũgĩ puts into practice his own beliefs: "Why can't African literature be at the centre so that we can view other cul-

tures in relationship to it? . . . The aim, in short, should be to orientate ourselves towards placing Kenya, East Africa, and then Africa in the centre"
(*Homecoming* 146).

Even in *The River Between* there are elements of this philosophy: the
novel centers on the Gikuyu people, and the colonists are only on the fringes
of the Gikuyu world. Ngũgĩ carefully depicts the land-centered consciousness of the Gikuyu, and uses their symbolic system to describe and interpret
the significance of the landscape. However, the form of the novel is Westernized, and Ngũgĩ gradually turns from this style to develop an African-centered approach not only to the content, but also to the structure of his novels.

Between the publication of *A Grain of Wheat* (1968) and *Petals of Blood*
(1977), Ngũgĩ published a collection of non-fiction essays, *Homecoming*
(1972), which describe his positions on colonialism, nationalism, capitalism,
and post-independence corruption in Africa, as well as his vision of an
African-centered world-view. The essays are focused on the present and the
future, rather than the past described in his early novels. Significantly, he
rejects the romanticism of the past typical of the Negritude poets:

> The African writer was in danger of becoming too fascinated by the yesterday
> of his people and forgetting the present. Involved as he was in correcting his
> disfigured past, he forgot that his society was no longer peasant, with common
> ownership of means of production, with communal celebration of joy and vic-
> tory, communal sharing of sorrow and bereavement; his society was no longer
> organized on egalitarian principles. (44)

Ngũgĩ claims that there are no longer any tribes in Africa: "the economic and
social forces that gave rise to various nations in pre-colonial Africa have collapsed" (xvii). In this new world, he urges Africans to look, not to the past,
but to the future: "For we are all involved in a common problem: how best to
build a true communal home for all Africans. Then all the black people, all
the African masses can truthfully say: we have come home" (xix). The Marxist
ideology and African-centered consciousness of *Homecoming* form the ideological context of *Petals of Blood*.

In *Petals of Blood,* Ngũgĩ moves from the primarily aesthetic and spiritual connection to the land evident in his early novels to an explicitly political
and economic relationship between the worker and the land. Instead of identifying characters as Gikuyu or Maasai, he calls them tillers, peasants and
herdsmen (Gurr 109), thus de-emphasizing the role of specific cultures in creating and maintaining the people's relationship to their environment. Rather,
the cycles of human life are seen as intricately interwoven with the cycles of
production:

> The peasant farmers of Ilmorog now went into the fields to idly earth up crops
> that no longer needed the extra earth, or to merely pull out the odd weed.
> Thistles, marigolds and forget-me-nots would stick to their clothes, and they

would now laugh and tell jokes and stories as they waited for the crops to ripen. (32)

The happiness of the peasant farmers is clearly linked to the time of year and idleness.

Earlier religious attitudes are rejected here:

A donkey has no influence on the weather. No animal or man can change the laws of nature. But people can use the laws of nature. The magic we should be getting is this: the one which will make this land so yield in times of rain that we can keep aside a few grains for when it shines. . . . Let us rather look to ourselves to see what we can do to save us from the drought. The labour of our hands is the magic and wealth that will change our world and end all droughts from our earth. (115)

While Karega, the protagonist, shares his community's vision of the land as belonging to the people as a whole, he rejects the magical beliefs of the community in favor of a socialist approach which relies on labor and communal action rather than on ancestral ties to preserve the productiveness of the land. Ngũgĩ even refigures the Gikuyu's reverence for ancestral spirits associated with the land through his revolutionary perspective: listening to stories of the Mau Mau, Karega becomes "aware of a new relationship to the ground on which they trod. . . . everything on the plains had been hallowed by the feet of those who had fought and died that Kenya might be free: wasn't there something, a spirit of those people in them too?" (143).

Godfrey Munira in *Petals of Blood* is a schoolteacher, like Waiyaki in *The River Between*. While Waiyaki was at the center of his people's conflict between Christianity and traditional culture, Munira is portrayed as an outsider, not only because he was not born in Ilmorog, but also because he does not work on the land: "Munira did not take part in such talk: he felt an outsider to [the peasants'] involvement with both the land and what they called 'things of blood.' . . . he seemed doomed to roam this world, a stranger" (18).

The figure of Munira, the Western-educated schoolteacher, serves as an indictment of a Western attitude toward nature. Munira's aesthetic appreciation of nature is divorced from practicalities: "He would watch the peasants in the fields going through the motions of working but really waiting for the rains, and he would vaguely feel with them in their anxieties over the weather. But the sun was nice and warm on his skin" (20). His attitude is similar to the traditional Western pastoral depiction of rural life, which elevated the picturesque qualities of rural scenes but tended to overlook the poverty of the rural people and their struggles to survive on marginal land. Munira shies away from anything beyond conventional Western aesthetic values. While on a nature walk, one of Munira's students says, "Look. A flower with petals of blood." Munira immediately corrects him: "There is no color called blood. What you mean is that it is red" (21). Just as he felt outside the "things of blood" the farmers discuss, Munira here avoids the implications of "petals of blood" which will be worked out throughout the novel. Only towards the end of the novel is Munira able to accept this image: after setting fire to a whorehouse, Munira

> stood on the hill and watched the whorehouse burn, the tongues of flame from the four corners forming petals of blood, making a twilight of the dark sky. He, Munira, had willed and acted, and he felt, as he knelt down to pray, that he was no longer an outsider, for he had finally affirmed his oneness with the Law. (333)

Action imbues the petals of blood with meaning. In the earlier scene, however, the children's questions about the relationships of man to nature only irritate him: "Man . . . law . . . God . . . nature [sic]; he had never thought deeply about these things, and he swore that he would never again take the children to the fields" (22).

Munira is an intruder in the community, a man who fails to establish any lasting ties. He is the image of the Western-educated African, aspiring to Western ideals but left out of the real centers of power. He fantasizes about being "lord" of Ilmorog: "he came to feel as if Ilmorog was his personal possession. . . . he felt as if the whole of Ilmorog had put on a vast flower-patterned cloth to greet its lord and master" (21). The language Munira uses, that of owner, master and lord, reveals Munira's desire for power and control; it is the language of the colonial masters. Yet Munira's fantasies about nature do not lead to any ties to the community or to a sense of belonging in Ilmorog, but only to frustration. Munira's alienation from the land represents the contradictions involved in a Kenyan accepting Western premises about nature, power, and community: Ngũgĩ implies that in an African context, these premises are irrelevant and futile.

Karega, the hero of the novel, is also a schoolteacher, but he is able to see the connection of the land to the labor of the people. In addition, he represents Ngũgĩ's desire to create an Afrocentric worldview. Karega asks, "How could he enlarge [the schoolchildren's] consciousness so that they could see themselves, Ilmorog and Kenya as part of a larger whole, a larger territory containing the history of African people and their struggles?" (109). This opinion is echoed later by the narrator, who comments that "the weakness of the resistance lay not in the lack of will or determination or weapons but in the African people's toleration of being divided into regions and tongues and dialects according to the wishes of former masters" (262). Africans, by accepting a Western-oriented worldview, accepted also the arbitrary divisions created by the colonial powers and then maintained by those in power. A new image of a united Africa would be, quite literally, revolutionary.

In *Homecoming,* Ngũgĩ claimed that "Now there are only two tribes left in Africa: the 'haves' and the 'have nots' " (xvii). In *Petals of Blood* the "haves" are the Europeanized blacks who work for foreign companies: "the new owners, master servants of bank power, money and cunning" (280). Ilmorog is divided into two parts—a wealthy residential area and the shanty town of the workers. This rift is not illustrated or supported by any split in the natural landscape—there is no river between them—which emphasizes the unnatural nature of the division. The only differences are in the man-made landscape, in which Ngũgĩ juxtaposes the luxuries of "Cape Town" (named after one of the centers of white South African power and privilege) with the open sewers and mud shanties of the "New Jerusalem" (whose hopes must lie in the future). Karega finally blames the system of private ownership for the destruction of the land:

> Why, anyway, should soil, any soil, which after all was what was Kenya, be owned by an individual? Kenya, the soil, was the people's common shamba, and there was no way it could be right for a few, or a section, or a single nationality, to inherit for their sole use what was communal. (302)

Ngũgĩ has moved from a description of a single people's connection with its ancestral homeland to a national, even pan-African, perspective. In the process, he has described how people's relationships to the land, and by extension, to Kenya and to Africa, are mediated by their cultural, racial, and economic situation. Ngũgĩ moves away from traditional descriptions of landscape, as in the opening of *The River Between,* towards descriptions that expose these mediating factors. For Ngũgĩ, peasants have the most authentic experience of the land, in that their work on the land gives them a connection to the landscape which is not based on ownership or aesthetic distance, but this must be supplemented by teachers like Karega who can provide a vision of Kenyan and African unity. This vision will only become a reality through the masses' struggle against capitalism:

> Imperialism:capitalism:landlords:earthworms. A system that bred hordes of round-bellied jiggers and bedbugs with parasitism and cannibalism as the highest goal in society. . . . The system and its gods and its angels had to be fought consciously, consistently and resolutely by all the working people! (344)

After *Petals of Blood,* Ngũgĩ co-authored a play in Gikuyu, *Ngaahika Ndeenda.* The play was staged in his home town, Limuru, and was acted by the *wananchi,* or peasants, of the area. By writing in Gikuyu, and choosing the theater over the form of the novel, Ngũgĩ was identifying himself with the African masses, trying to put into practice his idea of cultural and political commitment. As a result, he was detained under the Public Security Act of Kenya in December 1977. After his release, in December 1978, Ngũgĩ said "*Ngaahika Ndeenda* showed me the road along which I should have been travelling all these past seventeen years of my writing career" (*The Weekly Review* 32). Since that time, Ngũgĩ has been the leading proponent of writing in African languages.

The use of a foreign language creates a rift between the text and the author. By the time he wrote *Petals of Blood,* Ngũgĩ had already rejected Western techniques of description as implying Western, not African, relations to the land; now he rejected the language of the West also. Ngũgĩ's decision reflects his concern with the alienation of the African from his own society through the acceptance of Western culture and technology; Ngũgĩ claims that " [l]iterature published in African languages will have to be meaningful to the masses and therefore much closer to the realities of their situation" ("On Writing in Gikuyu" 151).

In *Devil on the Cross,* Ngũgĩ writes in Gikuyu from a Gikuyu perspective. The narrator of the story is a gicaandi singer, a traditional storyteller. He sprinkles his narrative with African proverbs: "the forest of the heart is never cleared of all its trees" (7); "aping others cost the frog its buttocks" (12); "just as a single bee is sometimes left behind by the others, one question in particular remained lodged in Wariinga's mind" (29); "a man who doesn't travel thinks that it's only his mother who cooks wild vegetables" (71). These proverbs connect the narrative with the oral tradition. They also provide a rhythm to the narrative development and a logic for conversations between characters different from that of traditional Western narratives. Proverbs are used in traditional African orature both to punctuate the narrative and as a form of persuasion: the character in the story who is most able to use proverbs to support his or her own argument usually prevails. In Ngũgĩ's novel, this strategy is used in conversations, as characters argue over the problems of modern Kenya. For example, Muturi argues for socialism in Kenya by referring to Gikuyu proverbs:

> That humanity is in turn born of many hands working together, for, as Gikuyu once said, a single finger cannot kill a louse; a single log cannot make a fire last through the night. . . . The unity of our sweat is what makes us able to change the laws of nature, able to harness them to the needs of our lives, instead of our lives remaining slaves of the laws of nature. That's why Gikuyu also said: Change, for the seeds in the gourd are not all of one kind. (52)

In another passage, a corrupt businessman also uses proverbs to support his own actions: "I have two mistresses, for you know the saying that he who keeps something in reserve never goes hungry, and when an European gets old, he likes to eat veal" (99). As in the last example, not all of the proverbs are traditional; some are taken from contemporary experience: "Money can flatten mountains" (117). Through these proverbs, Ngũgĩ directs his narrative to a Gikuyu audience. At the same time, he shows that traditional wisdom alone is not enough to guide contemporary African society; it can be called upon to support both African socialism and neo-colonial corruption. Readers must decide for themselves which argument is more persuasive.

In a similar manner, Ngũgĩ incorporates Christian rhetoric and imagery into the novel, beginning with the title, *Devil on the Cross*. This refers to a recurring dream that Warĩĩnga has:

> Instead of Jesus on the Cross, she would see the Devil, with skin as white as that of a very fat European she once saw near the *Rift Valley Sports Club,* being crucified by people in tattered clothes—like the ones she used to see in Bondeni—and after three days, when he was in the throes of death, he would be taken down from the Cross by black people in suits and ties, and, thus restored to life, he would mock Wariinga. (139)

In *Petals of Blood,* Ngũgĩ had rejected Christianity, and accepted traditional wisdom only insofar as it described a communal, socialist society. In *Devil on the Cross,* however, Ngũgĩ uses both traditional Gikuyu culture and Christianity as elements of contemporary Kenyan culture, and as sources for the rhetoric of his characters. Even the narrator, the *gĩcaandĩ* singer, describes a vision he has had in Biblical and apocalyptic terms:

> And after seven days had passed, the Earth trembled, and lightning scored the sky with its brightness, and I was lifted up, and I was borne up to the rooftop of the house, and I was shown many things, and I heard a voice, like a great clap of thunder, admonishing me: Who has told you that prophecy is yours alone, to keep to yourself? (8)

As in the figure of the Devil on the Cross, Biblical imagery is used to intensify Ngũgĩ's own argument; the range of diction and symbolic structures has expanded considerably from the narrowly socialist rhetoric of *Petals of Blood.*

The *gĩcaandĩ* singer's story begins with a description of the alienation of a working-class woman in Nairobi. Fired from her job for refusing sexual advances, then rejected by her boyfriend, Jacinta Warĩĩnga is thrown out of her apartment. All of these events make her lose her sense of perspective: "Instantly she felt dizzy. Nairobi—people, buildings, trees, motor cars, streets—began to swirl before her eyes" (12). Without a home, a lover, or a job, Warĩĩnga has no connection to her environment, and is alienated from it. Her dizziness is the result of the social and economic disruptions in her life.

Warĩĩnga then takes a *matatu,* a van, from Nairobi to Ilmorog. During this trip, several characters discuss the problems of modern Kenya, symbolized by an upcoming "Devil's Feast" for "Modern Thieves and Robbers" in a cave in Ilmorog. The bus trip provides a transition between the real Kenyan city and Ngũgĩ's fictional Ilmorog. Warĩĩnga asks:

> For today is there a single corner, even in the most far-flung reaches of Kenya, where a poor man can run to escape poverty? Ilmorog, Mombasa, Nairobi,

Nakuru, Kisumu—the water in all these places has become bitter for us peasants and workers. (41)

Ilmorog can stand for all of Kenya, because the same people control the economy and the political structure everywhere in Kenya.

The division of Ilmorog into two sections, which was described in *Petals of Blood,* has become even more exaggerated. The rich live in "Golden Heights," which "contains the homes of the wealthy and the powerful. But do you call them homes or residences! Homes or sheer magnificence?" (130). "New Jerusalem" has also gotten poorer: "The walls and the roofs of the shanties are made of strips of tin, old tarpaulin and polythene bags" (130).

In traditional Gikuyu stories, as in many African stories, ordinary and fantastic events take place side by side—the ordinary world and the spiritual universe are interconnected. In *Devil on the Cross,* Ngũgĩ utilizes this dimension of African literature for the first time in his fiction, going beyond the limits of Western realism. The best example of the author's use of fantastic elements is the feast in the sumptuous cave for the "Modern Thieves and Robbers." They have transformed the cave into a huge hall, with chandeliers and luxurious furniture. In this environment, Kenyan businessmen try to outdo one another in stories of white collar thievery and corruption in order to win prizes from the International Organization of Thieves and Robbers. Here, Ngũgĩ plays with Milton's description in *Paradise Lost* of the devils' first meeting in hell, in which each speaker tries to persuade the others how they should act in the future. The irony is that in Milton's version, the devils are ultimately powerless, subjected to God's will even in Hell, while the thieves and robbers in Ngũgĩ's cave have enormous power in Kenya: only a revolution could stop them.

Another parallel is, of course, Plato's cave in *The Republic,* in which people are chained to a wall and watch the shadows of figures and other objects carried by unseen people. This parallel is underlined in Ngũgĩ's novel when Wariinga steps out of the cave:

The sun shone brightly on the Ilmorog ridges and plains. The land lay quiet. No cold, no wind. "Although I have just been in the full glare of electric lights, I feel as if I have lived in darkness all my life," Wariinga sighed, and then she added in a sing-song voice: "Praise the sun of God! Hail the light of God!"

"You should be singing praises to the light of our country," Gatuiria told her. (128)

The electric lights, like the fire casting the shadows on the wall of Plato's cave, are artificial; the natural light of the sun, as in Plato's allegory, exposes the darkness of the cave. Wariinga's sing-song voice, as she praises God for this light, sounds childlike, a memorized chant. To Ngũgĩ, this Christian response to the evil of the cave is mechanical and pointless, as Wariinga's sighs will not lead to real change. Gatuĩria's claim that the light of truth is the light of the country foreshadows the protests of the peasants, students and workers against the robbers in the cave.

Inside Plato's cave, the people who create plausible fictions about the meaning of the shadows on the wall are praised, while the one who, like Socrates, frees himself and seeks the light of the sun is despised. In Ngũgĩ's novel, the businessmen/robbers in the cave create stories to convince the people that what they are doing is beneficial to the nation:

> It was said that I was a man who acted on his words; that I was able to get land for the poor and sold it to them cheaply; and that I did not even keep a plot back for myself because of my love for the people. They started singing my praises, calling me son of Gataanguru, a child imbued with love of the people. Do you see what can be achieved by cunning? (105)

As in Plato's cave, the stories that make people praise the ones who keep them from discovering the truth are the worst evil. Ngũgĩ's use of allusions to Western canonical figures emphasizes that the businessmen are practicing an unbridled Western capitalism, and are, at the banquet, trying to impress their European masters. They operate within a Western context.

There is a possibility for change. Warĩĩnga and Gatuĩria, wandering in the sunlight outside of the cave, enthusiastically sing a hymn to Kenya:

> Hail, Mount Kenya!
> Hail, our land.
> Never without water or food or green fields! (128)

Their love for each other is depicted as in harmony with the landscape: "Come to me my love! . . . The grass is a free bed given us by God, and the darkness is his blanket!" (241). As in the conclusion of *Petals of Blood,* the main characters decide to make "a new beginning for a new Earth" (246) through their own efforts. This new beginning is a violent one: Warĩĩnga discovers that Gatuĩria's father was her first seducer, and she shoots him with a pistol. Gatuĩria, the man who has been trying to write a new Kenyan opera, is at a loss: "he just stood in the courtyard, hearing in his mind music that led him nowhere" (254). Warĩĩnga "walked on, without once looking back" (254).

In *Devil on the Cross,* Ngũgĩ champions women's rights in Kenya. He argues for the education of women, especially practical education: Warĩĩnga trains to become an auto mechanic. Ngũgĩ is particularly concerned about the treatment of women as the sexual possessions of men:

> People love to denigrate the intelligence and intellectual capacity of our women by saying that the only jobs a woman can do are to cook, to make beds and to spread their legs in the market of love. The Wariinga of today has rejected all that. (218)

Ngũgĩ also deplores women's attempts to lighten their skin, straighten their hair, and follow the current fashions, and celebrates the beauty of African women who are strong and independent. Warĩĩnga, at the conclusion of the novel, is clearly the committed revolutionary, while her lover Gatuĩria hesitates, uncertain what path he will take.

At times, Ngũgĩ's novel seems too full of speeches, as each character gives his or her own autobiography and either boasts about his prowess (the thieves and robbers) or argues for a revolution. In the landscape of the novel, however, Ngũgĩ clearly broadens the horizons of his fiction, including surreal locations and exaggerated landscapes that heighten the impact of his story. This strategy also aligns his work with the tradition of oral African narratives. Thus Ngũgĩ has not only written *Devil on the Cross* in Gikuyu; he has also transformed the style and form of his novel, to create an Afrocentric narrative.

Ngũgĩ's most recent novel, *Matigari,* was published in Gikuyu in 1987. The novel is an allegory, a story of Everyman; as Ngũgĩ says in "To the Reader/Listener":

> This story is imaginary.
> The actions are imaginary.
> The characters are imaginary.
> The country is imaginary—it has no name even.
> Reader/listener: may the story take place in the country of your choice! (ix)

Compared to his earlier works, *Matigari* has a simplified landscape and a streamlined narrative. Matigari ma Njiruungi (his name means " 'the patriots who survived the bullets'—the patriots who survived the liberation war, and their political offspring," trans. note 20) has come out of the forests, and like a Kenyan Rip Van Winkle, wanders around the countryside looking for his children and asking, "My friends! Can you tell me where a person could find truth and justice in this country?" (72). Matigari's character represents everyone who toiled under the colonialists and fought in the war of independence; he says, "I tended the estates that spread around the house for miles. . . . I worked all the machines and in all the industries, but it was Settler Williams who would take the profits" (21). Rumors grow that he is the Angel Gabriel, or the Second Coming of Christ, and the government and the police become anxious to hunt him down. In the end, they accomplish this, chasing him into a river while they ride after their hounds, as if he were a fox, but meanwhile the boy Muriuki, who now calls himself and his friends "the children of the patriots," has picked up Matigari's gun and sword. Matigari ma Njiruungi remains undefeated.

The landscape of the novel is presented sparingly, as in an oral tale. There is a fig tree, where Matigari hid his rifle, a house he wishes to reclaim as his own with the estates surrounding it, a village, a city, and the country. The house is hardly described at all: "there on the top of the hill overlooking the whole country stood a huge house which seemed to stretch out for miles, as if, like the plantation itself, it had no beginning and no end" (42). It represents the shelter, food, and clothing which should be the result of the labor of the people, but which has been wrongly appropriated by those "who-reap-where-they-have-not-sown" (50). As Matigari talks to the current owners, the sun sets behind the house: "it had left behind a blood-red glow in the evening sky, lighting up the house, the gate and the road on which they stood" (47–48), foreshadowing the fire that will burn it down at the end of the story.

Matigari begins his journey by crossing the river and coming out of the forest. The forest was a haven for the freedom fighters in Kenya, protecting them from the British colonial soldiers. But when Matigari retreats to the forest to find the answer to his question, an old woman rebukes him: "My dear wanderer, you cannot find answers to your questions here where nobody lives. Truth and justice are to be found in people's actions" (87). The wilderness can provide shelter, but it cannot provide answers. It would have been plausible to use the wilderness as a symbol of spiritual renewal and dedication, because of its associations with the Mau Mau movement as the place of resistance to the colonial government. Ngũgĩ, however, explicitly turns away from it, and seeks renewal within the community.

Within the novel, there are enough details of the past history of the country and the freedom fighters to clearly identify the location as Kenya. Yet in his introductory poem, Ngũgĩ insists on the timelessness and placelessness of his story, connecting his narrative to traditional oral folktales. By doing so, Ngũgĩ also implies that the reading of his story should be like listening to a storyteller: each retelling is a reliving, a re-enactment of the story. In *Matigari,* this connection is particularly powerful: each reader/listener can ask him or herself if the patriots have returned, and where justice and truth can be found in the country. By reading, Ngũgĩ's audience participates in the awakening of the country.

In "A Note on the English Edition," Ngũgĩ relates some of the consequences of this blurring of fact and fiction:

> By January 1987, intelligence reports had it that peasants in Central Kenya were whispering and talking about a man called Matigari who was roaming the whole country making demands about truth and justice. There were orders for his immediate arrest, but the police discovered that Matigari was only a fictional character in a book of the same name. In February 1987, the police raided all the bookshops and seized every copy of the novel. (viii)

The readers of the book gave life, at least temporarily, to Matigari, whom the police tried to arrest. Failing in this, they arrested the book: "Matigari, the fictional hero, and the novel, his only habitation, have been effectively banned in Kenya" (viii). In this short note, Ngũgĩ shrinks the fictional landscape of the novel into the confines of the book, and then imagines both the book and Matigari as outcasts: "With the publication of this English edition, they have joined their author in exile" (viii). The place of this placeless, timeless book is the place of exile.

This brings us to the poignant ironies of Ngũgĩ's situation: passionately attached to the land of Kenya, he is in exile from it; committed to writing in Gikuyu, he publishes his novels in that language only to see them banned. The English language edition, translated not by Ngũgĩ himself but by Wangui wa Goro, is to him an exiled version of his text, enclosed in a non-African language. Thus, Ngũgĩ is distanced from his own work, at least from the only version in print. The event of the novel's publication and the circumstances surrounding it become part of the interpretation of the novel; it is only through his fictional character, Matigari, that Ngũgĩ can return to Kenya. The book's publication in Kenya had allowed the author's ideas to reappear in that country, and the landscape of the novel had allowed for the reappearance of heroes in Kenya. The banning of the novel reinforces and intensifies the author's own exile. The landscape of the novel, then, is not only the simplified allegorical landscape of the tale, but also the political landscape which places the author and the book in specific relations to the country, identifying Ngũgĩ and his novel as both Kenyan and expatriate, part of and excluded from the land.

In this examination of Ngũgĩ's fiction, we have moved from a consideration of traditional Western techniques of landscape description applied to an African landscape in *The River Between,* to a broadening of the concept of landscape to include the social and political environment surrounding the publication of the novel itself. The fictional and factual landscapes of Matigari influence and interpenetrate each other, creating a charged atmosphere that challenges the reader to go beyond a simple aesthetic appreciation of the novel and to engage the political landscape on his or her own terms. The intended audience of Ngũgĩ's later fiction is more and more clearly Kenyan, and African, not Western. The development of his style shows the possibilities and pitfalls of incorporating African elements into a Western form. Ultimately, Ngũgĩ chooses to model the form of the novel itself on the traditions of African orature. In *Matigari,* the subtle descriptions of the hills and valleys of Kenya have disappeared, but the symbolic, political and factual landscapes stand out more clearly. In this way, Ngũgĩ places his fiction squarely within the larger African political landscape, and outside the mainstream of the Western tradition.

Works Cited

Gurr, Andrew. *Writers in Exile: The Identity of Home in Modern Literature.* Atlantic Highlands, NJ: Humanities P, 1981.

Huxley, Elspeth. *The Flame Trees of Thika: Memories of An African Childhood*. New York: William Morrow, 1959.

————. *White Man's Country: Lord Delamere and the Making of Kenya*. Vol. 1 of *White Man's Country*. 2 vols. London: Chatto and Windus, 1953.

Ikiddeh, Ime. "James Ngugi as Novelist." *African Literature Today* 2 (1969): 3–10.

Kenyatta, Jomo. *Facing Mount Kenya: The Tribal Life of the Gikuyu*. London: Heinemann, 1961.

Moore, Gerald. "The Negro Poet and His Landscape" *Introduction to African Literature*. Ed. Ulli Beier. London: Longmans, Green and Co., 1967.

Ngũgĩ wa Thiong'o. *Devil on the Cross*. London: Heinemann, 1982.

————. *Homecoming: Essays on African and Caribbean Literature, Culture and Politics*. London: Heinemann, 1972.

————. *Matigari*. 1987. Trans. into English by Wangui wa Goro. Oxford: Heinemann, 1989.

————. "On Writing in Gikuyu." *Research in African Literatures* 16.2 (1985): 151–56.

————. *Petals of Blood*. New York: Dutton, 1978.

————. *The River Between*. London: Heinemann, 1965.

"Ngũgĩ Still Bitter over his Detention." Interview. *The Weekly Review* 203 (5 Jan. 1979): 30–32.

Nnolim, Charles E. "Background Setting: Key to the Structure of Ngũgĩ's *The River Between*." *Obsidian* 2.2 (1976): 20–29. Rpt. in *Critical Perspectives on Ngũgĩ wa Thiong'o*. Ed. G. D. Killam. Washington, DC: Three Continents, 1984. 136–45.

Robson, Clifford B. *Ngũgĩ wa Thiong'o*. New York: St. Martin's, 1979.

Roscoe, Adrian. *Uhuru's Fire: African Literature East to South*. Cambridge: Cambridge UP, 1977.

Wanjala, Chris. *The Season of Harvest: A Literary Discussion*. Nairobi: Kenya Literature Bureau, 1978.

Freedom's Children: Antiracist Juvenile Literature by Ngũgĩ wa Thiong'o and Other African Authors

YULISA AMADU MADDY AND DONNARAE MACCANN

"Poor mother . . . don't cry. I was right to choose the path of struggle. How else would I have looked you in the eyes?"
—Ngũgĩ wa Thiong'o and Micere Githae Mūgo, *The Trial of Dedan Kimathi*

Ngũgĩ's children's books, *Njamba Nene and the Flying Bus* and *Njamba Nene's Pistol,* contain a mother-son relationship that is central to the theme about political struggle. A social responsibility is also a personal responsibility. A literary technique that entails instruction is not rejected by Ngũgĩ nor is it downplayed in African artistic tradition generally. *Didactic* is not used as a disparaging term but relates to a forthright treatment of thematic material. Ngũgĩ's children's books are didactic in an expository sense but not coldly admonitory. They offer a blend of storytelling elements including the use of proverbs, fanciful excursions, and politically meaningful turns of plot.

This narrative richness, however, is not always what the Western or Westernized critic sees. Such critics do not incorporate an African perspective in their theory and practice, yet Ngũgĩ's liberationist stories benefit from such an approach. In the pages that follow we examine a set of antiracist, anticolonialist stories by Ngũgĩ (Kenya), Beverley Naidoo (South Africa), Peter Abrahams (South Africa), and Morgan Mahanya (Zimbabwe). We also discuss how Western or Westernized literary critics have handled some of these works.

Njamba Nene's Pistol and the story that preceded it, *Njamba Nene and the Flying Bus,* are not exclusively about gaining political independence and expelling the colonizer.[1] They are not about the glamour of leaders proclaiming "freedom" but failing to deliver true liberation. These two stories are about total liberation, the kind that frees from political and social strangulation. These stories are about the collective liberation that means enhancing a people's indigenous cultural growth and national development. Such development must be free from foreign influence. In *Njamba Nene and the Flying Bus* a teacher, Kigorogoru, tries to turn the young protagonist, Njamba Nene, into a "black-white" person, someone enamored by things white. Kigorogoru wants his pupils to identify, as he does, with foreign things and ideas. He wants the kind of students whom liberationists would dub "HMVs" (i.e., followers of "His Master's Voice"). But Njamba Nene cannot be coerced into a puppet's role. Readers who are conscious of how they have been "dragged up" rather than really educated by the colonial system will identify with this boy as they would identify with "bra Anansi" on different levels. They will respond with the unique perspective of people who have endured subjugation. They will understand the intensive program of brainwashing that Kigorogoru imposes on his young scholars. Njamba Nene's mother, who is "off-stage" but vital to her son's resistance to indoctrination, will be received as a countervoice.

In the story of the flying bus, the protagonist successfully lands a magical schoolbus where revolutionary and government forces are waging an armed battle. Njamba Nene shows his classmates how to use the resources of the forest for survival, and then he and some of his friends join the guerrilla army. He is thus expelled from school.

In the first sequel, *Njamba Nene's Pistol,* the hero experiences at an early age the deprivations of colonial-Christian intrigues. He meets humiliation and ostracization at every step of growing up. He witnesses the economic exploitation that forces him to scavenge and hustle to survive. The plotline revolves around this street child who is honest despite his desperate hunger. When he agrees to deliver a loaf of bread at the request of a stranger, he fulfills his mission without violating the trust of those depending on him. Only when he is detained in a camp for suspected revolutionaries does he discover that the bread contains a pistol and he can use it to bluff the government troops into submission.

This camp is where antiliberationist informers are identifying people to be tortured and imprisoned. Even a white boy of Njamba Nene's age is a government operative who is allowed to torment and insult the inmates. With Njamba Nene's pistol, the nationalist freedom fighters are able to rescue the detainees, commandeer a truck, disguise themselves in army uniforms, and escape to a makeshift guerrilla headquarters. Njamba Nene realizes that the stranger who initially sent him on his mission is the leader of the revolutionary army. Readers who know Ngũgĩ's play *The Trial of Dedan Kimathi* will associate this stranger with Kimathi; the martyred Kenyan leader. Both the play and the children's book use the story line about the gun encased in the bread.

What Ngũgĩ presents in these tales is a commentary on the remarriage of colonial and postcolonial Africa. This interpretation will not be lost on anticolonialist readers, even though the stories were written long after Kenya achieved independence. Additionally, such readers will not miss the significance of Njamba Nene's name.

In the African culture, children are named by the elders: grandparents, oldest living relatives, great uncles and aunts, and so forth. The naming ceremony is an important rite, and children are given names that will challenge them and bring out the best in them. The name *Njamba Nene* means Superman or Champ (literally Big Hero). In physical terms, Njamba Nene is far from Superman. His classmates tease this impoverished child with the name "Skinny Champ." He has "mosquito legs," they say, "but goes and gets himself a name as big as an elephant."[2] Handsome features, however, do not play a role in a communal rite that is intended to inspire the young. The African child belongs to the community and is the responsibility of that community; thus the first assigned name is symbolic, a designation alluding to how the child should grow up. Later the youth receives another name that will last him or her until death. In the Njamba Nene stories the naming sets the stage for the confrontation between traditional African culture and the alien culture that Westernized schools are designed to impart.

The schoolteacher represents the "I-am-here-to-help" spy-educators installed by colonial and neocolonial regimes. He manipulates the children on behalf of the multinationalist coalition that ultimately aims at reinstating cheap labor. Ngũgĩ exposes the truth about this imperialistic agenda vis-à-vis the schools; he disputes the myth of "independence" and thereby appears confrontational. Western academic critics have treated such exposés as examples of reverse racism, as a challenge to their supposed right to decide what the African thinks and needs.

Before we examine other liberationist children's tales, we will consider what two academic critics, Frederick Hale and Peter T. Simatei, have perceived in the Njamba Nene stories.

Misreading "Njamba Nene"

Frederick Hale charges Ngũgĩ with political bias, literary mediocrity, and unethical practices. His opposition is centered on the works' alleged propagandistic features and support for people Westerners call terrorists. He calls the stories "transparently propagandistic" and goes so far as to charge Ngũgĩ with "subordinat[ing] . . . ethical principles to the goals of the Mau Mau struggle."[3] Hale makes no effort to place the stories within a subgenre that defines liberationist fiction for what it is—namely, a storytelling tradition that celebrates struggles for national independence. In making these claims, Hale not only misinterprets the works generically, he also irrationally attacks a people's liberation wars for being warlike. Additionally, he applies a double

standard when he treats African wars as violations of "ethical principles."
Such a charge overlooks the way European wars are typically depicted as glorious events—as an ultimate example of principled national policy. This double standard turns the "literary" discussions about Njamba Nene into political statements with an anti-African political bias.

We need to pause here and say a further word about the intersecting
realms of art, politics, and education. Critics who see propaganda rather than
creativity in a liberationist tale are often assuming the role of child defenders.
They see references to an independence struggle as educationally inappropriate. They would keep government out of things, especially out of the spheres
of the intellect and the spirit. They would keep the liberationist voice muffled
if there are youngsters within earshot. Yet historically, colonizers have tar-
geted the young; the colonizer's voice has been directed toward the youthful
mind, and the message has been a familiar one. That is, in stories with a colonial slant, the slave or peon is typically so contented with his or her condition
that no opposition movement is conceivable. Throughout the eras of slavery,
colonialism, and neocolonialism, governments have exercised their teaching
power with this message.

In short, the government has hardly been a nonplayer or a neutral player
in the educational enterprise. Through its school authority, the government
has been deeply involved in the realm of the mind. And there is seldom any
so-called artistic "neutrality" tempering its messages. The nuances of technique have scarcely been of interest when the state has exercised its *self-gener-
ating power*—namely, its teaching power. Because colonialists have been
engaged in the preservation of the colonial state, they have not been inclined
to undermine their own security by tolerating opposition. Thus their educational systems are designed in ways inimical to the welfare of the African
child. This child is given a pariah status and placed in a labor force that is
entirely for the benefit of the colonizing nation. When Frederick Hale talks
about "ethical principles" and then faults Ngũgĩ for challenging this imperialistic system, one can only wonder whose ethics we should be examining.

In dismissing Ngũgĩ's stories for what he thinks they represent, Hale
states that "without exception they [the Europeans] are loathsome stereotypes who do nothing but oppress black Kenyans by imposing their language
and educational system on them, arresting and tormenting them, and capri-
ciously shooting black children."[4] Obviously, Hale has not witnessed colonial
and missionary destructiveness nor understood that the wounds are still raw.
And Africa has had no American-created Marshall Plan to help it recover. If
Ngũgĩ is guilty of any crime it is in being born at the "wrong time"—that is,
among leaders such as Kenyatta and Moi who have not known what their
responsibility entails. History tells us that the British, Dutch, French, German, Spanish, and Portuguese colonial systems did not hesitate to use
extreme force when confronted by the people who are rightful owners of the
land. And the people were often forced to work for little or no wages. Ngũgĩ

states his case succinctly in a line from his play *The Trial of Dedan Kimathi:* "We are not fighting the British people. We are fighting British colonialism and imperialist robbers of our land, our factories, our wealth."[5]

Hale charges Ngũgĩ with being "dogmatic in his perception of the Mau Mau struggle." He says that historians debate whether that "encounter with British colonialism .... helped to prompt or to impede Kenyan independence."[6] This explanation makes the war against imperialism seem ambiguous in principle and execution. But the British were not in the least ambiguous in arguing on behalf of British settlements in Africa, nor were they hesitant in employing massive force to oppose the liberation forces. The actions of Parliament, the Colonial Office, and the British governor speak for themselves. At the height of the "scramble for Africa," the former prime minister Lord Salisbury spoke glowingly about the wealth Britons could extract from the colonies. According to historian Herman Ausubel,

> Lord Salisbury was blunt in insisting that the government was duty-bound to use every opportunity to open new regions for English trade. Uganda, for example, a fertile and heavily populated area, had tremendous economic possibilities, and it was important that English businessmen have free access to the country. Hence he addressed to Lord Rosebery's Liberal Government these strong words: "You must open the path. It is for you to make the communication. It is for you to enable our people to get there. It is for you to enable capital to be invested and commerce to be extended."[7]

These frantic efforts to appropriate Africa were coupled with frantic efforts to retain this kind of economic advantage—thus, the enormous size of the British war machine (i.e., a bomber formation, a division of troops, 20,000 police officers, and both armored and artillery units) pitted against Mau Mau forces. Even more significant are the casualty figures: 11,503 independence activists killed versus 35 European civilians.[8] How could a committed Kenyan author see the Mau Mau forces as less than heroic?

Ngũgĩ has sent a wake-up call to his young readers. He relives and communicates a history that neocolonialist and foreign authorities would want to see buried and forgotten. Njamba Nene is not a character created to think and act as foreigners would want Africans to behave. This is what makes Hale angry. He wants Ngũgĩ to create a character that whites can identify with and pat on the shoulder without having any sense of guilt.

Besides the red-baiting technique that Hale uses in his analysis of Mau Mau, he goes further in chastising Ngũgĩ's morality; he accuses him of deriding Christianity. "Ngũgĩ," he says, "ridicules the faith that the boys have in Christianity."[9] Does Hale not know that it was the missionaries and colonial civil servants who ridiculed, mocked, and destroyed everything that was sacred to African spirituality and society? Is he unaware of the relics and sacred artifacts that were stolen for the benefit of the British, German, and other European museums? It was the missionaries who preached the invincibility of the white God, who taught that white power was great and that anything African or black was inferior and dispensable. The Western Christian is in no position to throw stones.

The stories *Njamba Nene and the Flying Bus* and *Njamba Nene's Pistol* are telling us that before the Christian missionaries and their colonizing partners came to Africa, African people had their own established sacred, spiritual, and ritual practices, their own sociopolitical institutions, their own moral principles. African traditions have their loose ends and their faults, but they were not based on land grabbing and the aggrandizement of wealth. They were not the irrationally restrictive practices that Western travelers (e.g., Livingstone, Stanley, and Kingsley) portrayed in their diaries and journals.

Hale sees a liberationist story as essentially inimical to the colonizer, which is, of course, what the storyteller intended. To many Western scholars, liberation that is not on the Westerner's terms has ethical flaws, and Hale serves as the quintessential mouthpiece for these scholars. He writes disapprovingly, "[Ngũgĩ's] sole ethical touchstone . . . is whether [decisions are in accord with] the pronouncements of the Gikuyu Mau Mau leadership." Being sympathetic to the Mau Mau movement makes Ngũgĩ, ipso facto, a producer of what Hale calls "a poorly developed . . . text."[10]

In treating Ngũgĩ as a mediocre children's author, Hale is in agreement with Peter T. Simatei (a Kenyan African) who entitles his essay "Ideological Inscription in Children's Fiction: Strategies of Encodement in Ngũgĩ and Achebe." This title is, of course, impressive, but it does not throw any light on the Ngũgĩ stories as creative pieces. Rather, the emphasis is on whether Ngũgĩ and Achebe introduce social themes as an "overt presence" or a "covert presence." Ngũgĩ is supposedly in the first category and is faulted for letting Njamba Nene stubbornly defend his indigenous language. When the child explains his preference by stating "Language is language. . . . No language is better than another," Simatei hears a shrill, overt intrusion. He explains his objection:

> Such intelligent remarks, uttered with the confidence of an adult tend to portray Njamba Nene as more of the author's mouthpiece than a typical character of children's fiction."[11]

By whose yardstick and standard is the boy being judged as intelligent? By whose rules is he lacking what a "typical character of children's fiction" must represent? Is Simatei telling us that only European children have the intelligence associated with precociousness? Is he saying that Njamba Nene should talk like the stereotyped African child created by white writers? Are characters in fiction not essentially the mouthpieces of their creators?

In their separate critical treatises, it seems clear that Hale and Simatei are trying to disguise their fears behind various academic conventions. Hale's fear is different from Simatei's, but they are two of a kind. They are both "experts" who do not understand that Ngũgĩ is making a simple point: that only when the oppressed can free themselves can the oppressor also be free. These critics have not recognized that those whose humanity is denied are not the ones negating humanity; it is the people who have denied others. In doing so, they negate their own humanistic character.

In particular Hale has trouble separating the actors in the independence struggle. When Ngũgĩ takes a stand on the side of the Mau Mau, he is illustrating that the helpless and the terrorized are not the ones initiating terror. Instead, it is those with power to create the concrete situations—to employ force. Power cannot be exerted by those who have been subjected to humiliation and deprivation but rather by those who have emasculated them. Nonetheless, Hale treats Ngũgĩ as a traitor. He refers to him as the Kenyan "who was baptized James Ngũgĩ." Did Ngũgĩ ask to be born and baptized under a system that treated people as slaves in their own country? The description continues sarcastically: "[Ngũgĩ] was the fifth child of the third wife of a polygamous tenant farmer."[12] Hale, it seems, cannot conceal his resentment of Ngũgĩ because Ngũgĩ is ingenious and bold in creating caricatured white characters—in naming them for what they really represent.

In another instance Hale fails to sort out the defenders and aggressors. He writes:

> Ngũgĩ leaves no room for settling conflicts through nonviolent protest, eventual reconciliation of members of opposing factions after the attainment of independence, or overarching moral norms that transcend ideologies and political loyalties.[13]

Is the critic here referring to the Njambe Nene stories, or is he indirectly telling readers that Ngũgĩ is a kind of subversive character who is using his creative talent to preach terrorism Mau Mau style? Actually, the sins attached to Ngũgĩ in that quotation could be more rationally tied to the European invaders. It is unlikely that the history of the Mau Mau can be truthfully told by the oppressor-colonizer. The story of colonialism and its devastation can and should be told in as many versions as possible from the point of view of Africans, just as the history of the West is being written and rewritten by Westerners.

A writer is not foreclosing other retellings of his story when he or she produces clear-cut symbols. And in parables about wars this seems self-evident. Moreover, children's literature is openly intentional as Simatei admits:

> [I]t is generally agreed that writing for children inevitably involves an attempt to inculcate in them norms and other ethical practices which the writer assumes are upheld by the society as its essential premises of cultural formation.[14]

Simatei allows for this involvement with "norms" in Achebe's stories for the young but sees Ngũgĩ as letting them "undercut the inscribing genre."[15] This criticism suggests a virtual denial of liberationist fiction as a much-used generic form. Ngũgĩ alludes to "norms and ethical practices," but they are not those typically packaged for export to the "Dark Continent." Ngũgĩ parts company with Hale and Simatei only in that he wants African children to learn about their history, culture, and nation. Is this not what every sincere educationist would do? Whatever Ngũgĩ's "ideological agenda" might be, he has a right to teach the history of the Mau Mau just as resistance against the Third Reich is widely taught in the West.

In fact, liberationist fiction is produced in many parts of the world, and by way of comparison, we turn now to examples related to the democratic struggles in South Africa and Zimbabwe. We will see that charges of literary mediocrity echo these same charges made against Ngũgĩ. Criticisms against Beverley Naidoo's *Journey to Jo'burg: A South African Story* (1984) are a case in point.

MISREADING A SOUTH AFRICAN NOVEL

One of the ironies connected with *Journey to Jo'burg* is that critics who point to the work's literary weakness are people who have not done their own literary homework. They compare two distinct genres as if their artistic principles were identical—that is, they judge an "easy reader" (*Journey to Jo'burg*) in the same way they judge standard novels. According to the *School Librarian*, Naidoo's short work belongs to the "Knockout" series created specifically for children with reading impairments or underdevelopment. The novel is thus generically simple; it is intentionally written without an extensive development of character and setting. Yet even within such limitations, *Journey* has its own truth, its own expressive means of conveying the emotions that the writer wishes to share. As in fiction generally, every revelation and emotion has its own peculiarities of character, plotline, and circumstance. This fictional web makes the story either interesting or uninteresting; it moves a reader from one culture to another, from the known to the unknown. In the case of *Journey,* the reader becomes an explorer in a region that has been isolated and widely misrepresented.

Naledi and Tiro, the sister and brother in *Journey,* are victims of dispossession. Their mother is three hundred kilometers away, working for a white family, while they are left with their grandma and other relatives. They must alert their mother to their younger sister's illness because they believe she is the only one who can save this child's life. Like Frederick Hale in his study of Ngũgĩ, critics Carla Hayden and Helen Kay Raseroka find Naidoo's tale underdeveloped and without spunk. Moreover, they see Naidoo as ethically culpable. They state their objection in terms of weak characterization, a flaw, they say, that suggests a denial of humanness. They write:

This charade denies the characters' individuality, which is the essence of humanness. It also leads us to the crux of the matter in South Africa—a denial of humanness, an inability and refusal to acknowledge blacks as feeling, thinking beings. *Journey,* ironically, makes the same mistake.[16]

For a book conceived as an "easy reader" (as is *Journey*), a lack of emphasis on character is not surprising. It does not imply a lack of humanness. What is ironic is that these critics fault Naidoo for including one chapter about the Soweto uprising of 1976—a rebellion that left 575 people dead, including numerous children. In a story about how apartheid affects the young, how could Naidoo overlook this tragedy? Hayden and Raseroka write with disapproval: "[Naledi's] awareness of the 1976 Soweto massacre is related in an entire chapter—in a slim volume—which is designed only to cram in facts regarding the uprising." These critics seem to imply that the details are an example of excess. What the critics ask for is a sense "that [Naledi] has had . . . deeper internal conflicts . . . caused by the policies of apartheid."[17] But how can the conflict be "deep" if the specifics of Soweto remain undescribed?

Naledi and Tiro do not embark on an unplanned, three-hundred-kilometer journey because they are foolish peasants, as the critics would want us to believe. They were children who had to make decisions that no others in a time of crisis would make. Their journey symbolizes a national imperative—a journey out of colonial and neocolonial subjugation. The illness that was threatening the baby sister is suggestive of plagues caused by the deprivations suffered under apartheid. But Hayden and Raseroka could see only a book that "stretches one's credulity," is "riddled with artificial plot devices," is stuck in the "mire of expediency," and was produced "merely to have something timely about a topic."[18] According to their critique, the novel is both mediocre and unprincipled.

This kind of analysis is seen also in Zena Sutherland's review of *Journey to Jo'burg* in the *Bulletin of the Center for Children's Books.* She notes that the story is weakened because it is "dwarfed by the horrors suffered by black South Africans."[19] Naidoo's goal was to do just that, to reveal the quality of suffering under apartheid. Sutherland's critique suggests a disinterest in that suffering, and it also shows a failure to understand the dimensions of liberationist fiction. If the criteria of Hayden, Raseroka, and Sutherland were to be generally followed, a large number of socially realistic stories would be condemned. Writers of "protest" fiction would be disallowed their rightful participation in a long-standing artistic tradition.

More Protesters: Peter Abrahams and Morgan Mahanya

"Crackling Day" by Peter Abrahams deals with another aspect of apartheid: the commonplace rituals that affirm white over black—white cruelty over black defenselessness.[20] This narrative is an excerpt from his autobiographical novel, *Tell Freedom,* and depicts the horrific abuse of both children and adults in black South African communities. Do the horrors overwhelm the narrative and thereby detract from the story's excellence? Horrors exist in nearly every line: hunger, exposure to freezing temperatures, insults, beatings, and death. This *is* South Africa as presented by a liberationist writer. Horrors do not "dwarf" a narrative, as Zena Sutherland would have us believe; they are sometimes the only possible means of truth telling. They are sometimes so basic as to be defining characteristics of a society. Abrahams leaves no detail unexposed. A black child who fights a white child for maligning the name of his deceased father is severely beaten by his own guardians. The whites insist that this punishment be carried out to whatever degree they dictate. They are in total command, acting as if blacks should be allowed to exist only through the sufferance of whites. The black child's uncle pleads for leniency, but the white man threatens him as well as his nephew:

> "You stubborn too, Sam?"
> "No *baas.*"
> Uncle Sam went into the other room and returned with a thick leather thong. . . .
> Bitterly, Uncle Sam said: "You must never lift your hand to a white person. No matter what happens, you must never lift your hand to a white person. . . ."
> He lifted the strap and brought it down on my back.[21]

Lee, the protagonist, has no choice but to defend the dignity and good name of his deceased father. If he runs away from this now, he will always live his life running away, even in his own country and from the people who have deprived him of his land, his parents, and his rights. He will have honored the invidious myth that white equals right. Like his uncle, he will live without strength enough to defend his own child.

Antiapartheid and anticolonialist narratives present the rationale for protests against oppressors. They exist for this purpose. The specific conditions call forth this response. Any other narrative mode would be dishonest, given the tyrannical conditions. But how can this theme be dealt with forthrightly if one believes that truthful details "dwarf" or "overwhelm" literary excellence? Or if one believes that truth telling is a mere "expediency"—a way to cash in on a timely topic?

Ngũgĩ, Naidoo, and Abrahams have created a platform for discussions between Africans and white Africanists, between Eurocentrists and Afrocentrists, between Assimilados and traditionalist Africans, between liberals and conservatives. Zimbabwean Morgan Mahanya joins this storytelling triumverate with a group of stories under the collective title *The Wound.* His collection is advertised as his "first junior book." Using a poem by Taban lo Liyong on his dedication page, Mahanya describes the sort of people liberationist writers are countering:

Perhaps they know these facts
but prefer the sweet lie
to the bitter truth
And are content
to pass through life
Acting a monstrous lie.[22]

The six stories illumine this theme. They present the activities of spies, informers, traitors; they set forth the anguishing choices that face Africans in a neocolonialist age—an age that often pits brother against brother and sister against sister.

We consider here "Betrayed by Trust" and "Day of Revenge." In the first of these stories a young nurse, Rhoda, has a brother connected with the Zimbabwean independence movement. She steals medicines for the guerrilla fighters, and eventually these men are killed by a bomb that demolishes their house. The reactionary security forces who perpetrate this attack keep a watch for any guerrilla accomplices, and when Rhoda arrives at the scene they exhibit a false sympathy to win her confidence. In the end they invade her home, rape her, and put her in prison for 12 years. "Betrayal," says Rhoda, "waited outside for anyone who tried to walk along freedom street."[23]

In "Day of Revenge" a young teacher, Chandiwana, is helped by a group of children when he is wounded. After the kids pull him to safety, he tells them the story of his wife's assault and murder by marauding soldiers. Then he becomes a liberationist recruit and earns a reputation as "a suicidal . . . fighter who would tackle anything."[24] The narrative presents the methodical way that he prepares to sabotage a truckload of enemy soldiers. As villagers wait for the expected counteroffensive, a cease-fire is mercifully declared.

Both Rhoda and Chandiwana, at the outset, are gainfully employed, law-abiding citizens; they did not get into the fight because they approve of destruction. They are drawn in as they fall victim to neocolonialist warfare. Rhoda is entrapped by her compatriots, by people she assumed would be fighting their common enemy. Chandiwana learns that the soldiers who are paid to protect citizens can become potential adversaries. The emphasis shifts from the external to the internal enemy, to leadership crises and the inhumanity that infects people living in a destabilized environment.

The Ngũgĩs, Naidoos, Abrahamses, and Mahanyas recognize that explorers and missionaries of the past have been long since replaced by experts, technocrats, and advisers—by outsiders offering advice on every conceivable African issue. In almost every African country a kind of independence has been granted, but Africans are economically and politically in a stranglehold by the colonial systems that once suppressed them. The modern Western mariners are fly-in–fly-out tourists, born-again environmentalists, and pedagogues who work with the omnipotent multinationalists. The gold and diamond tycoons have been superseded but not displaced in any meaningful sense. Free education, free health care, and other crucial social services were not part of the colonial "redemption," and postcolonial forces have achieved few substantive changes.

What the Ngũgĩs and Naidoos are telling us is that we need not take the great lie—the lie that says colonialism is dead—into the twenty-first century. But for being so outspoken, they have provoked negative outpourings from Eurocentric book critics. So the question remains: What critical principles and standards should we propose for liberationist fiction, for "protest" narratives, for authentic histories of slavery, colonial pillage, and postcolonial destabilization?

TOWARD A SOCIALLY RESPONSIBLE LITERARY THEORY

Images and messages help readers find their own interpretations and meanings. The work of the children's book critic is to retrace every step of the literary characters, to follow closely the paths that writers have mapped out. The characters have their own world and must move in their own time, space, and rhythm. The milieu created in stories by Africans is often meant to produce an awakening, and Africans will understand them because they speak directly to their own beleaguered lives.

To Western-oriented critics and theorists, this approach can make a writer such as Ngũgĩ seem like a nuisance, a voice that all too effectively exposes the imperialist foundation of underdeveloped Africa. Ngũgĩ's Njamba Nene is created in the spirit of the African mold, as every author writes out of his or her own culture. Ngũgĩ knows that the education of African children cannot be left in the care of foreign educators; an African lifestyle cannot be based on imported lifestyles. The irresponsible tendency among Western book theorists is the tendency to destroy the things that Westerners cannot create—to fail to accommodate thoughts, ideologies, and philosophies that have not come from white experience.

To remedy this narrow critical stance, an African perspective needs to inform literary practice. And there are many African sources that can aid in developing this perspective. Ngũgĩ is himself an educationalist as well as a literary artist. As a child he moved from a nationalist Gikuyu school to a school taken over by educational boards run by the English; he learned from direct experience the methods of colonialist indoctrination. Giving a general overview of education under Western rule, Ngũgĩ writes:

> Depending on who is wielding the weapon, education far from being a means of illuminating reality can be used as a means of masking reality to mystify the relations between man and nature and between man and man. . . .

[C]olonialism imposes an educational system which denies the colonized real knowledge about the wealth produced in the land while at the same time imparting a culture embodying a slave-consciousness.

Thus the colonized are taught that they have no history, meaning they have never acted on nature and changed it. . . . Denying that people had a history has one aim: to show that the colonized like animals had merely adapted themselves to nature and had made no attempt to put a human stamp on their natural environment. Hence they were really savages![25]

Having had such a colonial system imposed on him, Ngũgĩ urges on the literary world an interest in social relations. "Literature," he writes, "is of course primarily concerned with what any political and economic arrangement does to the spirit and the values governing human relationships."[26] And, as one important aspect of culture, literature and literary authenticity cannot be overestimated. "To control a people's culture is to control their tools of self-definition in relationship to others."[27]

This concern with cultural authenticity and self-definition is severely criticized in Western children's book circles. Its detractors range from those who call it too political to those who see it as a form of reverse racism. Both charges lead down the path of Eurocentric domination and constitute, in our view, an irresponsible approach. Perhaps because of the individualistic orientation in Western thought, literary critics view as authentic whatever anyone contrives. In contrast, societies that are community centered see authenticity as related to the particularities of time and place.

An example of the "too political" charge was analyzed in a recent issue of the *American Indian Libraries Newsletter*. A Native American book reviewer for the children's literature journal the *Horn Book* was told by the journal editor that she could not use the term *stereotype* in a review. She was told that the term suggested a "socio-political commentary that doesn't belong in a literary review of a children's book."[28] How would such a rule operate in books from South Africa, which has the most politically saturated children's literature in the world? Moreover, it is the racial ideology of apartheid that has, according to psychiatrist Robert Coles, "triumphed among all [South African] white children."[29] The pervasiveness of that ideology is, in part, the result of the white-dominated children's book industry. Yet the stereotypes circulated in apartheid-sponsored books would not be mentionable in *Horn Book* reviews, reviews that are among the most widely disseminated in schools and libraries. Thus the triumph of apartheid goes on—unscathed, unremarked, and unchallenged. In a response to the *Horn Book*'s demand for silence, Lisa Mitten (president of the American Indian Library Association) states her own simple rule about authenticity: "In reviews of books dealing with minority groups, I look for some indication that the author has a clue about what he is discussing."[30] Another response to the "keep quiet" rule comes from author Christine Nostlinger. She writes:

> It makes me suspect that what is really intended by those who are calling for such a thing is to make sure that no one is allowed to interfere with the sort of "politics" they want to fob off on the children![31]

The notion that cultural authenticity (as an evaluative criterion) borders on racism appears throughout the children's book press. This thesis is based in part on the misconception that cultural experiences are essentially overlapping. Postcolonial conditions are lumped together whether they are Caribbean, Canadian, Australian, African, or whatever. Similarly, in the United States, most immigrant experiences are seen as more or less identical. This premise about overlapping conditions is presented in Hazel Rochman's *Against Borders*. Rochman sees racial and cultural narrowness as characterizing people who call for authenticity. She writes disapprovingly:

> So what about those who say that an American can never write about Japan, that men can't write about women? In fact, some take it further. Only Indians can really judge books about Indians, Jews must review books about Jews. And . . . the ultimate extreme [is] that blacks should read only about blacks.[32]

Taking the same line of argument, fiction writer Ann Cameron advocates the "outsider" perspective. She states that "often the writer who is an outsider . . . sees in a way that enriches." Cameron claims "that people who advise 'write what you know' drastically underestimate the human capacity for imagining what is beyond our immediate knowledge."[33] *Knowledge,* however, is a very broad term. Chinua Achebe has countered this kind of carte blanche approach to artistic production with the Igbo proverb: "Odi be ndi adiro be ibe fa" ("What there is among one people is not among another").[34] Niyi Osundare addresses the insider-outsider debate when he rejects the idea of a uniform postcolonial condition:

> [T]o apply the "post-colonial" label so liberally to places such as Africa and Australia . . .—places whose colonial pasts are so fundamentally different—is tantamount to mocking the real wounds of the colonial infliction where they are deepest and most enduring. We certainly need to distinguish formal and superficial coloniality in places like Canada, Australia, and New Zealand from the systematic, exploitative—and, above all, racist—coloniality in the rest of the countries.[35]

Because a racist coloniality so permeates children's books published in the West, calls for more "imagination" and less "knowledge" seem utterly perverse. In fact, such racist books receive the highest accolades, while stories by Africans are summarily dismissed.[36] Phanuel Akubueze Egejuru summed up the dilemma for Africans:

[The] African writer was . . . in the unhappy position in which his success as a writer was determined not by his fellow Africans but . . . by European and American literary critics with preconceived ideas about what African writing should be.[37]

He is describing a situation in which the possibility of crossing borders is pure delusion. And in a place such as predemocratic, pre-1994 South Africa, African writer Peter Abrahams and Euro–South African writer Beverley Naidoo were either "detained" (a euphemism for arrested) or forced to flee the country when they exposed the specificities of the apartheid regime.[38]

When such writers come up against those disallowing a liberationist genre, they face a formalistic as well as a content-centered debate. They are being censured on matters of both tone and subject matter. Yet it is hard to separate these elements. In considering stories about liberation movements, we find them inherently polemical, but this does not mean they offer only a raw polemic. A polemic may or may not be noticeably shrill. The term *polemic* is defined in the *American Heritage Dictionary, New College Edition,* as an "argument, especially . . . one that is . . . an attack upon a specified opinion, doctrine, or the like." Appeals for political and social justice can be presented as dramas—as stories of ordinary people in ordinary situations. Human relationships, in the stories under discussion here, are presented in vivid images and dramatic scenes. The social vision is one that people can identify with. For readers on the other side of the struggle, however, the vision itself is often at the core of the objections being raised. Moreover, the detractors may well be telling us more about themselves than about the literature they are inveighing against. Dorothy Hammond and Alta Jablow have observed this phenomenon: "The literature on Africa does present a very clear self-view of the British in Africa."[39]

A socially responsible theory of literature will, in our view, reject this whole array of rationalizations: that the works are too political; they are too polemical; they limit individualism and the potential of the imagination. Such arguments function as essentially colonialist-supporting tactics. In contrast, a colonized people tend to start from a different perspective. Chinua Achebe states it in relation to literature:

[I]t is because [writers] see a vision of the world which is better than what exists; it is because they see the possibilities of man rising higher than he has risen at the moment that they write. So whatever they write, if they are true practitioners of their art, would be in essence a protest.[40]

He continues with an expansive view of the writer's role as an activist-protester: "I think protest will never end. . . . I don't think it's a question of protest against Europe or simply protest against local conditions. It is protest against the way we are handling human society in view of the possibilities for greatness and the better alternatives which the artist sees."[41] In our view, a responsible literary theory will reject attempts to muffle such protesters.

As children need the call for "better alternatives," they also need the stories of their own national liberation struggles. In the preface to their play, *The Trial of Dedan Kimathi* (1976), Ngũgĩ and Mũgo pose questions about Kenyan liberationist literature, but the queries echo far beyond national boundaries:

> [W]as the theme of Mau Mau struggles exhausted in our literature? Had this heroic . . . struggle against British forces of occupation been adequately treated in our literature? . . . Why were our imaginative artists not singing songs of praise to [Kimathi and others] and their epic deeds of resistance? Whose history and whose deeds were the historians and creative writers recording for our children to read?[42]

These questions ring with meaning for the next round of revolutionary storytellers.

Notes

1. Another sequel, *Njamba Nene and the Cruel Colonial Chief,* has not yet been translated into English.
2. Ngũgĩ wa Thiong'o, *Njambe Nene and the Flying Bus* (Nairobi: Heinemann Kenya, 1982), 2.
3. Frederick Hale, "Ngũgĩ wa Thiong'o's Mau Mau for Children," *Children's Literature Association Quarterly* 20, no. 3 (Fall 1995): 133.
4. Hale, "Ngũgĩ wa Thiong'o," 132.
5. Ngũgĩ wa Thiong'o and Micere Githae Mũgo, *The Trial of Dedan Kimathi* (Oxford, England: Heinemann, 1976), 64.
6. Hale, "Ngũgĩ wa Thiong'o," 130.
7. Herman Ausubel, *The Late Victorians: A Short History* (New York: Van Nostrand, 1955), 87.
8. Bruce Berman, *Control and Crisis in Colonial Kenya: The Dialectic of Domination* (London: James Currey, Nairobi: Heinemann Kenya; Athens: Ohio University Press, 1990), 352.
9. Hale, "Ngũgĩ wa Thiong'o," 133.
10. Hale, "Ngũgĩ wa Thiong'o," 133.
11. Peter T. Simatei, "Ideological Inscription in Children's Fiction: Strategies of Encodement in Ngũgĩ and Achebe," in *Other Worlds, Other Lives: Children's Literature Experiences. Proceedings of the International Conference on Children's Literature, April 4–6, 1995*, vol. 2, ed. Myrna Machet, Sandra Olen, and Thomas van der Walt (Pretoria: University of South Africa, 1996), 21.
12. Hale, "Ngũgĩ wa Thiong'o," 129.
13. Hale, "Ngũgĩ wa Thiong'o," 133.
14. Simatei, "Ideological Inscription," 17.
15. Simatei, "Ideological Inscription," 21. The two Achebe stories applauded by Simatei are *Chike and the River* (1981; originally published in 1966) and *The Drum* (1977). The first is an initiation tale about a young boy's move from rural to urban life. The second is an

animal fable about how power corrupts. Neither one lends itself to comparison with Ngũgĩ's use of a liberationist storytelling genre.

16. Carla Hayden and Helen Kay Raseroka, "The Good and the Bad: Two Novels of South Africa," *Children's Literature Association Quarterly* 13, no. 1 (Summer 1988): 58.

17. Hayden and Raseroka, "Good and Bad," 57–58.

18. Hayden and Raseroka, "Good and Bad," 57, 58.

19. Zena Sutherland, "Review of *Journey to Jo'Burg: A South African Story*, by Beverley Naidoo," *Bulletin of the Center for Children's Books* 39, no. 9 (May 1986): 175.

20. The title "Crackling Day" was added when this narrative was anthologized in Hazel Rochman's *Somehow Tenderness Survives: Stories of Southern Africa* (New York: Harper & Row, 1988). The story is actually a segment from Abraham's *Tell Freedom* (section 4, book 1). We are quoting from the "school edition" (London: George Allen & Unwin, 1963).

21. Abrahams, "Crackling Day," 33.

22. Morgan Mahanya, *The Wound* (Harare, Zimbabwe: Mambo Press, 1991), 3.

23. Morgan Mahanya, "Betrayed by Trust," in *The Wound*, 14.

24. Morgan Mahanya, "Day of Revenge," in *The Wound*, 33.

25. Ngugi wa Thiong'o *Barrel of a Pen: Resistance to Repression in Neo-Colonial Kenya* (Trenton, N.J.: Africa World Press, 1983), 90, 93.

26. Ngũgĩ wa Thiong'o (James Ngugi) *Homecoming: Essays on African and Caribbean Literature, Culture, and Politics* (London: Heinemann, 1972), xvi.

27. Ngũgĩ wa Thiong'o *Decolonising the Mind: The Politics of Language in African Literature* (London: James Currey; Nairobi: Heinemann Kenya; Portsmouth, N.H.: Heinemann, 1986), 16.

28. Lisa Mitten, "President's Column," *American Indian Libraries Newsletter* 19, no. 4 (Summer 1997): 3.

29. Robert Coles, *The Political Life of Children* (Boston: Atlantic Monthly Press, 1986), 200.

30. Mitten, "President's Column," 3.

31. Christine Nostlinger, "Doing It but Not Doing It," *Bookbird* 31, no. 2 (May 1993): 5.

32. Hazel Rochman, *Against Borders: Promoting Books for a Multicultural World* (Chicago: American Library Association, 1993), 22.

33. Quoted in Roger Sutton, "What Mean We, White Man?" *VOYA (Voice of Youth Advocates)* 15, no. 3 (August 1992): 156.

34. Kalu Ogbaa, "An Interview with Chinua Achebe," *Research in African Literatures* 12, no. 1 (Spring 1981): 2.

35. Niyi Osundare, "How Post-Colonial Is African Literature?" *Matatu* 12 (1994): 207.

36. For a detailed critique of many such novels, see *African Images in Juvenile Literature: Commentaries on Neocolonialist Fiction* by Yulisa Amadu Maddy and Donnarae MacCann (Jefferson, N.C., and London: McFarland & Company, 1996).

37. Phanuel Akubueze Egejuru, *Black Writers: White Audience: A Critical Approach to African Literature* (Hicksville, N.Y.: Exposition Press, 1978), 11.

38. After an upbringing as a privileged white South African, Beverley Naidoo joined the antiapartheid movement while a college student and in 1964 was detained by the government under the "Ninety Days" solitary confinement law. Since the age of 22 she has resided in England. (See *Something about the Author*, vol. 63, edited by Anne Commire, Detroit: Gale Research 1991.)

39. Dorothy Hammond and Alta Jablow, *The Africa That Never Was: Four Centuries of British Writing about Africa* (New York: Twayne, 1970), 9.

40. Ogbaa, "Chinua Achebe," 4–5.

41. Ogbaa, "Chinua Achebe," 10.

42. Ngũgĩ wa Thiong'o and Micere Githae Mũgo, *Trial of Dedan Kimathi*, i.

Bibliography

Abrahams, Peter. Excerpt from book 1 of *Tell Freedom*. School edition edited by W. G. Bebbington, 26–35. London: George Allen & Unwin, 1963. Reprinted as "Crackling Day" in Hazel Rochman, *Somehow Tenderness Survives: Stories of Southern Africa*, 7–18. New York: Harper & Row, 1988.

Ausubel, Herman. *The Late Victorians: A Short History*. New York: Van Nostrand, 1955.

Berman, Bruce. *Control and Crisis in Colonial Kenya: The Dialectic of Domination*. London: James Currey; Nairobi: Heinemann Kenya; Athens: Ohio University Press, 1990.

Coles, Robert. *The Political Life of Children*. Boston: Atlantic Monthly Press, 1986.

Egejuru, Phanuel Akubueze. *Black Writers: White Audience: A Critical Approach to African Literature*. Hicksville, N.Y.: Exposition Press, 1978.

Hale, Frederick. "Ngũgĩ wa Thiong'o's Mau Mau for Children," *Children's Literature Association Quarterly* 20, no. 3 (Fall 1995): 129–34.

Hammond, Dorothy, and Alta Jablow. *The Africa That Never Was: Four Centuries of British Writing about Africa*. New York: Twayne, 1970.

Hayden, Carla, and Helen Kay Raseroka. "The Good and the Bad: Two Novels of South Africa," *Children's Literature Association Quarterly* 13, no. 1 (Summer 1988): 57–60.

Mahanya, Morgan. *The Wound*. Harare, Zimbabwe: Mambo Press, 1991.

Mitten, Lisa. "President's Column," *American Indian Libraries Newsletter* 19, no. 4 (Summer 1997): 3–4.

Naidoo, Beverley. *Journey to Jo'burg: A South African Story*. Illustrated by Eric Velasquez. New York: J. B. Lippincott, 1986.

Ngugi wa Thiong'o. *Homecoming: Essays on African and Caribbean Literature, Culture, and Politics*. London: Heinemann, 1972.

———. *Njamba Nene and the Flying Bus*. Illustrations by Emmanuel Kariuki. Nairobi: Heinemann Kenya, 1982; first English translation, 1986.

———. *Barrel of a Pen: Resistance to Repression in Neo-Colonial Kenya*. Trenton, N.J.: Africa World Press, 1983.

———. *Njamba Nene's Pistol*. Illustrations by Emmanuel Kariuki. Nairobi: Heinemann Kenya, 1984; first English translation, 1986.

———. *Decolonising the Mind: The Politics of Language in African Literature*. London: James Currey; Nairobi: Heinemann Kenya; Portsmouth, N.H.: Heinemann, 1986.

Ngũgĩ wa Thiong'o and Micere Githae Mũgo. *The Trial of Dedan Kimathi*. Oxford: Heinemann, 1976.

Nostlinger, Christine. "Doing It but Not Doing It," *Bookbird* 31, no. 2 (May 1993): 4.

Ogbaa, Kalu. "An Interview with Chinua Achebe," *Research in African Literatures* 12, no. 1 (Spring 1981): 1–13.

Osundare, Niyi. "How Post-Colonial Is African Literature?" *Matatu* 12 (1994): 203–16.

Rochman, Hazel. *Against Borders: Promoting Books for a Multicultural World*. Chicago: American Library Association, 1993.

Simatei, Peter T. "Ideological Inscription in Children's Fiction: Strategies of Encodement in Ngugi and Achebe." In *Other Worlds, Other Lives: Children's Literature Experiences. Proceedings of the International Conference on Children's Literature, April 4–6, 1995*. Vol. 2, 17–31. Edited by Myrna Machet, Sandra Olen, and Thomas van der Walt. Pretoria: University of South Africa, 1996.

Sutherland, Zena. Review of *Journey to Jo'burg: A South African Story*, by Beverley Naidoo. *Bulletin of the Center for Children's Books* 39, no. 9 (May 1986): 175.

Sutton, Roger. "What Mean We, White Man?" *VOYA (Voice of Youth Advocates)* 15, no. 3 (August 1992): 155–58.

Ngugi wa Thiong'o and
the Writing of Kenyan History

Carol Sicherman

When Heinemann decided to reissue some of the most successful titles of its African Writers Series in a new format, Ngugi wa Thiong'o took advantage of the opportunity to revise certain details and to add significantly new passages in *A Grain of Wheat*.[1] Two of the revisions, a change in political terminology and a correction of a historical detail, hint suggestively at my topic: the emergence of Ngugi's mature understanding of the role of history in African literature and of his own role in the rewriting of Kenyan history. Regarding a writer as the "conscience of the nation" (Darling 16), Ngugi intends to make his compatriots see the history of Kenya for the last hundred years as the story of resistance to colonialism—and to neocolonialism.

First, in revising *Grain* Ngugi has changed the term "the Party" to "the Movement." Bitter at the betrayal by the Kenyan African National Union (KANU) of its own ideals, he refuses to see it as the inheritor of the nationalistic movement. The narrator's explanation at the beginning of chapter 2 of *Grain* reflects popular perception of KANU (founded in 1960) as the culmination of a political evolution stemming from Harry Thuku's East African Association (founded in 1921):

> ... to most people, especially those in the younger generation, the Party [Movement] had always been there, a rallying centre for action. It changed names; leaders came and went but the Party [Movement] remained, opening new visions, gathering greater and greater strength, till on the eve of Uhuru, its influence stretched from one horizon touching the sea to the other resting on the great Lake. (11, 10)

But from the moment of Uhuru, as illustrated by the local MP in *Grain,* KANU bid good-bye to revolution and embraced neocolonialism. A self-serving Party—since 1969 the *only* party, and *de jure* the only party since 9 June 1981—it cannot be linked with the idealistic Movement whose martyrs

Reprinted with permission from Indiana University Press from Carol M. Sicherman, "Ngugi wa Thiong'o and the Writing of Kenyan History," *Research in African Literatures* (Indiana University Press) 20, no. 3 (Fall 1989): 347–70.

Ngugi celebrates. Hence the pointed addition given to General R. in the revised *Grain*. Following his comment "We get Uhuru today," he says in the revision; "But what's the meaning of 'Uhuru'? It is contained in the name of our Movement: Land and Freedom" (192, 221); thus the Movement is explicitly identified not with KANU but with Dedan Kimathi's Land and Freedom Army, commonly known as Mau Mau, which is of course the great historical theme of Ngugi's writing.

Second, Ngugi has corrected a historical error. In chapter 2 the elderly Warui is reminiscing about the brutal suppression of the crowd demonstrating on behalf of Harry Thuku in 1922;[2] the first version reads: "Three men raised their arms in the air. . . . Within a few seconds the big crowd had dispersed; nothing remained but *fifteen crooked watchers* on the ground, outside the State House" (14, emphasis added). The term "crooked watchers" for the slain demonstrators is startlingly evocative, but the error in number is just as startling. Even the official coroner's figure—twenty-one—was higher; the most widely accepted figure is 150, which is what Ngugi uses in the revision (13) as well as in *Detained* (82) and *Barrel of a Pen* (30). This revision, like the change from "Party" to "Movement," implies not mere devotion to detail but a larger mission that has come to dominate Ngugi's thinking as a creative writer. Promising monuments to the Mau Mau fighters, the members of the Uhuru government instead busied themselves accumulating private wealth. Rather than enact the ideal of the Land and Freedom Army, the government memorialized its leader by renaming one of the principal shopping streets of central Nairobi, lined with expensive stores and businesses, "Kimathi Avenue." Kimathi's prophecy in 1954 that "portraits and statues of our heroes" would stand in Kenyan cities while "those of the Colonialists which stand there now will be pulled down" (qtd. in Itote, *"Mau Mau" General* 146) has remained unfulfilled. If the government reneged on its promise, Ngugi determined to fulfill it: his works constitute a developing monument to the freedom struggle, a struggle that Ngugi now sees as stretching from the early resistance of Waiyaki (d. 1892) right into the underground movement that (he hints in *Devil on the Cross*) took shape in the late 1970s and that now, called Mwakenya, challenges the government of President Daniel arap Moi. Although there is no evidence of Ngugi's participation in Mwakenya activities,[3] accusations of such participation by the Moi government contain a symbolic truth, for his writing has unquestionably been a major inspiration to the current Kenyan resistance.

In order to understand Ngugi's deploying of the history of Kenyan resistance, we need to know its political, cultural, and historiographical context. We need, further, to recognize that Ngugi blurs the lines between history and literature and that, perhaps as a consequence of this blurring of the two genres, the distinction between Ngugi and his narrators and certain characters also becomes blurred. This is certainly the case in the work on which I will focus, *Petals of Blood,* in which Ngugi's ideas are voiced by

Karega and the lawyer (as well as by the collective "we" that at times assumes the narrative function). I will need first to sketch the evolution of Ngugi's handling of history and his emerging perceptions of the kind of history needed for Kenya, then to discuss his challenge to Kenyan historians (and to Ngugi himself as erstwhile historian), and finally to assess his critique of the first generation of Kenyan historians—who are, of course, Ngugi's age-mates. Having described this background, I can proceed to discuss interpretations of resistance, focusing first on Waiyaki, perceived as progenitor of the pre-presidential Kenyatta and of Mau Mau as well, and then on Mau Mau as the largest example. In both cases we will see an intermingling of history and legend—indeed, a transformation of legend into history—as well as fierce ideological disputes. A brief reflection on Ngugi's readership will bring this essay to an end if not a conclusion; no conclusion is possible, for the story continues.

1

The "ideal" African novel, Ngugi told an interviewer in 1969, would "embrace the pre-colonial past[,] . . . the colonial past, and the post-indepen-dence period with a pointer to the future" (Friedberger ii)—a description of *Petals of Blood,* the novel that he started to write the following year. By then he knew that, like his character Munira, he "had to take a drastic step that would restore me to my usurped history, my usurped inheritance, that would reconnect me with my history" (*Petals of Blood* 227). Whereas Munira eventu-ally retreats into religious fundamentalism, Ngugi has accomplished the reconnection.

Preoccupied with history from the start, Ngugi has gradually altered his view of the relationship of literature to history and the relationship of himself as creative writer to Kenyan historians. From the nationalist enthusiasm of a student writer living abroad, he has moved through the middle ground of *A Grain of Wheat* to the forthright evangelism of *The Trial of Dedan Kimathi, Petals of Blood,* and the later works—a writer tested by mature combat with the forces of neocolonialism at home. It must not be forgotten that *The River Between* and *Weep Not, Child* were both written while he was an undergraduate at Makerere College in Uganda and *A Grain of Wheat* while he was an MA student at Leeds University in England. The burgeoning of his political awareness during his years at Leeds (1964–67) certainly affected *Grain* but did not fully blossom until *Trial.*

Ngugi's first three novels, which look back in time, form a quasi trilogy in chronological progression that runs from *The River Between* (1965; drafted in 1960), *Weep Not, Child* (1964; drafted in 1962), and *A Grain of Wheat* (1967; completed in 1966)—running from the female circumcision controversy that came to a head in 1929 and led to the development of Gikuyu independent schools (*River*), through the Emergency (1952–56) declared to suppress Mau Mau (*Weep*), to the critical moment of Independence (*Grain*). The next novel picks up chronologically where *Grain* leaves off: set during the twelve years up to and including the very years when Ngugi was writing it (1970–75), *Petals* looks at the present in the light of the past. *Petals* contains not only many reminiscences of Mau Mau but also panoramic allusions to the more distant African past and to the black diaspora, going back through what Ngugi calls "a huge space of time" to show "three different phases of social formations: a long period of precapitalist, precolonialist, relations," then colonialism, and finally neocolonialism ("RW Interview" 10). The way in which past and present are viewed is reversed in the play *The Trial of Dedan Kimathi* (1976; written 1974–76), which looks at the past in the light of the present in an attempt to assess the enduring legacy of Mau Mau to independent Kenya. *I Will Marry When I Want*—the English title of Ngugi's first Gikuyu play, *Ngaahika Ndeenda*—looks squarely at the present, with an implied agenda for change. Finally, *Devil on the Cross,* his first Gikuyu novel (*Caitaani Mutharaba-ini*), looks at the present in the light of the future, setting a satiric critique of contemporary Kenya against a vision of a socialist Kenya purged of neocolonialism—the fulfillment of Ngugi's early requirement that the writer "be prepared to suggest" a future (Nagenda and Serumaga, "A Discussion" iii).

References to historical figures and events of earlier periods are nearly as important as the historical settings. Except for his apprentice plays and earlier short stories, Ngugi's works are dense with allusions to historical personages and events, the density becoming most marked in *Petals of Blood*. Even where the allusions are general rather than exact—"Siriana," for example, although modeled on Alliance High School, is founded some years before the actual founding of Alliance in 1926—the fiction is deeply imbued with history.

From the beginning Ngugi deliberately mixed fictional names with those of historical characters, hoping to heighten the illusion of fictional "reality";[4] as he says in the author's note to *Grain*, "fictitious" characters exist in a real "situation and [among] . . . problems [that] are real." Even so, he apparently felt some uneasiness about intermixing history and fiction; the author's note also explains that historical figures "like . . . Jomo Kenyatta and Waiyaki are unavoidably mentioned." In his subsequent works, there are no such apologies and certainly no avoidance; increasingly, the fictional characters intermingle with historical characters and events, functioning as illustrators of history.

In the earlier books, historical allusions are vague and inaccurate. The representation of the 1922 demonstration and massacre in the first version of *Grain,* faulty though it is, at least reduced the extraordinary understatement of *Weep:* "People were shot and three of them died" (42). After *Grain,* it would seem, Ngugi read Kenyan history more attentively, unimpeded by the blinders of his colonial education. With Micere Mugo he conducted secondary research in English and primary research in Gikuyu while writing on *The Trial of Dedan Kimathi,* a work of the imagination that purports to contribute to the revision of Kenyan history that Ngugi regards as essential to his country's liberation from the colonial legacy. Perhaps doing historical research helped hone the awareness of history and of Kenyan historiography permeating his fourth novel.

Petals of Blood is thick with allusions to world black history and contains a number of pointed historiographical disquisitions. Indeed, the aesthetics of his fiction changes (for the worse, some critics argue), and there is often little difference between the writing in certain passages of the novel and in the closely related nonfiction written soon after (in particular, *Detained*). The scope of historical reference has widened in both time and space, ranging from the distant, legendary past "of Ndemi and the creators from Malindi to Songhai" to the nineteenth and twentieth centuries—"the past of L'Ouverture, Turner, Chaka, *Abdulla,* Koitalel, *Ole Masai,* Kimathi, Mathenge" (*Petals* 214; my italics indicate fictional characters). Against a backdrop of broadly sketched grandeur achieved long before by "the creators," the fictional characters take their place among not only the heroes of Kenyan resistance—from the early twentieth century (Koitalel arap Samoei) to Mau Mau (Dedan Kimathi, Stanley Mathenge)—but also among the heroes of resistance a century earlier elsewhere in Africa (Chaka) and the New World (Toussaint L'Ouverture, Nat Turner). To contrast with the heroes, Ngugi lists a demonology, with three historical figures from the earlier twentieth century preceding their fictional analogues from the later twentieth century: "Kinyanjui, Mumia, Lenana, *Chui, Jerrod, Nderi wa Riera*" (*Petals* 214).

The purpose of such collocations of historical and fictional characters is to make Kenyan readers reflect on their own place in the continuum of history. Sounding like a miniature Karega, the wise young hero of Ngugi's first children's book advises his classmates how to find their way out of the forest: "We must . . . find out where we are, in order to decide where we will go next. We cannot know where we are, without first finding out where we come from" (*Njamba Nene and the Flying Bus* 19; cf. *Petals* 127–28). The Kenyan view of the past, Ngugi said in a 1978 interview, "up to now has been distorted by the cultural needs of imperialism"—needs that led historians to show "[first,] that Kenyan people had not struggled with nature and with other men to change their natural environment and create a positive social environment . . . [and second, that they] had not resisted foreign domination" ("Interview" 10).

The first omission to which Ngugi calls attention concerns the history of common people, who were completely ignored by colonial and postcolonial historians despite the professed interest of the latter in "the history of the inarticulate" (Temu and Swai 3–5). Ngugi's call for a history of the anonymous masses reacts to the commonplaces of his early education, when it was

in the interest of colonial historians "to stress what they claimed was the natural logic of Europeans in colonizing and dominating the Kenyan" (Wanjohi
668). Sir Philip Mitchell (governor of Kenya, 1944–52) saw "the Native as
hampered by a past in which he has been notoriously slow to meet what Dr.
Toynbee has described as the challenge of his environment," evincing "a sin-
gular incapacity either to devise for himself or to adopt from others the means
of improving his material or intellectual life" (Lord Hailey, in Mitchell xiii).
"Nothing, except a little gradual change," had occurred to the "ignorant and
primitive population" in East Africa during the thirty thousand years
between Stone Age man and Dr. Livingstone (Mitchell 18–19)—a conception of Africa as "primitive, static, and asleep or in a Hobbessian state of
nature" that has long since been exploded (Boahen 23). Given his premise,
Mitchell naturally celebrates "what an enlightened colonialism can do for the
dark places" that still preserve the static barbaric past (268). In contrast,
Kenyan historians today note the ability of precolonial peoples to adapt to
difficult material conditions.

The second element neglected by colonial historians—resistance to foreign incursions—divides into two parts: the history of mass movements and
the history of heroes. A focus on certain heroes and on the creation of nation-
states can help support the newly independent African states, led by heroes
like Kenyatta, so that the postcolonial becomes, in Ngugi's terms, the neocolonial. Thus the new historians, wittingly or not, become servants of the
state: ". . . we are," William R. Ochieng' has rather pompously but correctly
declared, "the founding fathers of the Kenya nation" ("Colonial African
Chiefs" 46). Nation building necessarily involves myth building, and myths,
as the Tanzanian historian Nelson Kasfir has said, may "decolonise African
peoples by restoring their dignity" (qtd. in Neale 48). It is the choice of myth
that is crucial. Many of the intellectual clashes in contemporary Kenya are
between rival mythologies—very often between conflicting myths of Mau
Mau but also between the historians' myth of a past splendid insofar as it
rivaled white successes, and Ngugi's myth of the people's centuries-long
"heroic resistance . . . their struggles to defend their land, their wealth, their
lives" (see Neale 49, 106; Were and Wilson 44; Ngugi *Petals* 67).

2

Although Ngugi's conception of Kenyan history and his charges against the
historians are open to some question, the call for action with which he concluded the interview quoted earlier has obvious relevance to his own practice
as a novelist:

> Kenyan intellectuals must be able to tell these stories, or histories, or history of
> heroic resistance to foreign domination by Kenyan people . . . looking at ourselves

as . . . as a people whose history shines with the grandeur, if you like, of heroic resistance and achievement of the Kenyan people. . . . I feel that Kenyan history, either pre-colonial or colonial[,] has not yet been written. ("Interview" 11)

That history, he says in *Detained,* will show the "history of Kenyan people creating a . . . fight-back, creative culture" (64). Because of the deficiencies of professional historians, Ngugi argues, at the present time this story can be better told through literature.

Petals of Blood insists at some length on revising Kenyan historiography, first through the futile efforts of Karega to find suitable history texts for his pupils—a genuine difficulty, according to Neale (see ch. 2)—and then in Karega's appeal to the lawyer for help in his quest for "a vision of the future rooted in a critical awareness of the past," an awareness more specifically of economic history (198). The lawyer sends him "books and a list of other titles written by professors of learning at the University," the same university where Ngugi taught. But the books fail to answer his questions.

In a calmly magisterial review of "Three Decades of Historical Studies in East Africa, 1949–1977," Professor Bethwell A. Ogot, doyen of Kenyan historians, remarks ironically on those who have been disappointed in their search for "a usable past," people who "are seeking freedom to tackle present-day problems . . . without constantly looking over their shoulder for precedents from the dead and irrelevant past" (31). But the past is neither dead nor irrelevant to the searcher who seeks the roots of the present in the past. Ogot forgets that the past may become "usable" if suitably constructed. His own mainly biographical *Historical Dictionary of Kenya* (1980), useful for what it contains, is badly marred by its omissions, lacking any mention of the notorious detention camps and significantly omitting some of the "heroes" and "traitors" whom Ngugi has increasingly invoked—Laibon Turugat, Stanley Mathenge, Fenner Brockway (Kenyanized as Fenna Brokowi in *Grain* 56; 63), and many others—as well as some of the important episodes of resistance, such as the Giriama Rising of 1914. In other "neocolonialist" texts, the past is, from Ngugi's point of view, distorted: Mau Mau fighters are depicted as "extremists"; the colonial government, as an agent of "constitutional advance" leading to "a multi-racial society" (Were and Wilson 270–72; cf. Buijtenhuijs, *Mau Mau* 75). Precolonial history, according to the Mitchell-like "professors of learning," depicts "wanderlust and pointless warfare between peoples" evincing "primitivity" or "undercivilization" (*Petals* 199). Ngugi may allude here to Ochieng', who sees African history up to 1900 as the story of "migrating hordes" and says that Africa failed to become "civilized" ("Undercivilization" 2–3, 5, 8, 16).

In contrast to this approach, there is Karega's capsule history of Africa:

In the beginning he [Mr. Blackman] had the land and the mind and the soul together. On the second day, they took the body away to barter it for silver coins. On the third day, seeing that he was still fighting back, they brought priests and educators to bind his mind and soul so that these foreigners could more easily take his land and its produce. (*Petals* 236)

The binding of mind and soul, Ngugi maintains, still exists and is the reason Kenya needs a new historiography. Karega speaks for his creator when he tells Munira:

Our children must look at the things that deformed us yesterday, that are deforming us today. They must also look at the things which formed us yesterday, that will creatively form us into a new breed of men and women who will . . . struggle against those things that dwarf us. (*Petals* 247)

Ngugi's understanding of his major theme, the history of resistance, has broadened since his undergraduate writing when his knowledge was limited to the Mau Mau rising and to a few major figures or episodes—Waiyaki's resistance and death in the early 1890s, Harry Thuku's campaign against colonial restrictions in 1921–22, the female circumcision controversy of 1929–31. In these works, legend carries equal weight with documentable history. Particularly in *The River Between* and *Weep Not, Child,* he emphasizes the prophecy of the seer Mugo wa Kibiro, with its dual message of the coming of the white man and the folly of resistance; there is an implication here, as Gitahi-Gititi has observed, that aside from Mau Mau and a few other episodes, "the Gikuyu people offered no resistance to colonial penetration" (36)—an implication that Ngugi began to correct in *A Grain of Wheat* and wholeheartedly attacked in *The Trial of Dedan Kimathi* and *Petals of Blood.*

From 1976 on Ngugi has made plain his determination to participate in the decolonizing of Kenyan history. Indeed, in his later works he deliberately has dealt with periods and figures neglected by professional historians, as when he set his suppressed musical *Maitu Njugira* ("Mother Sing to Me"), in the 1930s, a period "almost totally ignored by Kenyan historians" (Gachie 13). *Maitu Njugira* dramatizes "actual history" based on Ngugi's research into "the actual laws and ordinances" of the 1930s (Gachie 13). "These things of the past cement the present," said one of the actors (qtd. in Gachie 19); they create links to the future and at the same time implications too unpleasant for the government to countenance. "Writers are surgeons of the heart and souls of a community" (*Decolonising* ix), but official Kenya declines the operation, retaining the old Kenyan history.

But what does the phrase "Kenyan history" mean? Karari Njama describes the pre-high school curriculum at Alliance High School in the 1940s, where Ngugi studied a decade later:

In History we had been taught all the good the white man had brought us— the stopping of tribal wars, guaranteeing security . . . , good clothings, education and religion, easy ways of communication and travel . . . and, finally, better jobs that would make it easy to raise the standard of living above the uned-ucated Africans. . . . In teaching Kenya History, the question of land was cun-ningly omitted. (Barnett and Njama 96)

This is the background for the school strike in *Petals:* "We wanted to be taught African literature, African history, for we wanted to know ourselves better" (170). Why should a student seeking an "education that will fit [him] in [his] own environment" be given instead "a lot about English Pirates and English Kings, and practically nothing of his local geography and history"—an education that makes him "a misfit in his own community?" (Kakembo 7).

History was the field that offered the most scope to African intellectual initiatives in the 1940s and 1950s, but these had to take place outside of offi-cial confines because for an African to take "an interest in his people's past was unhealthy, . . . a betrayal of the civilization to which he attached himself when he was educated and baptized a Christian" (Rosberg and Nottingham 132). Well before Independence, however, nationalist stirrings provided unof-ficial alternative education at Alliance High School, where a secret political and educational organization taught "how the English people acquired their supremacy, how they came to our country, how they alienated our lands, and how hypocritical they are in their Christianity" (Barnett and Njama 100).

Although the official history of colonial times has gone, no comparably assured version has replaced it,[5] for three main reasons: first, the particular historical bias imparted in the waning days of colonialism to the first post-Independence generation of African intellectuals, a bias incorporated in lan-guage; second, the absence of substantial written documentation for much of the precolonial past, which poses formidable problems of reconstruction from oral, linguistic, and archaeological sources; and, third and most important, the continued politicizing of intellectual discourse in the period following Independence.

The colonial view of history did not simply disappear at Independence, when European scholars of African history began to be replaced by their African pupils. "The history of East Africa," wrote Sir Reginald Coupland in 1938, "is only the history of its invaders"; it is thus the history of "the com-ings and goings of brown men and white men on the coast," behind which stretches the Conradian "impenetrable darkness" of Black Africa (14). Trevor-Roper's now-classic formulation of this attitude (9), uttered only two months before Kenya's Independence, is, as Feuser has shown (53–54), typical enough of European attitudes then and for more than a hundred previous years.

Deeply imbued with European values, the nationalist historians who emerged in the 1960s often took their mentors' history and produced "the older version turned upside down, with many of its faults intact" (Neale 4; cf. Temu and Swai 154). They took it for granted that progress was evolutionary and that "unity is the basis of progress" (Neale 3–21, 155), the latter assumption familiar in Kenyatta's theme-slogan, "We all fought for Uhuru" (cf. the Politician in *Trial* 47 and Kimeria in *Petals* 153). The carryover of European assumptions was, however, masked by an appearance of African nationalism. In the 1960s—the "golden age of consensus" (Temu and Swai 63)—historians dwelt on three themes: "the bliss that was African life before the coming of the Europeans"; "the injustice of colonialism"; and "how gloriously the African fought his way to *Uhuru*" (Atieno Odhiambo, " 'Mind Limps' " 7–8).

Ngugi himself, with his automatic adjective "glorious," seems to fall into this self-congratulatory pattern of thinking when he has his narrator reflect:

> [Ilmorog] had had its days of glory: thriving villages with a huge population of sturdy peasants who had tamed nature's forest. . . . And at harvest time . . . the aged would sip honey beer and tell the children, with voices taut with prideful authority and nostalgia, about the founding patriarch. (*Petals* 120)

Although the phrases roll out automatically in this passage, later Karega rejects such "worship" of the past in a passage that sounds like Ngugi's own recantation: "Maybe I used to [worship] it: but I don't want to continue worshipping in the temples of a past without tarmac roads, without electric cookers, a world dominated by slavery to nature"; the people who "tamed nature's forest," he feels, had become nature's slaves (*Petals* 323; cf. *Trial* 72). Furthermore, Ngugi's sharp distinction between traitors and collaborators saves him from the tendency of historians as well as politicians to paint *all* colonial peoples as somehow resisters (see Neale 107–08).

"Neocolonial" historians—Ngugi names "[Bethwell A.] Ogot, [Godfrey] Muriuki, [Gideon] Were and [William R.] Ochieng"—are merely "following on similar theories yarned out by defenders of imperialism" who "insist that we only arrived here yesterday" (*Petals* 67). "Arrival" for such historians, Ngugi implies, means arrival of the "modern" (i.e., Western-style) nation—even though, as John Lonsdale has remarked, "the most distinctively African contribution to human history could be said to have been precisely the civilized art of living fairly peaceably together *not* in states" ("States and Social Processes" 139). There are, consequently, "many questions about our history which remain unanswered," such as the history of international trade *before* the Portuguese "ushered in an era . . . that climaxed in the reign of imperialism over Kenya" and the resultant "heroic resistance" (*Petals* 67).

An evaluation of Ngugi's charges against Kenyan historians should start with the correction implied in his own more recent work. *Detained,* indeed, stands in mild reproof to the author of *Petals of Blood,* for in the later book Ngugi demonstrates research in books like Ghai and MacAuslan's *Public Law and Political Change in Kenya* (see *Detained* 44) and, more significantly, in works by the very historians he reviles in *Petals,* including Ogot and Ochieng'.[6] A work by another of the supposed "neocolonial" historians,

Gideon Were's *Western Kenya Historical Documents,* stands as an example of important research in oral history; Were's use of the word "documents" to describe the contents of his book implicitly challenges the notion that historians depend on *written* documents (see also Vansina 173–202; Mazrui, *Cultural Engineering* 4–7; Temu and Swai 113). Finally, the treatment by Godfrey Muriuki of the early colonial paramount chief Kinyanjui, in a widely respected study focusing on precolonial Gikuyu history, stands as a good example of precisely the kind of history that Ngugi calls for. Muriuki makes plain that Kinyanjui—one of the "traitors" who were "collaborators with the enemy" (*Detained* 55) to whom Ngugi repeatedly refers (*Petals* 214, *Trial* 32, *Detained* 82)—was typical of those chiefs created by the British out of "nonentities in the traditional society": men who, in gratitude for their masters' donation of power, were willing to support British interest "at all costs in order to bolster up their position and influence outside the traditional structure" (Muriuki, *History* 93). Yet while Muriuki's own accomplishment as a historian is impressive, he himself acknowledges that historical studies in Kenya have accomplished little and, in fact, are in crisis, with student enrollment plummeting and research funds nonexistent ("Historiography" 205, 213).

Besides the ideological or political-prudential reason for the absence of consensus on Kenyan history, there is another and very practical cause: events and people lacking a connection with Europeans were also often lacking written documentation, and the historian must unravel oral history and analyze physical and linguistic evidence in order to assemble a coherent account of historical developments. Ngugi's narrator explains: "Just now we can only depend on legends passed from generation to generation by the poets and players . . . supplemented by the most recent archaeological and linguistic researches and also by what we can glean from between the lines of the records of the colonial adventurers" (*Petals* 67–68). It remains to be seen whether this kind of history, necessarily local and tribal, can be incorporated in a truly "national" history, one that would achieve Ngugi's goal of unifying the country.

These problems of documentation, although imposing, pale before the third cause of historiographical difficulty: contemporary politics, which of course involves the dominant neocolonial ideology. What one of Ngugi's principal intellectual antagonists, William R. Ochieng', has said of *Detained*—"to Ngugi history is simply a propaganda instrument in the service of a chosen ideology" ("Autobiography" 97)—could be said generally of historical writing, although in both genres the best writing rejects propaganda for legitimate and knowledgeable interpretation. A month before Kenyan Independence, Ali Mazrui observed (echoing Ernest Renan) "that one essential factor in the making of a nation is 'to get one's history wrong,' " to be *"selective* about what did happen" so as to build national unity (*On Heroes* 21). Characteristic of the 1960s and early 1970s, the vigorous tone of the statement, as well as its content, is a direct contradiction of the colonialist historians' claim that knowledge is neutral, a claim that deflected any challenge on ideological grounds.

There are no "pure facts"; everything "involve[s] interpretation" (*Petals* 246). But writers must be conscious that they *are* interpreting. Writers on history must recognize that the basic terms of historical writing—"collaboration," "resistance," "nationalism"—still need definition, and Ngugi gives them a nudge in this direction. "The government says we should bury the past," the betrayer Mugo says in *A Grain of Wheat*, but Gikonyo cries: "I can't forget. . . . I will never forget" (59; 67). It is therefore essential to "choose your side" (*Petals* 200). This injunction marks a distinct change in Ngugi's fiction; the experience of detention and his more extensive reading in Kenyan history have helped him recognize that "an intellectual is not a neutral figure in society" (Omari 1).

Interviewing Ngugi shortly after the publication of *Detained*, Emman Omari suggested provocatively that in his "extremity the objectivity is buried": "You have melodiously clapped hands for active resisters like the Kimathis; and . . . you have snapped at the Mumias" (Mumia, an early colonial chief patronized by the British, was their enthusiastic ally). Ngugi acknowledged Omari's implications: "When writing history for our children, which things do we want them to admire? Should they emulate traitors or heroes?" (1). And Ngugi knows who is who, with Waiyaki foremost in the pantheon of heroes and Kinyanjui, Waiyaki's betrayer, prominent among the traitors. This either/or mentality unfortunately characterizes much of the intellectual and political discourse in Kenya today, despite appeals for finer discriminations.

The issue, as Ngugi sees it, is whether Kenya's rulers wish to lead a truly independent country, or whether they are—as he charges—merely lackeys for multinational businesses, the "thieves and robbers" of *Devil on the Cross*. Although historians have a particular responsibility to attempt clearheaded analysis, most remain partisan: like their own colonial teachers, they "delighted in abusing and denigrating the efforts of the people and their struggles in the past" (*Petals* 199). Despite his bias, Ngugi's challenge makes *Petals of Blood* "compulsory reading" for African historians (Neale 144), while at the same time his own efforts have met with considerable criticism, partly for scholarly reasons and partly for political ones. Establishment critics accuse him of negativism in his earlier works and lack of artistry in his more recent, "committed" writing: as soon as he "seemed to have an axe to grind"—that is, after *A Grain of Wheat*—"he . . . ceased to be a creative writer" and wrote mere "propaganda" (" 'Exiled' Dissidents" 4, 7).

3

Displaying their profession's common inability to accept literary interpretations of their field—rejecting that "blending of fact and fiction [that] . . . is precisely what makes it important" (Fleming 20)—historians object both to Ngugi's carelessness with details and to his promoting myth as history. Ngugi is conscious of this element in his writing: "This Harry Thuku [whose followers, demonstrating against his arrest, were massacred by police] has already moved into patriotic heroic legends and I have treated him as such in the early chapters of *A Grain of Wheat*" (*Detained* 82). But Ngugi also knows the historical Thuku, who fought against "forced labour, female and child slavery, high taxation without even a little representation, low wages, and against the oppressive *kipande* [pass] that the workers were obliged to carry with chains around their necks" (*Detained* 81)—all, except for the mention of "slavery," elements of Thuku's campaign frequently mentioned by historians. Literary treatments of history include legend as well as "facts" because writers seek to discover "not only what has happened"—the historians' task—"but the *ways* in which things are felt to happen in history" (Neale 187). And the ways in which things are *felt* to happen may actually affect the way things *do* happen. Ngugi's Kenyan readers know full well how indistinguishable the exploits of Dedan Kimathi the historical figure (1920–57) are from those of Dedan Kimathi the legendary figure, and how the legend in turn inspired military action—facts—by Kimathi's followers.

Another major twentieth-century historical figure who became mythologized is Jomo Kenyatta, who is referred to a number of times in *A Grain of Wheat* and *Weep Not, Child*—often by his popular name, "The Burning Spear," a characteristic mythologizing appellation. Ngugi's treatment of Kenyatta was the subject of another paper by Ochieng' at the 1984 conference, a reproof for the mythologizing portrayal in the early novels and an attack on Ngugi's later analysis of Kenyatta as a failed hero, one who betrayed his country. Again controversy ensued, with Ochieng' defended by his colleague Henry Mwanzi through the same technique that Ochieng' had used in attacking Ngugi's depiction of the Mau Mau as a national liberation movement—bald assertion. It is difficult to write history about legends. Kenyatta may not have been the "fire-spitting nationalist that Ngugi imagined him to be" (Ochieng', "Ghost" 10), but Ngugi's imagination was not peculiar to himself, as Ochieng' acknowledges; he grew up with "myths" and "tribal gossip" about Kenyatta that then became part of history when people acted upon their beliefs (Ochieng', "Ghost" 3, 10).

A fascinating example of such mythologizing occurs in the history—or story—of Waiyaki, a Gikuyu leader of resistance against the British in the early 1890s. Whether Waiyaki was consistently such a leader is open to doubt, as are the circumstances of his death. But in *A Grain of Wheat*, doubts matter far less that what Ochieng' disparagingly calls "rumor" or "gossip"— the legend of "Waiyaki and other warrior-leaders [who] took arms" against the "long line of other red strangers who carried, not the Bible, but the sword" (*Grain* 12; 12). Defeated by the superior technology of "the whiteman with bamboo poles that vomited fire and smoke," Waiyaki was arrested and taken to the coast, bound hands and feet. Later, *so it is said,* Waiyaki was buried alive at Kibwezi with his head facing to the centre of the earth. . . . Then nobody noticed it; but looking back we can see that Waiyaki's blood contained within it a seed, a grain, which gave birth to a political party. (*Grain* 12–13; 12; emphasis added)

The weight Ngugi gives to what "is said," to "rumor" and "gossip" as agents in forming the imaginative life of his people, makes it clear that he knows that actual historical force of what "is said"—its role in politics. Myths made things happen during the Emergency.

The "facts" regarding Waiyaki are difficult to come by. He probably was not buried alive head downward. The most plausible hypothesis to account for the legend is that of T. C. Colchester, a colonial official, in an unpublished note. Colchester observes that until the 1930s the Gikuyu did not ordinarily bury their dead; Waiyaki's burial would have seemed so abnormal as to suggest that he had been "killed by burial," and, as Colchester adds, the coincidental death and burial at Kibwezi some years later of Waiyaki's antagonist, William J. Purkiss, might have fed the legend (2). As far as Waiyaki's character goes, Muriuki is no doubt historically correct: "He was neither the 'scheming rogue'—breathing treachery, fire and brimstone—of the company officials, nor was he the martyr" imagined by nationalists (149). But what is finally most important, where Ngugi is concerned, is not the evaluation of historians but Waiyaki's role in Gikuyu folklore—Waiyaki as martyr, "tortured . . . fighting for his country," an avatar of "the second disciple of God . . . Jomo Kenyatta" (Mau Mau song qtd. in McIntosh 99 n. 129).

Waiyaki—or his legend—caused future events: "When he died, he left a curse that we should never sell our land or let it be taken from us" (Gikoyo 35). The impossibility of confirming the deathbed curse is less important than the belief that people had in its truth, a belief that influenced events sixty years after Waiyaki's death. Waruhiu Itote (a leading Mau Mau general known as "General China") describes a Mau Mau reprisal modeled on Waiyaki's legendary martyrdom, a reprisal that particularly inflamed European opinion. Having been told by a witch doctor that to win the war the Mau Mau "must bury a European alive with a black goat," a Mau Mau did precisely that in 1954: "They buried him [Arundell Gray Leakey] with his face downwards, *as we hear* Waiyaki was buried by the Europeans at Kibwezi" (Itote, *Mau Mau in Action* 26–27; emphasis added). The phrase, *as we hear,* like Ngugi's *so it is said,* testifies both to the strong Gikuyu awareness of their own history in the Mau Mau period and to the power of myth to affect events.

The nearer to the present day the historians get, the more obviously embroiled in controversy their task becomes. The most immediate questions about the relationship of past to present have been provoked by the Mau Mau rising; among the most urgent is the question whether Mau Mau was merely a manifestation of local (Gikuyu) nationalism or, as Ngugi argues, a central and catalytic event in the struggle for Kenyan independence. Whereas Europeans spoke of Mau Mau as a barbaric and atavistic reversion and many educated Africans recognized intelligent and ruthless adaptation, the fighters themselves, agreeing with neither view, commonly saw a mainly laudable and certainly necessary re-creation of the past—a mistake, in the opinion of Karari Njama, himself one of the few educated Mau Mau leaders (Barnett and Njama 413, 336–37). To counter that view, part of the job of first-generation historians was to develop comprehension of the past as not static (the view of illiterate Africans as well as of Europeans) but dynamic.

In their common enterprise of national interpretation historians and writers should support one another, carrying out what the American scholar St. Clair Drake told Ochieng' was the "sacred duty . . . to redeem our race through the written word" (Ochieng', "The Scholar"). Such cooperation does exist; one testimony, indeed, to Ngugi's skill as a literary-historical artist has been citation of his novels by social scientists to illustrate their points (see, for two of many examples, Wanjohi 668 and Furedi 355). But too often the two professions manifest a kind of sibling rivalry evident during a 1984 conference of the Kenya Historical Association devoted to "The Historiography of Kenya: A Critique," which included analyses of literary treatments of history. The literary critics who attended the sessions were quick to point out their colleagues' deficiencies as literary analysts. The historians, said the critic Chris Wanjala, "showed lack of basic understanding about the way literature worked" (31). In a riposte to Wanjala, the historian Henry Mwanzi dismissed "Ngugi's fans" for having "an emotional attachment to the man" that blinded them to "his falsification of our history." In fact, some historians' political antipathy to Ngugi prevents rational discourse. Ochieng' roundly admits that he cannot bear to read Ngugi (his "style bores me to death"), but his aversion did not stop him from writing a review of *Detained* that concludes: "Ngugi is operating beyond the limits of his role as a writer. He is terrorising us ("Dignitaries Not Spared" 47–48). Ochieng's difficulty in reading Ngugi stems partly from the disabling effect of his animus and partly from too narrow a conception of "history," excluding the contribution of legend from its purviews.

The wars of the intellectuals and the post-Uhuru battle for recognition of the ex-freedom fighters were linked in February 1986 during the first commemorative meeting of ex-Mau Mau fighters. One purpose of the meeting was "to find ways to write the history of the Mau Mau movement" as a national phenomenon, refuting non-Gikuyu historians' allegations "that the Mau Mau was a tribal movement or a civil war" (Mutahi 13). To the veterans their history seemed to have vanished. Ngugi's career-long emphasis on Mau Mau has to be seen as a form of resistance to this betrayal by oblivion, as a monument in words to the heroes of the forests.

Remembering for Ngugi requires the painful acknowledgment of imperfection. The heroic Mau Mau model, as readers of *A Grain of Wheat* know, fits few actual freedom fighters; for every Kimathi-style Kihika, there may be dozens or hundreds of Mugos. If the writing of history depends on the truth-telling of the survivors, how dependent are we on the Mugos who conceal the truth? There are records: even while in the forest, the freedom fighters kept "records [that] would form a book of history which would be read by our future generations," a leitmotif in Karati Njama's memoirs (Barnett and Njama 326, cf. 334). These records showed an effort to place contemporary history in a wider context, although the ill-educated writers often knew little of that context. The writer of "A Book of Forest History"—a Mau Mau document captured by British forces—reported a meeting in the forest on 5 December 1953 during which he "learnt a lot of new things and ideas," chiefly concerning alleged English parallels to Mau Mau activities: from the Roman period through the seventeenth century, it seems, the British took oaths and entered the forest, staying "about 120 years" under the Romans ("Book" 2–3).[7] British resistance to Roman imperialism, by offering a precedent to Kenyan resistance, validated the later resistance to British imperialism.

But Kenyan historians have either avoided the Mau Mau records as political hot potatoes or have been so partisan and careless—as in Maina wa Kinyatti's *Kenya's Freedom Struggle,* which omits essential documentation—that they have not advanced our understanding. When previously secret official documents relating to Mau Mau became available in 1984 under the thirty-year rule, the *Standard,* a Nairobi daily, published reports of the "top-secret Mau Mau papers" that focused on British policy. Despite their fairly innocuous content—the first article, with front-page banner headlines, discussed British thinking behind the June 1953 banning of the Kenya African Union—the dispatches aroused such official ire that the *Standard* ceased its reports (see 14 Feb., 1, 6; and 20 Feb., 20). Popular distrust of professional historians is consequently endemic. One speaker at the Mau Mau commemorative meeting urged "that the books and papers authored by Professor Ochieng be banned from Kenyan schools, a proposal that was thunderously supported" (Mutahi 14) although hardly likely to take effect, especially since Ochieng' had just published the first textbook of Kenyan history and was shortly to assume the chair in history at Moi University. Furthermore, President Moi contributed to the 1986 controversy by declaring that the history of the Mau Mau should not be written.

In the same year, a time of sharply escalated repression of intellectuals, Moi made clear his choice of patriotic historian by naming Professor Ogot, who sees Mau Mau as a narrowly tribal rather than as a national struggle, to the position of chairman of the Posts and Telecommunications Corporation.[8] There could be no better confirmation of Temu and Swai's assertions that the so-called "new history . . . has resulted in the production of history to serve a new class of exploiters" (53, 81; cf. Wrigley 123). "Small wonder, then," add Temu and Swai, "that side by side with the development of postcolonial Africanist historiography has developed a crescendo of intellectual McCarthyism" (53)—a remark particularly apt to Kenya in the period following

Ngugi's necessary self-exile, imposed in 1982. One of the sad if understand-able results of the repressive political climate in Kenya has been the drying up of creative writing, a theme of R. N. Ndegwa's reviews (or "laments," as she calls them) of the year's work, published in the *Journal of Commonwealth Literature* (see 20.2 [1985]: 2 and subsequent years).

These are not merely professional but deeply personal matters. Ngugi's political ideas result from an effort to foster an organic connection between his past as the child of peasants steeped in tradition and his present as an international author, the kind of connection that Karega has maintained and that Munira has lost. A spectator of both public and his own private history, Munira suffers from an inability to feel an organic and constructive link to the past: "The repetition of past patterns had always frightened him. It was the tyranny of the past that he had always tried to escape" (*Petals* 249).

Involvement in personal history seems to be a prerequisite for involve-ment in public history. Munira asks, "Could I resurrect the past and connect myself to it, graft myself on the stem of history even if it was only my family's history outside of which I had grown? And would the stem really grow, sprouting branches with me as part of the great resurgence of life?" (244). But Munira hardly knows his siblings, feels both rejection and admiration of his father, is remote from his mother. Nonetheless, despite his claim to be dis-connected from his past, he is overwhelmed by his discovery that Karega was the lover of his sister (the only sibling with whom he felt any connection) and that she killed herself soon after being told by her father to choose between Karega and her family. He also is distressed by the link between Karega's family and his own: Karega's mother was an *ahoi* on his father's land, and Karega's brother Ndung'iri was probably a member of the Mau Mau gang that cut off his father's ear. Only by working through these connections, by converting distress into understanding, could Munira become reintegrated; instead, he retreats into a crazed, ahistorical religiosity.

And there is a societal parallel to Munira's dislocation, in the transfor-mation of the religious center of Ilmorog, "where Mwathi had once lived guarding the secrets of iron works and native medicine" (*Petals* 281), into an archaeological museum, "a site for the curious about the past, long long before East Africa traded with China and the Indies" (266). "The mythical Mwathi" (302) in one sense does not exist and in another exists perennially, his traditional wisdom voiced, we deduce, by his spokesperson, Muturi; he thus stands for the continuity of past with present, which is broken by the earth-moving machines and the archaeologists' scientific labeling. It is the voice of Mwathi that Ngugi's later work strives to transmit.

4

The very density and casualness of Ngugi's allusions to Kenyan historical events and figures in his work published after 1975—as well as the proliferation of untranslated Gikuyu words and phrases—accords with the decision he made, upon completing *Petals of Blood* in October 1975, to write his creative work in Gikuyu. Further, he asserts that "the true beginning of my education" took place in "the six months between June and November of 1977" when, developing his first Gikuyu work in concert with Kamiriithu peasants, he "learnt [his] language anew" and "rediscovered the creative nature and power of collective work" (*Detained* 76). With *Decolonising the Mind* in 1986, he said farewell to all writing in English (except, his practice has shown, journalism.) Some months later, in September 1986, Heinemann Kenya published his second Gikuyu novel, *Matigari ma Njiruungi,* but readers of Gikuyu had little chance to buy it: in February 1987, in yet another act of intellectual suppression, the Kenyan government confiscated all copies in bookshops.

Implicitly, the main audience for Ngugi's work now in both his languages is Kenyan—not just readers of Gikuyu but those Kenyans who must rely on English (there have, however, been some translations into Kiswahili, encouraged by Ngugi). With the switch to Gikuyu or Kiswahili, "I can directly have dialogue with peasants and workers," for he is now "not only writing *about* peasants and workers but . . . *for* peasants and workers" (Omari 15). This change in audience clearly has had an effect on the intermixed genres of *Devil on the Cross.* Readers unacquainted with Gikuyu will increasingly depend not only upon translation but—in the case of nonKenyans at least—upon a more extensive cultural interpretation. The book is not closed on the interrelationships between literature and history; Ngugi has, however, turned a new leaf.[9]

Notes

1. The additions and corrections are included in MS 337272 in the library of the School of Oriental and African Studies, University of London. This is actually a number of separate items; I refer here to the copy of the first version of *Grain,* marked by Ngugi for revision, and the typed list of corrections to be incorporated in the revised 1986 edition. The manuscript is fully described in my *Ngugi wa Thiong'o: A Bibliography of Primary and Secondary Sources: 1957–1987* (Oxford: Hans Zell, 1989). Page references given here to *Grain* are first to the first edition, second to the revision.

2. Oddly, Ngugi does not correct the erroneous date of 1923, which he uses in *Grain* (13, 73, and 208) and *Secret Lives* (43).

3. He is, however, currently the chairman of Umoja, an umbrella organization of dissident groups abroad that supports Mwakenya.

4. Ngugi wa Thiong'o, interview, New York, 20 Oct. 1986.

5. Ochieng''s *A History of Kenya* is a text intended for Kenyan O-level students; the article *A* in the title is significant, acknowledging the impossibility of writing *The History.*

6. For example, Ogot and Ochieng' published their article on Mumboism in 1972, nine years before Ngugi completed *Detained,* in which he mentions "the Mumboist leaders Muraa wa Ngiti, Oteyno, Ongere and others in the 1920s" (49); all of these relatively obscure

figures are treated by Ogot and Ochieng' (153, 157, 160–61, 172), whose article may be the source of Ngugi's allusion.

7. I am grateful to W. H. Thompson, who "captured" this document and deposited it at Rhodes House, Oxford (Mss. Afr. s. 1534), for permission to quote it.

8. He has since been named chairman of Kenya Railways. For his view of Mau Mau, see "Politics."

9. This research was supported (in part) by two grants from the PSC-CUNY Research Award Program of the City University of New York, number 6-66038 and number 667040. In revising the essay, I have benefited from conversations with academics and others in Kenya whom I cannot thank by name because of the political sensitivity of the topic, as well as from readers' reports. Two major historiographical studies that have appeared since completion of this essay in mid-1987 are Bogumil Jewsiewicki's immense paper "African Historical Studies as Academic Knowledge: Radical Scholarship and Usable Past, 1956–1986" commissioned by the ACLS/SSRC Joint Committee on African Studies for presentation at the African Studies Association meeting 20–22 November 1987, and the June 1987 issue of the *African Studies Review* (30.2, published in 1988), devoted to "African History Research Trends and Perspectives on the Future." A work awaiting non-Gikuyu readers at the time of writing this essay was Wangui wa Goro's English translation of *Matigari ma Njiruungi* (Heinemann, 1989), which promised to carry on Ngugi's concern with history; speaking as a choric voice, the title character, Matigari, declaims: ". . . I was there at the time of the Portuguese, and the time of the Arabs, and the time of the British," provoking the black neocolonialist to whom he speaks to interrupt: "Look, I don't want history lessons" ("Matigari" 93).

Works Cited

Atieno Odhiambo, E. S. " 'Mind Limps after Reality': A Diagnostic Essay on the Treatment of Historical Themes in Kenyan Writings since Independence." Paper delivered at the annual conference of the Historical Association of Kenya, 1976. Typescript. Pp. 1–33.

———. "Seven Theses on Nationalism." Lecture delivered 16 Oct. 1981 at Nairobi branch of the Historical Society of Kenya. Typescript, Northwestern University Library.

Barnett, Donald L., and Karari Njama. *Mau Mau from Within: Autobiography and Analysis of Kenya's Peasant Revolt.* New York: Monthly Review Press, 1966.

Boahen, A. Adu. *African Perspectives on Colonialism.* Baltimore: Johns Hopkins UP, 1987.

"A Book of Forest History or War in the Forest and Attacks Here and There." English version of paper captured from Mau Mau during battle. Mss. Afr. s.1534. Rhodes House, Oxford U. 8 pp.

Buijtenhuijs, Robert. *Mau Mau Twenty Years After: The Myth and the Survivors.* Foreword by Ali A. Mazrui. The Hague: Mouton, 1973.

Colchester, T. C. "A Note on the Association between the Death of Chief Waiyaki in 1893 [sic] and the Leakey Sacrifice during the Mau Mau Emergency." Typescript dated 16 Mar. 1966. MSS. Afr. s.742(3). Rhodes House, Oxford U.

Coupland, Reginald. *East Africa and Its Invaders from Earliest Times to the Death of Seyyid Said in 1856.* Oxford: Clarendon, 1938.

Darling, Peter. "My Protest Was against the Hypocrisy in the College." *Sunday Nation,* 16 Mar. 1969: 15. [Interview with Ngugi.]

" 'Exiled' Dissidents Come under Fire." *Weekly Review* 26 Oct. 1984: 3–5, 7.

Feuser, Willfried F. "Reflections of History in African Literature." *World Literature Written in English* 24.1 (1984): 52–64.

Fleming, Thomas. "Inventing Our Probable Past." *New York Times Book Review* 6 July 1986: 1, 20–21.

Friedberger, Heinz. "Kenyan Writer James Ngugi Interviewed by Heinz Friedberger in Nairobi." *Cultural Events in Africa* 50 supp. (1969): i–ii.

Furedi, Frank. "The Development of Anti-Asian Opinion among Africans in Nakuru District, Kenya." *African Affairs* 73.292 (1974): 347–58.

Gachie, Wariara. "The New Departure in Kenyan Theatre Is . . . 'A Learning Experience.' " *Standard* 29 Jan. 1982: 13, 19.

Ghai, Yash P., and J. P. W. B. MacAuslan. *Public Law and Political Change in Kenya: A Study of the Legal Framework of Government from Colonial Times to the Present.* Nairobi: Oxford UP, 1970.

Gikoyo, Gucu G. *We Fought for Freedom.* Trans. Ciiri Cerere. Nairobi: East African Publishing House, 1979.

Gitahi-Gititi, V. L. "The Development of a Writer's Social Perspective: An Assessment of Ngugi wa Thiong'os [sic] Selected Texts." MA thesis. U of Nairobi, 1980–81.

Itote, Waruhiu (General China). *"Mau Mau" General.* Nairobi: East African Publishing House, 1967.

———. *Mau Mau in Action.* Nairobi: Transafrica, 1979.

Kakembo, Robert S. *An African Soldier Speaks.* Foreword George C. Turner. Kampala: [East African Literature Bureau], 1944.

Lonsdale, John. "States and Social Processes in Africa: A Historiographical Survey." *African Studies Review* 24.2–3 (1981): 139–225.

McIntosh, Brian G. "The Scottish Mission in Kenya, 1891–1923." PhD diss. U of Edinburgh, 1969.

Maina-wa-Kinyatti, ed. *Kenya's Freedom Struggle: The Dedan Kimathi Papers.* London: Zed, 1986.

———, ed. *Thunder from the Mountains: Mau Mau Patriotic Songs.* London: Zed, 1980.

Martin, E. F. "Documents concerning Home Guard Duties during Mau Mau in Kenya, 1952–53." MSS. Afr. s.721. Rhodes House, Oxford U.

Maughan-Brown, David. *Land, Freedom, and Fiction: History and Ideology in Kenya.* London: Zed, 1985.

Mazrui, Ali A. *Cultural Engineering and Nation-Building in East Africa.* Evanston: Northwestern UP, 1972.

———. *On Heroes and Uhuru-Worship: Essays on Independent Africa.* London: Longman, 1967.

Mboya, Tom. *Freedom and After.* London: Andre Deutsch, 1963.

Mitchell, Sir Philip. *African Afterthoughts.* Foreword by Lord Hailey. London: Hutchinson, 1954.

Muriuki, Godfrey. "The Historiography of East Africa." In *Into the 80's: The Proceedings of the Eleventh Annual Conference of the Canadian Association of African Studies, Vol. 2.* Ed. Donald I. Ray, Peter Shinnie, and Donovan Williams. B. C. Geographical Series 32. Vancouver: Tantalus Research, 1981.

———. *A History of the Kikuyu, 1500–1900.* Nairobi: Oxford UP, 1974.

Mutahi, Wahome. "Ex-Mau Mau Meet to Commemorate a Struggle They Won." *Daily Nation* 28 Feb. 1986: 13–14.

Mwanzi, H. A. "Men of Literature and Kenya's History." *Weekly Review* 5 Oct. 1984: 39.

Nagenda, John, and Robert Serumaga. "A Discussion between James Ngugi, . . . John Nagenda, . . . and Robert Serumaga." *Cultural Events in Africa* 15 supp. (1966): i–iii.

Neale, Caroline. *Writing "Independent" History: African Historiography, 1960–1980.* Stanford: Stanford UP, 1985.

Ngugi wa Thiong'o. *Barrel of a Pen: Resistance to Oppression in Neo-Colonial Kenya.* London: New Beacon Books; Trenton, NJ: Africa World P, 1983.

———. *Decolonising the Mind: The Politics of Language in African Literature.* London: James Currey; Nairobi: Heinemann Kenya; Portsmouth, NH: Heinemann; Harare: Zimbabwe Publishing House, 1986.

———. *Detained: A Writer's Prison Diary.* London: Heinemann, 1981.

———. *Devil on the Cross*. Trans. author. London, Ibadan, Nairobi: Heinemann, 1982.

———. *A Grain of Wheat*. London, Nairobi, and Ibadan: Heinemann, 1967; rev. ed. 1986.

———. "A Grain of Wheat." MS 337272. School of Oriental and African Studies, University of London.

———. "An Interview with Ngugi." *Weekly Review* 9 Jan. 1978: 9–11.

———. "Matigari: An Extract from a Forthcoming Novel." [Trans. Wangui wa Goro.] *Index on Censorship* 17.5 (May 1988): 91–94.

———. *Njamba Nene and the Flying Bus*. Adventures of Njamba Nene 1. Trans. Wangui wa Goro. Illustrations by Emmanuel Kariuki. Nairobi: Heinemann Kenya, 1986.

———. *Petals of Blood*. 1977; New York: Dutton, 1978.

———. "The RW Interview: Ngugi wa Thiong'o." *Revolutionary Worker* 15 Dec. 1986: 8–10.

———. *The River Between*. 1965; London, Ibadan, Nairobi: Heinemann, 1975.

———. *This Time Tomorrow*. Rpt. Nairobi: Kenya Literature Bureau, 1982.

———. *The Trial of Dedan Kimathi*. 1976; London, Ibadan, Nairobi: Heinemann, 1977.

———. *Weep Not, Child*. 1964; London, Ibadan, Nairobi: Heinemann, 1976.

Ochieng', William R. "Autobiography in Kenyan History." *Ufahamu* 14.2 (1985): 80–101.

———. "Colonial African Chiefs: Were They Primarily Self-Seeking Scoundrels?" *Hadith 4: Politics and Nationalism in Colonial Kenya* (1972): 46–70.

———. "Dignitaries Not Spared." *Weekly Review* 24 July 1981: 47–48.

———. "The Ghost of Jomo Kenyatta in Ngugi's Fiction." Paper delivered at annual conference of the Historical Association of Kenya, 23–26 Aug. 1984, University of Nairobi. Typescript. Melville E. Herskovits Library, Northwestern University.

———. *A History of Kenya*. Nairobi: Macmillan Kenya, 1985.

———. "The Scholar and the Populariser." *Weekly Review* 22 Dec. 1978: 3. [Review of St. Clair Drake's *The Redemption of Africa and Black Religion*.]

———. "Undercivilization in Black Africa." In William R. Ochieng'. *The First Word: Essays on Kenya History*. Kampala, Nairobi, and Dar-es-Salaam: East African Literature Bureau, 1975. 1–19.

Ogot, Bethwell A. *A Historical Dictionary of Kenya*. African Historical Dictionaries, no. 29. Metuchen, NJ: Scarecrow P, 1981.

———. "Politics, Culture, and Music in Central Kenya: A Study of Mau Mau Hymns, 1951–56." *Kenya Historical Review* 5.2 (1977): 275–86.

———. "Three Decades of Historical Studies in East Africa, 1949–1977." *Kenya Historical Review* 6 (1978): 22–33.

———. "Towards a History of Kenya." *Kenya Historical Review* 4.1 (1976): 1–9.

Ogot, Bethwell A., and William Ochieng'. "Mumboism: An Anti-Colonial Movement." In *War and Society in Africa: Ten Studies,* ed. Bethwell A. Ogot. London: Frank Cass, 1972. 149–72.

Okoth, P. Godfrey. "Autobiography in Kenyan History: A Critique." *Ufahamu* 14.2 (1985): 102–12.

Omari, Emman. "Ngugi wa Thiong'o Speaks!: 'I Am Not above the Contradictions Which Bedevil Our Society.' " *Weekend Standard* 28 Aug. 1981: 1, 15.

Rosberg, Carl G., Jr., and John Nottingham. *The Myth of "Mau Mau": Nationalism in Kenya*. New York: Praeger, 1966.

Temu, Arnold, and Bonaventure Swai. *Historians and Africanist History: A Critique*. London: Zed, 1981.

Trevor-Roper, Hugh. *The Rise of Christian Europe*. London: Thames and Hudson, 1965.

Vansina, Jan. *Oral Tradition as History*. Madison: U of Wisconsin P, 1985.

Wachanga, H. K. *The Swords of Kirinyaga: The Fight for Land and Freedom*. Ed. Robert Whittier. Nariobi, Kampala, and Dar-es-Salaam: East African Literature Bureau, 1975.

Wanjala, Chris. "What Is Literature to Kenya Historians?" *Weekly Review* 7 Sept. 1984: 30–31.

Wanjohi, N. Gatheru. "Historical Scholarship in the East African Context." *International Social Science Journal* 33.4 (1981): 667–74.

Were, Gideon S. *Western Kenya Historical Texts: Abaluyia, Teso, and Elgon Kalenjin.* Nairobi, Dar-es-Salaam, and Kampala: East African Publishing House, 1967.

Were, Gideon S., and Derek A. Wilson. *East Africa through a Thousand Years: A History of the Years A.D. 1000 to the Present Day.* New York: Africana, 1968.

Publishing Ngugi:
The Challenge, the Risk, and the Reward

HENRY CHAKAVA

The history of Ngugi wa Thiong'o as a published writer goes back to the late 1950s when he was a student at Alliance High School in Kenya. His story "Try Witchcraft" was published in the school magazine in 1957, when he was in the second form; another, "Voluntary Service Camp," appeared in the 1958 issue. Commercial success did not come until he was at Makerere University College in Kampala, which he entered in 1959. While there he wrote many stories, beginning with "The Fig Tree" ("Mugumo"), and won prizes for several of these in competitions organized within and around the college. His first contact with a commercial publisher appears to have been in 1961 when his story, "The Black Messiah," won first prize in a competition organized by the East African Literature Bureau. By this time his potential as a writer of great promise had already been recognized and Heinemann was able to publish his second novel *Weep Not, Child* in the African Writers Series in 1964, followed almost immediately with *The River Between,* which was a rewritten version of his earlier story "The Black Messiah." His more ambitious work, *A Grain of Wheat,* was published in the same series in 1967.

My own involvement with Ngugi started in the late 1960s when I was a literature student at the University of Nairobi. He was my tutor. In my final year, I elected to write my thesis on his novels, using the title "The Element of Guilt and Betrayal in Ngugi's Novels." I have never seen this thesis, nor have I come across any reference to it after it satisfied my examiners in 1972. Perhaps it is best left forgotten, as its contents might affect my present relationship with Ngugi. But Ngugi gave me every support I needed and the student/tutor relationship disappeared during that time and has never come back. After securing my degree and doing a brief stint as a tutor in the Department of Philosophy and Religious Studies, I joined Heinemann in Nairobi in 1972 as an editor-in-training.

Reprinted, with permission, from Henry Chakava, "Publishing Ngugi: The Challenge, the Risk, and the Reward," in *Ngũgĩ wa Thiong'o: Texts and Contexts* (Trenton, N.J.: Africa World Press, 1995), 13–28.

During this period, 1972–1986, I was responsible for receiving, evaluating and selecting materials for publication in Heinemann's London-based African Writers Series, in close consultation with my colleagues in London and Ibadan. I was able to introduce new East African voices such as Meja Mwangi, Mwangi Ruheni, Sam Kahiga, Martha Mvungi, Mukotani Rugyendo, and Thomas Akare into the series, while also publishing more established writers such as Okot p'Bitek, Taban lo Liyong, Joe de Graft, Rebeka Njau, and Micere Mugo. Not only did we publish many more new books by Ngugi over the same period, but we also witnessed a transformation in the author/publisher relationship that had existed between Ngugi, Heinemann London and Heinemann Kenya, and finally the transformation of Heinemann Kenya itself into an independent African imprint with the new name of East African Educational Publishers. *Petals of Blood* was the last of Ngugi's novels to be published by Heinemann in London in 1977. Even then I insisted on a copublication arrangement and was able to fly a few hundred copies into Nairobi so that the title was launched there in July 1977 in the presence of Heinemann representatives from London and Ibadan. I shall return to the crucial author/publisher relationship later.

THE GREAT LITERATURE DEBATE

Much written about, this debate started in the University of Nairobi's Department of English in the late 1960s. While victory meant changing the name to Department of Literature-in-English and later Department of Literature, the goal was to give meaning to this change and to attend to its ramifications in the teaching of English and Literature in Kenyan schools. At a conference of literature teachers held in Nairobi in 1974, Ngugi and his colleagues were able to persuade secondary school teachers of English and literature to work towards a new curriculum. Although agreement to formulate a new curriculum was accepted in principle, the Ministry of Education was slow in carrying out these changes; even today, certain aspects of those wide-ranging recommendations have yet to be implemented. During the debate Ngugi, who was now chairman of the Department of Literature at the University of Nairobi, was constantly reminding me of the need to "localize" my publishing program to fulfil better the needs of the new curriculum and to show everybody that "it can be done." In response, I commissioned a textbook of oral literature, the first ever, and this received enthusiastic reviews when it finally came out in 1982, becoming an instant bestseller and remaining to this day one of our most successful titles. In addition, I started a series of oral literature studies in Kenya's major languages. Although the running text was in English, the oral texts themselves were rendered in the original language, with English translations alongside. I have to date published the oral literatures of the Gikuyu, Maasai and Kalenjin. The Dholuo and Miji-Kenda are in process. A number of supplementary books useful for the learning and teaching of oral literature have also been published. Sales of these books were slow at first, but they have now established themselves as standard reference books both in schools and colleges and universities. In addition, other publishers have followed our lead and oral literature is now a popular publishing subject area. This, therefore, is what the Great Literature Debate meant for me: besides opening up new publishing vistas, it took me and others back to our roots and restored the role of our parents and grandparents as the real sources of knowledge.

THE GREAT LANGUAGE DEBATE

This debate emerged naturally out of the first one. If we accept that our literatures are to be found among our own communities, in what language(s) must we express them? How should we share them among ourselves? Doubts were expressed about the suitability of English to perform this role, in a society which had only recently freed itself from British colonialism and which is basically oral and with a high rate of illiteracy. Although it was agreed that English is vital for international communication, it was felt strongly that our writers should write for our own people and that if the rest of the world saw any merit in what we were producing, they could access that material through translation into their own languages. We felt that it was time to prepare our communities and awaken them to the reality that they were the creators of their own literature. It was at this time (1976) that Ngugi (with his namesake Ngugi wa Mirii) wrote *Ngaahika Ndeenda* with the full critical participation of the people of Kamiriithu, who were later to stage it at the Kamiriithu Community Centre before large audiences.

But publishing in African languages was quite another proposition. What orthographies would we use, since some communities had none while others, reacting against those prepared for them by missionaries, were busy compiling new ones? Who would buy these books, in view of the fact that the majority of mother-tongue speakers were poor peasants who lived below the bread line, and only a small percentage of whom had achieved literacy beyond the three R's? As a publisher, how was I going to promote and distribute these books, in view of the fact that the majority of readers would be people from the rural areas where the roads were nonexistent or impassable for most of the year? In the absence of newspapers, journals, and other promotional outlets in those languages, how was I going to advertise these books?

Ngugi and I agonized over these matters for long hours, he optimistic, I skeptical. In the end we began to realize the power of translation. Who ever remembers that *War and Peace* and *Anna Karenina* were written in Russian?

What about other classics like *Dead Souls, The Idiot, The Cherry Orchard, The Caucasian Chalk Circle, Hedda Gabbler, The Plague, God's Bits of Wood* and all those many books that we so much enjoyed reading in English? Ngugi regretted that he had enriched the English language and culture with his novels *Weep Not, Child, The River Between, A Grain of Wheat* and *Petals of Blood* without giving anything back to the community, culture and language that had inspired them. He swore that he would never write any more novels in English, but would henceforth write in the Gikuyu language. I agreed to be his publisher. That was in 1977.

In the years 1977–1982, before and after Ngugi's detention (which was during the whole of 1978), we spent much time together. The University of Nairobi administration had refused to allow him to resume his teaching duties, so I gave him a desk at my office where he could do his writing. After many discussions together, we were able to interpret the results of the Great Literature Debate and the Great Language Debate as follows: *every community, every nationality, has its own language, its own codified body of knowledge, its own literature, music, drama and dance, etc. Every community must accept the duty to preserve its own heritage, and should not rely on anyone else for this. Every community is a concentric circle, complete in itself, and the good from it will flow and be absorbed into a broader national circle, which will in turn flow into a regional or continental circle, with only the best reaching the global circle.* We saw translation as the bridge across those concentric circles and imagined a world where the Dholuo would be able to access materials written in Gikuyu, and vice-versa, and the Luhya and Miji-Kenda would be able to compare their literatures. In our plan, works which transcended the first circle would be translated into Kiswahili and finally into English for dissemination nationally, regionally and internationally. If people from countries where English is not spoken, such as France, Germany, Russia, Japan, Scandinavia, etc., expressed interest in any of our works, we would grant them rights to translate that work into their own language, and assist them, as much as possible, with the original language. In this way Africa would be exposing only the best of its creative output to the rest of the world.

I decided to start with children's books in mother tongues and Ngugi himself volunteered to write the first three. I commissioned more children's books from the nation's leading writers, among them David Maillu, Francis Imbuga, Asenath Odaga and Grace Ogot. I published six new titles within a couple of years. Yet in all sincerity, and in spite of the enthusiasm displayed by all my writers, I have to admit that these books did not do well and, to date, none of them has reprinted. I decided to skip our second circle (i.e., issuing them in Kiswahili translation) and commissioned English translations with some good results. International rights have been sold in only a few, including Ngugi's own. No research has been carried out to show why these mother-tongue books proved commercially unviable, but some of the questions I asked earlier might be instructive.

Publishing Ngugi

Publishing Ngugi is a pleasurable and enriching experience. My direct publishing association with him dates back to 1975–76, when we worked together on *Petals of Blood*. Contrary to popular belief among academics and other creative writers who think we automatically accept Ngugi's books for publication, the script of *Petals*, then under the working title *Wrestling with God* or *Wrestlers with God*, was sent out for readers' reports in the normal way. I personally gave it an in-depth house report. Although all the reports recommended publication, they raised serious issues about the timing, movement and content of the story; they noted constant repetition, felt some scenes had been contrived to achieve certain desired effects, and decried the predictability or inevitability of the plot.

Ngugi took all these criticisms seriously and with great humility. He retrieved the script and reworked it for a long time, constantly coming back to seek clarification about some of our readers' criticisms. He listened to, even solicited, every comment, however casual, from my editors and other friends to whom he had given the script at his own initiative. I once made a casual observation to the effect that Wanja's matatu journey from Nairobi to Ilmorog, which was then identifiably Limuru, was too long and packed with too many incidents. I made a similar criticism of the delegation of workers and peasants from Ilmorog to Nairobi to meet their "lost" M.P., which I again felt was overstretched and loaded with content which seemed to come out of Ngugi's mouth rather than his characters'. He responded to these criticisms by leaving all the incidents intact but "moving" Ilmorog so that it was now much further away from Nairobi, and its new description had changed from the lush green of Limuru to a drier place resembling Nyandarua, Kinangop or Lari, or somewhere deeper into the Rift Valley. As for Wanja and her matatu journey, he seems to have edited it out of the novel altogether, later to reuse it in a much more integrated and creative manner in his next novel, *Devil on the Cross*, where Wanja becomes Wariinga. Quite frankly, I cannot tell you which edition of *Petals of Blood* is in print, having read several versions of that novel both in manuscript and in proof.

I eventually came to accept Ngugi as being fastidious in his writing style, and I now know that unless you stop him, he can go on rewriting a novel ceaselessly, responding to his critics not by following their laid-down recommendations but by adopting a new approach which somehow takes care of their criticisms. The same story applies to proofs, which Ngugi changes beyond his normal allocation, forcing a publisher to incur heavy correction costs. Yet Ngugi treats his publisher as an equal partner in his creative process, cooperates fully in carrying out the publisher's assignments and meets his deadlines promptly. I have never seen Ngugi lose his temper during our long publishing association. When we disagreed completely over the introduction to *The Trial of Dedan Kimathi*, which he had coauthored with Micere Mugo, the matter was amicably resolved to our mutual satisfaction.

My experience with the Gikuyu books was different although equally enriching. It started with *Ngaahika Ndeenda,* the community-based effort in writing and producing a play. When he handed me the final script, Ngugi informed me that it had undergone a lot of fine tuning by members of the cast and that he doubted we needed to do any more work on it. Beginning with *Ngaahika,* I established a pattern which was to repeat itself in the assessment of all works submitted by Ngugi in Gikuyu. Being a non-Gikuyu speaker myself, I had to find ways of overcoming my linguistic handicap before I could feel confident enough to offer his works for acceptance to our editorial board. The fact that we had no Gikuyu speaking editor on our staff at that time meant that I could not benefit from an in-house assessment. We devised a strategy which was able to satisfy me as well as Ngugi and all those writers who participated in our "Return to Mother Tongue" program. First, Ngugi would describe the plot in as much detail as possible, inviting comments from me at each stage. I would then give him the go-ahead to proceed with the writing. When the final script was ready, we would go through it together, page by page, with Ngugi explaining the story in meticulous detail. Once satisfied, I would submit the script to one or two Gikuyu readers for reports, and offer it for acceptance if the reports were positive, which they usually were.

Ngugi was determined that the Gikuyu editions of his books should be of the same production quality as their English counterparts, to forestall any thoughts that local language publications were inferior or second-rate. For this reason, we were compelled to import new fonts for our typesetter to enable him to do justice to the Gikuyu alphabet. We had to use the best designers and illustrators available for his books. Once our designer produced a cover for *Caitani Mutharaba-ini.* It depicted a Mau Mau warrior stepping on a dead white soldier and with his AK47 rifle held up high in victory. Ngugi admired this cover for a long time and finally, in his modesty, declared it "too strong" for *Caitani.* He asked me to keep that cover safely for he would write a new novel specifically for it. That novel was *Matigari.*

Ngugi is one of the few writers who believe that publishers can be honest and decent people. He usually doesn't haggle over the terms that I propose to him. He will accept the percentage royalty proposed and the advance offered and might even agree to forego some benefit in order "to get the book started." Unlike other writers I know, he doesn't complain and fret that he has been to so-and-so bookshop and has not seen copies of his books, although he will from time to time suggest ideas as to how we might promote or distribute our books better. Again, unlike some writers, he does not go behind our back to visit the warehouse to check the bin cards or visit our Accounts Department to inspect the records to ensure that we are not holding back any royalties. He has absolute faith in people and their good intentions. For example, when in 1985, I diverted some of his "idle" royalties and used the money to buy him shares in our company which was then undergoing localization, all he could say when I later informed him was, "You mean I am now a capitalist? Anyway, that was good."

Publishing Ngugi: The Challenge

The challenge of publishing Ngugi is the same as that faced by any publisher who publishes an internationally renowned writer. I started working with Ngugi when he already had a formidable reputation and my challenge was to raise my stature, my professionalism and my services to his level so as to be worthy of the trust he had placed in me. He knew the publishing game well through his previous dealings with Heinemann and expected similar services from me. Of course I could not match London in paying royalty advances and investing heavily in publicity and marketing promotion, but Ngugi understood and accepted this. Even though it was a favor for him to be giving me his books, rather than me pleading to publish him, Ngugi treated me and continues to treat me with all respect. It is always a matter of great pride for him and for me when he introduces me as "my publisher" in a manner that suggests that he does not recognize anyone else for that role.

As I pointed out earlier, Ngugi is a serious and committed writer with a vision. He expects you as his publisher to share and participate in that vision. He will engage you in long discussions to win you over and will expect an equally enlightened and sensitive—even critical—response from you. In other words, as Ngugi's publisher you are not simply a businessman but an intellectual sparring partner. You are his tuning fork, the litmus test that will gauge the readers' response to his views and convictions. He expects a "creative" response from you and his ideas refine themselves in the course of your discussions. As I have explained above, my input was sought during the literature and language debates, and my publishing in oral literature and mother tongues was shaped and informed by our regular "discourses." His keen attention and the animated manner in which he responds inspire a feeling of conquest, of great satisfaction and fulfillment.

Distribution of Ngugi's books internationally in the way that he was used to at Heinemann was a real challenge. I had already had some experience with *Petals of Blood,* published in London, but for which I had asked Heinemann to grant me East African rights in view of the role I had played in "developing" it with Ngugi. Second, when Heinemann declined to copublish Ngugi and Micere's *The Trial of Dedan Kimathi* because the African Writers Series was supposed to be for anthologies, and not single collections of plays, I decided to publish the play in Nairobi. Ngugi and Micere had written it in anger because they were appalled by the manner in which Kenneth Watene had depicted Kimathi in his play, then just published and entitled *Dedan Kimathi*. Furthermore, Ngugi and Micere wanted a quick answer from us. Heinemann soon realized their mistake and eventually purchased rights from me to sell the play outside East Africa. I decided that as I did not have the marketing and distribution reach, I was going to sell rights, including translation rights, as widely as possible. The African Writers Series was the automatic choice for English language rights and, in the case of *Matigari,* for example, I was able to successfully sell French, Dutch, German, Danish, Swedish, American and Japanese rights with assistance from Heinemann U.K. It is my belief and conviction that the books I have published with Ngugi are as well marketed and distributed as when he was published by Heinemann in London.

PUBLISHING NGUGI: THE RISK

I shall narrate in detail three incidents that demonstrate the risk of publishing Ngugi in Kenya. There is, of course, the social stigma of being isolated and branded "controversial," "rebel," "antigovernment," "collaborator with the forces of destruction," etc., etc. There is the loss that my business suffered (especially in the years 1976–86) and continues to suffer, albeit on a smaller scale today, because of my association with Ngugi. My books (including Ngugi's own) have been taken off school reading lists; bookshops stocking Ngugi's books have been harassed and some stocks impounded, and the government's response to textbooks published by my firm has been lukewarm at best, because they do not want to recommend books submitted by Ngugi's publisher.

A few weeks before the publication of *Ngaahika Ndeenda* and *Caitani Mutharaba-ini* in 1980, I began to receive threatening death calls from anonymous callers, first through our switchboard and later through my private line and house. The callers were usually women who would variously introduce themselves as friends of mine. They used names like Jane, Rose, or Esther. The pattern of the calls was always the same. They would request to speak to me, and when I confirmed I was the one they would ask me to "hold on for my boss." They would then put the telephone down, and I would begin to hear echoes of music and conversation in the background as if they were calling from a large hall. After a minute or so, the same woman would come back on the phone, click and then whisper a rude word like "jinga" (stupid) or some other unprintable words. If I made the error of disconnecting the call, they would ring back immediately to say that they had not yet finished with me. Whenever I took a stroll in the streets, which was usually during lunch time, I would notice that I was being watched and sometimes followed. Strangers would collide with me, apologize profusely and attempt to engage me in conversation. When I got home in the evening after work, the callers would be on the phone to welcome me, claiming that they had "escorted" me all the way from town, "for my own safety."

I alerted the police and recorded statements at the police station but the harassment did not stop. I sought assistance from friends in the post office who agreed to block off all calls to my office and house so that all callers had to go through the central exchange and identify themselves first. One evening in March, 1980, on the 17th, to be precise, two days before the printers were due to deliver printed copies of *Ngaahika* and *Caitani*, I had just had a meeting with the post office official monitoring the calls to my house, and had pulled in at my gate at about 7:30 PM. When I was waiting for the gate to be opened, I noticed a car behind mine which was now so close to me that I was virtually sandwiched between that car and my own gate. With lightning speed, four people armed with simis, pangas, and clubs set upon me, broke the windows of my car and cut me badly in my face and hands. They eventually took possession of my car and pushed me onto the floor of the front passenger seat. Two of them firmly held me down with their heavy boots on my neck. The third tried to drive the car away while the fourth returned to their getaway car. I was saved by the screams from my house and the alarms that all my neighbors raised. The driver seemed to have a problem handling my brand new car. I heard him reprimanded in one of our local languages, "You told us you knew how to drive a BMW." My attackers escaped, leaving me trapped in my car, and good Samaritan neighbors drove me to Nairobi Hospital at once. In spite of excellent medical attention, I lost use of my index finger because the tendons had been severed in two places by a simi. My attackers were never apprehended. But two months later, the day the post office removed the bugs on my phones, I got another call from my lady friends, and it went as follows:

> CALLER: Have you learned your lesson?
>
> HC: What lesson?
>
> CALLER: You mean we should come again?
>
> HC: You didn't tell me when you came the first time, so don't tell me when you will be coming back.

I immediately disconnected. The second incident happened in 1982, shortly before the aborted coup. I was working out a detailed itinerary for Ngugi, who had finally decided to travel abroad after spending three years in Kenya unsuccessfully trying to regain his teaching job at the University of Nairobi. I received a long letter from a group describing themselves as the Moonday Gang, saying they were part of a hit squad headquartered in South America. I had been earmarked for destruction, but having studied me and my family closely, they had concluded that I was "innocent," and they had decided to spare my life if I could pay them a ransom of KSh 200,000. They warned me not to play any tricks, described everything about me and my family in great and accurate detail, and said they would start by eliminating Sharon, my 6-year-old daughter who was at school at Loreto Convent, Msongari in Nairobi. They explained what time she left the house in the morning, what time she left school in the evening, in what car, and the name of the driver who picked her up.

When the people finally made telephone contact, I had already reported the matter to police and was getting "maximum cooperation." When they made the call to instruct me as to how the ransom money should be delivered, I had two senior scene-of-the-crime officers listening in at my house. My brother was at the exchange, trying to trace the origin of the call with the assistance of friends. The police were encouraging me to talk as long as possible to facilitate this exercise, and I used this time to bargain with the gangsters and reduce the ransom money to KSh 100,000. The source of the call or the number they were calling from was never established, but both the police and post office suspected the call had come from Thika, a town 50 km north of Nairobi and the same place I was expected to take the money that night.

Although I had been warned not to have any other person in the car, the scene-of-the-crime officers led me to Parklands Police Station, Nairobi, where I collected false money and two policemen armed with "patchets," which they described as automatic rifles capable of spraying bullets in all directions and therefore able to hit any target without necessarily aiming. They asked me to drive my car at 180 kph, "just in case these people are following us," and told me they would shoot dead anybody who approached me once we got to the scene. "If the press should ask you how it happened, please remember to say the gangsters attacked us first, and we simply fired back in self-defence." I agreed to cooperate in this.

We arrived at Thika Bridge (the appointed place) at 8:30 PM, half an hour late according to their instruction. As soon as I stopped the car, I saw a sharp blue light emitted into the sky and whispered to the policemen flat on the back seat of my car that that was the promised signal. As I drove slowly forward, another blue light was emitted and this time all of us saw it. The third light was aimed directly at us, and it lit up the car as blue lightning would do. One of the police officers then started screaming, claiming that he had been shot. He insisted that we should go back to Nairobi or to Thika Police Station for reinforcements. "This thing is too big for the two of us. I already have one bullet lodged in my stomach and I do not want another one." We managed to persuade our friend that he had not been shot, and that perhaps we should make another attempt. He agreed. When we went back to the bush where my extortioners were hiding, things did not work out as planned. I was made to come out of the car and conduct a dialogue with these people. Eventually I took out the money and dropped it according to their instructions. Meanwhile the police were still lying flat on the back seat contrary to their earlier promises. When I returned to the car and pleaded with them to act, they immediately flung the doors of the car open and I saw five armed people immediately put down their weapons and raise their hands holding what appeared to be identity cards. The policemen's first priority was to retrieve the false money which I had dropped on the road, so that by the time they turned to the gangsters, only three were left. In the course of their arrest a third escaped and we were left with two. The police then beat up these two thoroughly, asking them to say where their accomplices were. The suspects eventually led us to a boy in a nearby school. He confessed that he was the one who had been writing their letters in a girl's handwriting and who afterwards had been telephoning me using different women's names. We brought the three suspects to Nairobi in my car that night and they were locked up at Parklands Police Station.

These three people were never charged in a court of law. The police kept moving them from one station to another. Eventually I was informed that one of them was a minor, had been released on special bond, and had gone back to school. Then I was told that the prosecutor in charge of the case had gone on long leave and they did not want to assign the case to another officer. Things continued in this way until the file vanished and the police were "forced" to close the case.

The third and final incident I will mention happened in 1986 when I published *Matigari*. The book had been on the market for four months and was enjoying a steady sale. One afternoon, I received a visit from a senior superintendent of police, a haughty gentleman dressed in a smart civilian suit. He asked me general questions about publishing and finally wanted to know if I had published anything recently that might have offended the Kenyan public. When I answered in the negative, he spoke into a walkie-talkie and two fierce-looking uniformed officers stepped into my office with a plainclothes escort who had made no effort to conceal his pistol. The offending book was called "Mabaki," according to one of the policemen, and was written in Gikuyu by Ngugi wa Thiong'o.

I was told that the people "from above" were very unhappy with the book and did not want to see it in circulation. "Why do you publish books which only a certain section of the Kenyan society can read?" they wanted to know. They asked how many copies I had printed and I said 4,000. They wanted to know how many copies were left and I replied, "Maybe 1,500." They insisted on knowing the actual number. I begged leave of them and went into my warehouse in the basement to check. Then I realized that the whole area had been sealed and was swarming with security agents—close to sixty, I learned later. The actual balance of books was just over 600 and they told me they were going to take all those copies away, there and then. They were at pains to explain that they were not banning the book, and yet they warned me against daring to reprint it. They wanted to know how much money I had spent on the book, and how much revenue I was going to lose by not selling it.

I did not answer the latter question, but informed them that my cost of production had been around KSh 200,000. The smart officer assured me that the government would compensate me for this loss. I was relieved when there was no cheque nor any other follow-up on this matter.

There have been many other threats, direct or indirect, that my company or I have suffered because of our association with Ngugi. I have already related how Ngugi's books and our other textbooks have been removed from official government reading lists. There have been other forms of censorship and harassment and the constant threat of litigation from members of the public who have felt libelled by Ngugi in his writings. Thankfully, with the exception of our lawyers' fees which we have had to pay, none of these claimants have felt able to pursue their cases in a court of law. Obviously Ngugi himself has suffered on a much larger scale, and it is that suffering that still keeps him in exile today.

PUBLISHING NGUGI: THE REWARD

In spite of the problems I have been through, my association with Ngugi has been very rewarding, both intellectually and commercially. First and foremost, I must admit that my linkage with Heinemann's African Writers Series and with Ngugi in particular has played an important part in establishing and enhancing my reputation and that of EAEP as the leading fiction publisher in the region, if not in the entire African continent. My fiction list consists of drama, poetry, plays, novels and works of oral literature, works in their mother tongue, Kiswahili, and in English, not to mention children's books, all-in-all numbering 190 titles to date. Further, there is not a single Ngugi book I have published (except the children's books in Gikuyu) which has not been an instant best seller. *Ngaahika Ndeenda* and *Caitani Mutharaba-ini* reprinted two times within the first year of publication. Their Kiswahili and English translations have performed equally well. I recently released an English translation of *Matigari* and it is performing well and will most likely reprint. The original *Matigari* remains in limbo, as we have not yet ascertained if we would be breaking the law by reissuing it. The essays, *Writers in Politics* and *Decolonising the Mind,* are in great demand, especially in our academic institutions, and are regularly reprinted. *Moving the Centre* promises to be similarly successful. Rights have been acquired from Heinemann London on the earlier novels and these, too, are published in Nairobi and continue to do well. Ngugi's long absence from Kenya and the propaganda campaign that has been waged against him and his writings have certainly affected the momentum of the sales of his books, but, excepting *Matigari,* all of them are in print and are not officially banned as is sometimes claimed in other circles.

What I have valued most is my intellectual association with Ngugi. He is a lot more committed, serious, idealistic and ideologically inclined than I am, but we share the same philosophical and temperamental worldview. Ngugi's advice and our exchange of views have encouraged me to give priority to oral literature in my publishing program. Ngugi's conviction and my own willingness to experiment with some of his ideas have made me venture into publishing in African languages. Had Ngugi continued to live in Kenya, write more books in this line, and encourage his colleagues to support this venture, the program would have succeeded. In spite of my present setbacks in publishing in this area, I am waiting for the day when he will return home so that we can continue.

Although my association with Heinemann gave me a lot of international exposure, much of this has been sustained by the fact that I am the publisher of one of Africa's greatest and certainly its most controversial avant-garde writer, Ngugi wa Thiong'o. In selling rights to his books, I have had to interact with international publishers from all over the world: Japan, Russia, Germany, France, Scandinavia, U.S.A., and some African countries such as Zimbabwe and South Africa. At home, I enjoy quiet respect from serious-minded Kenyans who acknowledge the courageousness of keeping Ngugi's books in print under very difficult circumstances. The strong messages contained in his writings are much appreciated locally, even though this appreciation hardly finds public expression nowadays.

Much of what I have said in this paper is being said for the first time. Some things were too raw, too painful to write about when they happened, but I have realized that I might never have another similar opportunity to share this part of my private life and tribulations. My presentation might appear gratuitous since it draws rather too much attention to myself. I have resisted mentioning additional, very personal incidents to present broader national and academic issues. If I have misrepresented Ngugi in any way, I would request his forgiveness, while reserving my right to interpret our interaction over all those years in my own way.

Index

♦

The Volume Editor

◆

Peter Nazareth is Professor of English and African-American World Studies and Adviser to the International Writing Program at the University of Iowa. He was born in Uganda and studied at Makerere University College and Leeds University. He was Seymour Lustman Fellow at Yale University and Honorary Fellow in the International Writing Program. He received the 1984 Distinguished Independent Study Course Award from the National University Continuing Education Association for his course and study guide, *Literatures of the African Peoples.* His "Brave New Cosmos," "The Hospital," and "X" were broadcast by the BBC program African Theatre. Since 1992, he has taught "Elvis as Anthology," which received a great deal of media attention, including stories on *World News Tonight with Peter Jennings* and *The Today Show,* sparked off by an article in the *Wall Street Journal.*

Nazareth's books include *In a Brown Mantle, The General Is Up, The Third World Writer: His Social Responsibility,* and *In the Trickster Tradition: The Novels of Andrew Salkey, Francis Ebejer, and Ishmael Reed,* the last of these carrying a blurb by Ngũgĩ. His other works include "Elvis as Anthology," in Vernon Chadwick, ed., *In Search of Elvis: Music, Race, Art, Religion* (Boulder: Westview, 1997); "Heading Them Off at the Pass," in Bruce Allen Dick, ed., *The Critical Response to Ishmael Reed* (Westport, Conn., and London: Greenwood Press, 1999); and "The Confessor" and "Moneyman," in Manohar Shetty, ed., *Ferry Crossing: Short Stories from Goa* (New Delhi: Penguin, 1998). His essays on African literature have been translated into Hungarian and Serbo-Croatian and his fiction into Bengali, Hungarian, Japanese, Korean, Polish, Malay, Arabic, and Hebrew.

The General Editor

♦

Robert Lecker is professor of English at McGill University in Montreal. He received his Ph.D. from York University. Professor Lecker is the author of numerous critical studies, including *On the Line* (1982), *Robert Kroetch* (1986), *An Other I* (1988), and *Making It Real: The Canonization of English-Canadian Literature* (1995). He is the editor of the critical journal *Essays on Canadian Writing* and of many collections of critical essays, the most recent of which is *Canadian Canons: Essays in Literary Value* (1991). He is the founding and current general editor of Twayne's Masterwork Studies and the editor of the Twayne World Authors Series on Canadian writers. He is also the general editor of G. K. Hall's Critical Essays on World Literature series.